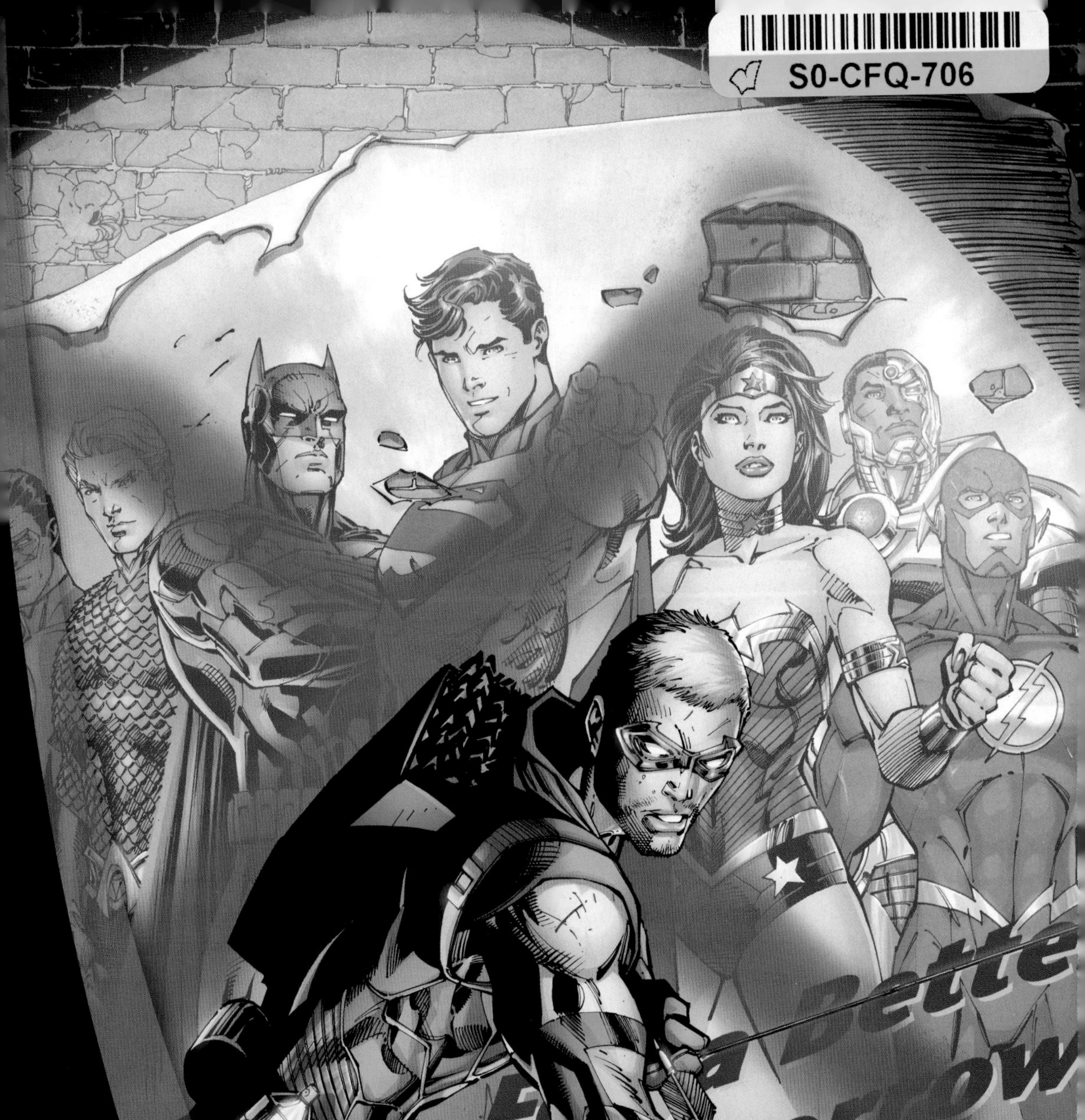

JUSTICE LEAGUE

VOLUME 2 THE VILLAIN'S JOURNE

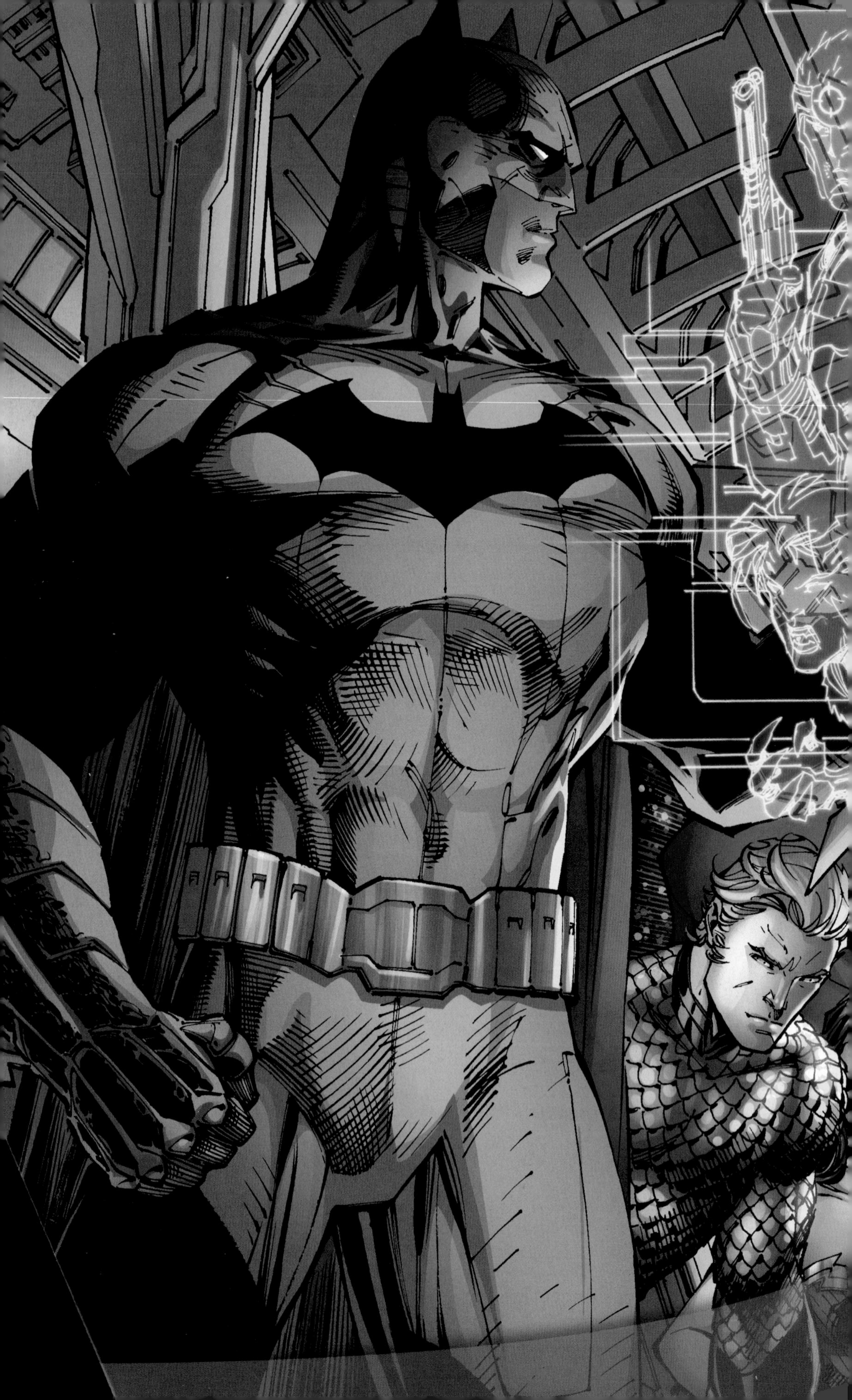

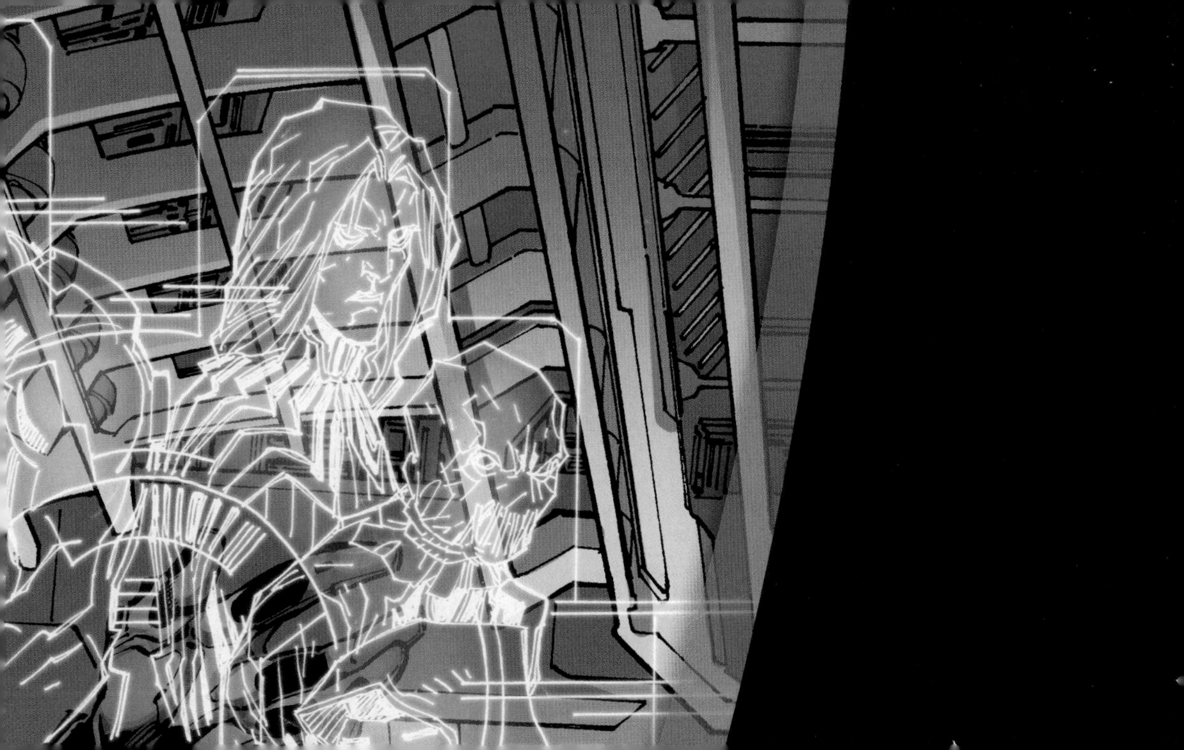

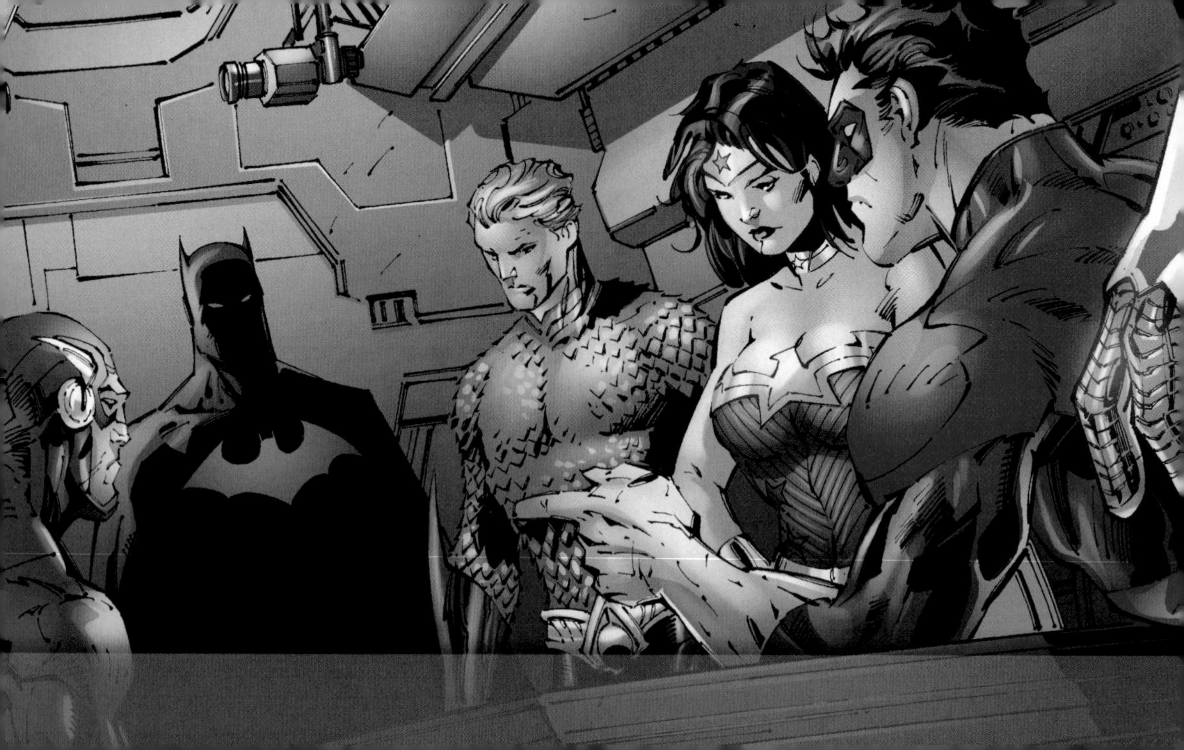

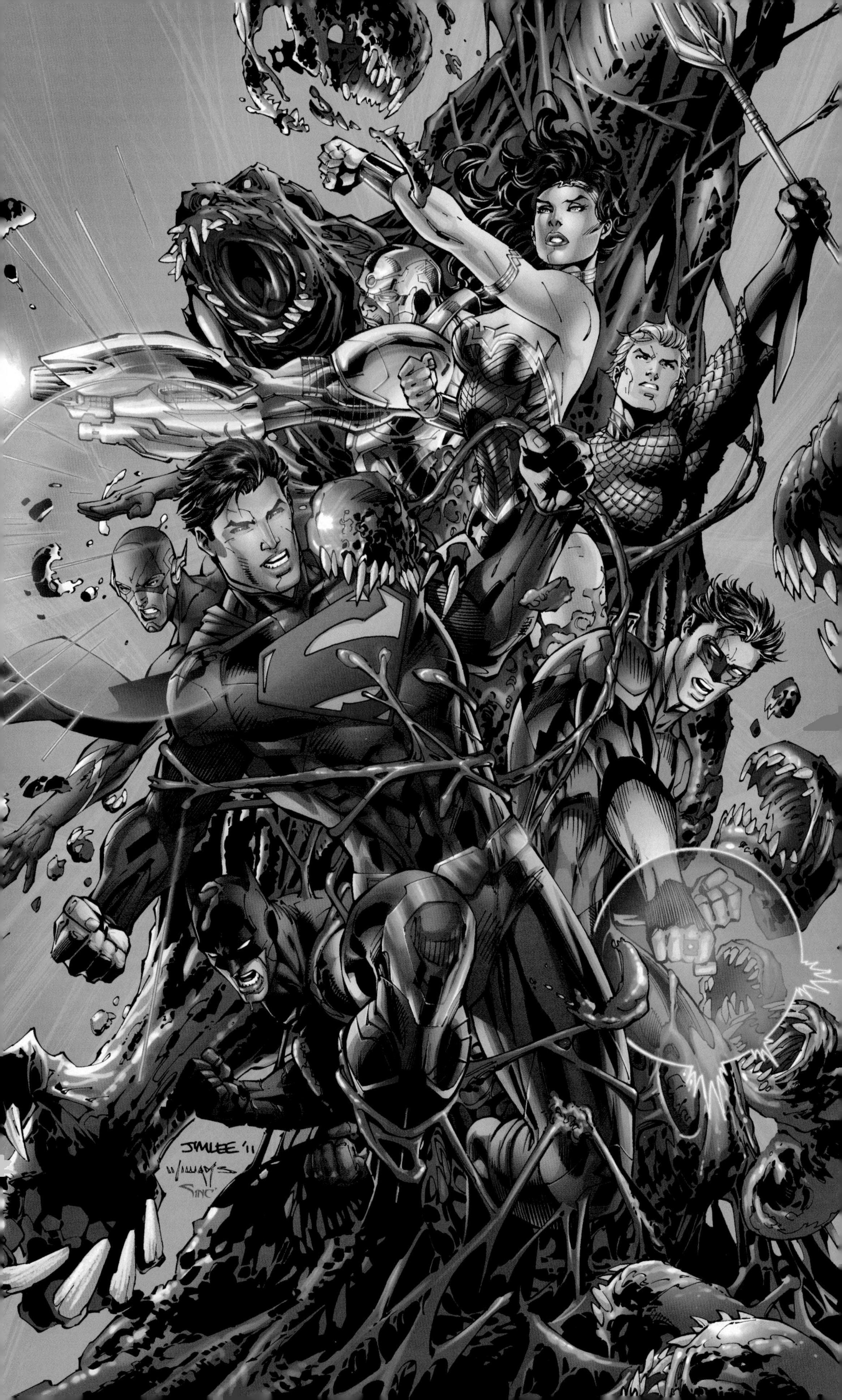
JIMLEE '11
WILLIAMS
SINC

THE VILLAIN'S JOURNEY PROLOGUE

GEOFF JOHNS writer **GENE HA** artist cover by **JIM LEE, SCOTT WILLIAMS & ALEX SINCLAIR**

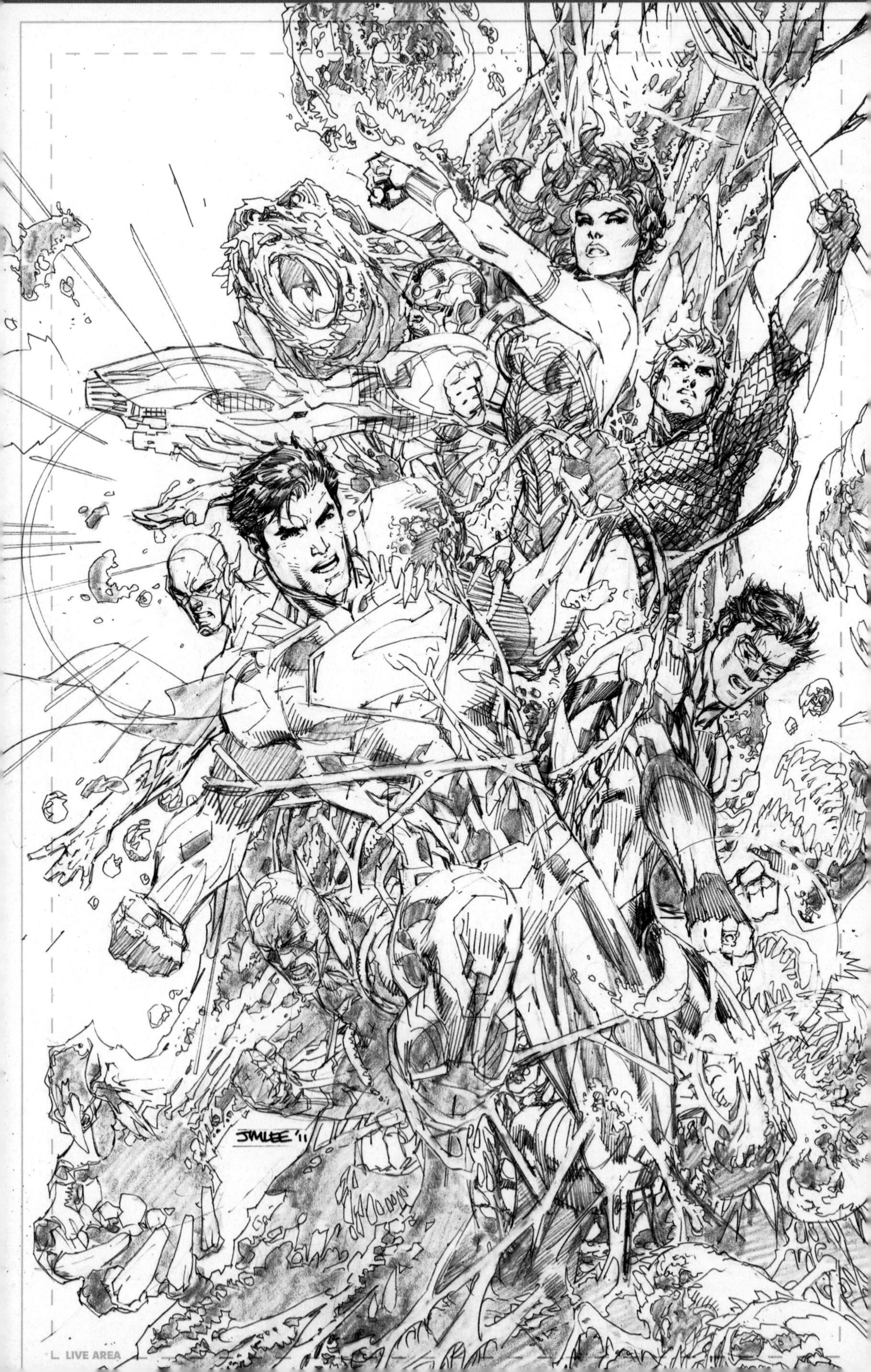
JIMLEE '11
LIVE AREA

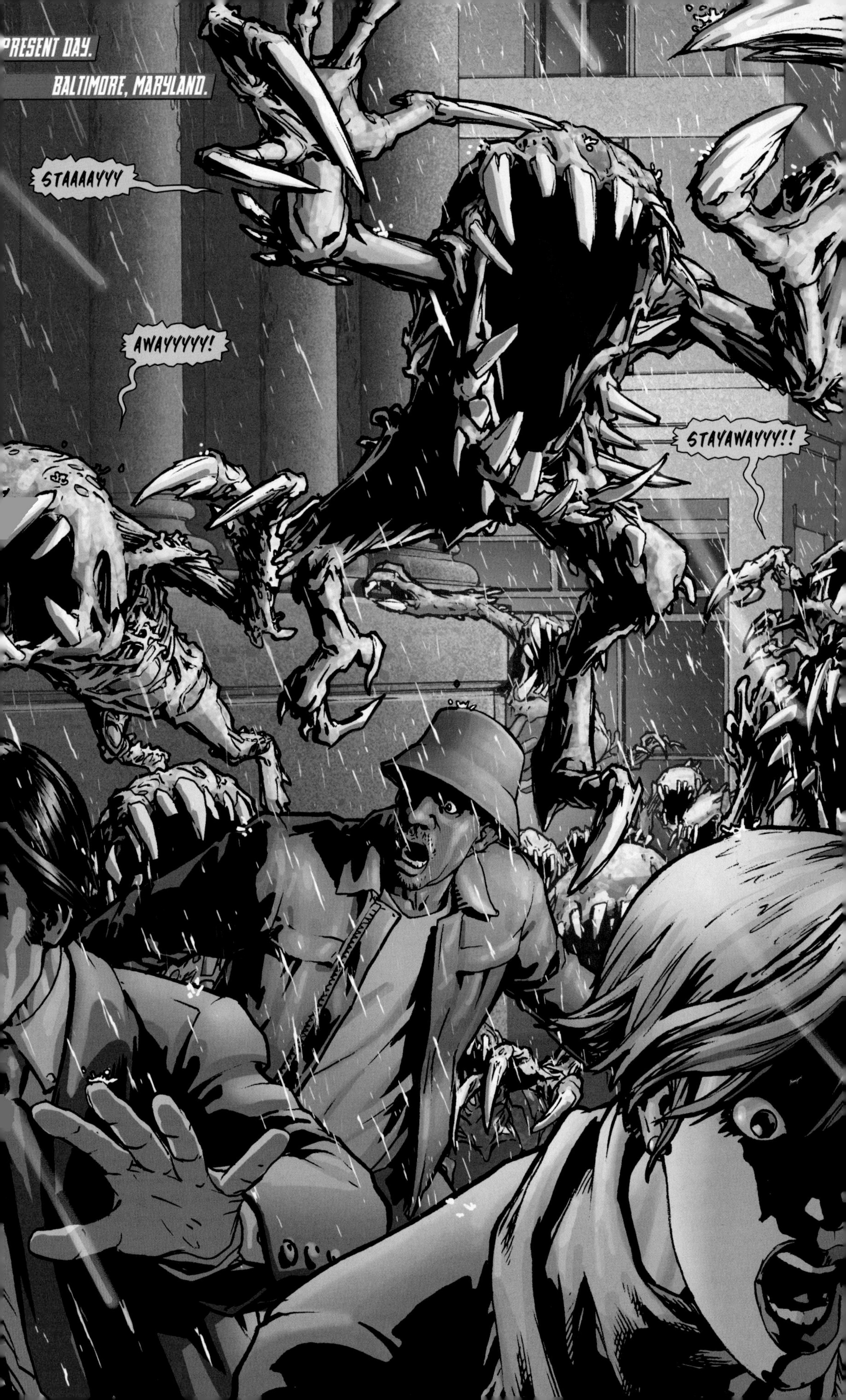
PRESENT DAY.
BALTIMORE, MARYLAND.
STAAAAYYY
AWAYYYYY!
STAYAWAYYY!!

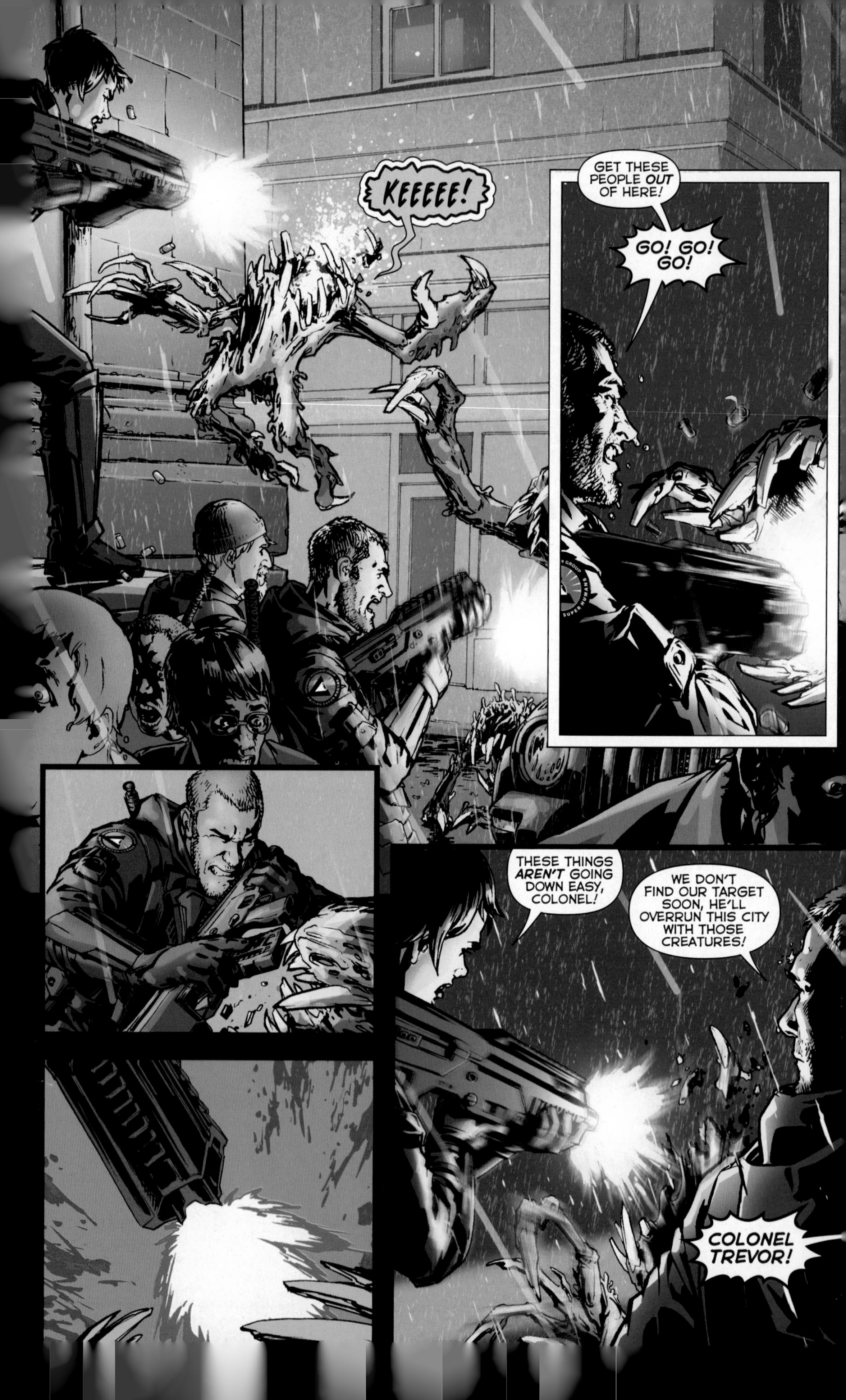
KEEEEE!
GET THESE PEOPLE OUT OF HERE!
GO! GO! GO!
THESE THINGS AREN'T GOING DOWN EASY, COLONEL!
WE DON'T FIND OUR TARGET SOON, HE'LL OVERRUN THIS CITY WITH THOSE CREATURES!
COLONEL TREVOR!

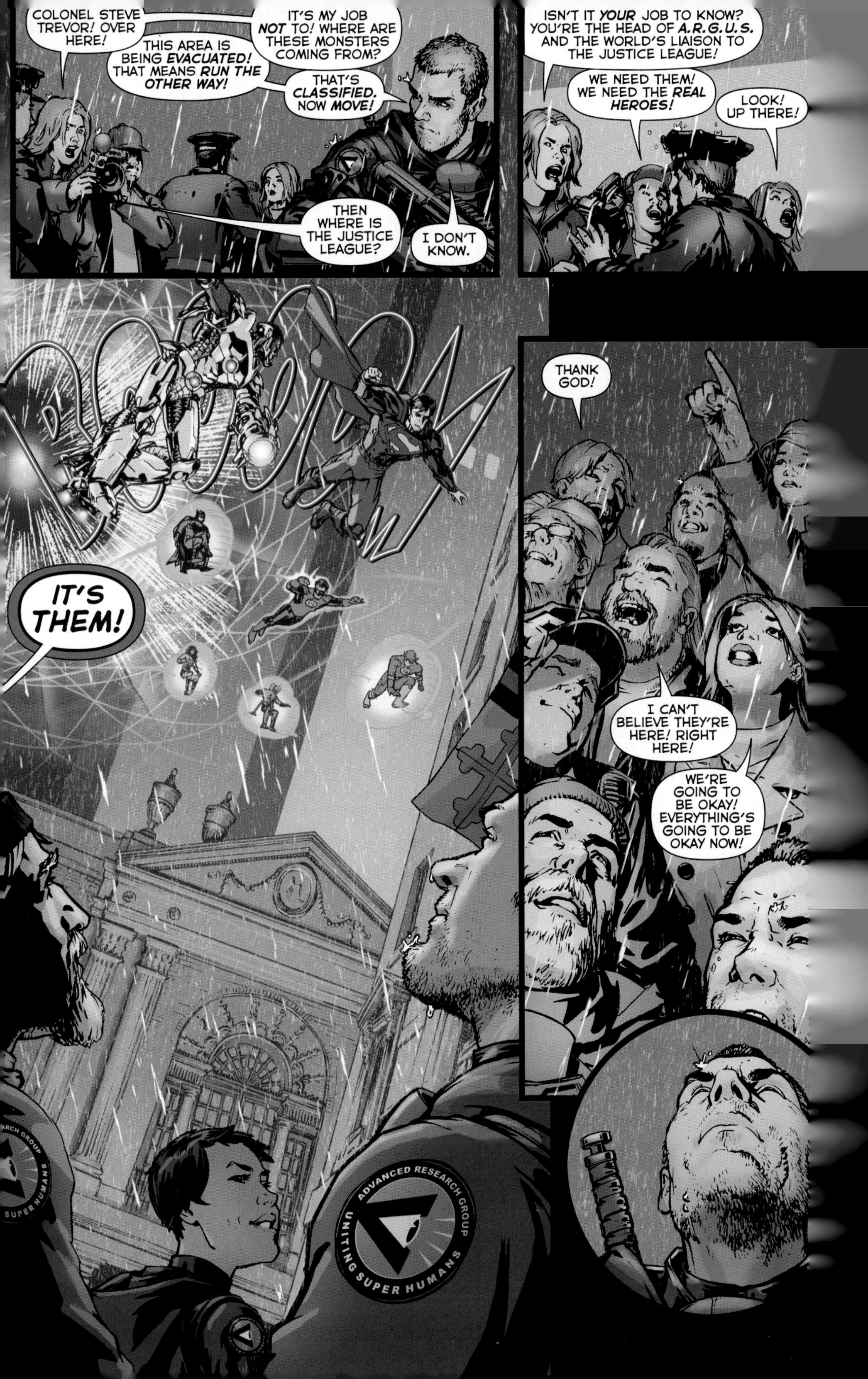

COLONEL STEVE TREVOR! OVER HERE!
THIS AREA IS BEING *EVACUATED!* THAT MEANS *RUN THE OTHER WAY!*
IT'S MY JOB *NOT* TO! WHERE ARE THESE MONSTERS COMING FROM?
THAT'S *CLASSIFIED.* NOW *MOVE!*
THEN WHERE IS THE JUSTICE LEAGUE?
I DON'T KNOW.
ISN'T IT *YOUR* JOB TO KNOW? YOU'RE THE HEAD OF *A.R.G.U.S.* AND THE WORLD'S LIAISON TO THE JUSTICE LEAGUE!
WE NEED THEM! WE NEED THE *REAL HEROES!*
LOOK! UP THERE!
IT'S THEM!
THANK GOD!
I CAN'T BELIEVE THEY'RE HERE! RIGHT HERE!
WE'RE GOING TO BE OKAY! EVERYTHING'S GOING TO BE OKAY NOW!
ADVANCED RESEARCH GROUP
UNITING SUPER HUMANS

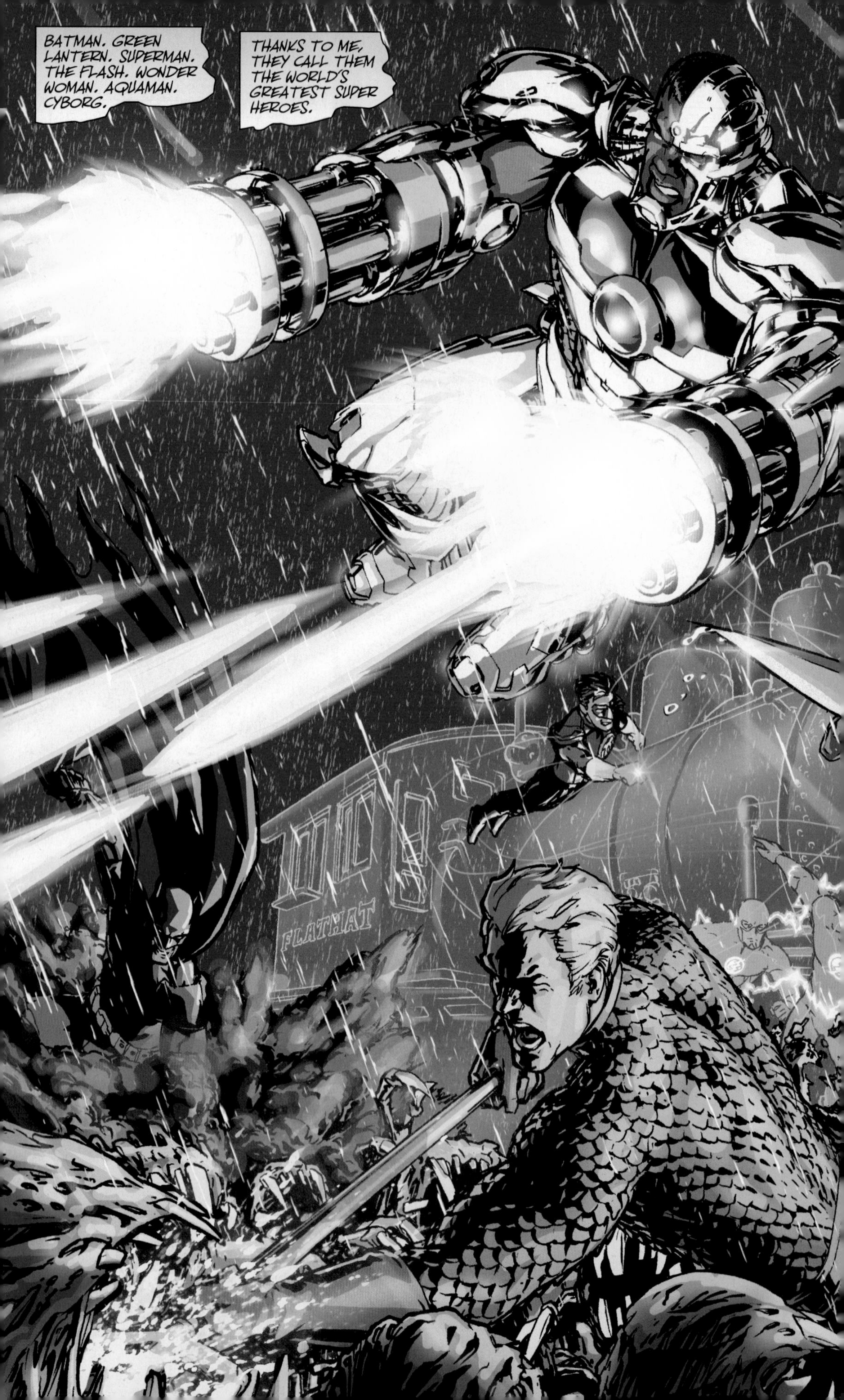
BATMAN. GREEN LANTERN. SUPERMAN. THE FLASH. WONDER WOMAN. AQUAMAN. CYBORG.
THANKS TO ME, THEY CALL THEM THE WORLD'S GREATEST SUPER HEROES.
FLATHAT

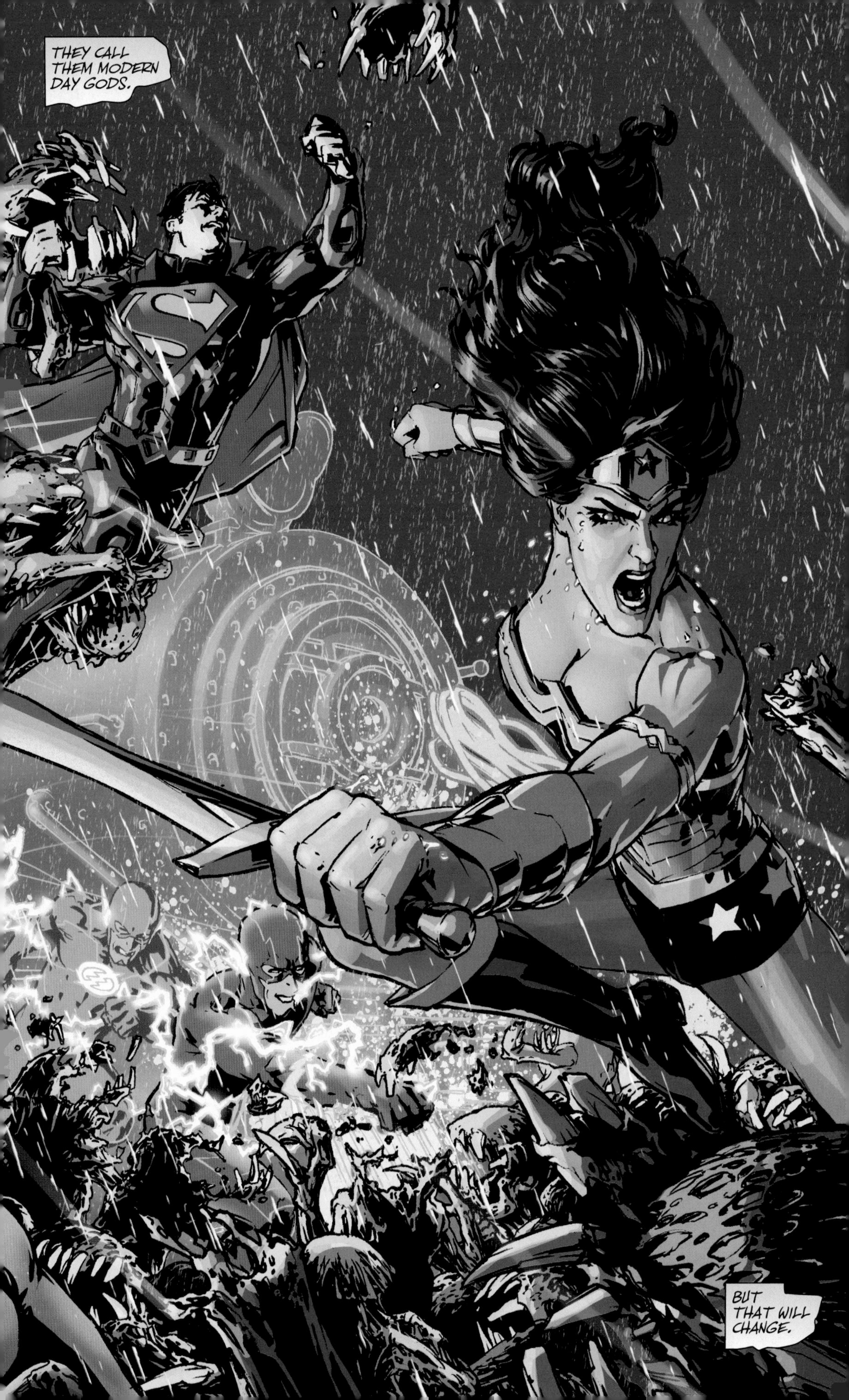
THEY CALL THEM MODERN DAY GODS.
BUT THAT WILL CHANGE.

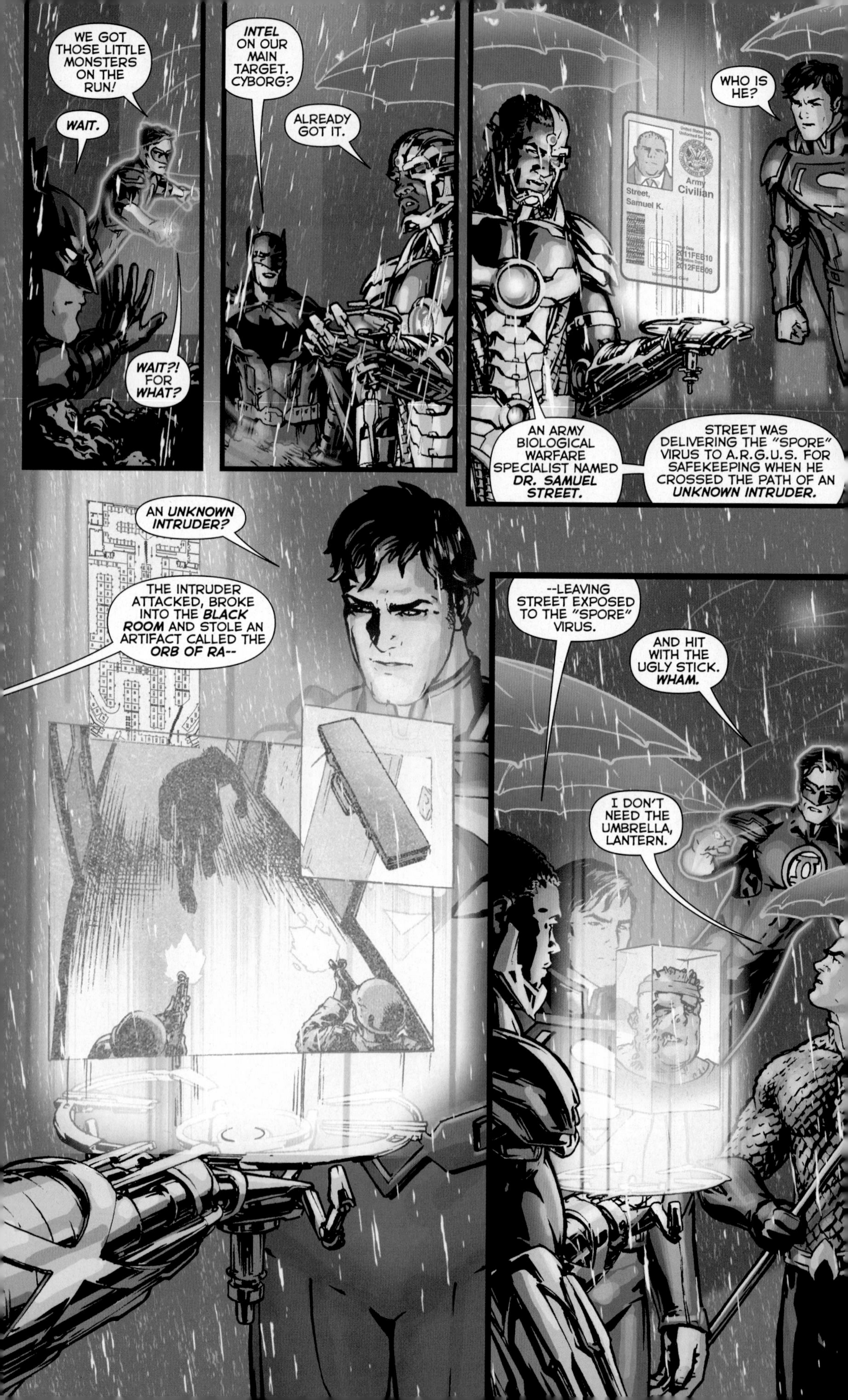

WE GOT THOSE LITTLE MONSTERS ON THE RUN!
WAIT.
WAIT?! FOR WHAT?
INTEL ON OUR MAIN TARGET. CYBORG?
ALREADY GOT IT.
WHO IS HE?
Street, Samuel K.
Army Civilian
2011FEB10
2012FEB09
AN ARMY BIOLOGICAL WARFARE SPECIALIST NAMED DR. SAMUEL STREET.
STREET WAS DELIVERING THE "SPORE" VIRUS TO A.R.G.U.S. FOR SAFEKEEPING WHEN HE CROSSED THE PATH OF AN UNKNOWN INTRUDER.
AN UNKNOWN INTRUDER?
THE INTRUDER ATTACKED, BROKE INTO THE BLACK ROOM AND STOLE AN ARTIFACT CALLED THE ORB OF RA--
--LEAVING STREET EXPOSED TO THE "SPORE" VIRUS.
AND HIT WITH THE UGLY STICK. WHAM.
I DON'T NEED THE UMBRELLA, LANTERN.

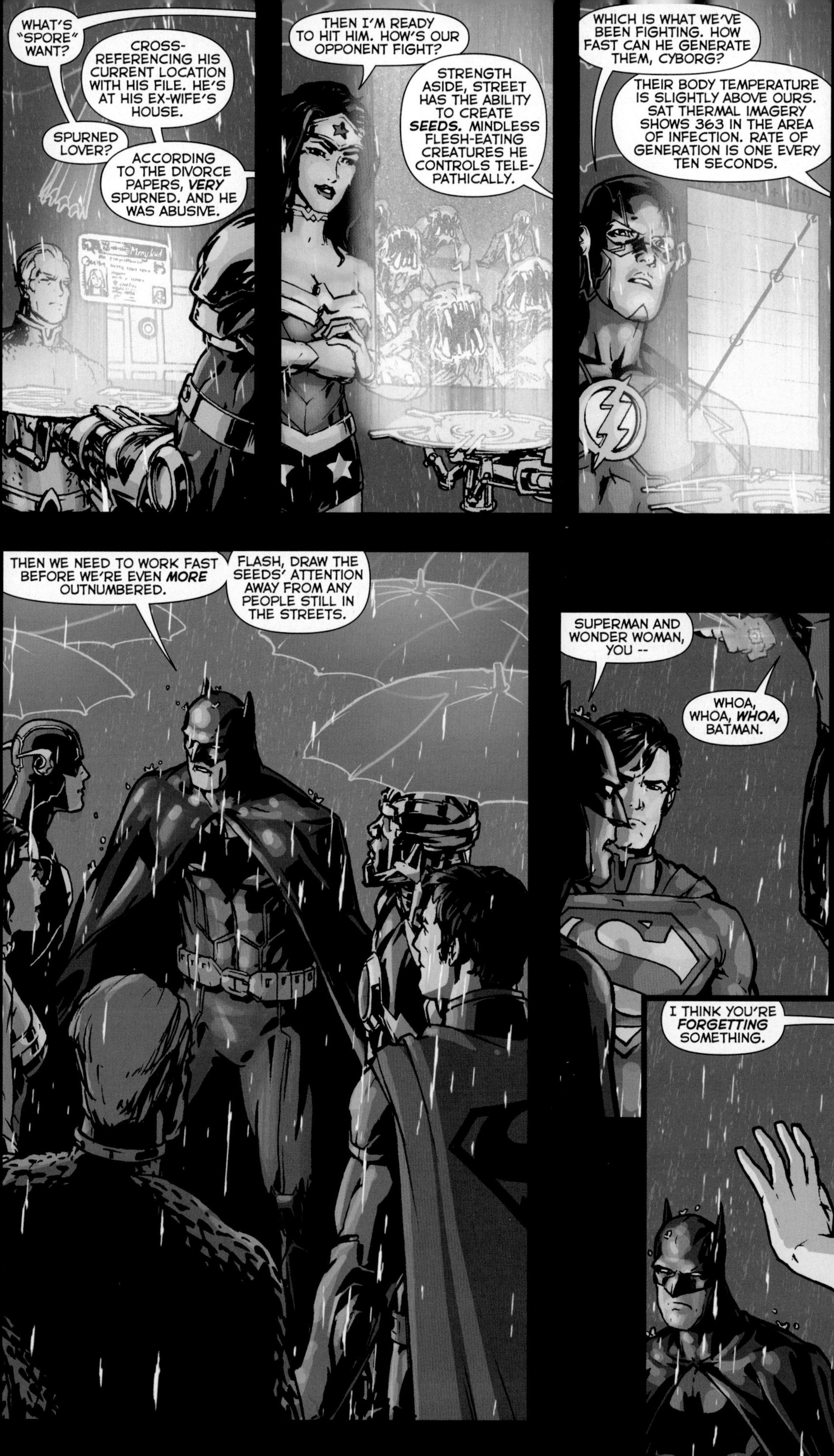
WHAT'S "SPORE" WANT?
CROSS-REFERENCING HIS CURRENT LOCATION WITH HIS FILE. HE'S AT HIS EX-WIFE'S HOUSE.
SPURNED LOVER?
ACCORDING TO THE DIVORCE PAPERS, *VERY* SPURNED. AND HE WAS ABUSIVE.
THEN I'M READY TO HIT HIM. HOW'S OUR OPPONENT FIGHT?
STRENGTH ASIDE, STREET HAS THE ABILITY TO CREATE *SEEDS.* MINDLESS FLESH-EATING CREATURES HE CONTROLS TELE-PATHICALLY.
WHICH IS WHAT WE'VE BEEN FIGHTING. HOW FAST CAN HE GENERATE THEM, CYBORG?
THEIR BODY TEMPERATURE IS SLIGHTLY ABOVE OURS. SAT THERMAL IMAGERY SHOWS 363 IN THE AREA OF INFECTION. RATE OF GENERATION IS ONE EVERY TEN SECONDS.
THEN WE NEED TO WORK FAST BEFORE WE'RE EVEN *MORE* OUTNUMBERED.
FLASH, DRAW THE SEEDS' ATTENTION AWAY FROM ANY PEOPLE STILL IN THE STREETS.
SUPERMAN AND WONDER WOMAN, YOU --
WHOA, WHOA, *WHOA,* BATMAN.
I THINK YOU'RE *FORGETTING* SOMETHING.

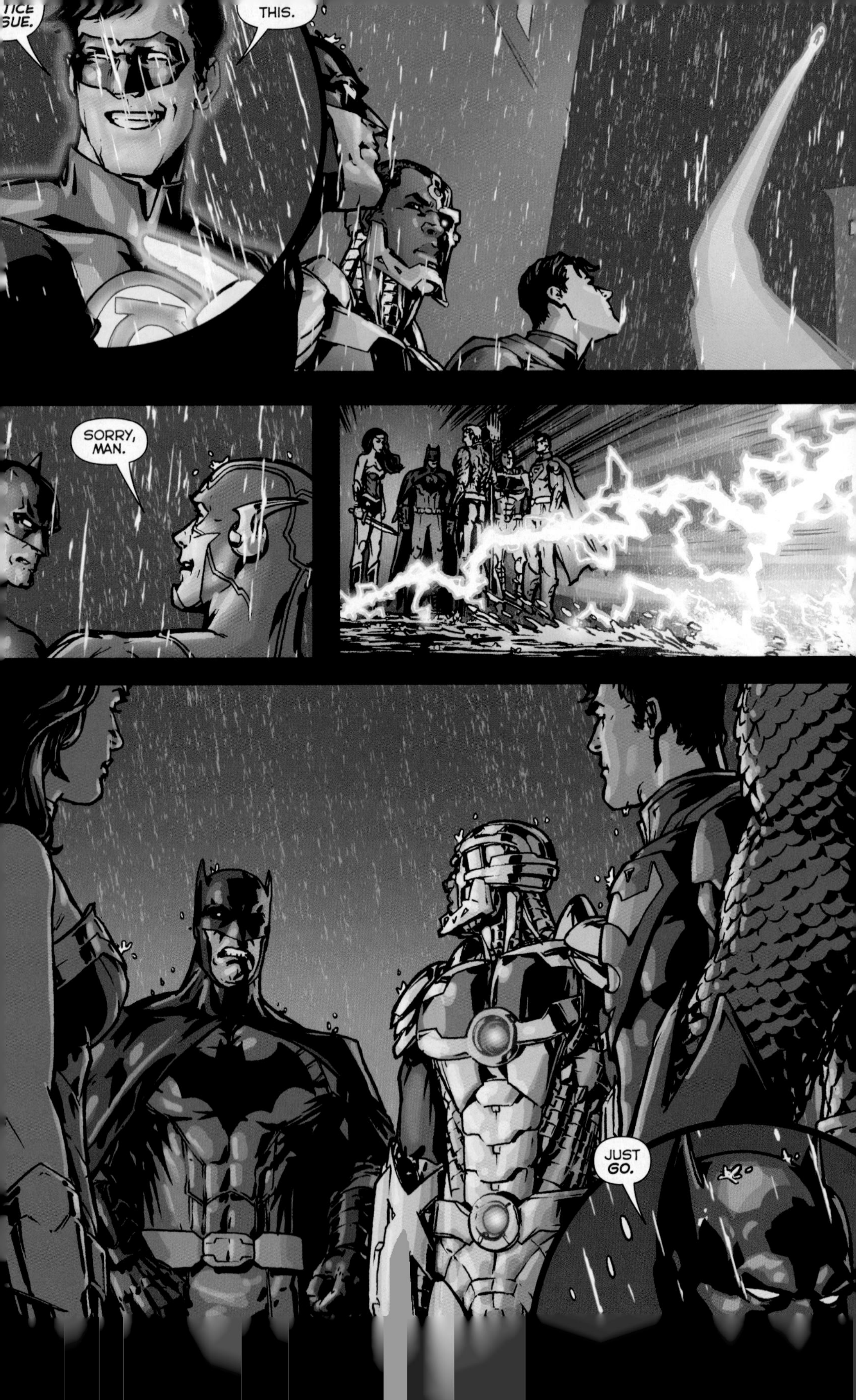
TICE
GUE.
THIS.
SORRY, MAN.
JUST GO.

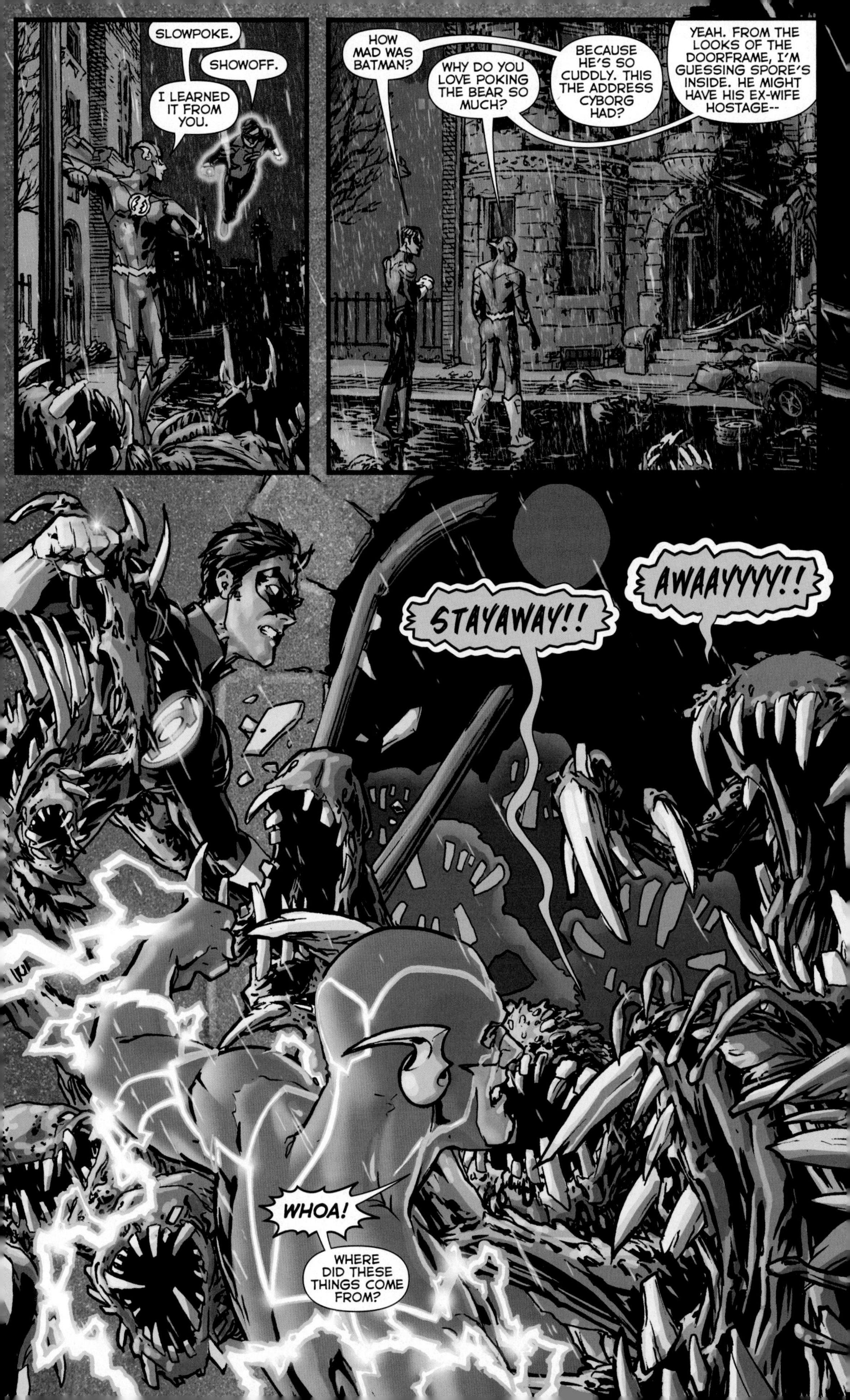
SLOWPOKE.
SHOWOFF.
I LEARNED IT FROM YOU.
HOW MAD WAS BATMAN?
WHY DO YOU LOVE POKING THE BEAR SO MUCH?
BECAUSE HE'S SO CUDDLY. THIS THE ADDRESS CYBORG HAD?
YEAH. FROM THE LOOKS OF THE DOORFRAME, I'M GUESSING SPORE'S INSIDE. HE MIGHT HAVE HIS EX-WIFE HOSTAGE--
STAYAWAY!!
AWAAYYYY!!
WHOA!
WHERE DID THESE THINGS COME FROM?

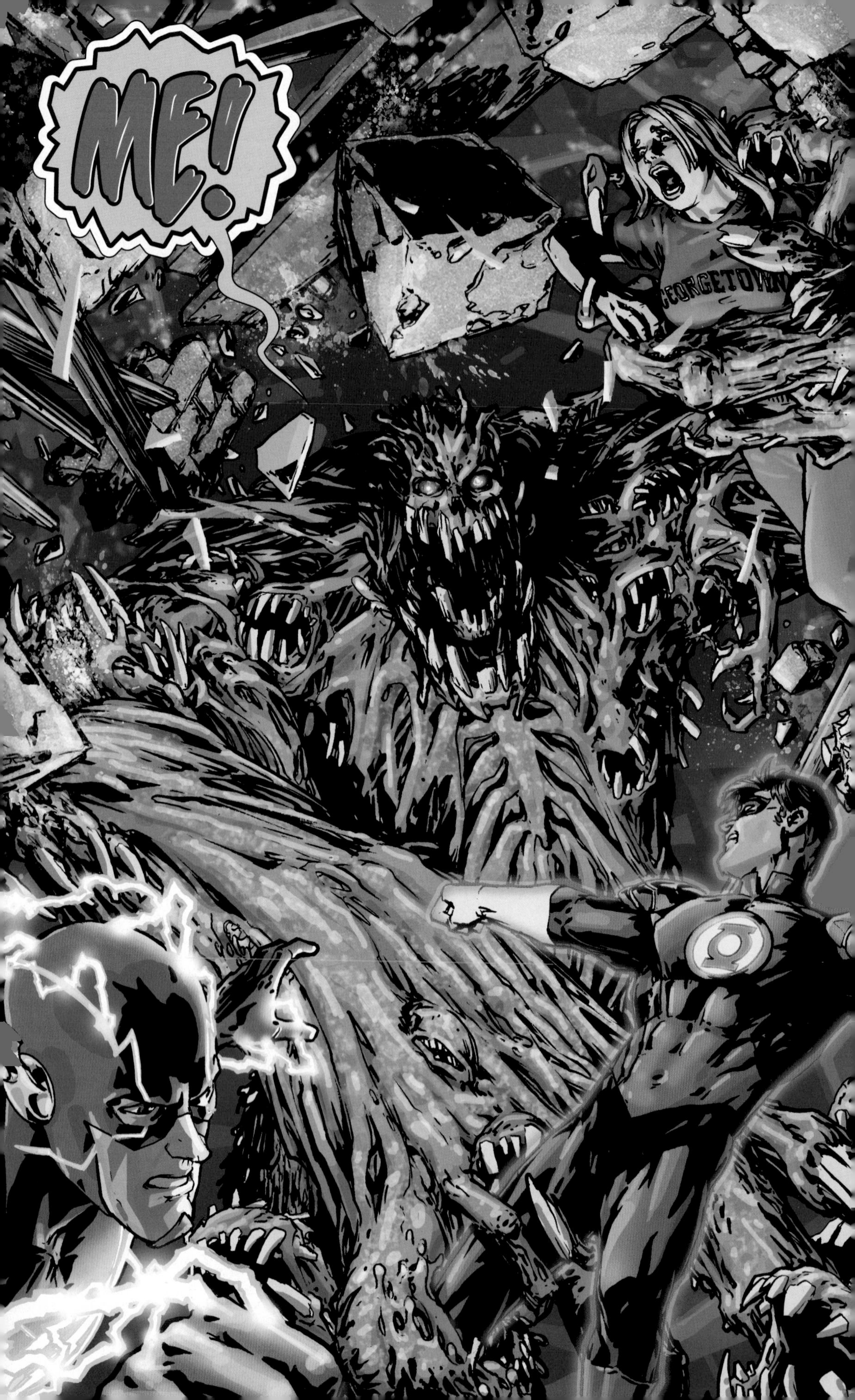
ME!
GEORGETOWN

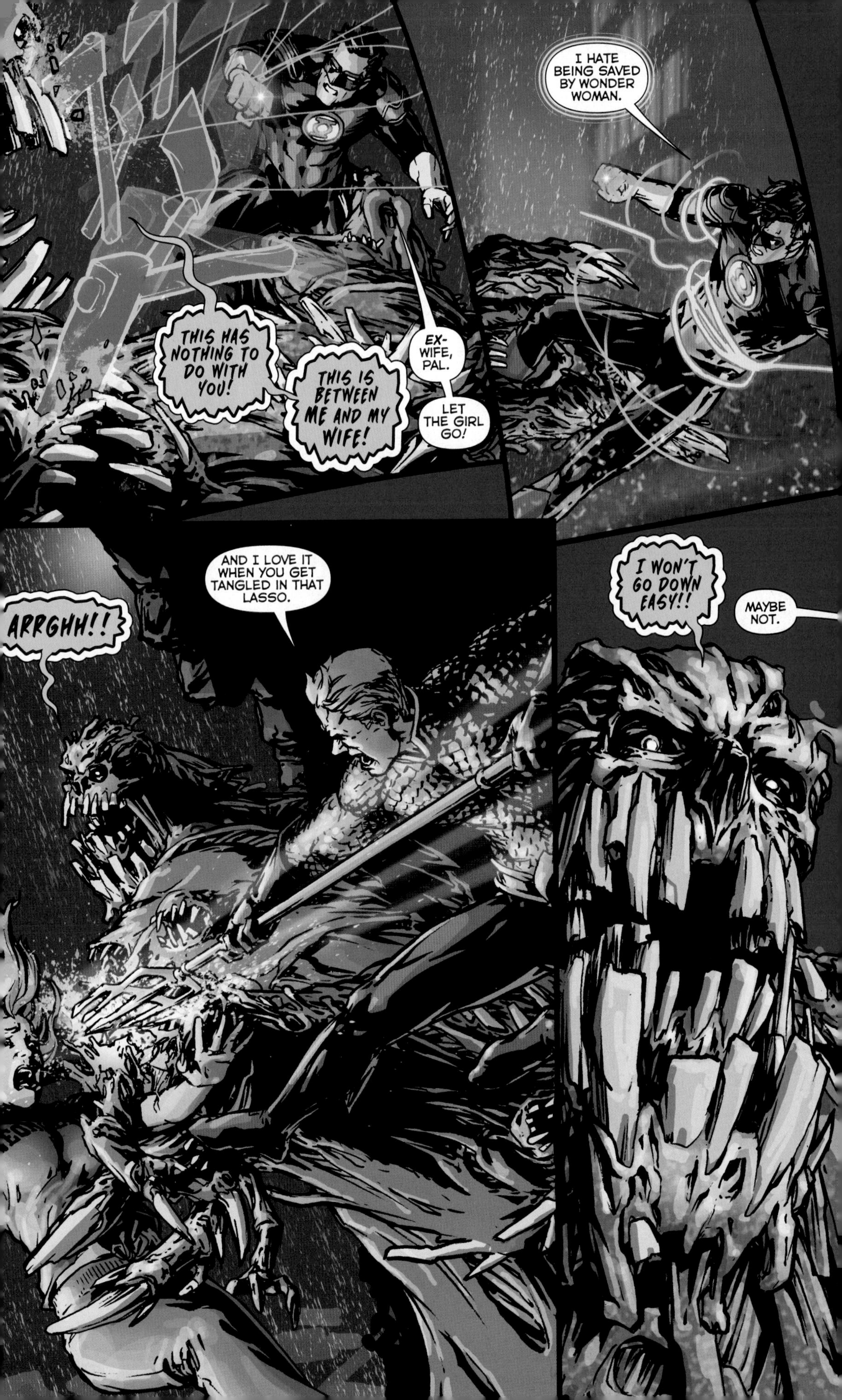
THIS HAS NOTHING TO DO WITH YOU!
THIS IS BETWEEN ME AND MY WIFE!
EX-WIFE, PAL.
LET THE GIRL GO!
I HATE BEING SAVED BY WONDER WOMAN.
ARRGHH!!
AND I LOVE IT WHEN YOU GET TANGLED IN THAT LASSO.
I WON'T GO DOWN EASY!!
MAYBE NOT.

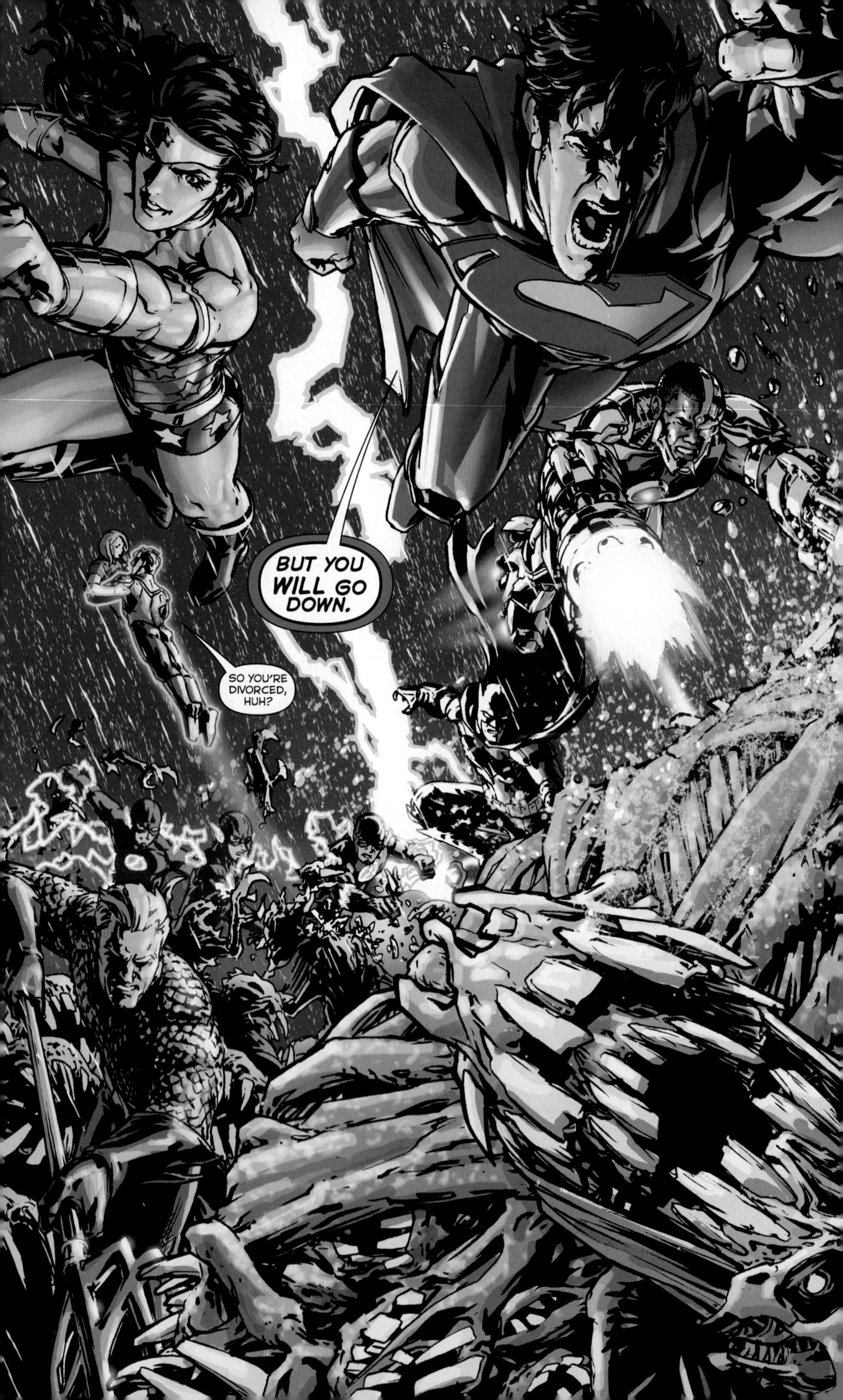
BUT YOU WILL GO DOWN.
SO YOU'RE DIVORCED, HUH?

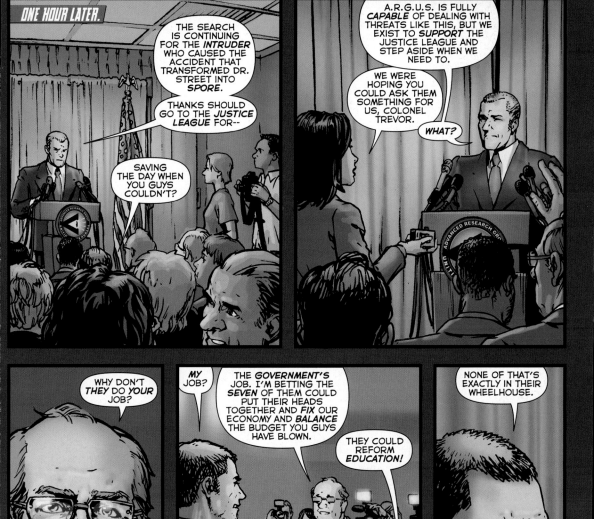

THE SEARCH IS CONTINUING FOR THE *INTRUDER* WHO CAUSED THE ACCIDENT THAT TRANSFORMED DR. STREET INTO *SPORE*.

THANKS SHOULD GO TO THE *JUSTICE LEAGUE* FOR--

SAVING THE DAY WHEN YOU GUYS COULDN'T?

A.R.G.U.S. IS FULLY *CAPABLE* OF DEALING WITH THREATS LIKE THIS, BUT WE EXIST TO *SUPPORT* THE JUSTICE LEAGUE AND STEP ASIDE WHEN WE NEED TO.

WE WERE HOPING YOU COULD ASK THEM SOMETHING FOR US, COLONEL TREVOR.

WHAT?

WHY DON'T *THEY* DO *YOUR* JOB?

MY JOB?

THE *GOVERNMENT'S* JOB. I'M BETTING THE *SEVEN* OF THEM COULD PUT THEIR HEADS TOGETHER AND *FIX* OUR ECONOMY AND *BALANCE* THE BUDGET YOU GUYS HAVE BLOWN.

THEY COULD REFORM *EDUCATION!*

NONE OF THAT'S EXACTLY IN THEIR WHEELHOUSE.

WHAT *ISN'T?* COME ON, COLONEL. THE LEAGUE'S RECORD IS *SPOTLESS.* AND THE WAY THEY WORK *TOGETHER.*

THEY GIVE US HOPE!

THEY'RE NOT AT EACH OTHER'S THROATS. THEY'RE FRIENDS.

THEY'RE *SUPER-FRIENDS!*

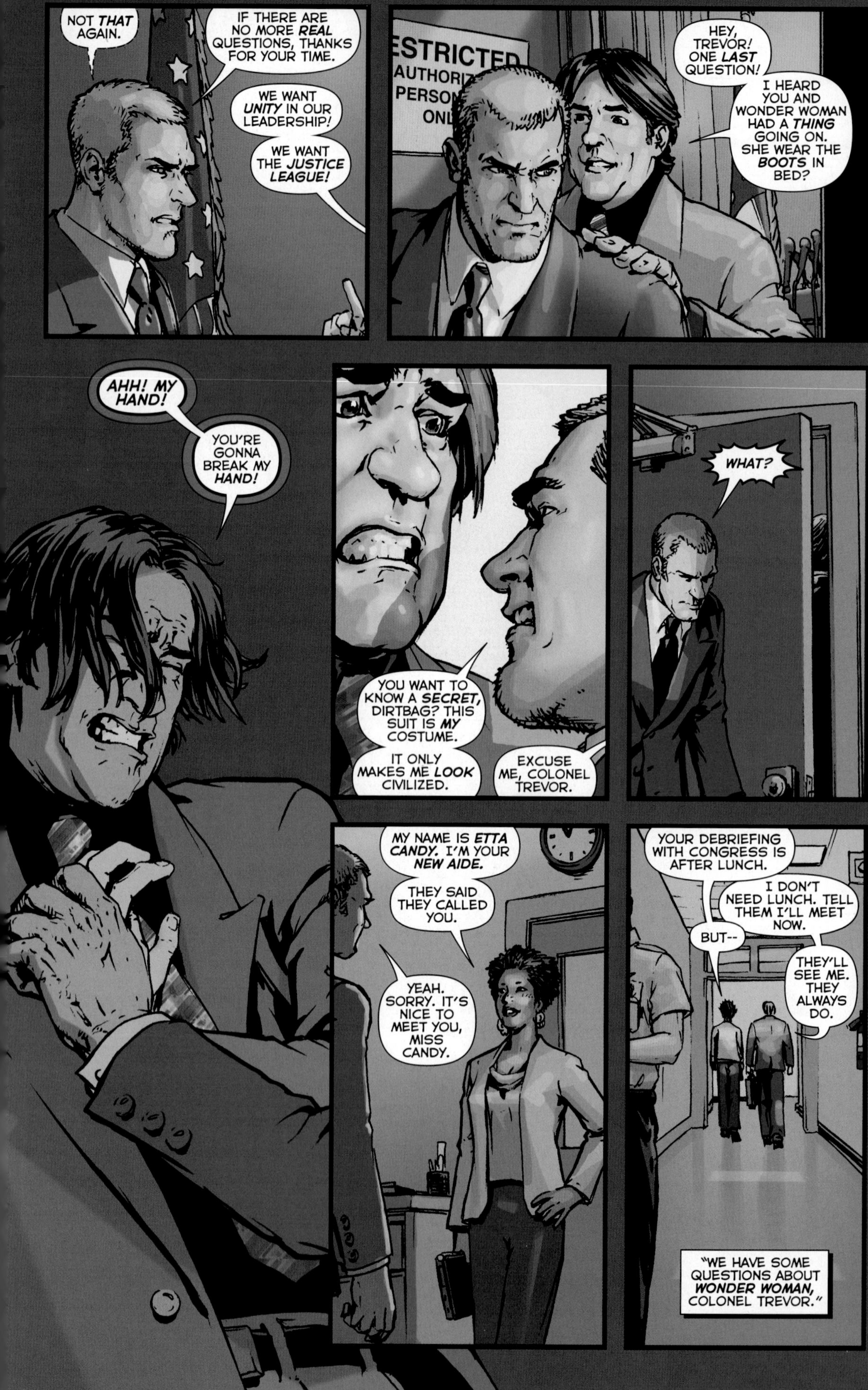
NOT THAT AGAIN.
IF THERE ARE NO MORE REAL QUESTIONS, THANKS FOR YOUR TIME.
WE WANT UNITY IN OUR LEADERSHIP!
WE WANT THE JUSTICE LEAGUE!
ESTRICTED AUTHORIZ PERSON ONL
HEY, TREVOR! ONE LAST QUESTION!
I HEARD YOU AND WONDER WOMAN HAD A THING GOING ON. SHE WEAR THE BOOTS IN BED?
AHH! MY HAND!
YOU'RE GONNA BREAK MY HAND!
YOU WANT TO KNOW A SECRET, DIRTBAG? THIS SUIT IS MY COSTUME.
IT ONLY MAKES ME LOOK CIVILIZED.
EXCUSE ME, COLONEL TREVOR.
WHAT?
MY NAME IS ETTA CANDY. I'M YOUR NEW AIDE.
THEY SAID THEY CALLED YOU.
YEAH. SORRY. IT'S NICE TO MEET YOU, MISS CANDY.
YOUR DEBRIEFING WITH CONGRESS IS AFTER LUNCH.
I DON'T NEED LUNCH. TELL THEM I'LL MEET NOW.
BUT--
THEY'LL SEE ME. THEY ALWAYS DO.
"WE HAVE SOME QUESTIONS ABOUT WONDER WOMAN, COLONEL TREVOR."

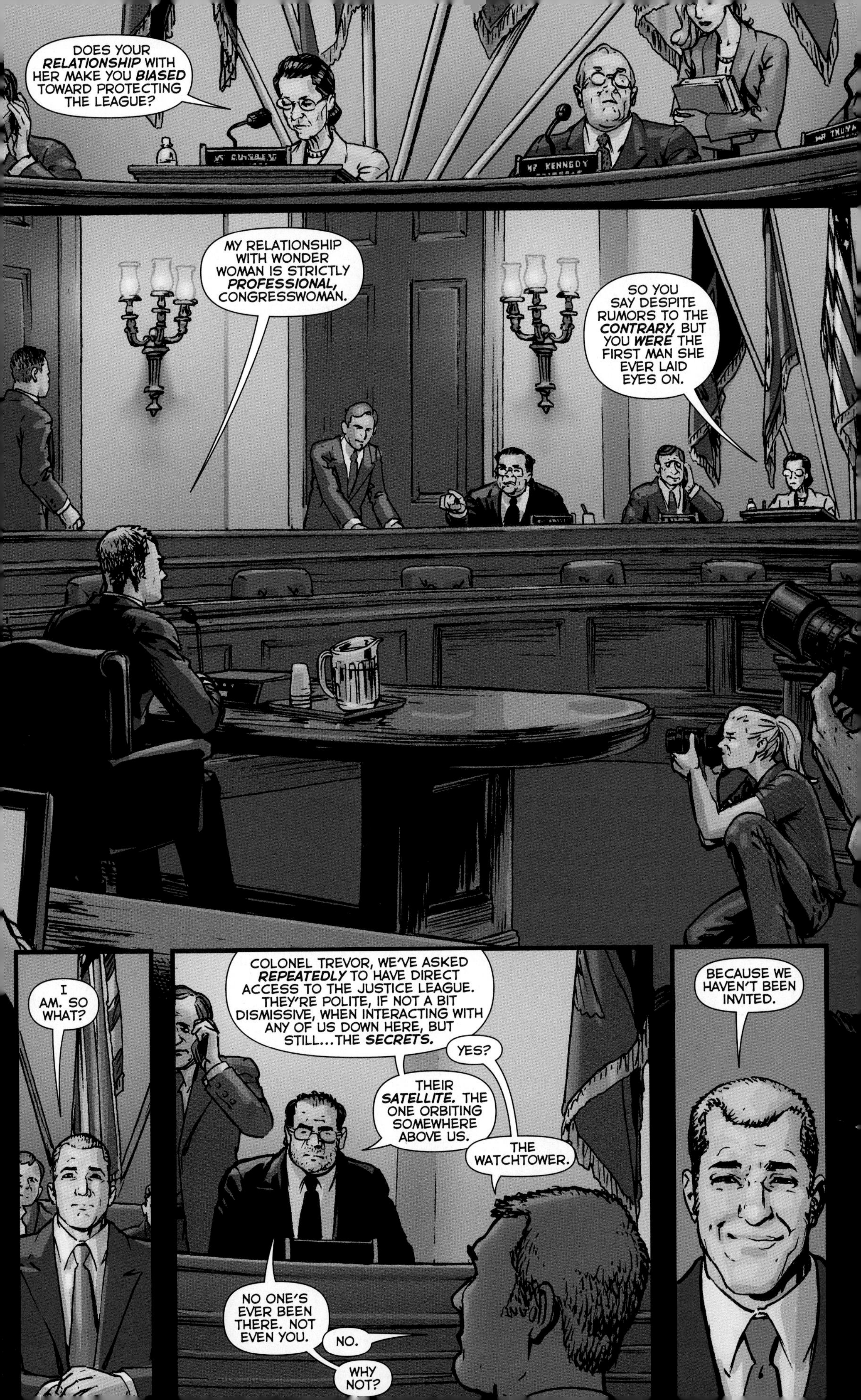
DOES YOUR RELATIONSHIP WITH HER MAKE YOU BIASED TOWARD PROTECTING THE LEAGUE?
MR KENNEDY
MY RELATIONSHIP WITH WONDER WOMAN IS STRICTLY PROFESSIONAL, CONGRESSWOMAN.
SO YOU SAY DESPITE RUMORS TO THE CONTRARY, BUT YOU WERE THE FIRST MAN SHE EVER LAID EYES ON.
I AM. SO WHAT?
COLONEL TREVOR, WE'VE ASKED REPEATEDLY TO HAVE DIRECT ACCESS TO THE JUSTICE LEAGUE. THEY'RE POLITE, IF NOT A BIT DISMISSIVE, WHEN INTERACTING WITH ANY OF US DOWN HERE, BUT STILL...THE SECRETS.
YES?
THEIR SATELLITE. THE ONE ORBITING SOMEWHERE ABOVE US.
THE WATCHTOWER.
NO ONE'S EVER BEEN THERE. NOT EVEN YOU.
NO.
WHY NOT?
BECAUSE WE HAVEN'T BEEN INVITED.

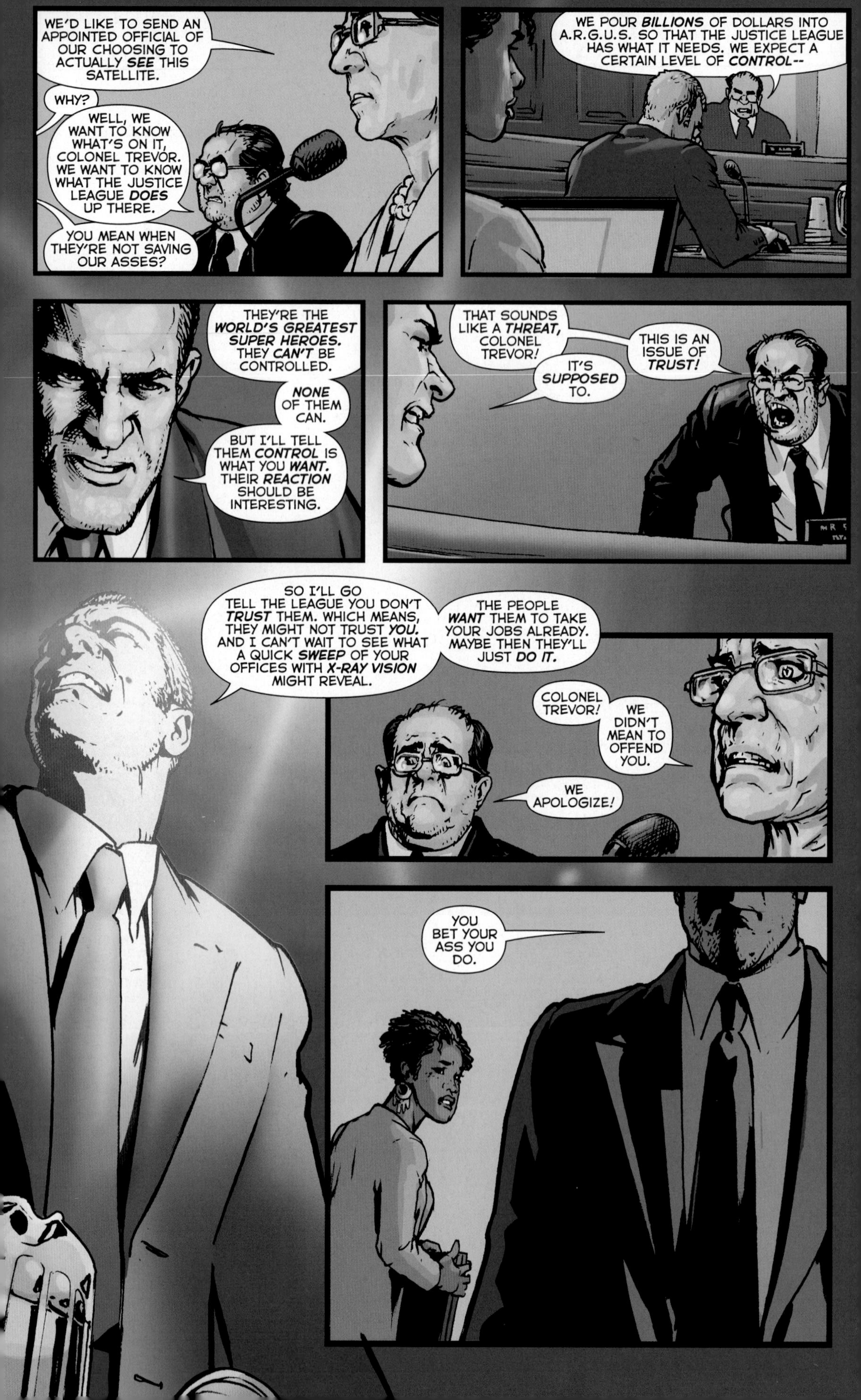
WE'D LIKE TO SEND AN APPOINTED OFFICIAL OF OUR CHOOSING TO ACTUALLY SEE THIS SATELLITE.
WHY?
WELL, WE WANT TO KNOW WHAT'S ON IT, COLONEL TREVOR. WE WANT TO KNOW WHAT THE JUSTICE LEAGUE DOES UP THERE.
YOU MEAN WHEN THEY'RE NOT SAVING OUR ASSES?
WE POUR BILLIONS OF DOLLARS INTO A.R.G.U.S. SO THAT THE JUSTICE LEAGUE HAS WHAT IT NEEDS. WE EXPECT A CERTAIN LEVEL OF CONTROL--
THEY'RE THE WORLD'S GREATEST SUPER HEROES. THEY CAN'T BE CONTROLLED.
NONE OF THEM CAN.
BUT I'LL TELL THEM CONTROL IS WHAT YOU WANT. THEIR REACTION SHOULD BE INTERESTING.
THAT SOUNDS LIKE A THREAT, COLONEL TREVOR!
IT'S SUPPOSED TO.
THIS IS AN ISSUE OF TRUST!
SO I'LL GO TELL THE LEAGUE YOU DON'T TRUST THEM. WHICH MEANS, THEY MIGHT NOT TRUST YOU. AND I CAN'T WAIT TO SEE WHAT A QUICK SWEEP OF YOUR OFFICES WITH X-RAY VISION MIGHT REVEAL.
THE PEOPLE WANT THEM TO TAKE YOUR JOBS ALREADY. MAYBE THEN THEY'LL JUST DO IT.
COLONEL TREVOR!
WE DIDN'T MEAN TO OFFEND YOU.
WE APOLOGIZE!
YOU BET YOUR ASS YOU DO.

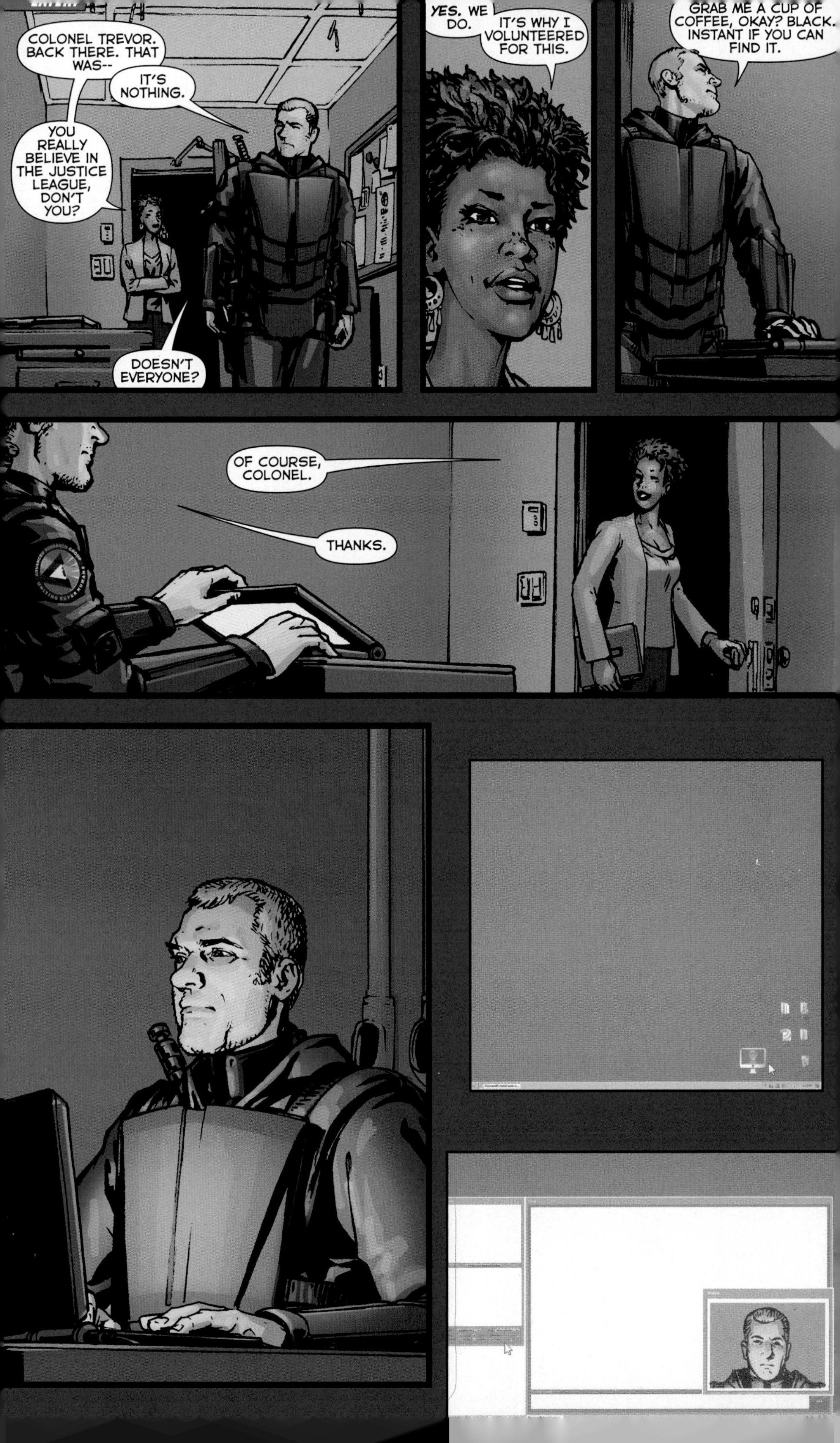
COLONEL TREVOR. BACK THERE. THAT WAS--
IT'S NOTHING.
YOU REALLY BELIEVE IN THE JUSTICE LEAGUE, DON'T YOU?
DOESN'T EVERYONE?
YES. WE DO.
IT'S WHY I VOLUNTEERED FOR THIS.
GRAB ME A CUP OF COFFEE, OKAY? BLACK. INSTANT IF YOU CAN FIND IT.
OF COURSE, COLONEL.
THANKS.

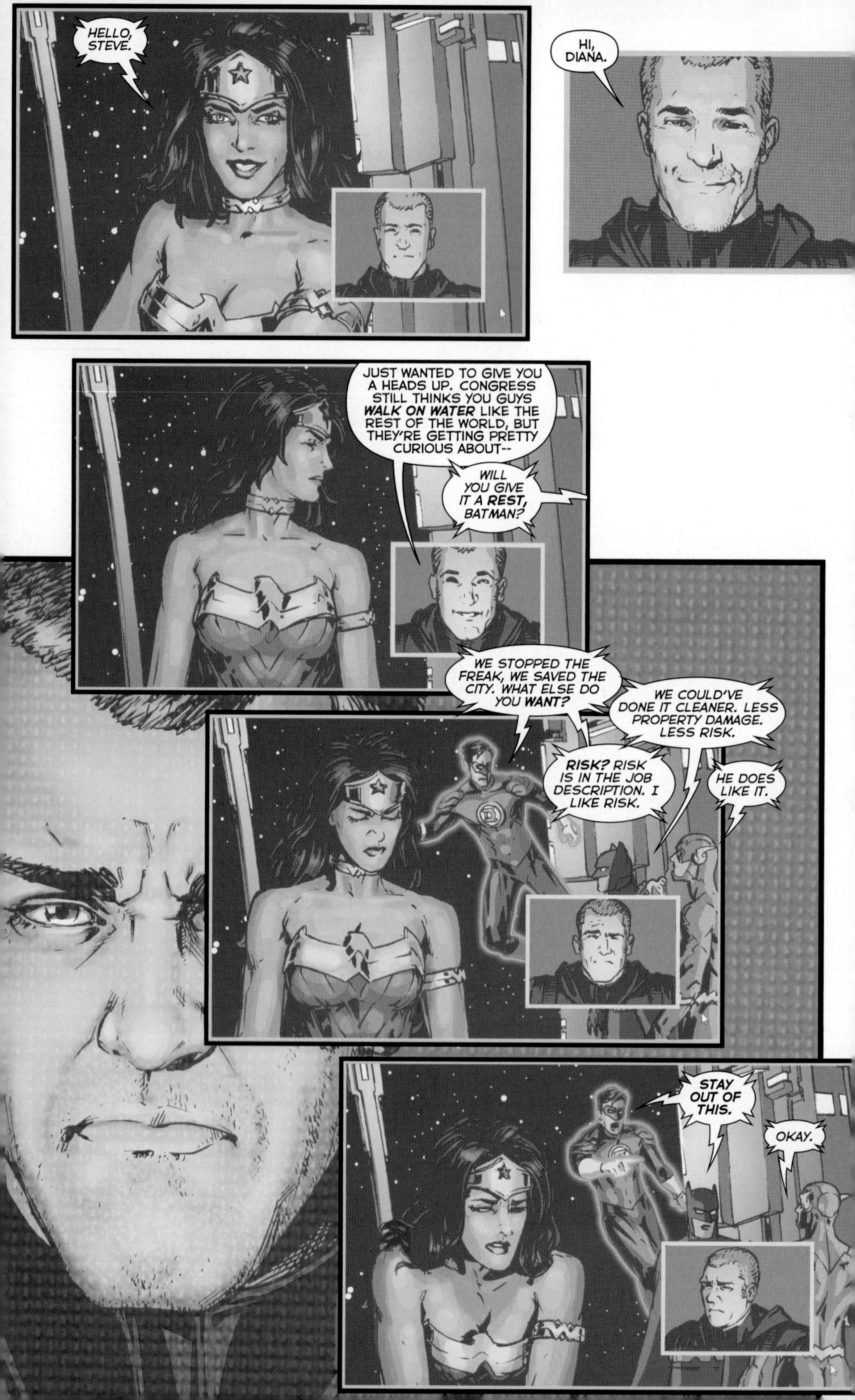
HELLO, STEVE.
HI, DIANA.
JUST WANTED TO GIVE YOU A HEADS UP. CONGRESS STILL THINKS YOU GUYS WALK ON WATER LIKE THE REST OF THE WORLD, BUT THEY'RE GETTING PRETTY CURIOUS ABOUT--
WILL YOU GIVE IT A REST, BATMAN?
WE STOPPED THE FREAK, WE SAVED THE CITY. WHAT ELSE DO YOU WANT?
WE COULD'VE DONE IT CLEANER. LESS PROPERTY DAMAGE. LESS RISK.
RISK? RISK IS IN THE JOB DESCRIPTION. I LIKE RISK.
HE DOES LIKE IT.
STAY OUT OF THIS.
OKAY.

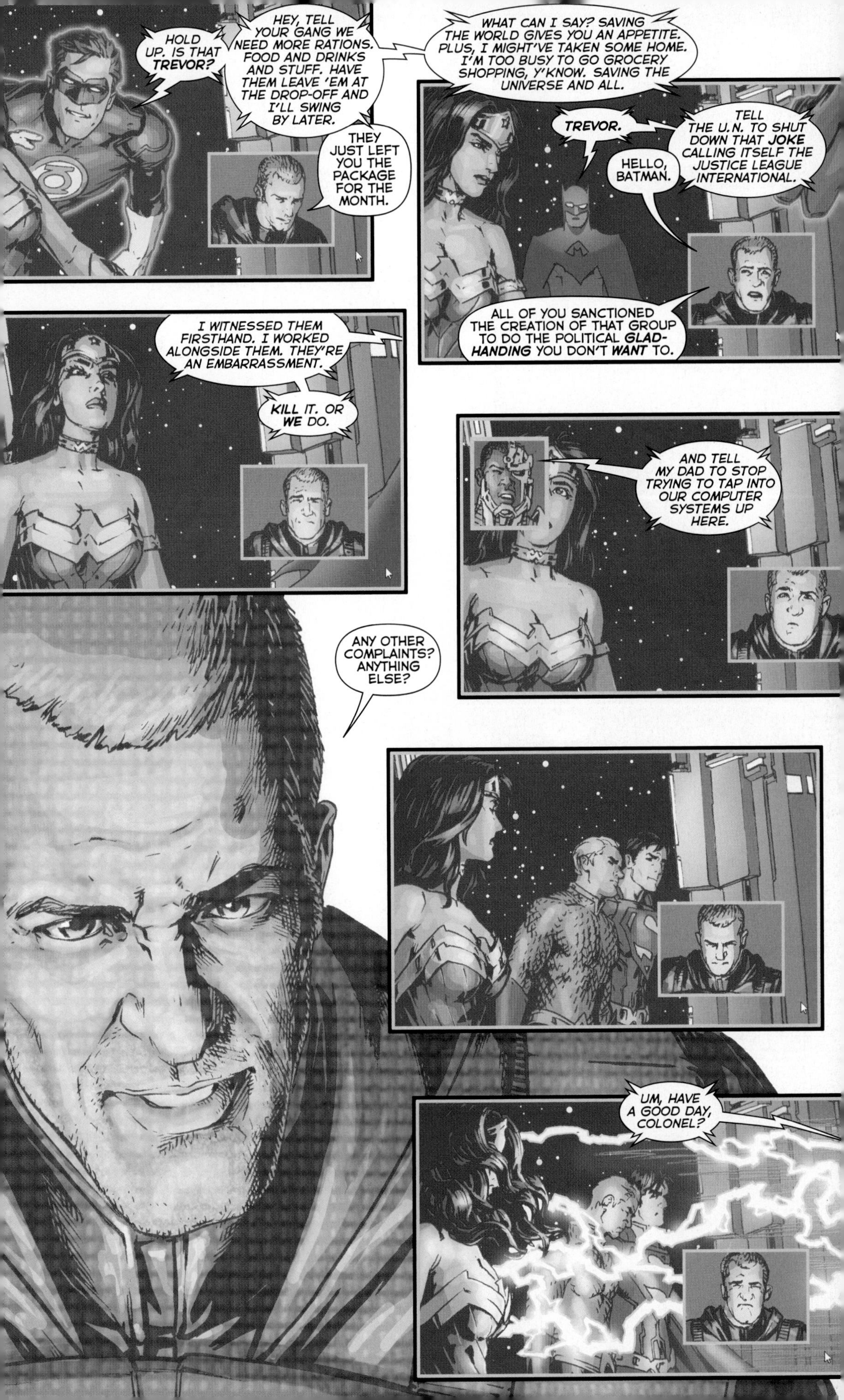
HOLD UP. IS THAT TREVOR?
HEY, TELL YOUR GANG WE NEED MORE RATIONS. FOOD AND DRINKS AND STUFF. HAVE THEM LEAVE 'EM AT THE DROP-OFF AND I'LL SWING BY LATER.
THEY JUST LEFT YOU THE PACKAGE FOR THE MONTH.
WHAT CAN I SAY? SAVING THE WORLD GIVES YOU AN APPETITE. PLUS, I MIGHT'VE TAKEN SOME HOME. I'M TOO BUSY TO GO GROCERY SHOPPING, Y'KNOW. SAVING THE UNIVERSE AND ALL.
TREVOR.
TELL THE U.N. TO SHUT DOWN THAT JOKE CALLING ITSELF THE JUSTICE LEAGUE INTERNATIONAL.
HELLO, BATMAN.
ALL OF YOU SANCTIONED THE CREATION OF THAT GROUP TO DO THE POLITICAL GLAD-HANDING YOU DON'T WANT TO.
I WITNESSED THEM FIRSTHAND. I WORKED ALONGSIDE THEM. THEY'RE AN EMBARRASSMENT.
KILL IT. OR WE DO.
AND TELL MY DAD TO STOP TRYING TO TAP INTO OUR COMPUTER SYSTEMS UP HERE.
ANY OTHER COMPLAINTS? ANYTHING ELSE?
UM, HAVE A GOOD DAY, COLONEL?

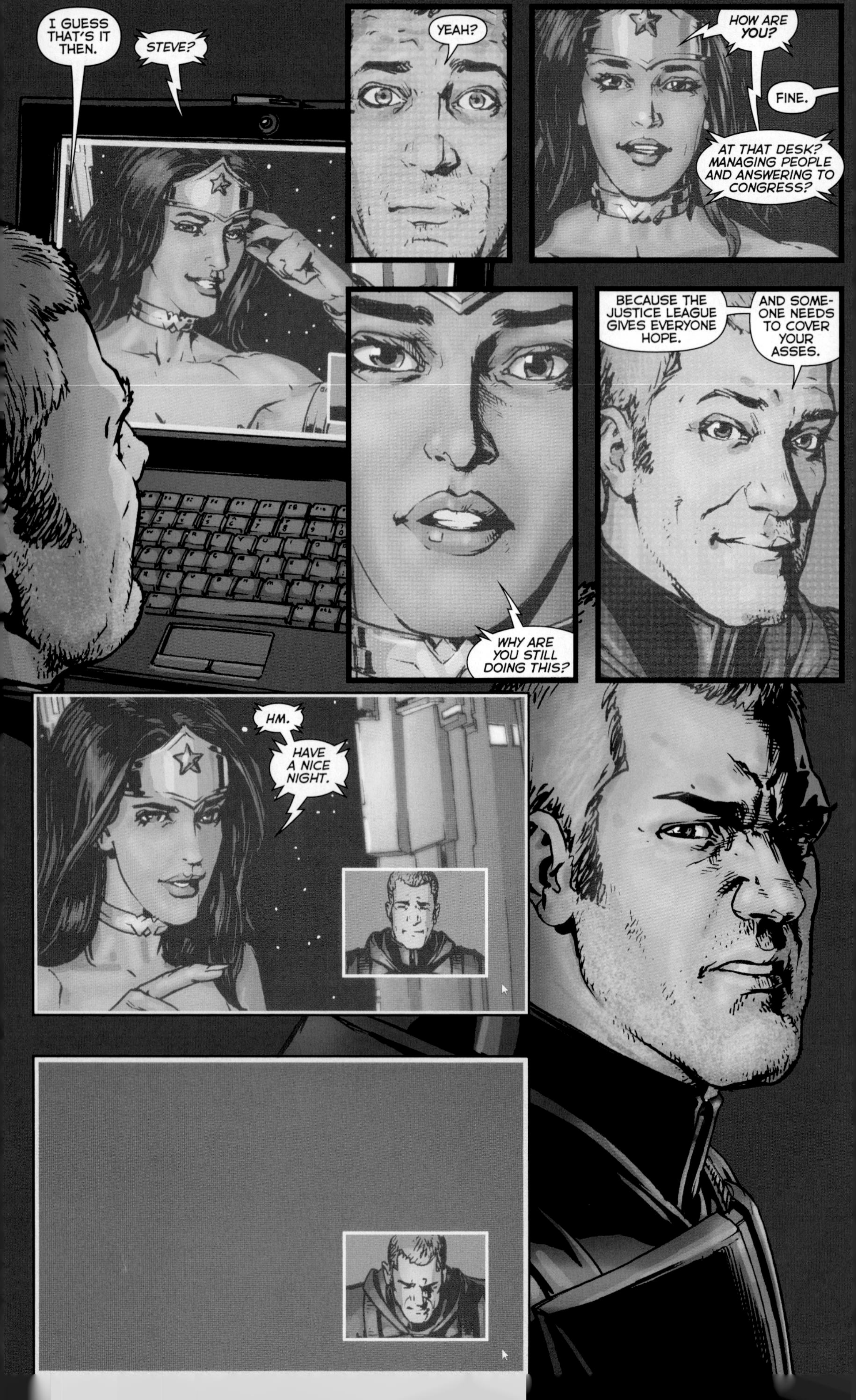
I GUESS THAT'S IT THEN.
STEVE?
YEAH?
HOW ARE YOU?
FINE.
AT THAT DESK? MANAGING PEOPLE AND ANSWERING TO CONGRESS?
WHY ARE YOU STILL DOING THIS?
BECAUSE THE JUSTICE LEAGUE GIVES EVERYONE HOPE.
AND SOME-ONE NEEDS TO COVER YOUR ASSES.
HM.
HAVE A NICE NIGHT.

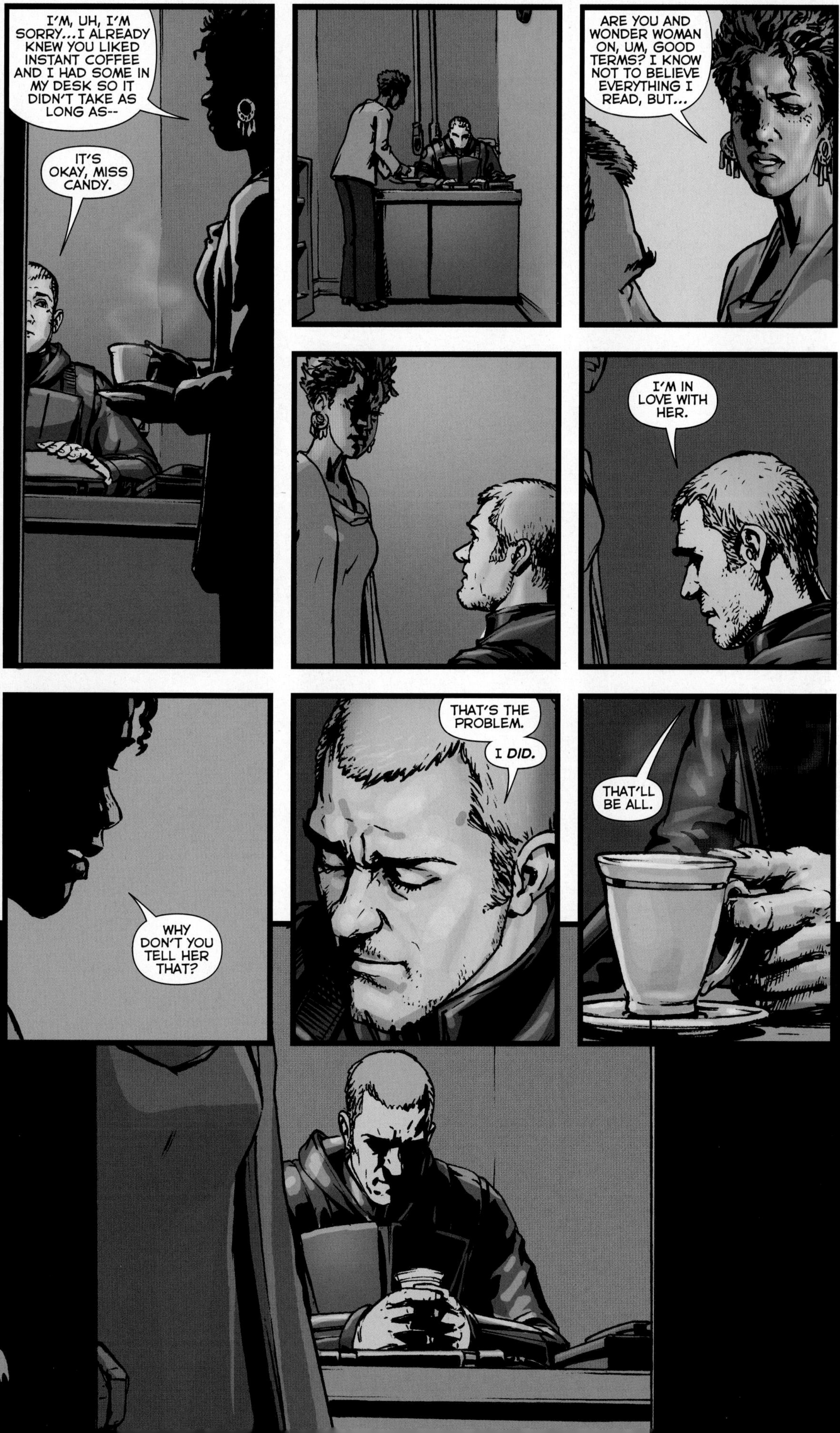
I'M, UH, I'M SORRY...I ALREADY KNEW YOU LIKED INSTANT COFFEE AND I HAD SOME IN MY DESK SO IT DIDN'T TAKE AS LONG AS--
IT'S OKAY, MISS CANDY.
ARE YOU AND WONDER WOMAN ON, UM, GOOD TERMS? I KNOW NOT TO BELIEVE EVERYTHING I READ, BUT...
I'M IN LOVE WITH HER.
WHY DON'T YOU TELL HER THAT?
THAT'S THE PROBLEM.
I DID.
THAT'LL BE ALL.

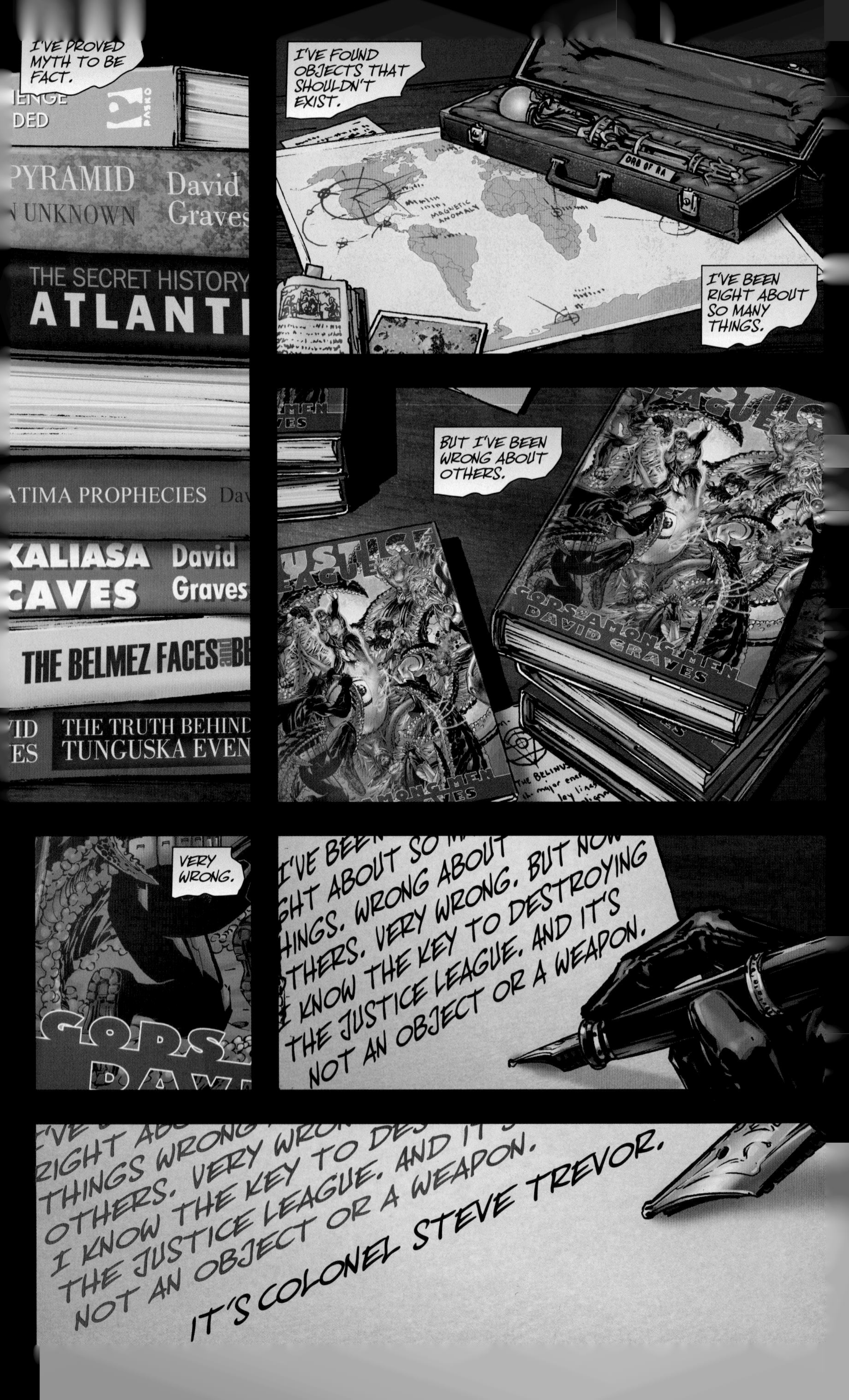

I'VE PROVED MYTH TO BE FACT.
PYRAMID
David Graves
THE SECRET HISTORY
ATLANTI
ATIMA PROPHECIES
KALIASA CAVES
David Graves
THE BELMEZ FACES
THE TRUTH BEHIND TUNGUSKA EVEN
I'VE FOUND OBJECTS THAT SHOULDN'T EXIST.
ORB OF RA
MAGNETIC ANOMALY
I'VE BEEN RIGHT ABOUT SO MANY THINGS.
BUT I'VE BEEN WRONG ABOUT OTHERS.
JUSTICE LEAGUE
GODS AMONG MEN
DAVID GRAVES
VERY WRONG.
THINGS. WRONG ABOUT OTHERS. VERY WRONG. BUT NOW I KNOW THE KEY TO DESTROYING THE JUSTICE LEAGUE. AND IT'S NOT AN OBJECT OR A WEAPON.
IT'S COLONEL STEVE TREVOR.

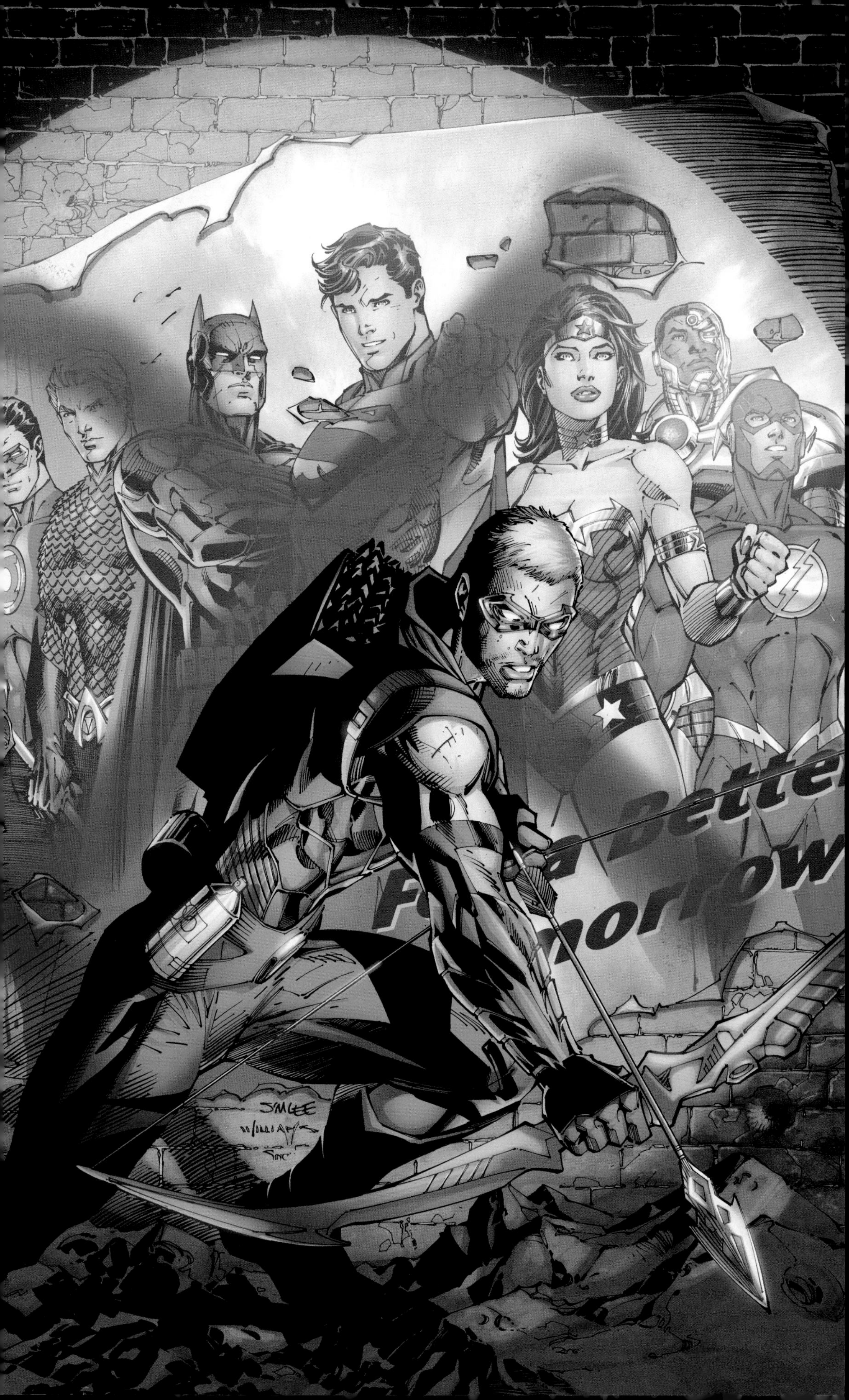

JUSTICE LEAGUE TEAM-UP: GREEN ARROW

GEOFF JOHNS writer **CARLOS D'ANDA WITH IVAN REIS & JOE PRADO** artists cover by **JIM LEE, SCOTT WILLIAMS & ALEX SINCLAIR**

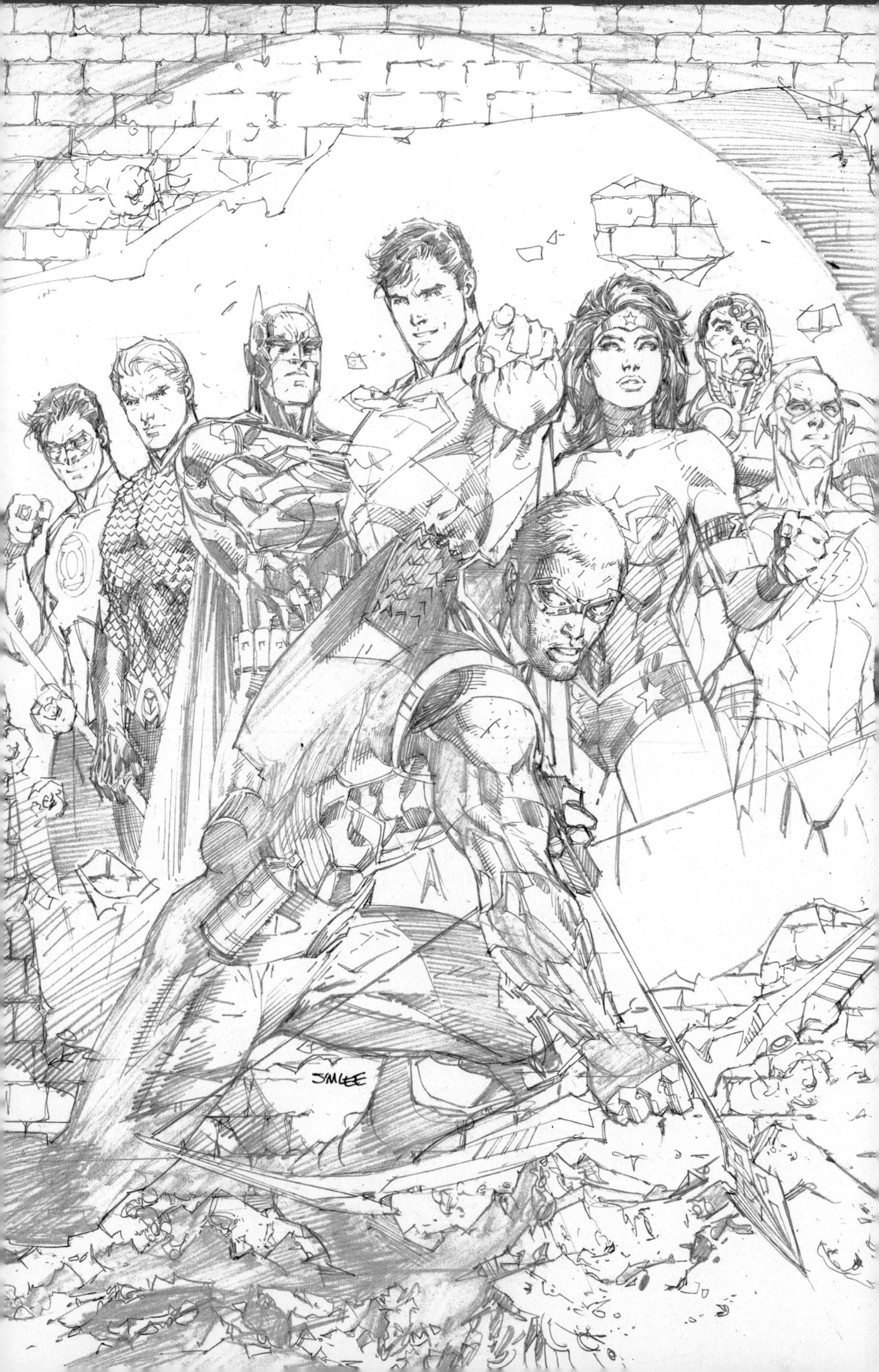
JIMLEE

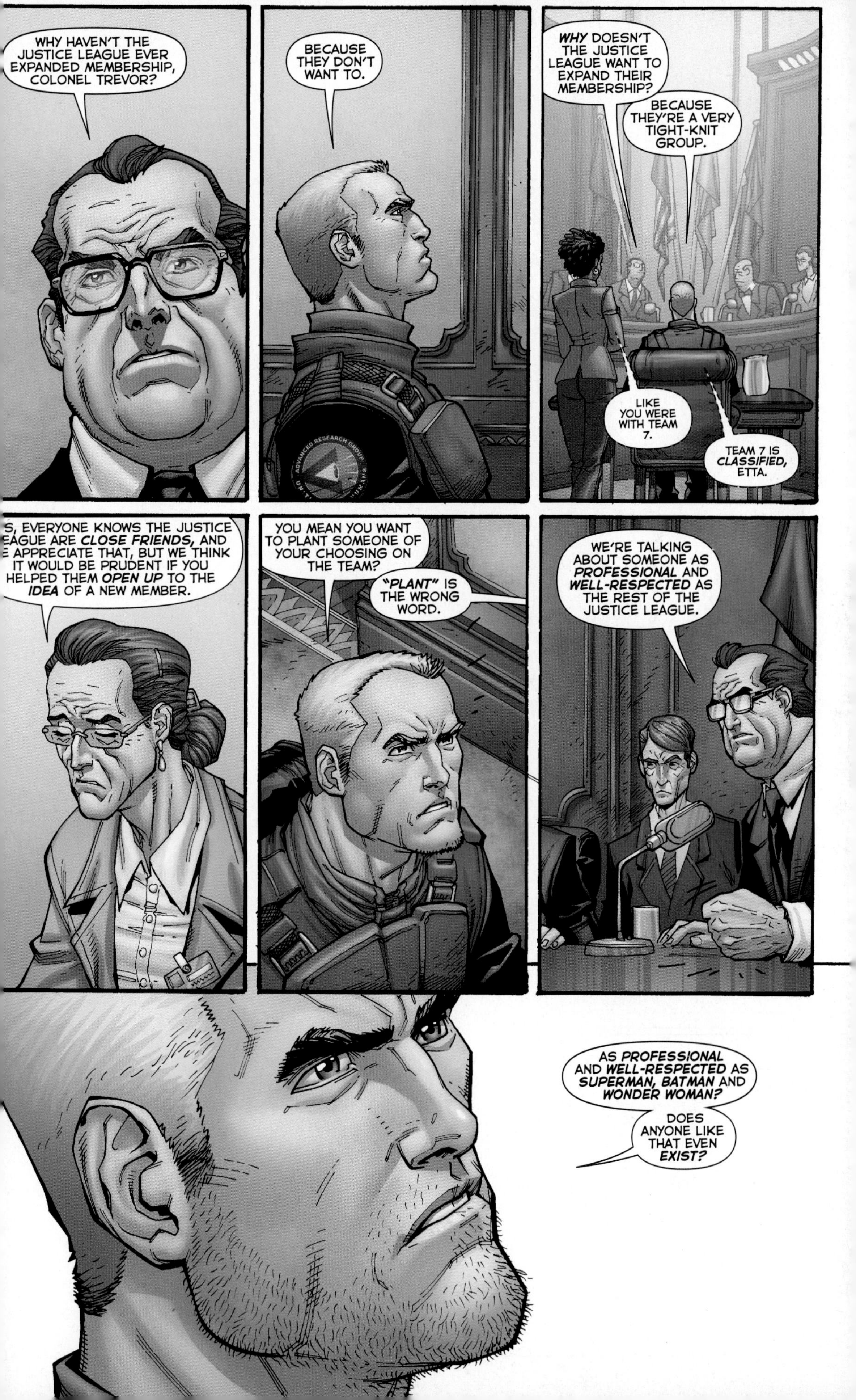
WHY HAVEN'T THE JUSTICE LEAGUE EVER EXPANDED MEMBERSHIP, COLONEL TREVOR?
BECAUSE THEY DON'T WANT TO.
ADVANCED RESEARCH GROUP
WHY DOESN'T THE JUSTICE LEAGUE WANT TO EXPAND THEIR MEMBERSHIP?
BECAUSE THEY'RE A VERY TIGHT-KNIT GROUP.
LIKE YOU WERE WITH TEAM 7.
TEAM 7 IS *CLASSIFIED,* ETTA.
S, EVERYONE KNOWS THE JUSTICE EAGUE ARE *CLOSE FRIENDS,* AND E APPRECIATE THAT, BUT WE THINK IT WOULD BE PRUDENT IF YOU HELPED THEM *OPEN UP* TO THE *IDEA* OF A NEW MEMBER.
YOU MEAN YOU WANT TO PLANT SOMEONE OF YOUR CHOOSING ON THE TEAM?
"PLANT" IS THE WRONG WORD.
WE'RE TALKING ABOUT SOMEONE AS *PROFESSIONAL* AND *WELL-RESPECTED* AS THE REST OF THE JUSTICE LEAGUE.
AS *PROFESSIONAL* AND *WELL-RESPECTED* AS *SUPERMAN, BATMAN* AND *WONDER WOMAN?*
DOES ANYONE LIKE THAT EVEN *EXIST?*

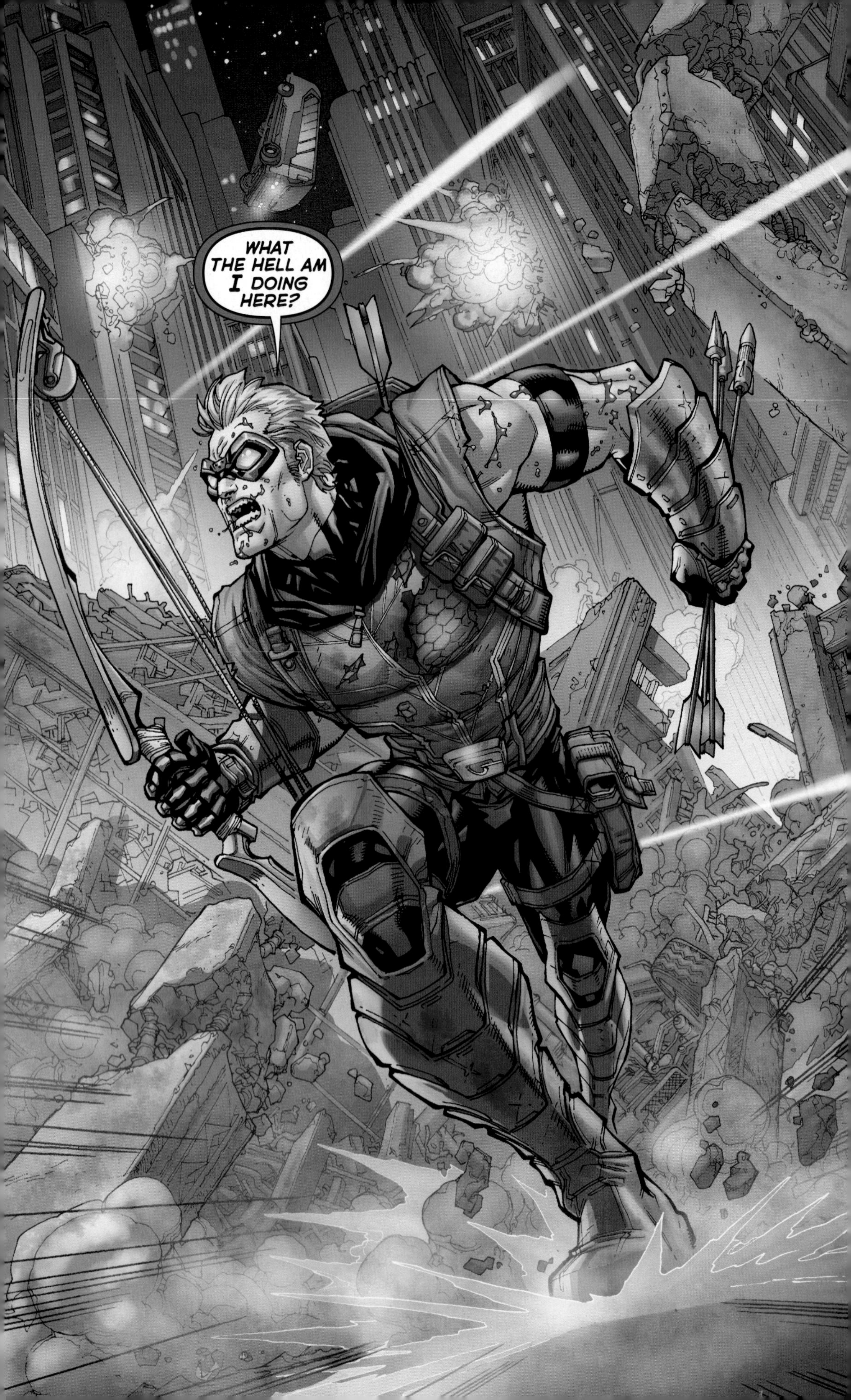
WHAT THE HELL AM I DOING HERE?

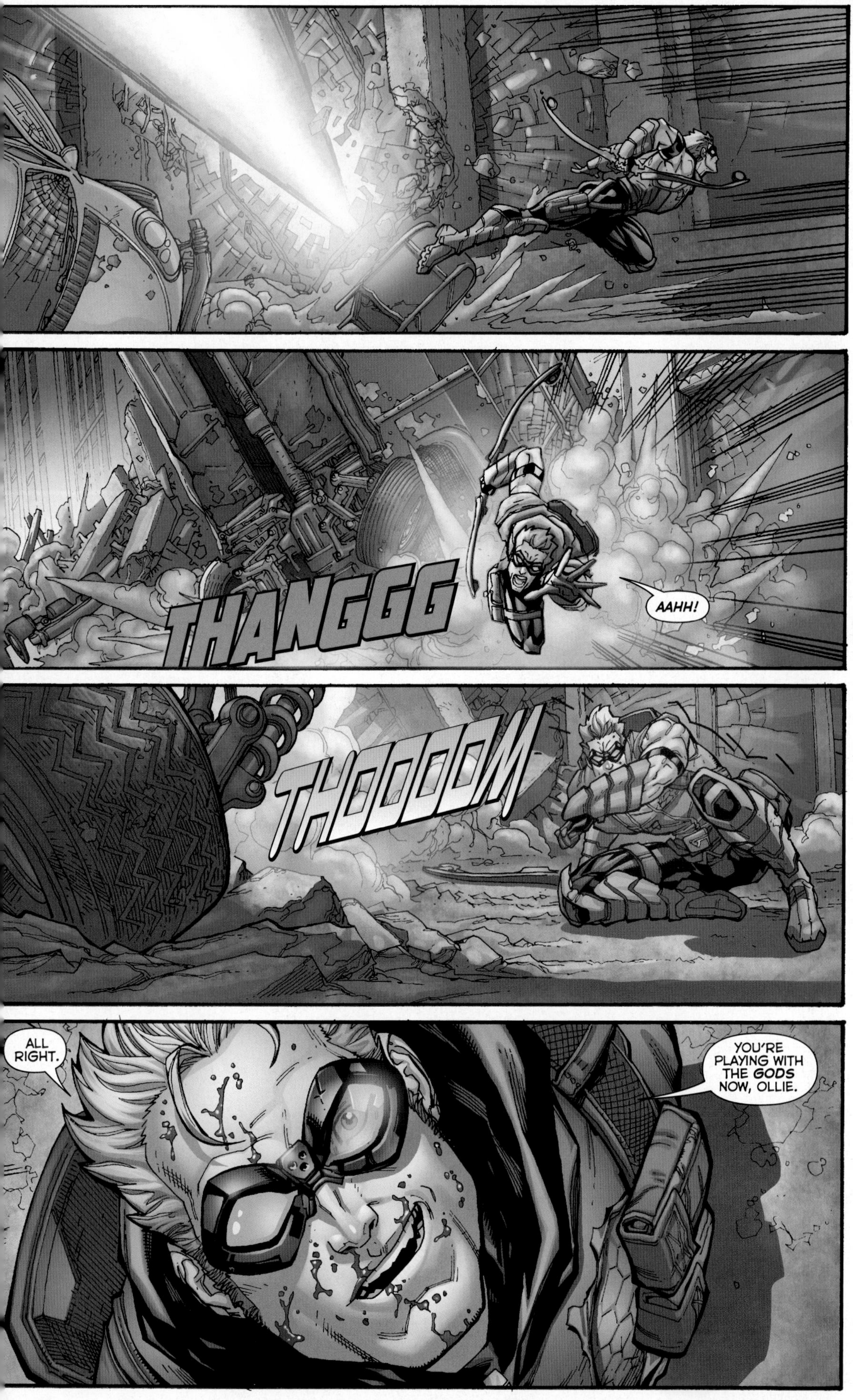
THANGGG
AAHH!
THOOOOM
ALL RIGHT.
YOU'RE PLAYING WITH THE GODS NOW, OLLIE.

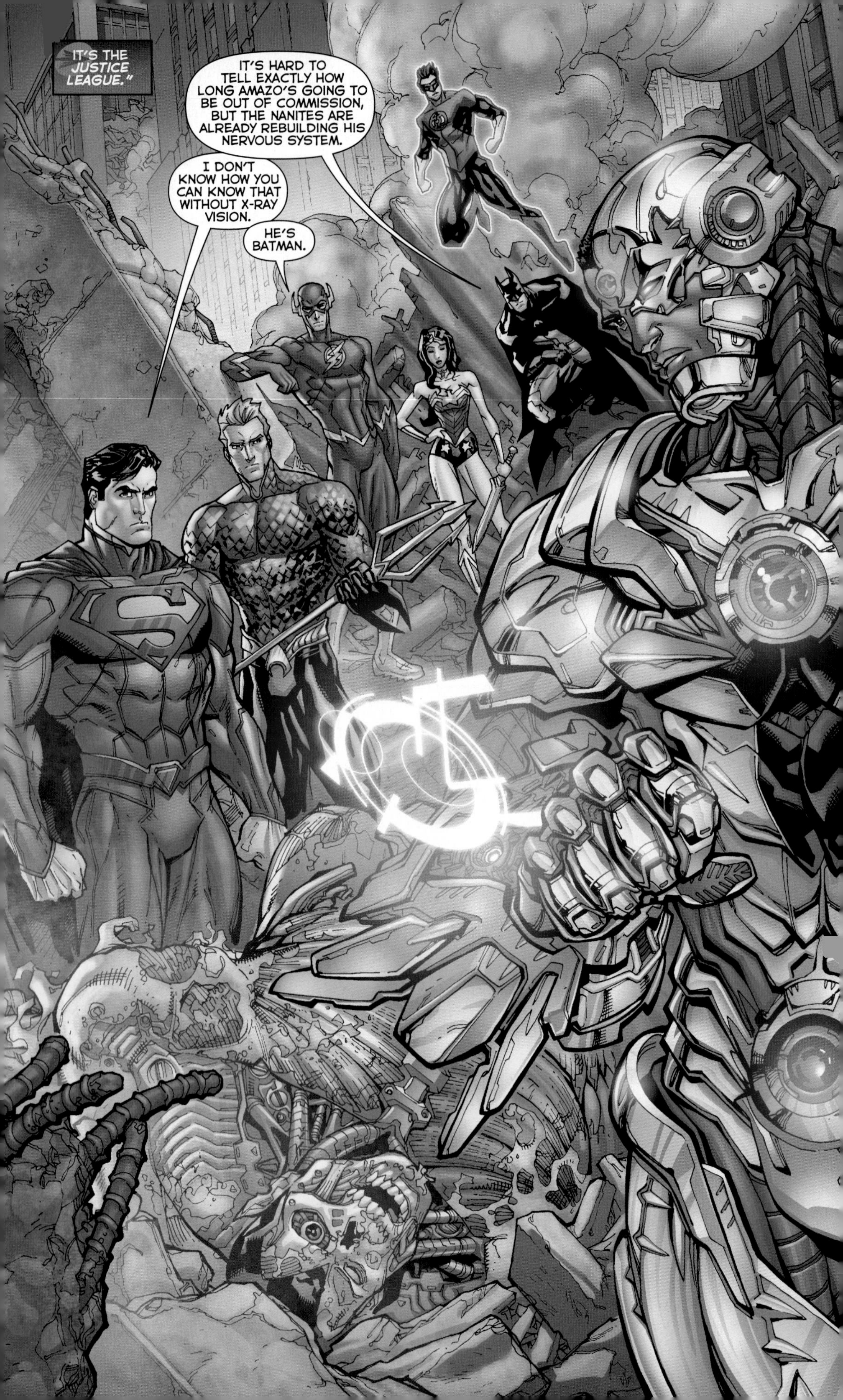
IT'S THE JUSTICE LEAGUE."
IT'S HARD TO TELL EXACTLY HOW LONG AMAZO'S GOING TO BE OUT OF COMMISSION, BUT THE NANITES ARE ALREADY REBUILDING HIS NERVOUS SYSTEM.
I DON'T KNOW HOW YOU CAN KNOW THAT WITHOUT X-RAY VISION.
HE'S BATMAN.

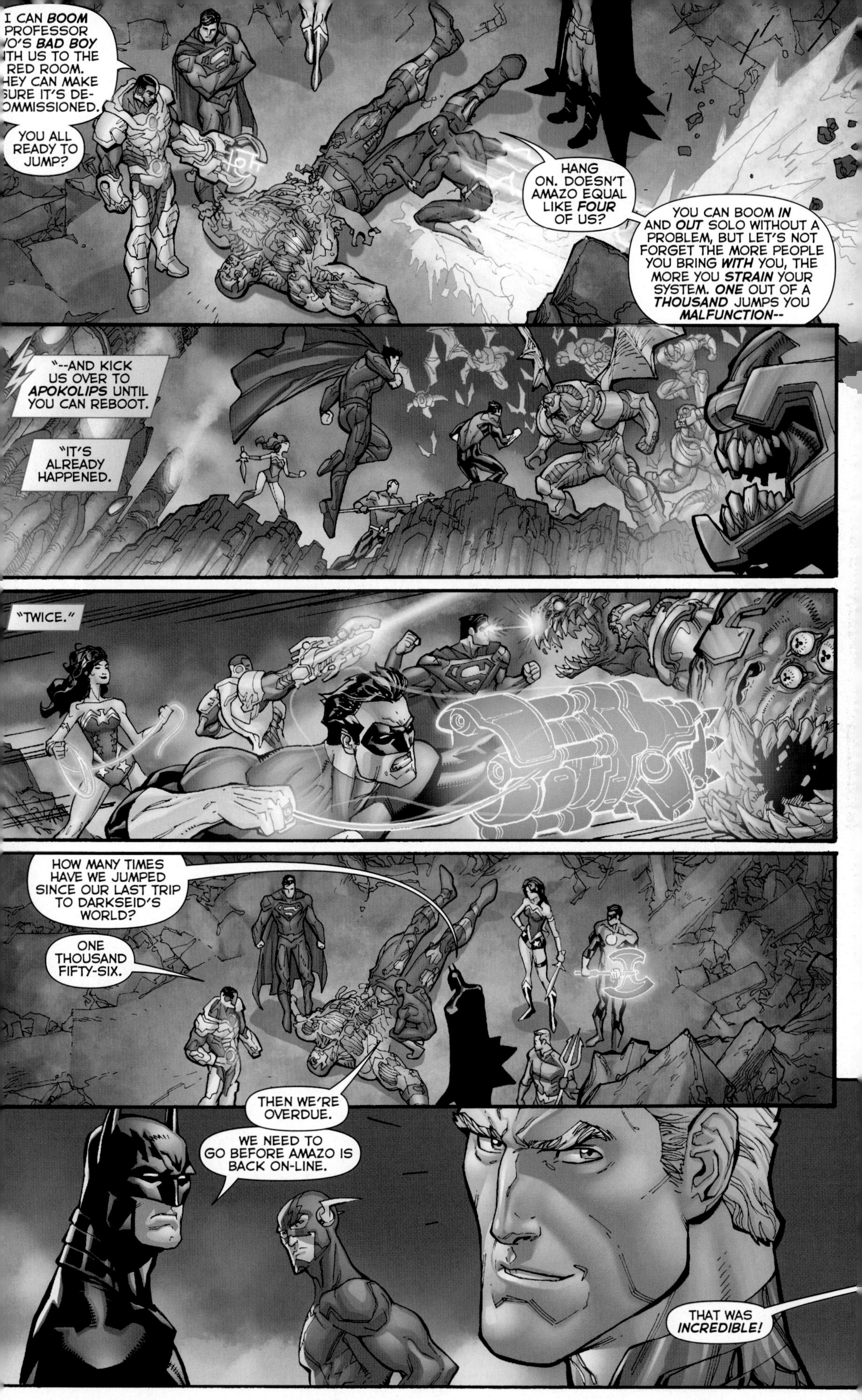
I CAN BOOM
PROFESSOR
IVO'S BAD BOY
WITH US TO THE
RED ROOM.
THEY CAN MAKE
SURE IT'S DE-
COMMISSIONED.
YOU ALL READY TO JUMP?
HANG ON. DOESN'T AMAZO EQUAL LIKE FOUR OF US?
YOU CAN BOOM IN AND OUT SOLO WITHOUT A PROBLEM, BUT LET'S NOT FORGET THE MORE PEOPLE YOU BRING WITH YOU, THE MORE YOU STRAIN YOUR SYSTEM. ONE OUT OF A THOUSAND JUMPS YOU MALFUNCTION--
"--AND KICK US OVER TO APOKOLIPS UNTIL YOU CAN REBOOT.
"IT'S ALREADY HAPPENED.
"TWICE."
HOW MANY TIMES HAVE WE JUMPED SINCE OUR LAST TRIP TO DARKSEID'S WORLD?
ONE THOUSAND FIFTY-SIX.
THEN WE'RE OVERDUE.
WE NEED TO GO BEFORE AMAZO IS BACK ON-LINE.
THAT WAS INCREDIBLE!

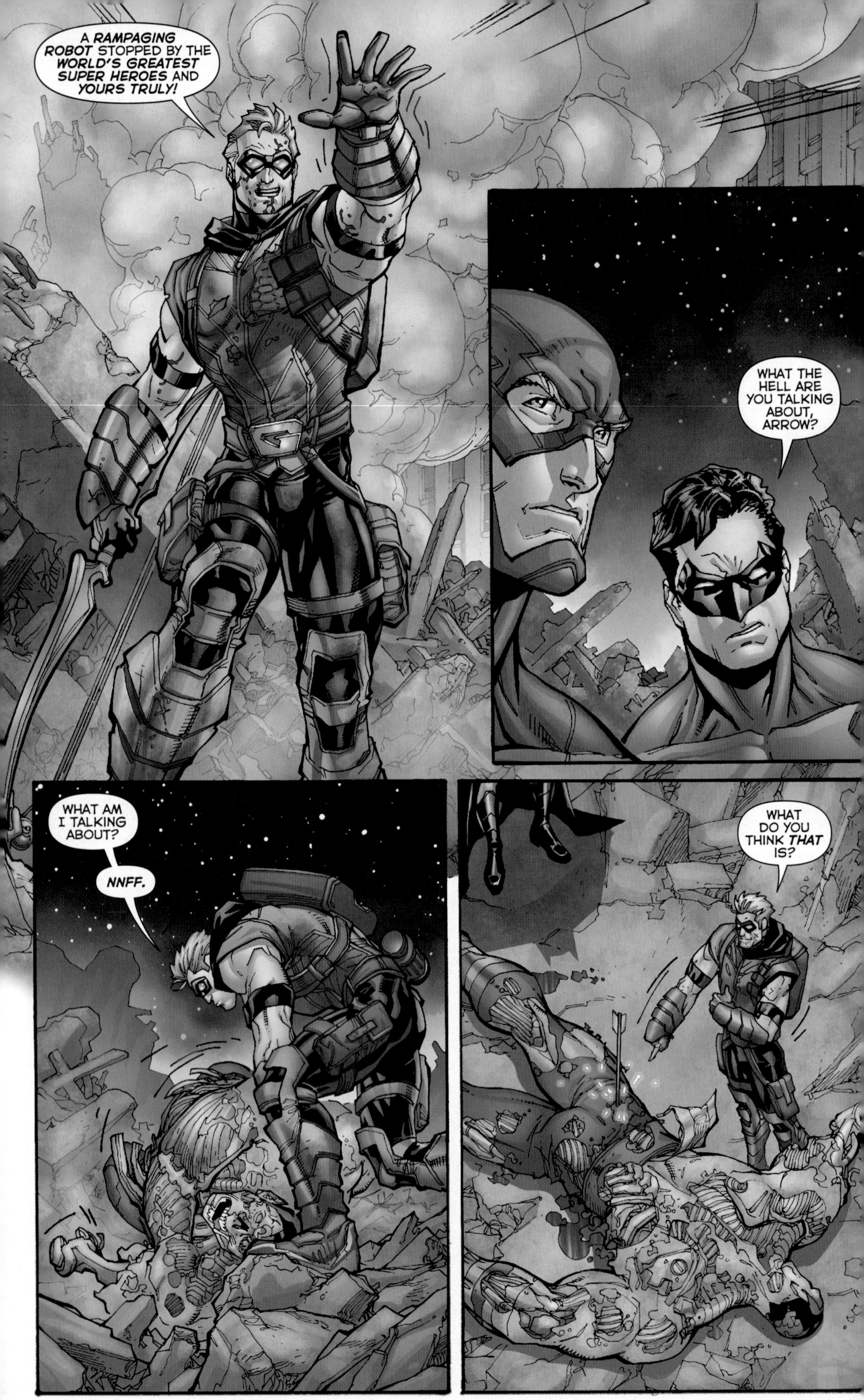
A *RAMPAGING ROBOT* STOPPED BY THE *WORLD'S GREATEST SUPER HEROES* AND *YOURS TRULY!*
WHAT THE HELL ARE YOU TALKING ABOUT, ARROW?
WHAT AM I TALKING ABOUT?
NNFF.
WHAT DO YOU THINK *THAT* IS?

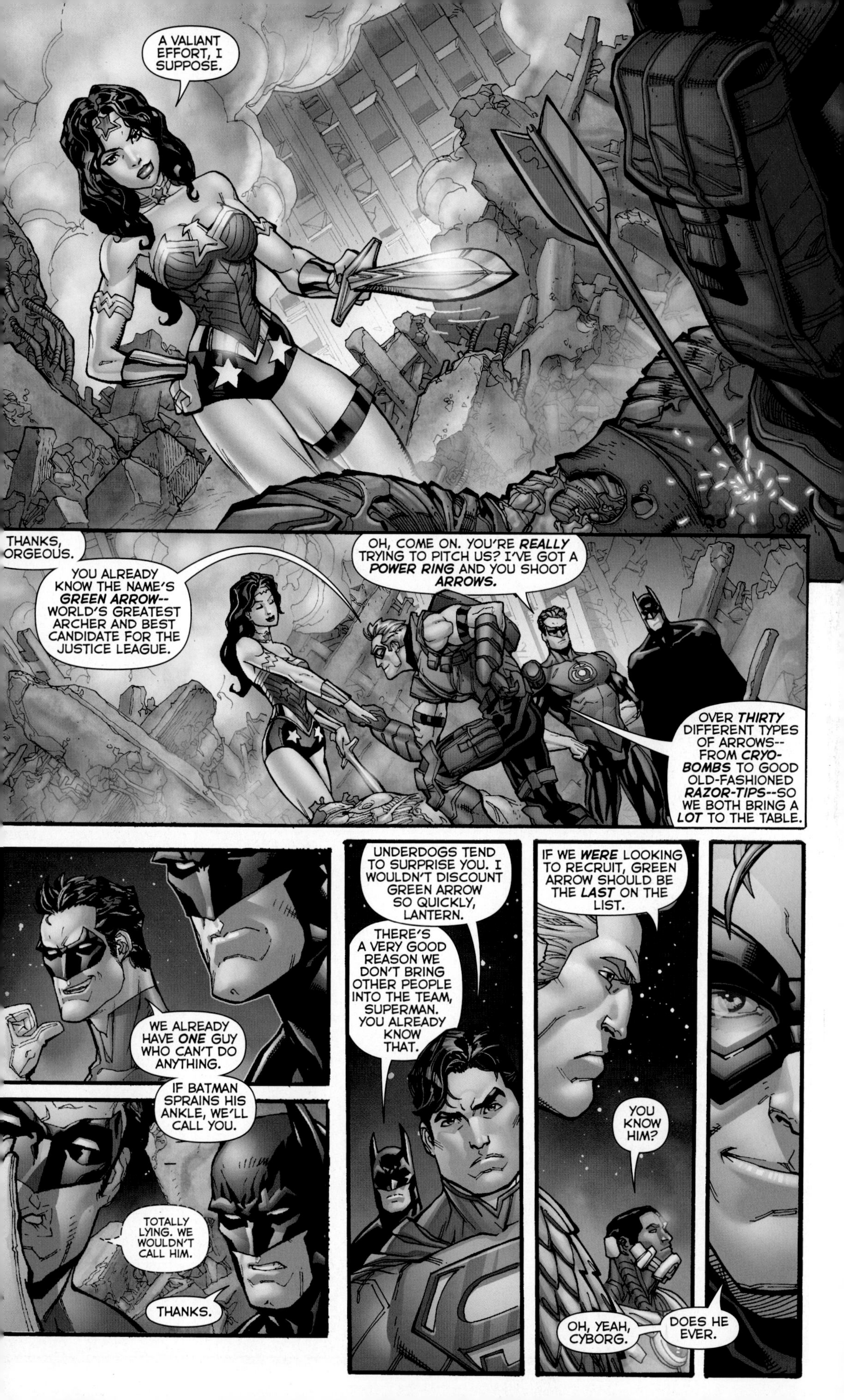
A VALIANT EFFORT, I SUPPOSE.
THANKS, GORGEOUS.
YOU ALREADY KNOW THE NAME'S GREEN ARROW-- WORLD'S GREATEST ARCHER AND BEST CANDIDATE FOR THE JUSTICE LEAGUE.
OH, COME ON. YOU'RE REALLY TRYING TO PITCH US? I'VE GOT A POWER RING AND YOU SHOOT ARROWS.
OVER THIRTY DIFFERENT TYPES OF ARROWS-- FROM CRYO-BOMBS TO GOOD OLD-FASHIONED RAZOR-TIPS--SO WE BOTH BRING A LOT TO THE TABLE.
WE ALREADY HAVE ONE GUY WHO CAN'T DO ANYTHING.
IF BATMAN SPRAINS HIS ANKLE, WE'LL CALL YOU.
TOTALLY LYING. WE WOULDN'T CALL HIM.
THANKS.
UNDERDOGS TEND TO SURPRISE YOU. I WOULDN'T DISCOUNT GREEN ARROW SO QUICKLY, LANTERN.
THERE'S A VERY GOOD REASON WE DON'T BRING OTHER PEOPLE INTO THE TEAM, SUPERMAN. YOU ALREADY KNOW THAT.
IF WE WERE LOOKING TO RECRUIT, GREEN ARROW SHOULD BE THE LAST ON THE LIST.
YOU KNOW HIM?
OH, YEAH, CYBORG.
DOES HE EVER.

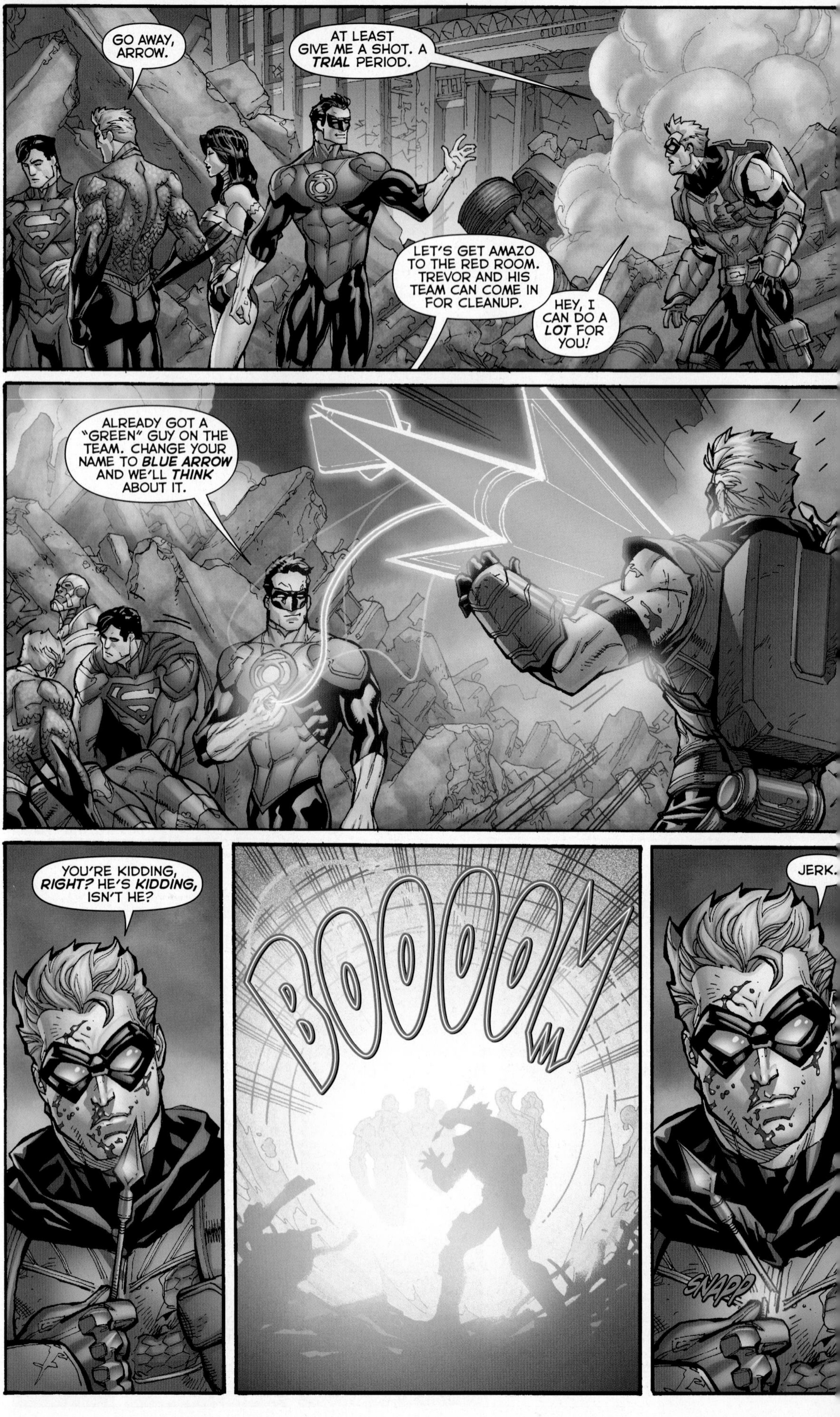
GO AWAY, ARROW.
AT LEAST GIVE ME A SHOT. A TRIAL PERIOD.
LET'S GET AMAZO TO THE RED ROOM. TREVOR AND HIS TEAM CAN COME IN FOR CLEANUP.
HEY, I CAN DO A LOT FOR YOU!
ALREADY GOT A "GREEN" GUY ON THE TEAM. CHANGE YOUR NAME TO BLUE ARROW AND WE'LL THINK ABOUT IT.
YOU'RE KIDDING, RIGHT? HE'S KIDDING, ISN'T HE?
BOOOOOM
JERK.
SNAPP

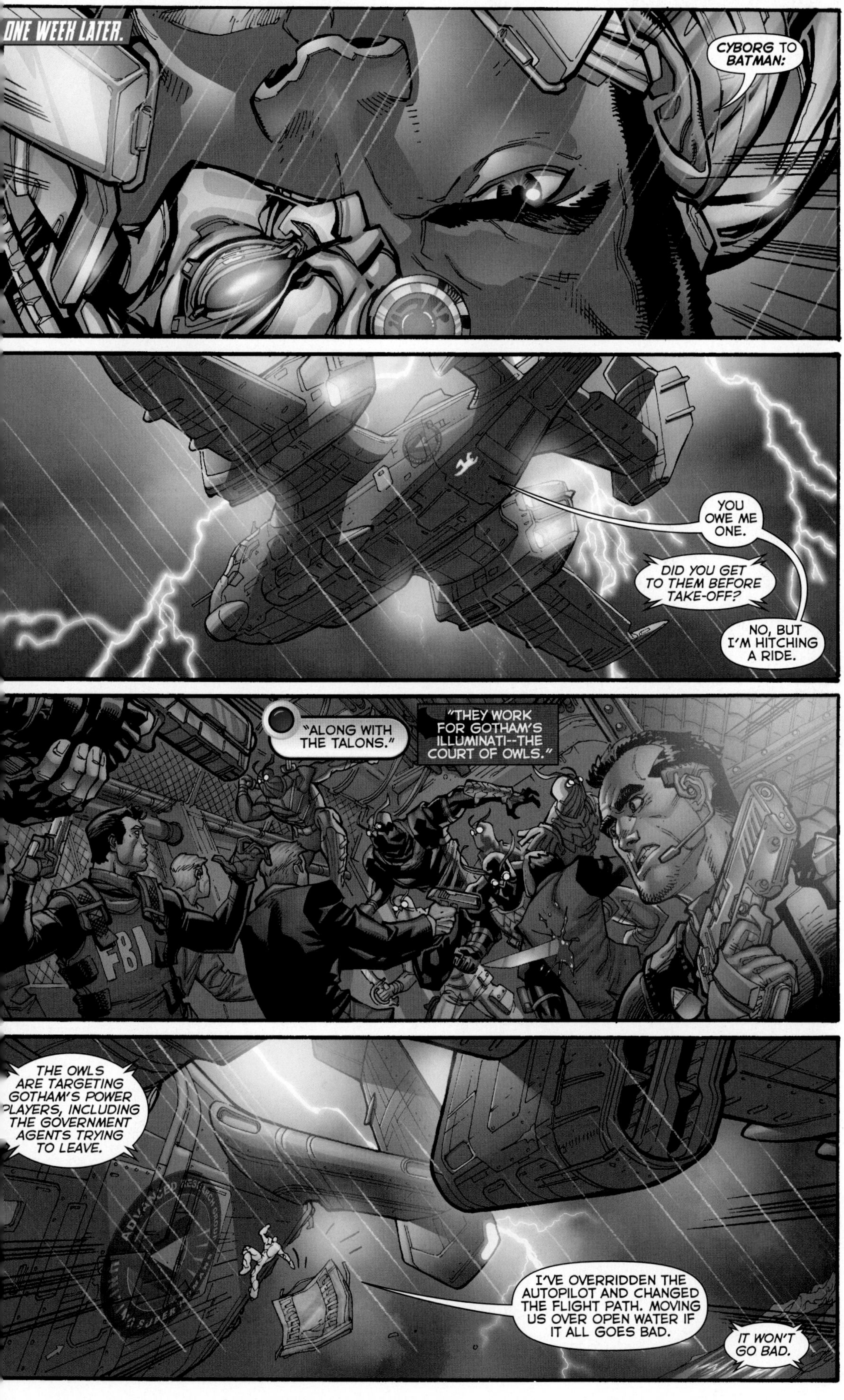
ONE WEEK LATER.
CYBORG TO BATMAN:
YOU OWE ME ONE.
DID YOU GET TO THEM BEFORE TAKE-OFF?
NO, BUT I'M HITCHING A RIDE.
"ALONG WITH THE TALONS."
"THEY WORK FOR GOTHAM'S ILLUMINATI--THE COURT OF OWLS."
FBI
THE OWLS ARE TARGETING GOTHAM'S POWER PLAYERS, INCLUDING THE GOVERNMENT AGENTS TRYING TO LEAVE.
I'VE OVERRIDDEN THE AUTOPILOT AND CHANGED THE FLIGHT PATH. MOVING US OVER OPEN WATER IF IT ALL GOES BAD.
IT WON'T GO BAD.

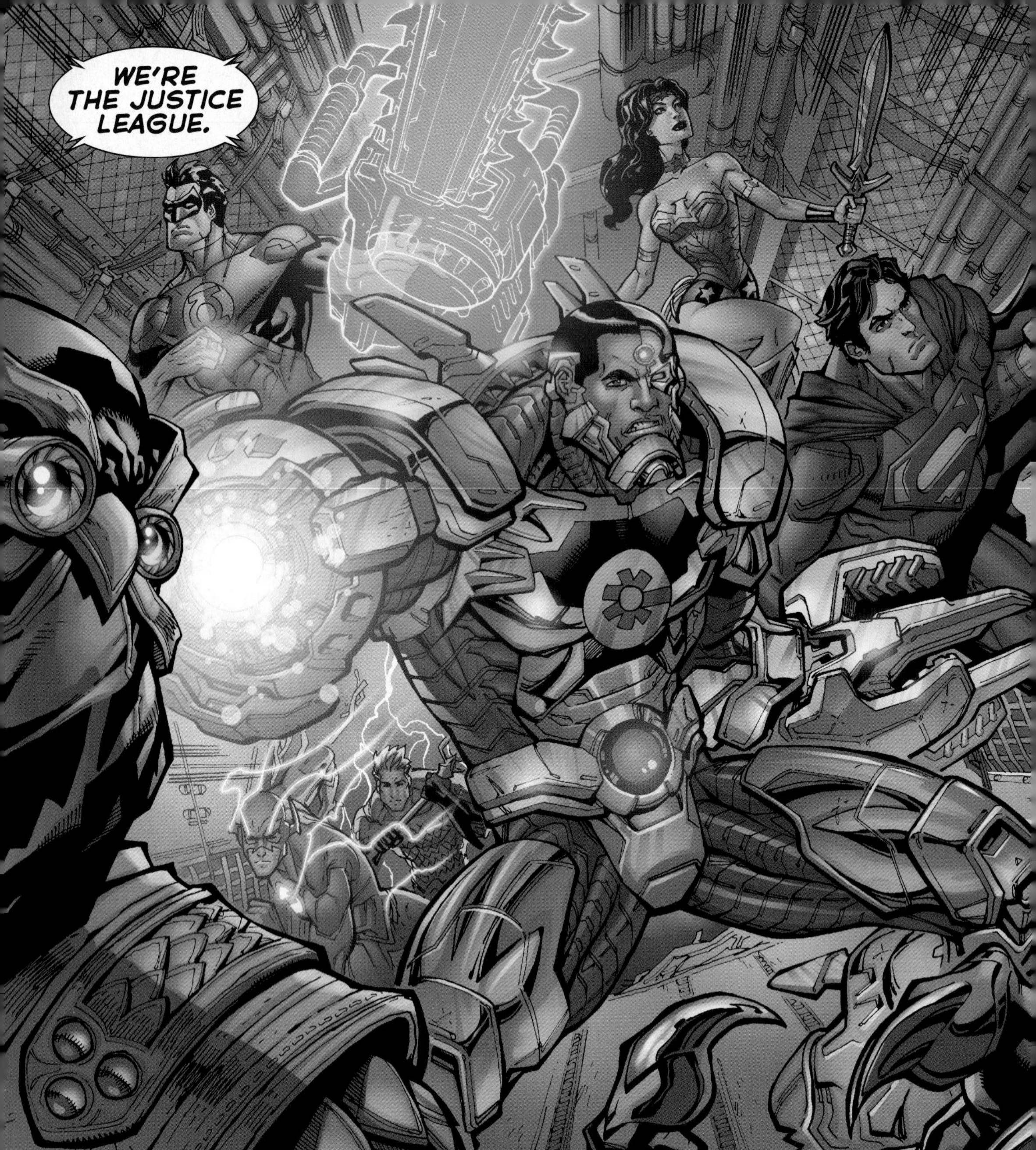
WE'RE THE JUSTICE LEAGUE.

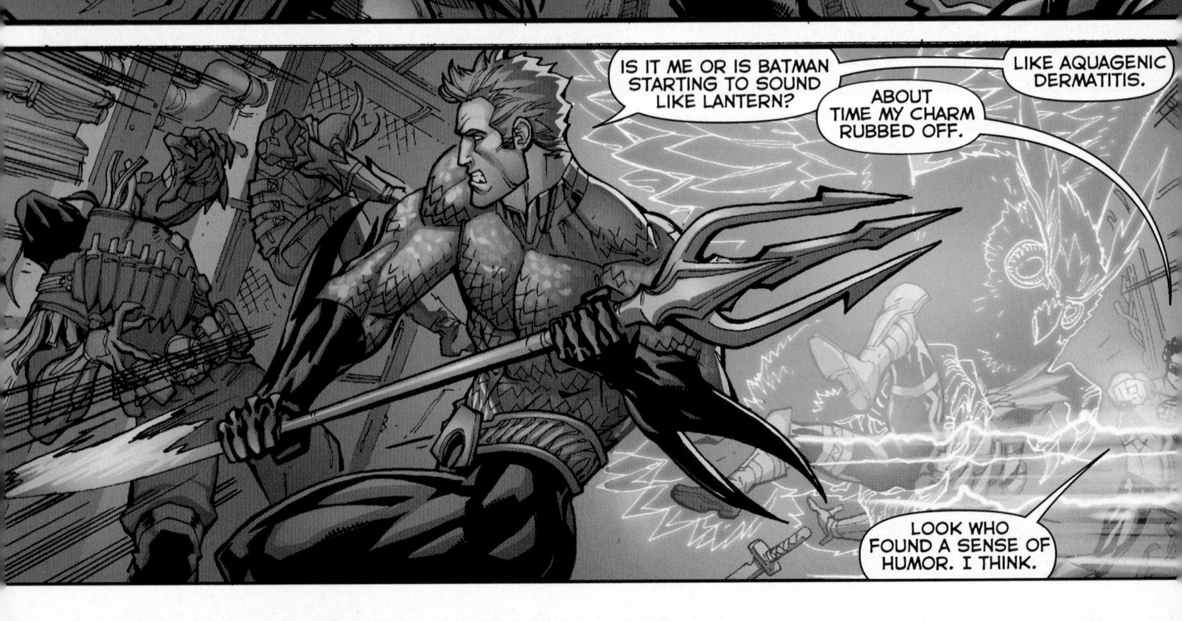
IS IT ME OR IS BATMAN STARTING TO SOUND LIKE LANTERN?
LIKE AQUAGENIC DERMATITIS.
ABOUT TIME MY CHARM RUBBED OFF.
LOOK WHO FOUND A SENSE OF HUMOR. I THINK.

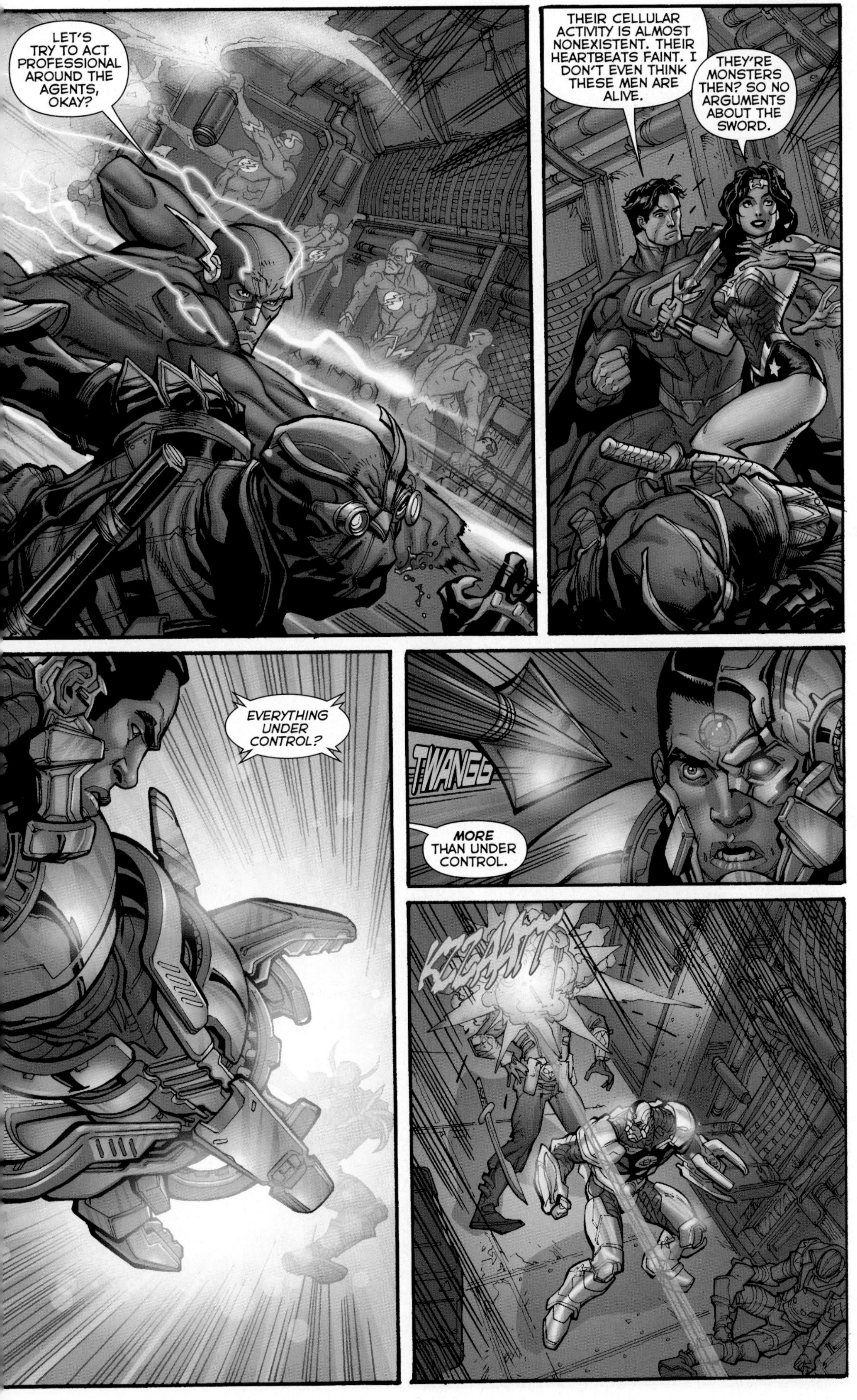
LET'S TRY TO ACT PROFESSIONAL AROUND THE AGENTS, OKAY?
THEIR CELLULAR ACTIVITY IS ALMOST NONEXISTENT. THEIR HEARTBEATS FAINT. I DON'T EVEN THINK THESE MEN ARE ALIVE.
THEY'RE MONSTERS THEN? SO NO ARGUMENTS ABOUT THE SWORD.
EVERYTHING UNDER CONTROL?
TWANGG
MORE THAN UNDER CONTROL.
KZZAAKT

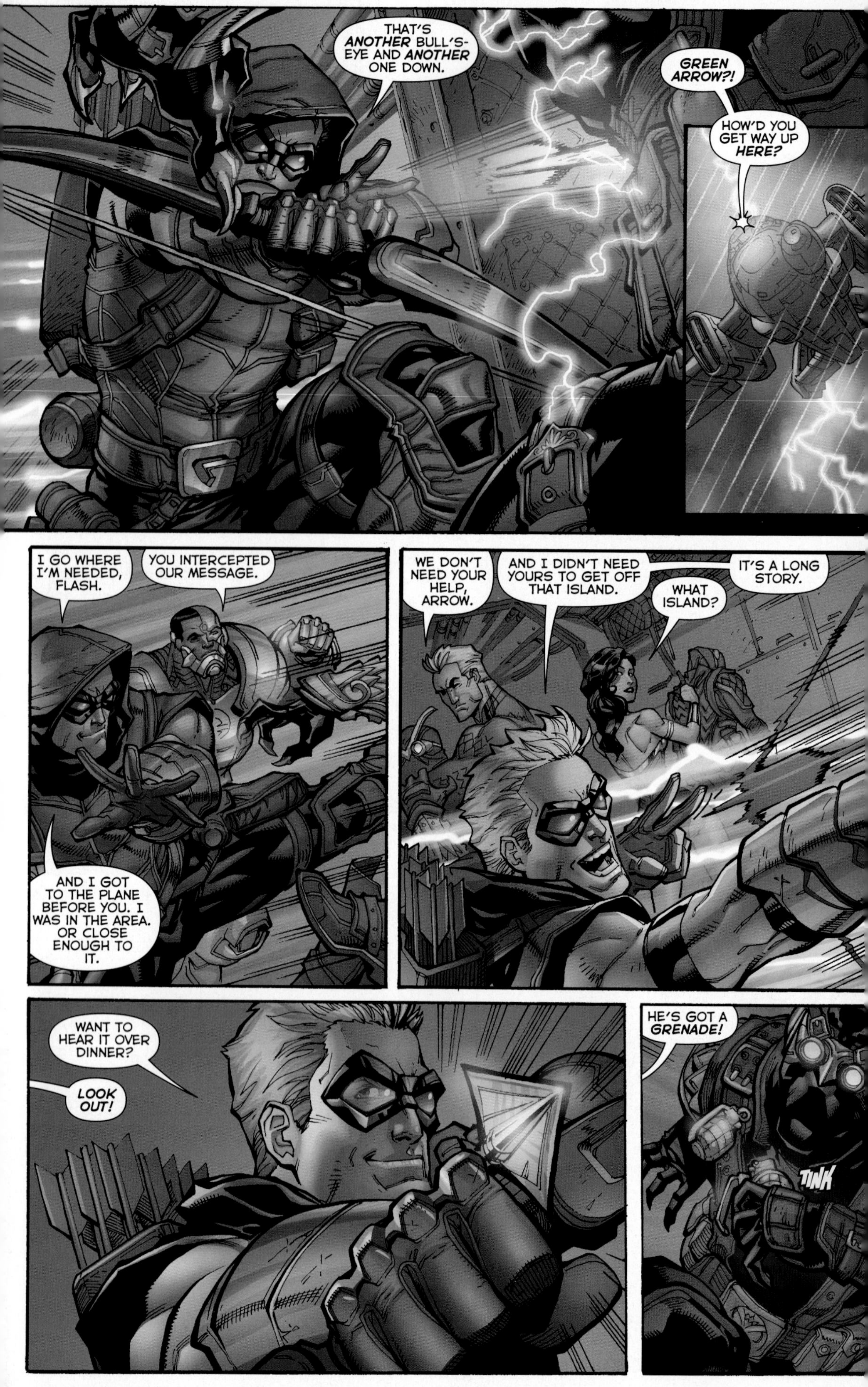

THAT'S ANOTHER BULL'S-EYE AND ANOTHER ONE DOWN.
GREEN ARROW?!
HOW'D YOU GET WAY UP HERE?
I GO WHERE I'M NEEDED, FLASH.
YOU INTERCEPTED OUR MESSAGE.
AND I GOT TO THE PLANE BEFORE YOU. I WAS IN THE AREA. OR CLOSE ENOUGH TO IT.
WE DON'T NEED YOUR HELP, ARROW.
AND I DIDN'T NEED YOURS TO GET OFF THAT ISLAND.
WHAT ISLAND?
IT'S A LONG STORY.
WANT TO HEAR IT OVER DINNER?
LOOK OUT!
HE'S GOT A GRENADE!
TINK

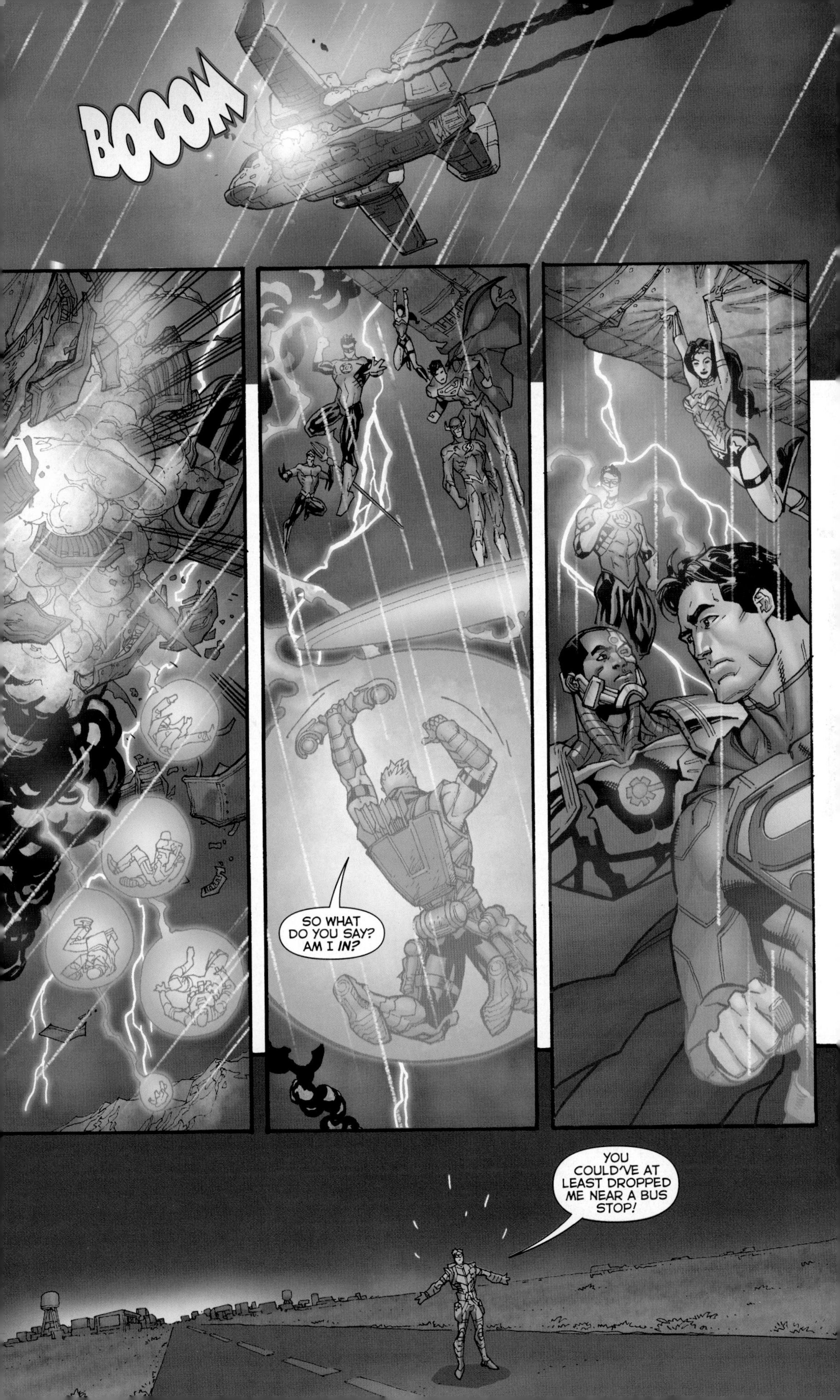
BOOOM
SO WHAT DO YOU SAY? AM I *IN?*
YOU COULD'VE AT LEAST DROPPED ME NEAR A BUS STOP!

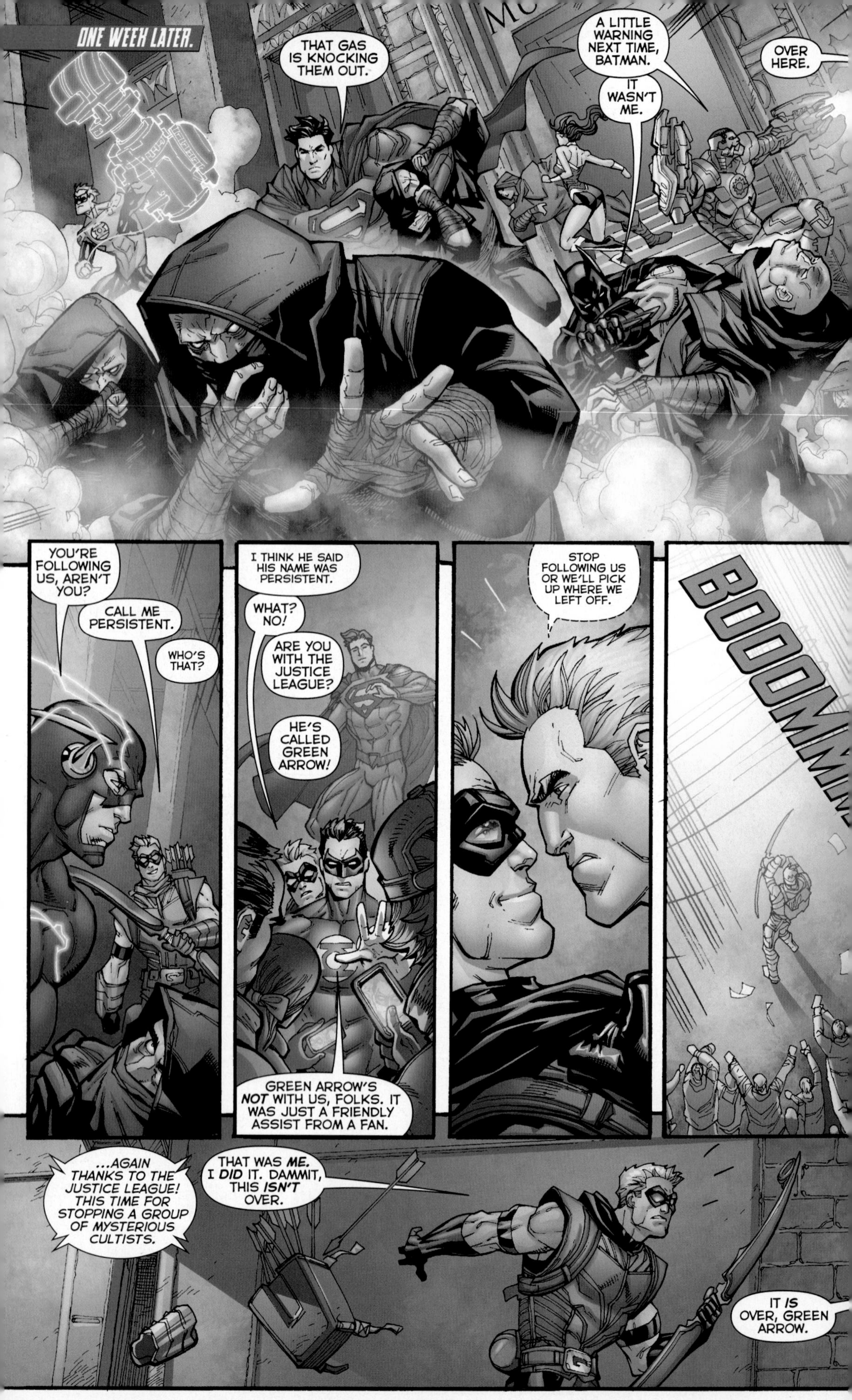
ONE WEEK LATER.
THAT GAS IS KNOCKING THEM OUT.
A LITTLE WARNING NEXT TIME, BATMAN.
IT WASN'T ME.
OVER HERE.
YOU'RE FOLLOWING US, AREN'T YOU?
CALL ME PERSISTENT.
WHO'S THAT?
I THINK HE SAID HIS NAME WAS PERSISTENT.
WHAT? NO!
ARE YOU WITH THE JUSTICE LEAGUE?
HE'S CALLED GREEN ARROW!
GREEN ARROW'S **NOT** WITH US, FOLKS. IT WAS JUST A FRIENDLY ASSIST FROM A FAN.
STOP FOLLOWING US OR WE'LL PICK UP WHERE WE LEFT OFF.
BOOOMMM
...AGAIN THANKS TO THE JUSTICE LEAGUE! THIS TIME FOR STOPPING A GROUP OF MYSTERIOUS CULTISTS.
THAT WAS **ME.** I **DID** IT. DAMMIT, THIS **ISN'T** OVER.
IT **IS** OVER, GREEN ARROW.

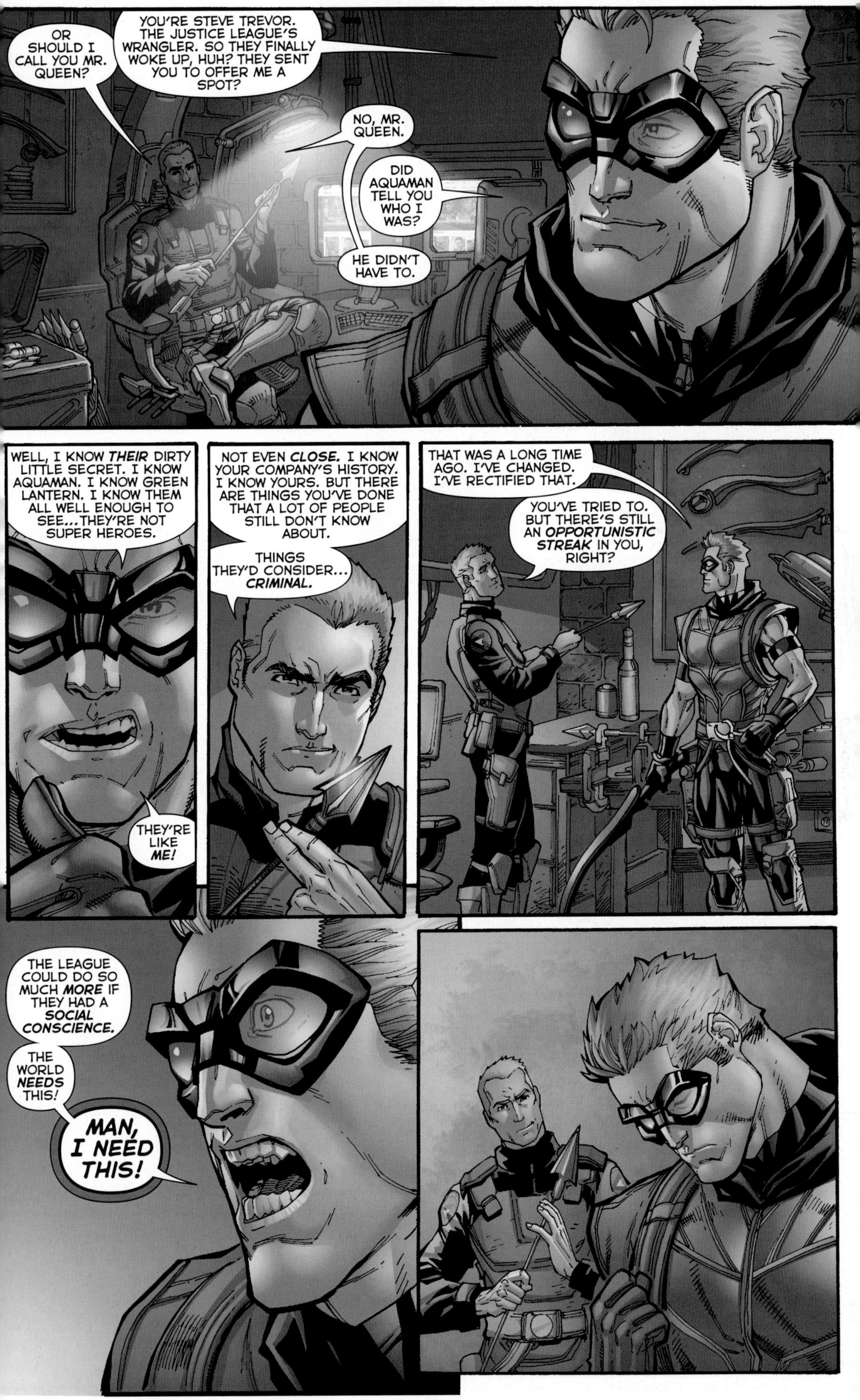

OR SHOULD I CALL YOU MR. QUEEN?
YOU'RE STEVE TREVOR. THE JUSTICE LEAGUE'S WRANGLER. SO THEY FINALLY WOKE UP, HUH? THEY SENT YOU TO OFFER ME A SPOT?
NO, MR. QUEEN.
DID AQUAMAN TELL YOU WHO I WAS?
HE DIDN'T HAVE TO.
WELL, I KNOW *THEIR* DIRTY LITTLE SECRET. I KNOW AQUAMAN. I KNOW GREEN LANTERN. I KNOW THEM ALL WELL ENOUGH TO SEE...THEY'RE NOT SUPER HEROES.
THEY'RE LIKE *ME!*
NOT EVEN *CLOSE.* I KNOW YOUR COMPANY'S HISTORY. I KNOW YOURS. BUT THERE ARE THINGS YOU'VE DONE THAT A LOT OF PEOPLE STILL DON'T KNOW ABOUT.
THINGS THEY'D CONSIDER... *CRIMINAL.*
THAT WAS A LONG TIME AGO. I'VE CHANGED. I'VE RECTIFIED THAT.
YOU'VE TRIED TO. BUT THERE'S STILL AN *OPPORTUNISTIC STREAK* IN YOU, RIGHT?
THE LEAGUE COULD DO SO MUCH *MORE* IF THEY HAD A *SOCIAL CONSCIENCE.*
THE WORLD *NEEDS* THIS!
MAN, I NEED THIS!

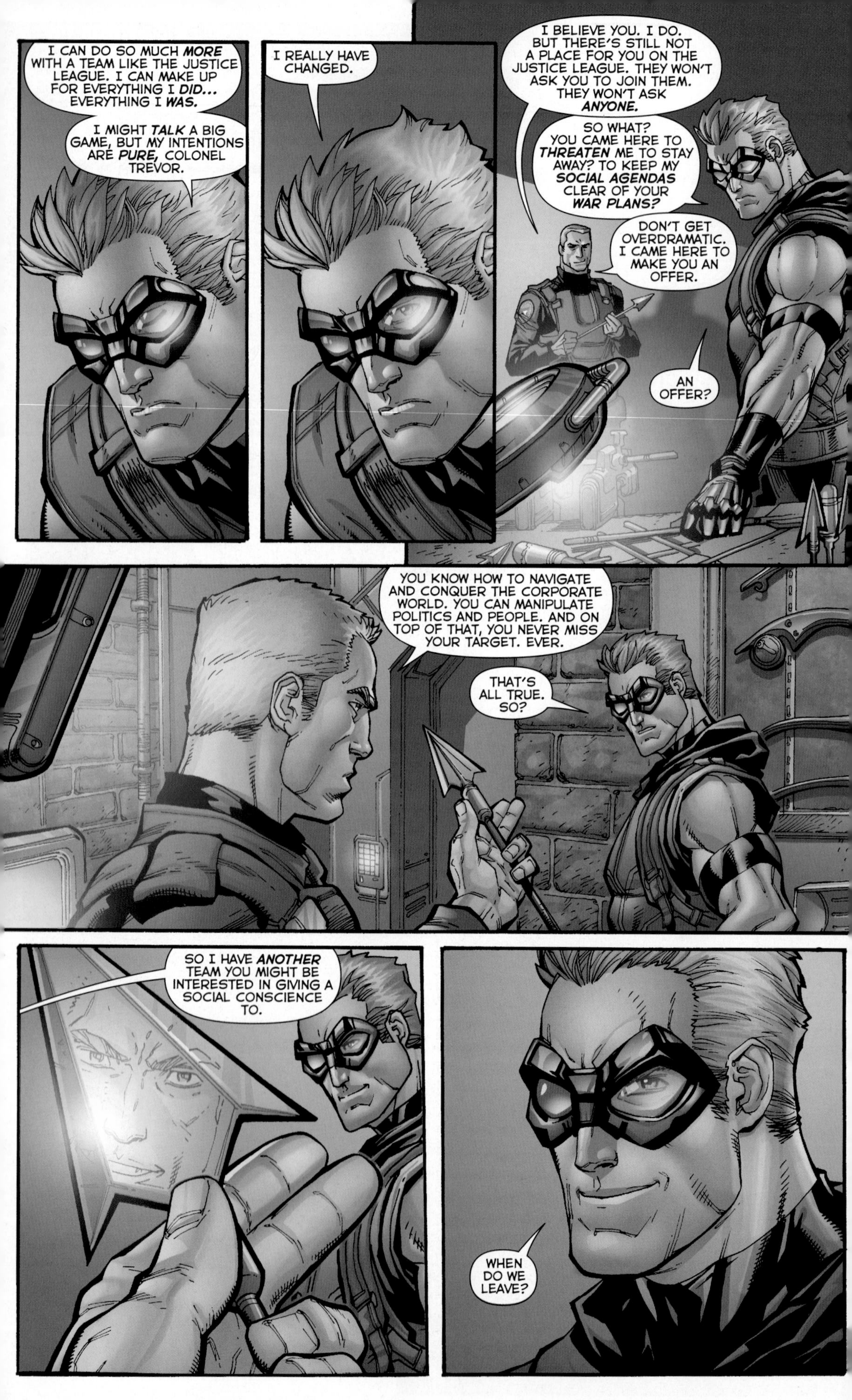
I CAN DO SO MUCH MORE WITH A TEAM LIKE THE JUSTICE LEAGUE. I CAN MAKE UP FOR EVERYTHING I DID... EVERYTHING I WAS.
I MIGHT TALK A BIG GAME, BUT MY INTENTIONS ARE PURE, COLONEL TREVOR.
I REALLY HAVE CHANGED.
I BELIEVE YOU. I DO. BUT THERE'S STILL NOT A PLACE FOR YOU ON THE JUSTICE LEAGUE. THEY WON'T ASK YOU TO JOIN THEM. THEY WON'T ASK ANYONE.
SO WHAT? YOU CAME HERE TO THREATEN ME TO STAY AWAY? TO KEEP MY SOCIAL AGENDAS CLEAR OF YOUR WAR PLANS?
DON'T GET OVERDRAMATIC. I CAME HERE TO MAKE YOU AN OFFER.
AN OFFER?
YOU KNOW HOW TO NAVIGATE AND CONQUER THE CORPORATE WORLD. YOU CAN MANIPULATE POLITICS AND PEOPLE. AND ON TOP OF THAT, YOU NEVER MISS YOUR TARGET. EVER.
THAT'S ALL TRUE. SO?
SO I HAVE ANOTHER TEAM YOU MIGHT BE INTERESTED IN GIVING A SOCIAL CONSCIENCE TO.
WHEN DO WE LEAVE?

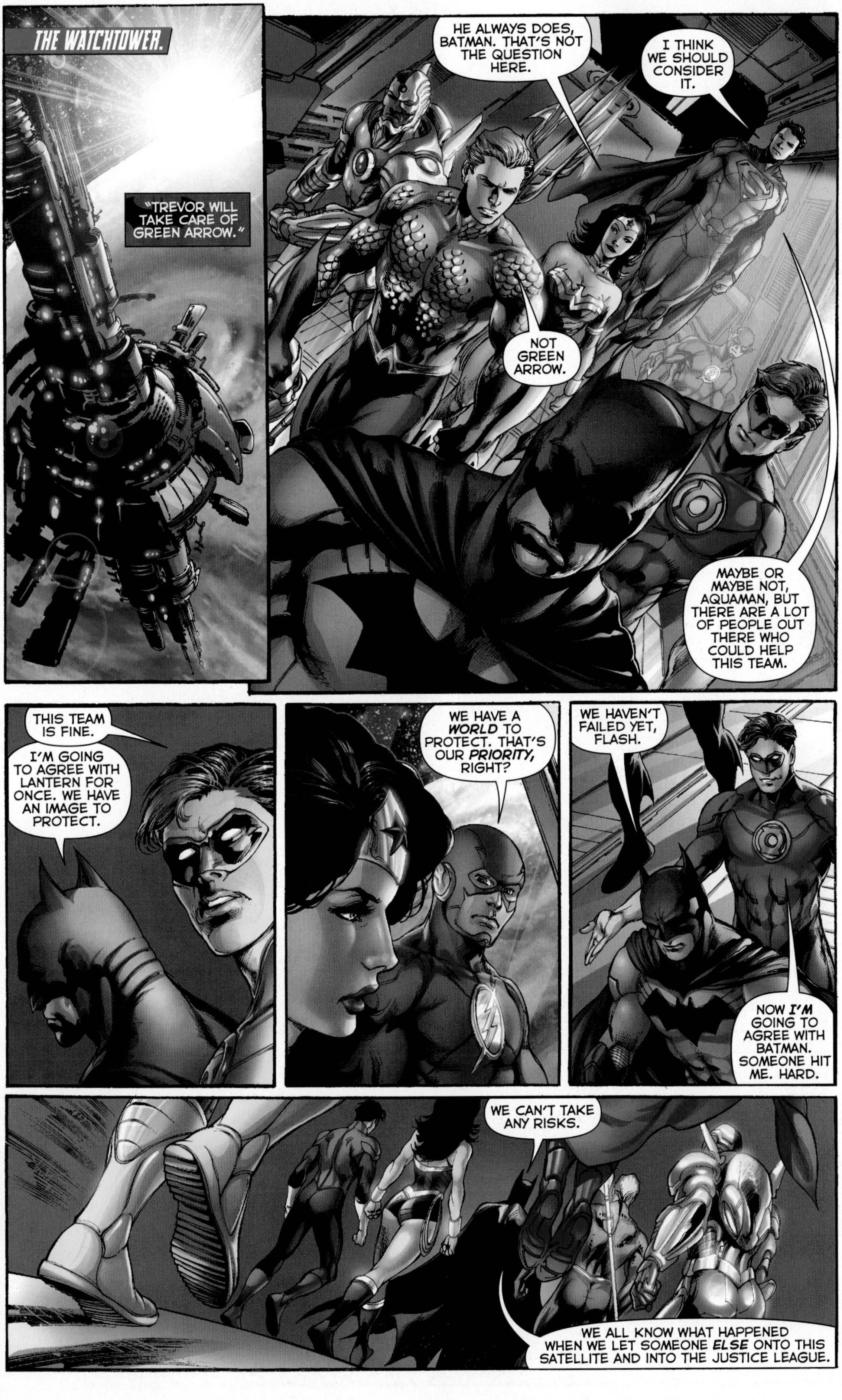
THE WATCHTOWER.
"TREVOR WILL TAKE CARE OF GREEN ARROW."
HE ALWAYS DOES, BATMAN. THAT'S NOT THE QUESTION HERE.
I THINK WE SHOULD CONSIDER IT.
NOT GREEN ARROW.
MAYBE OR MAYBE NOT, AQUAMAN, BUT THERE ARE A LOT OF PEOPLE OUT THERE WHO COULD HELP THIS TEAM.
THIS TEAM IS FINE.
I'M GOING TO AGREE WITH LANTERN FOR ONCE. WE HAVE AN IMAGE TO PROTECT.
WE HAVE A WORLD TO PROTECT. THAT'S OUR PRIORITY, RIGHT?
WE HAVEN'T FAILED YET, FLASH.
NOW I'M GOING TO AGREE WITH BATMAN. SOMEONE HIT ME. HARD.
WE CAN'T TAKE ANY RISKS.
WE ALL KNOW WHAT HAPPENED WHEN WE LET SOMEONE ELSE ONTO THIS SATELLITE AND INTO THE JUSTICE LEAGUE.

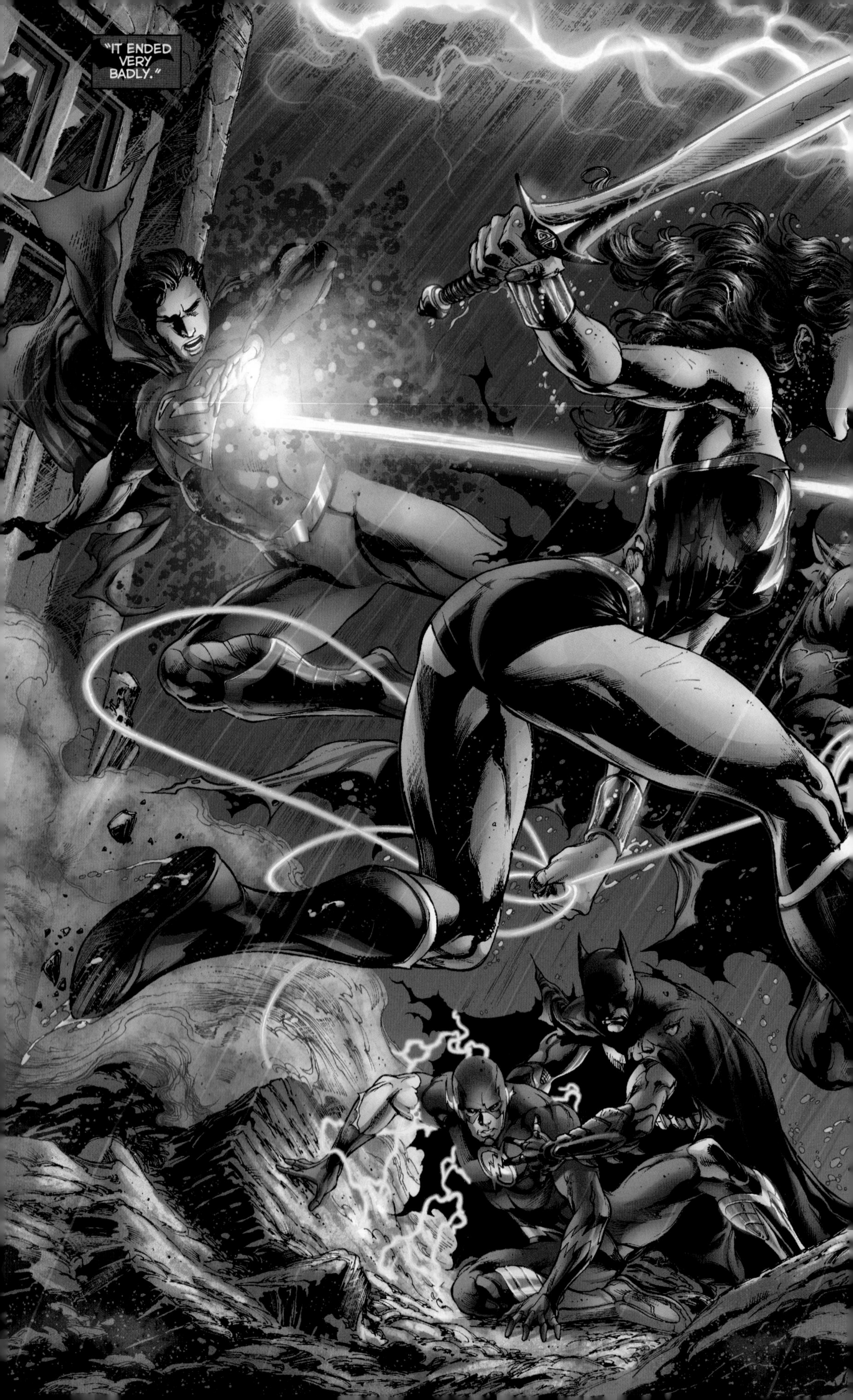
"IT ENDED VERY BADLY."

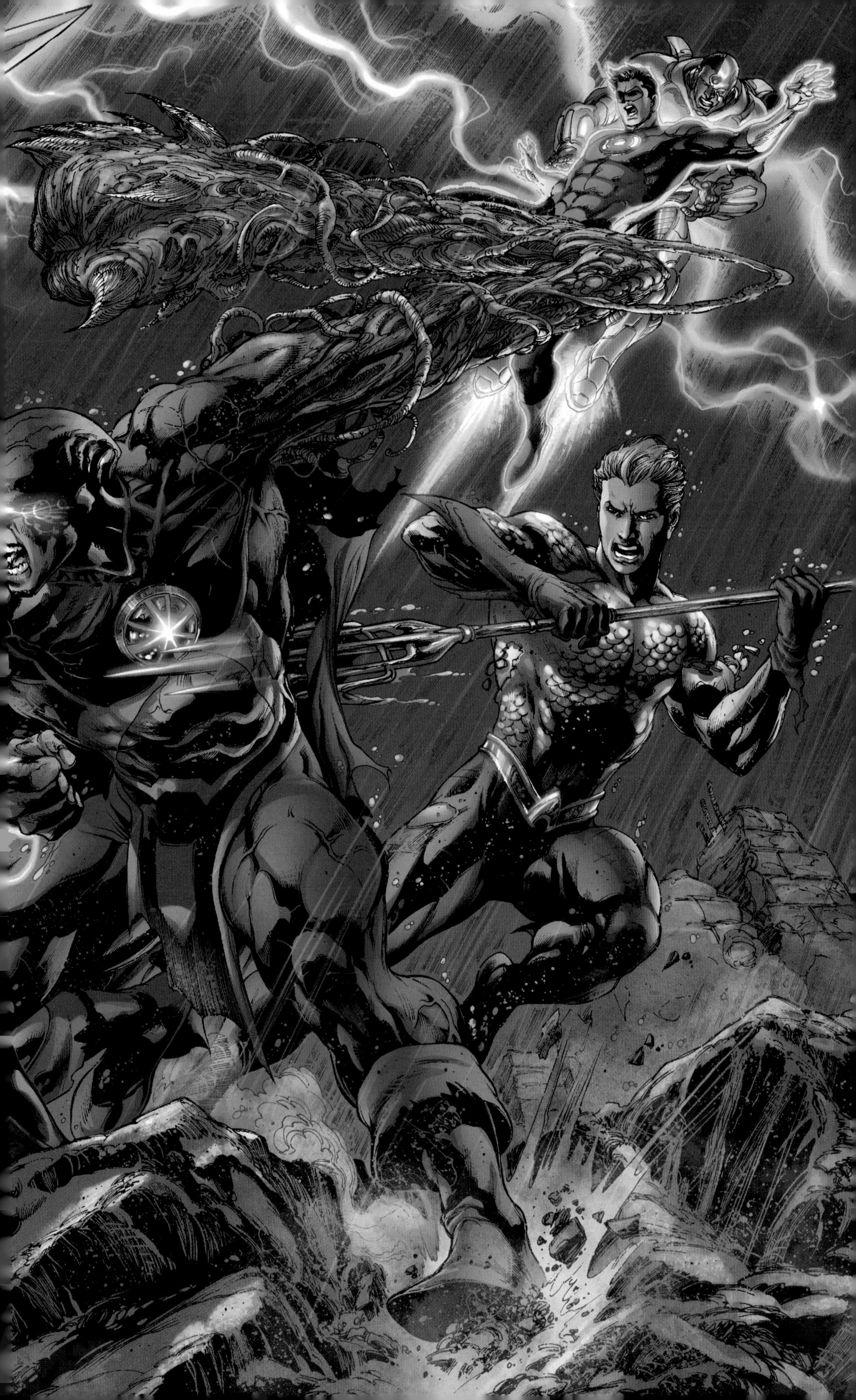

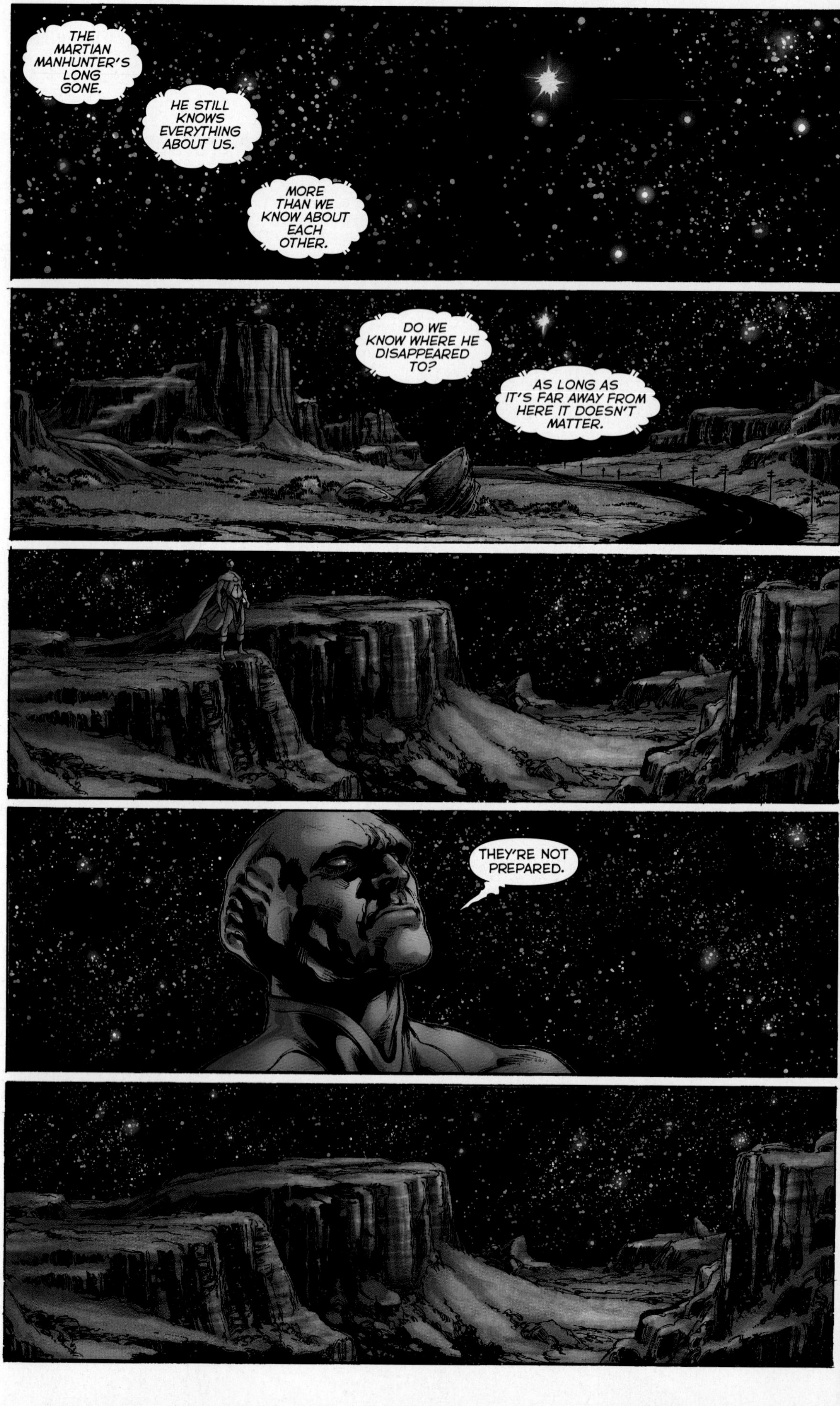
THE MARTIAN MANHUNTER'S LONG GONE.
HE STILL KNOWS EVERYTHING ABOUT US.
MORE THAN WE KNOW ABOUT EACH OTHER.
DO WE KNOW WHERE HE DISAPPEARED TO?
AS LONG AS IT'S FAR AWAY FROM HERE IT DOESN'T MATTER.
THEY'RE NOT PREPARED.

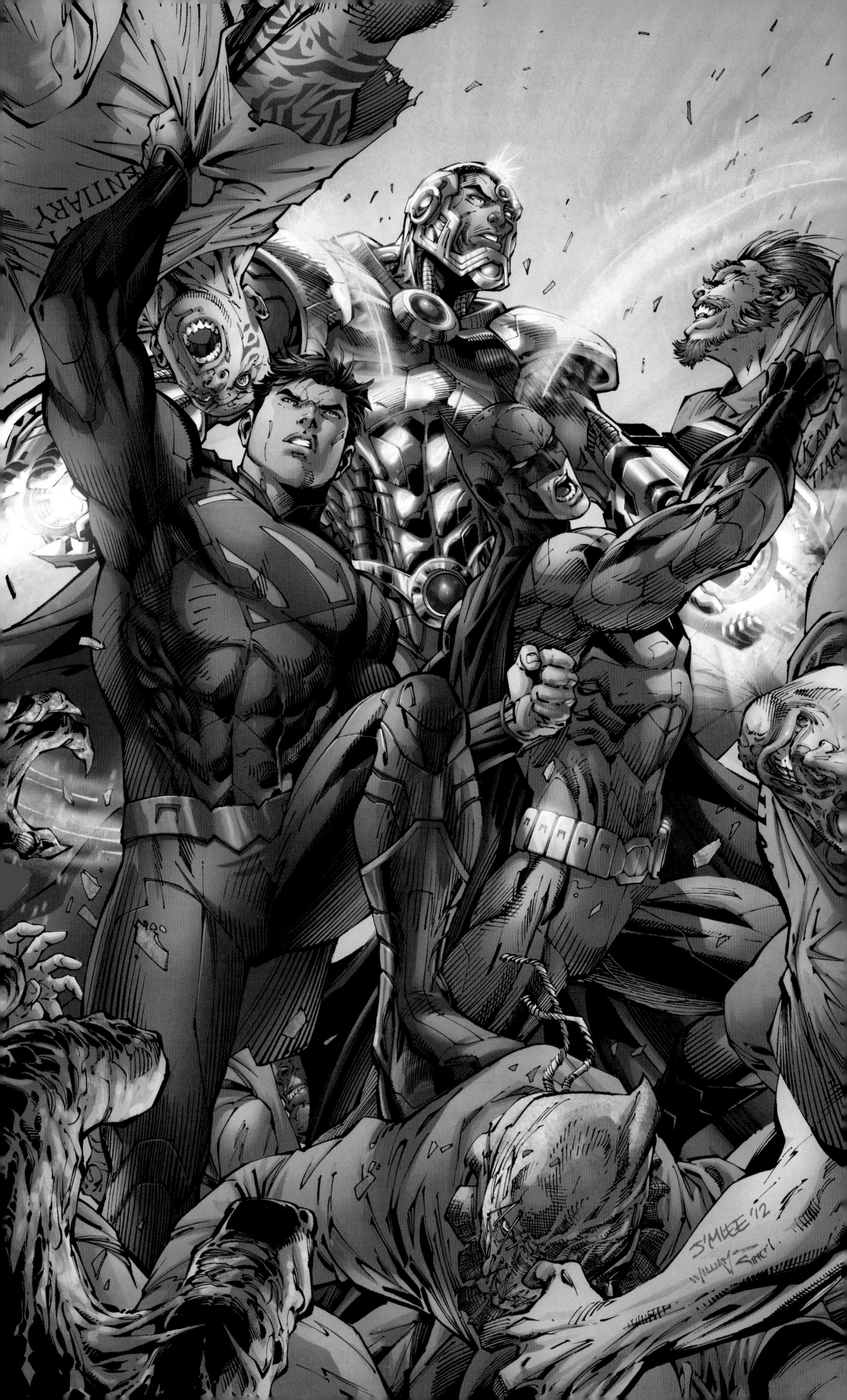

THE VILLAIN'S JOURNEY CHAPTER ONE: THE CALL FOR ADVENTURE

GEOFF JOHNS writer **JIM LEE** penciller **SCOTT WILLIAMS** inker cover by **JIM LEE, SCOTT WILLIAMS & ALEX SINCLAIR**

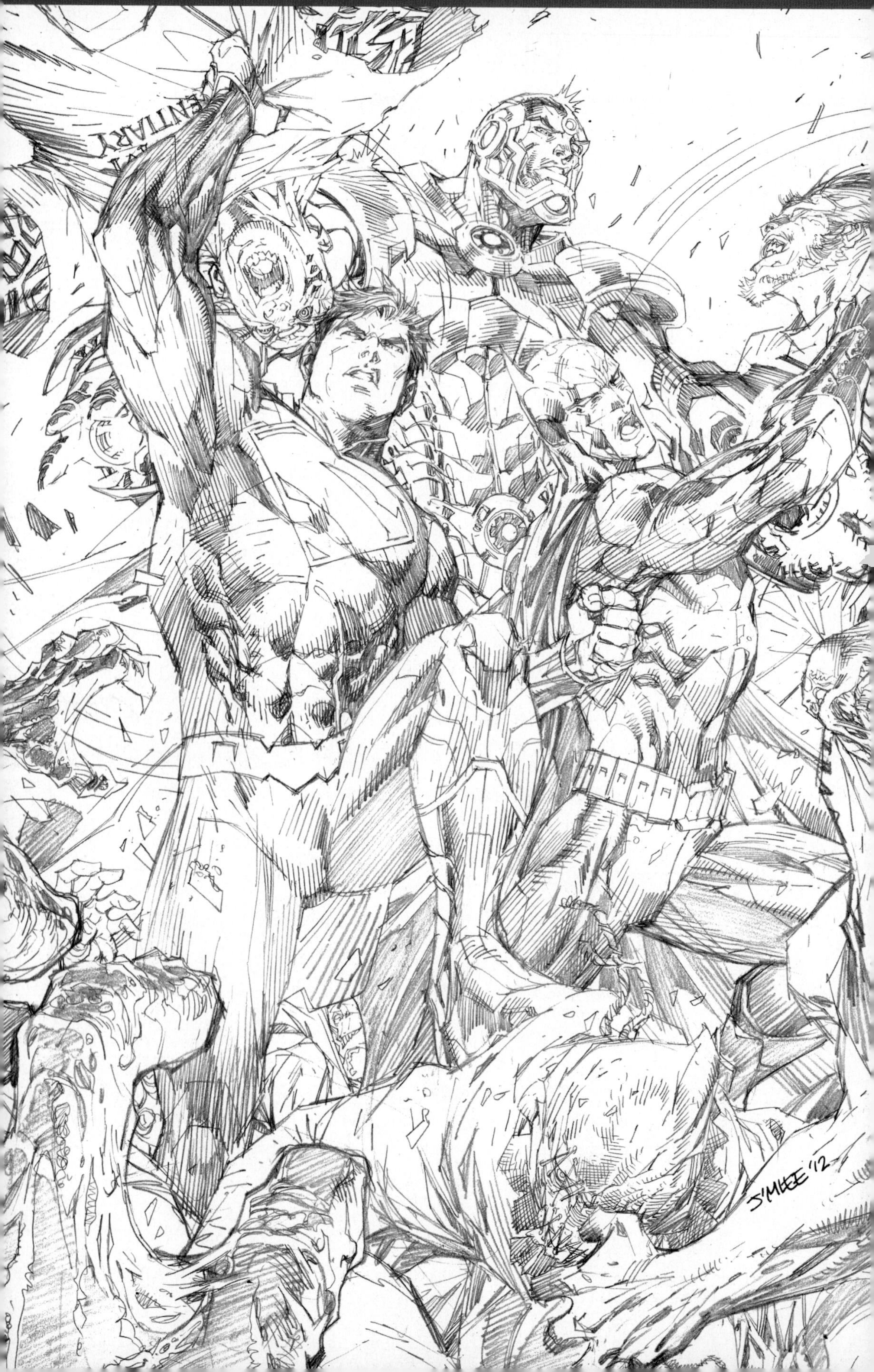

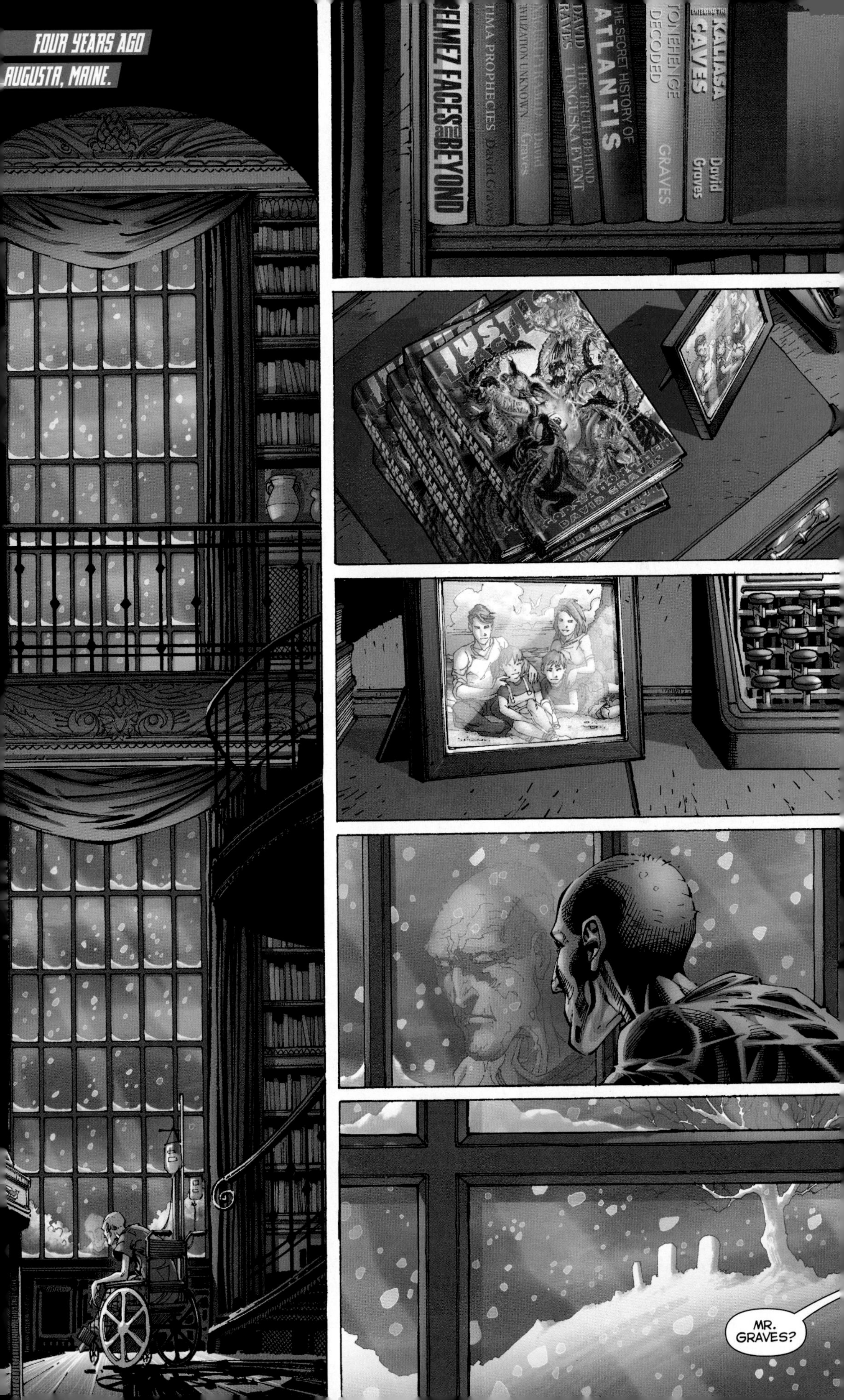
FOUR YEARS AGO
AUGUSTA, MAINE.
THE SECRET HISTORY OF ATLANTIS
THE TRUTH BEHIND TUNGUSKA EVENT
David Graves
MR. GRAVES?

YES, DOCTOR WHITE?

I WAS SAYING DESPITE EVERYTHING WE'RE ATTEMPTING, YOUR NEUTROPHIL COUNT IS STILL WELL BELOW FIVE HUNDRED CELLS PER MICROLITER--

JUST TELL ME WHAT IT MEANS.

IT MEANS YOUR BODY IS FAILING.

HAVE YOU TRIED TO CONTACT THE JUSTICE LEAGUE YET?

THEY DON'T RESPOND TO PROBLEMS LIKE MINE, DOCTOR WHITE.

I KNOW THEY'RE DIFFICULT TO REACH, BUT IF THEY KNEW WHAT *YOU* WERE GOING THROUGH AND *WHY* THEY'D SURELY OFFER HELP IN ANY WAY THEY COULD.

THEY *CAN'T* HELP ME. I WAS... WRONG.

THEY'RE... NOT GODS.

WHAT ABOUT STEVE TREVOR? ACCORDING TO YOU, HE HAS A DEEPER CONNECTION TO THE JUSTICE LEAGUE THAN ANYONE. HE COULD REACH THEM.

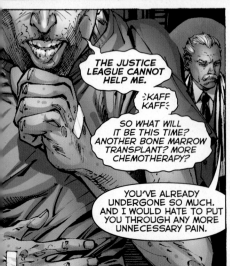

THE JUSTICE LEAGUE CANNOT HELP ME.

≤KAFF KAFF≥

SO WHAT WILL IT BE THIS TIME? ANOTHER BONE MARROW TRANSPLANT? MORE CHEMOTHERAPY?

YOU'VE ALREADY UNDERGONE SO MUCH. AND I WOULD HATE TO PUT YOU THROUGH ANY MORE UNNECESSARY PAIN.

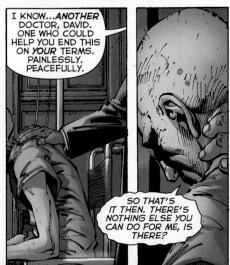

I KNOW...ANOTHER DOCTOR, DAVID. ONE WHO COULD HELP YOU END THIS ON *YOUR* TERMS. PAINLESSLY. PEACEFULLY.

SO THAT'S IT THEN. THERE'S NOTHING ELSE YOU CAN DO FOR ME, IS THERE?

I'M SO SORRY, DAVID.

THERE'S NOTHING ELSE I CAN DO.

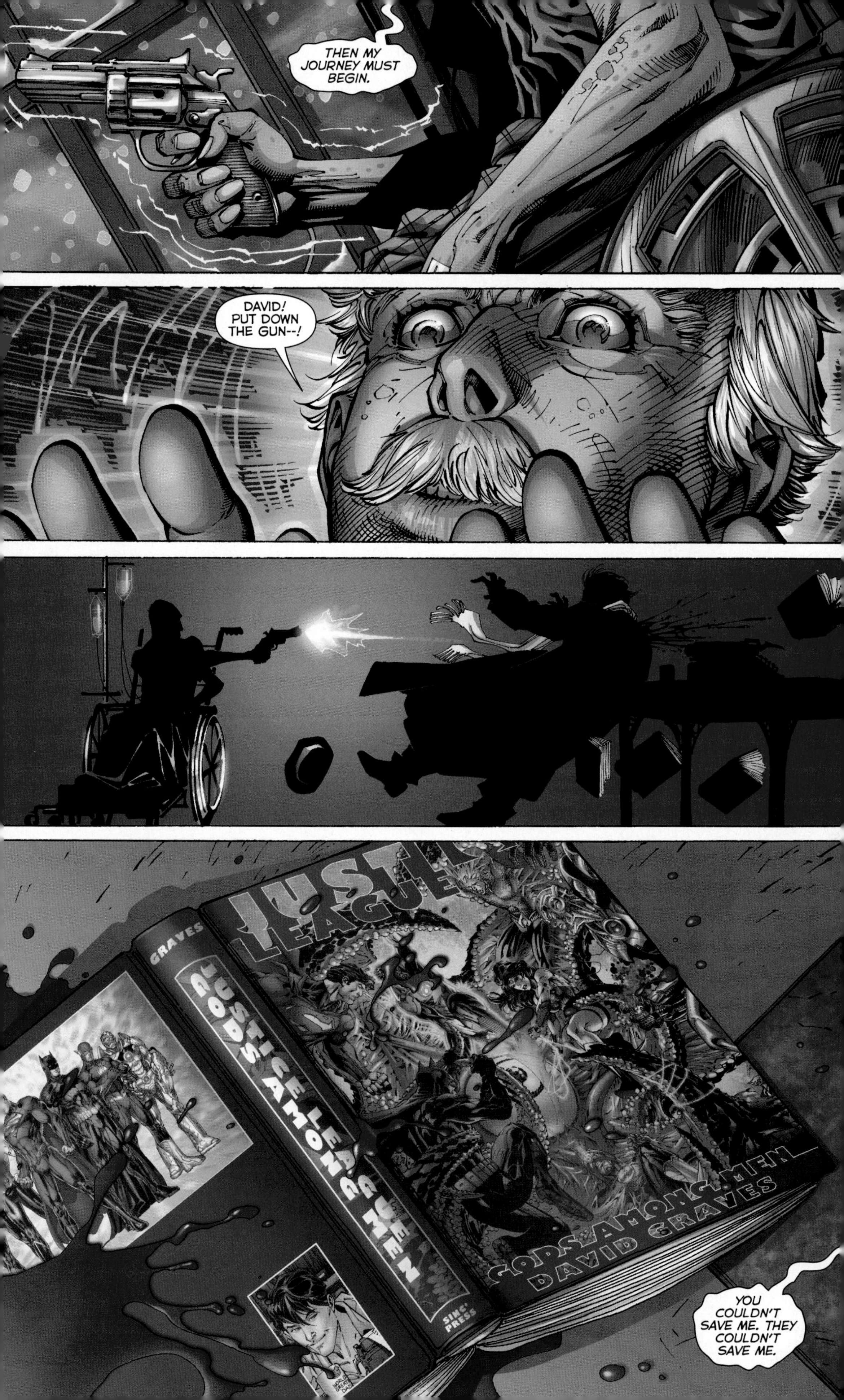
THEN MY JOURNEY MUST BEGIN.
DAVID! PUT DOWN THE GUN--!
JUSTICE LEAGUE
GRAVES
JUSTICE LEAGUE GODS AMONG MEN
GODS AMONG MEN DAVID GRAVES
YOU COULDN'T SAVE ME. THEY COULDN'T SAVE ME.

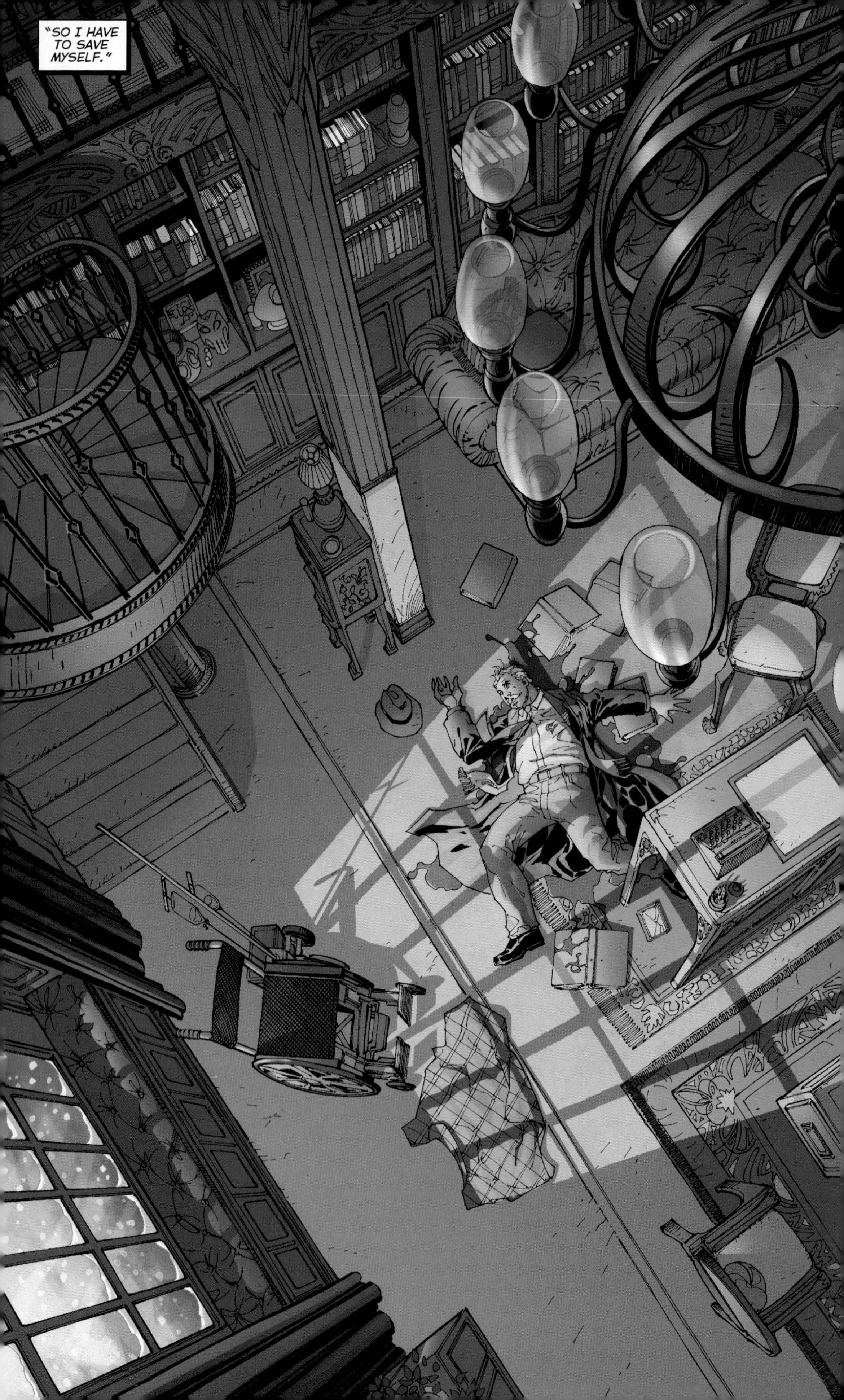
"SO I HAVE TO SAVE MYSELF."

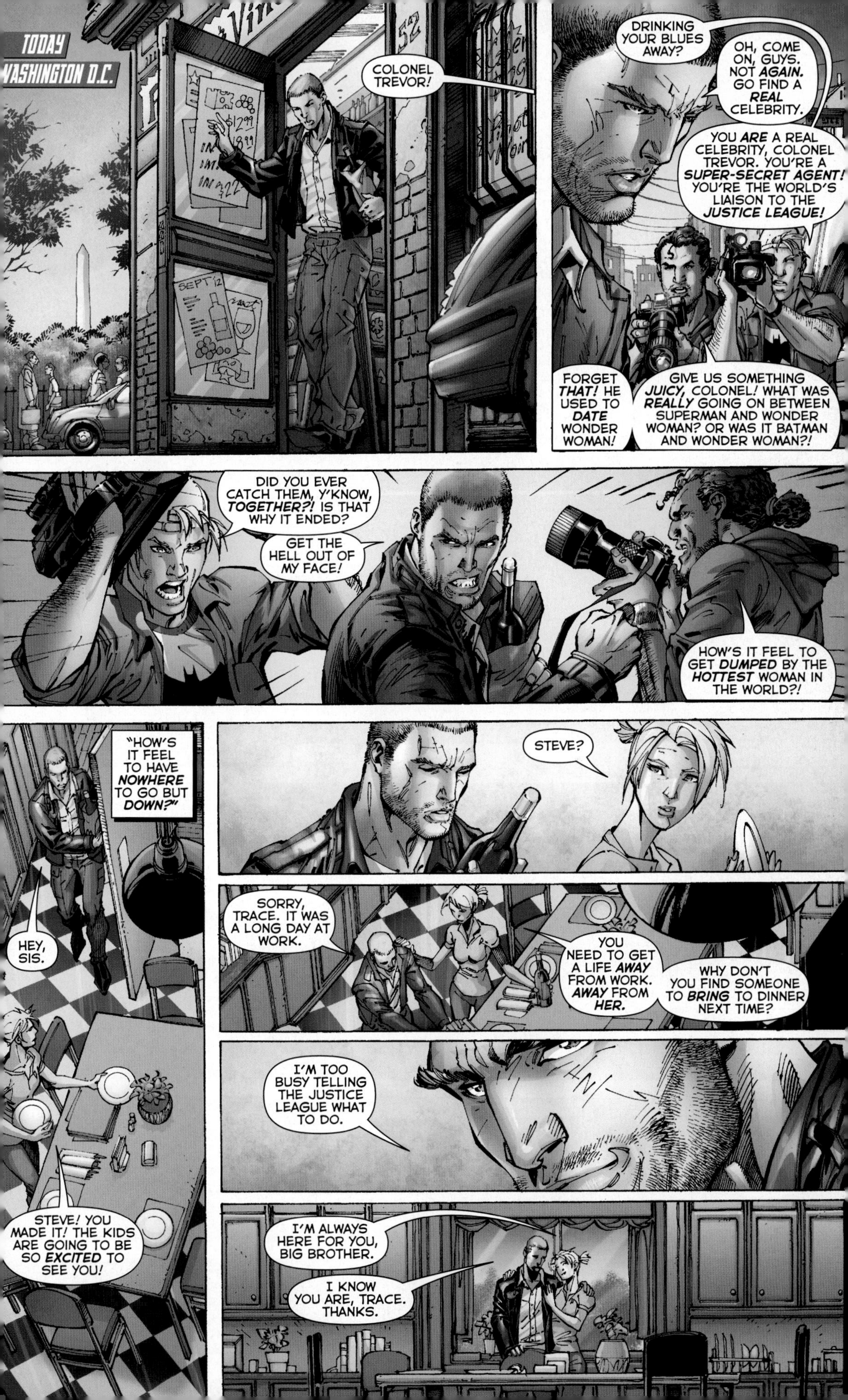
TODAY
WASHINGTON D.C.
COLONEL TREVOR!
DRINKING YOUR BLUES AWAY?
OH, COME ON, GUYS. NOT AGAIN. GO FIND A REAL CELEBRITY.
YOU ARE A REAL CELEBRITY, COLONEL TREVOR. YOU'RE A SUPER-SECRET AGENT! YOU'RE THE WORLD'S LIAISON TO THE JUSTICE LEAGUE!
FORGET THAT! HE USED TO DATE WONDER WOMAN!
GIVE US SOMETHING JUICY, COLONEL! WHAT WAS REALLY GOING ON BETWEEN SUPERMAN AND WONDER WOMAN? OR WAS IT BATMAN AND WONDER WOMAN?!
DID YOU EVER CATCH THEM, Y'KNOW, TOGETHER?! IS THAT WHY IT ENDED?
GET THE HELL OUT OF MY FACE!
HOW'S IT FEEL TO GET DUMPED BY THE HOTTEST WOMAN IN THE WORLD?!
"HOW'S IT FEEL TO HAVE NOWHERE TO GO BUT DOWN?"
HEY, SIS.
STEVE! YOU MADE IT! THE KIDS ARE GOING TO BE SO EXCITED TO SEE YOU!
STEVE?
SORRY, TRACE. IT WAS A LONG DAY AT WORK.
YOU NEED TO GET A LIFE AWAY FROM WORK. AWAY FROM HER.
WHY DON'T YOU FIND SOMEONE TO BRING TO DINNER NEXT TIME?
I'M TOO BUSY TELLING THE JUSTICE LEAGUE WHAT TO DO.
I'M ALWAYS HERE FOR YOU, BIG BROTHER.
I KNOW YOU ARE, TRACE. THANKS.

There's on[ly] [one] thing I kn[ow] about life[.] [I] know some[thing] happen by [...] And some [...] happen be[cause] we make t[hem] happen.

Barry Allen wa[...]

YES, BATMAN KNOCKED THE MAD HATTER'S TEETH OUT AND FREED THE JUDGE AND HIS STAFF, BUT LOOK AT THE BIG PICTURE FOR A SECOND.

GOTHAM CITY MIGHT HAVE BATMAN, BUT WE ALSO HAVE THE HIGHEST MURDER RATE IN THE COUNTRY. STILL.

BATMAN KNOWS CRIME IS IN THIS CITY'S DNA. IT AIN'T GONNA CHANGE! SO YOU HAVE TO ASK YOURSELF...

...WHY DOES HE BOTHER WITH IT? WHY DOESN'T HE SPEND ALL HIS TIME SAVING THE WORLD WITH THE JUSTICE LEAGUE?

BRUCE? THAT SMELL-- WHAT ARE YOU DOING?

I'M PAINTING MY ROOM, ALFRED.

YOUR MOTHER PAINTED YOUR ROOM. YOU'RE COVERING UP YOUR FAVORITE COLOR.

I DON'T HAVE A FAVORITE COLOR ANYMORE.

...INTERRUPT THIS PROGRAM TO BRING YOU BREAKING NEWS: CHAOS AGAIN AT ARKHAM ASYLUM.

AN EXPLOSION MINUTES AGO RIPPED OPEN THE CONTROVERSIAL INSTITUTION. AUTHORITIES SAY THE JUSTICE LEAGUE'S TELEPATHIC ENEMY KNOWN AS THE KEY IS RESPONSIBLE.

SIR, YOU'RE GOING TO BE LATE TO YOUR MEETING WITH STAGG INDUSTRIES.

THE KEY
REAL NAME: UNKNOWN
ABILITIES: PSYCHO-CHEMICALS ALLOW THE KEY TO FEED OFF VICTIMS' PSYCHOLOGICAL STATE.
WANTED FOR: CAPITAL MURDER, MURDER AND TORTURE.

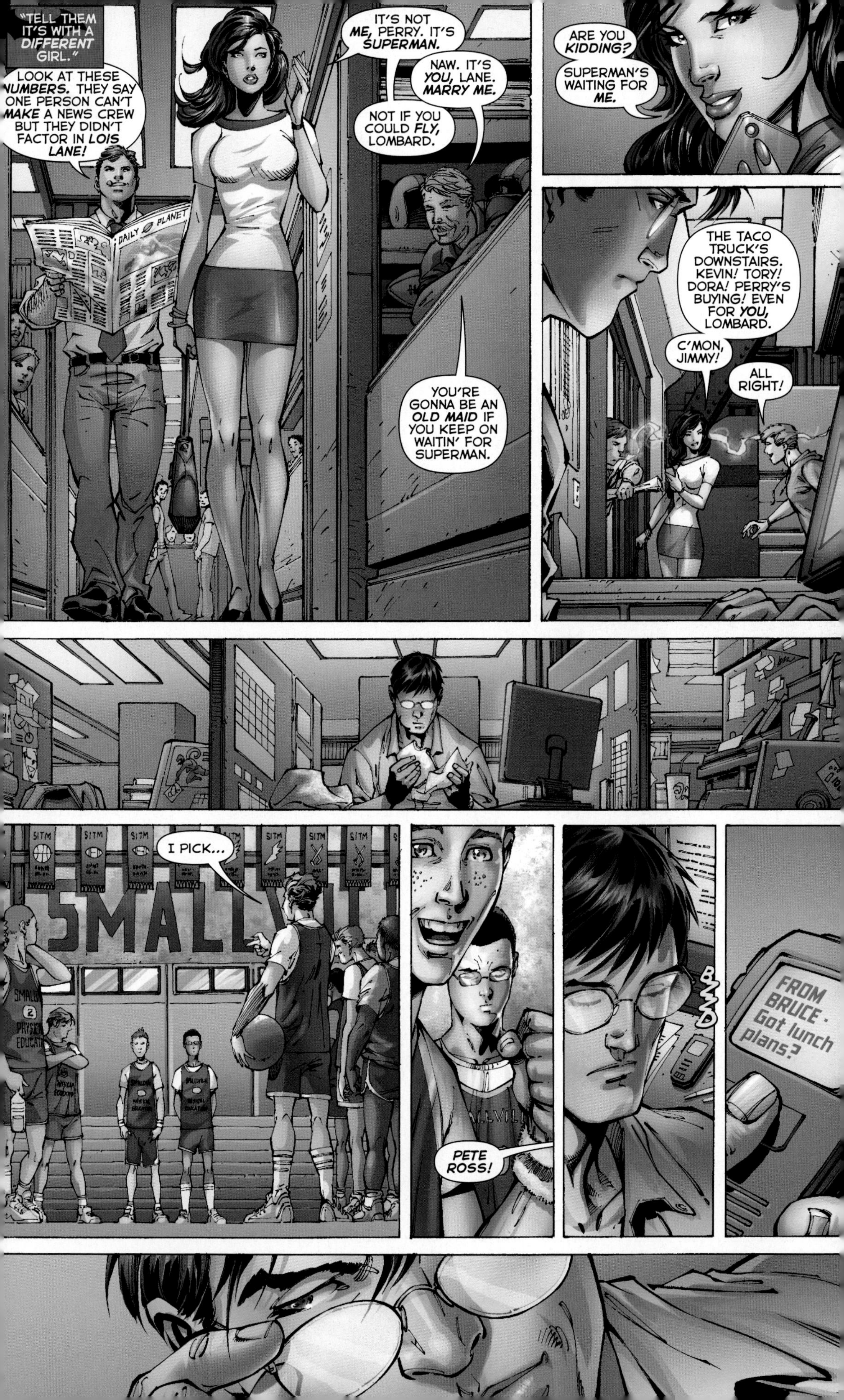
"TELL THEM IT'S WITH A DIFFERENT GIRL."
LOOK AT THESE NUMBERS. THEY SAY ONE PERSON CAN'T MAKE A NEWS CREW BUT THEY DIDN'T FACTOR IN LOIS LANE!
DAILY PLANET
IT'S NOT ME, PERRY. IT'S SUPERMAN.
NAW. IT'S YOU, LANE. MARRY ME.
NOT IF YOU COULD FLY, LOMBARD.
YOU'RE GONNA BE AN OLD MAID IF YOU KEEP ON WAITIN' FOR SUPERMAN.
ARE YOU KIDDING?
SUPERMAN'S WAITING FOR ME.
THE TACO TRUCK'S DOWNSTAIRS. KEVIN! TORY! DORA! PERRY'S BUYING! EVEN FOR YOU, LOMBARD.
C'MON, JIMMY!
ALL RIGHT!
I PICK...
SMALL
PETE ROSS!
BZZZD
FROM BRUCE - Got lunch plans?

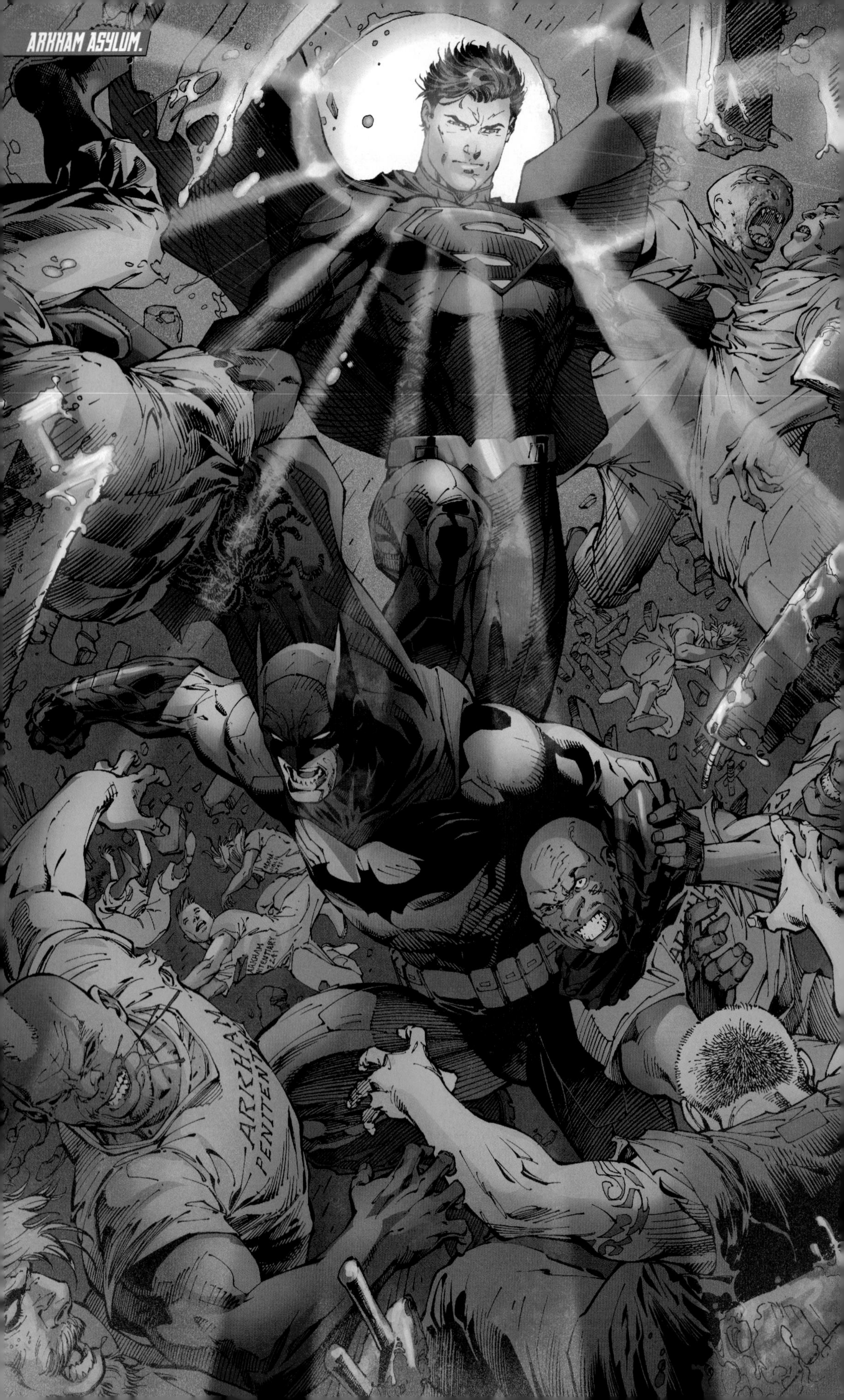
ARKHAM ASYLUM.

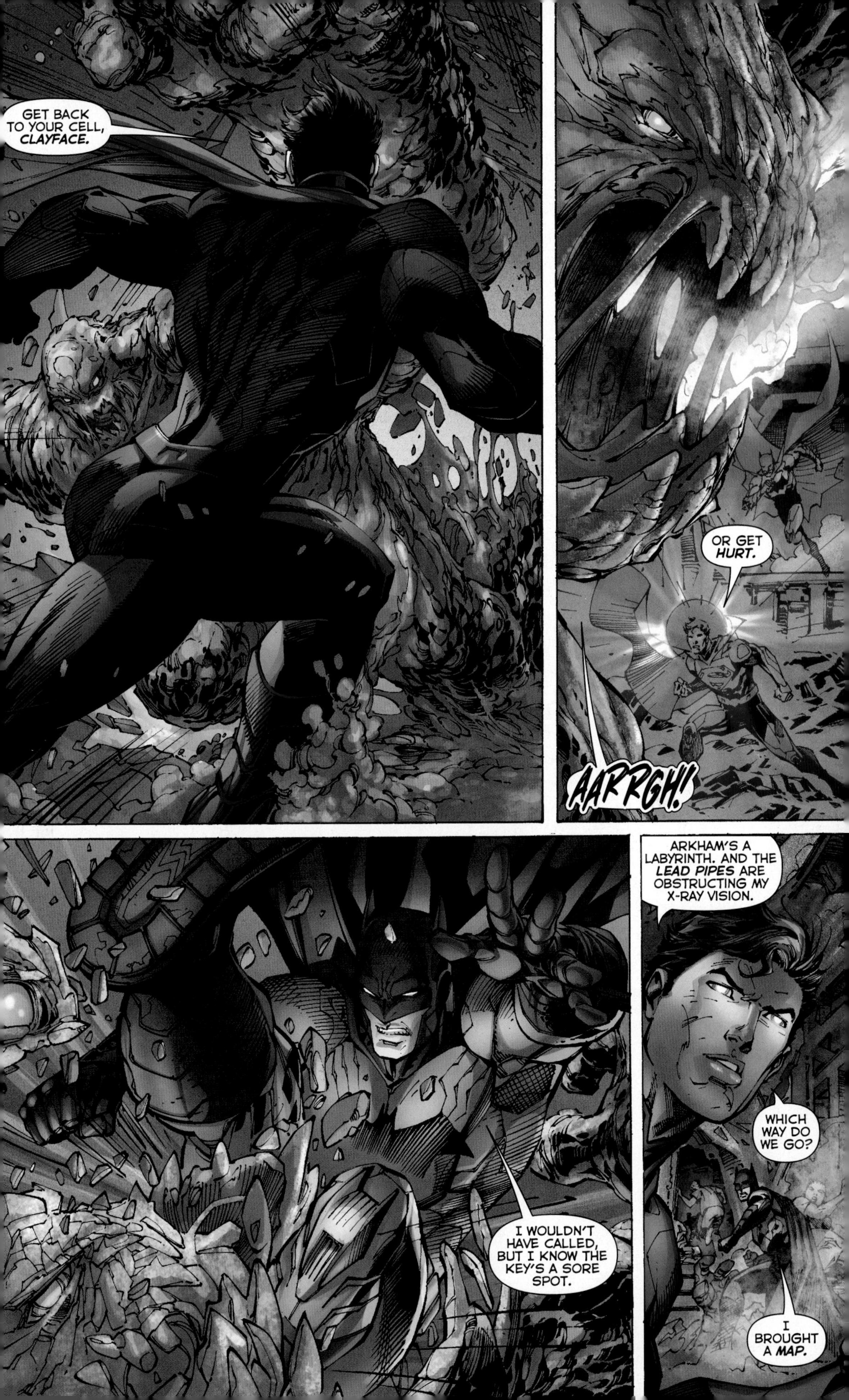
GET BACK TO YOUR CELL, CLAYFACE.
OR GET HURT.
AARRGH!
I WOULDN'T HAVE CALLED, BUT I KNOW THE KEY'S A SORE SPOT.
ARKHAM'S A LABYRINTH. AND THE LEAD PIPES ARE OBSTRUCTING MY X-RAY VISION.
WHICH WAY DO WE GO?
I BROUGHT A MAP.

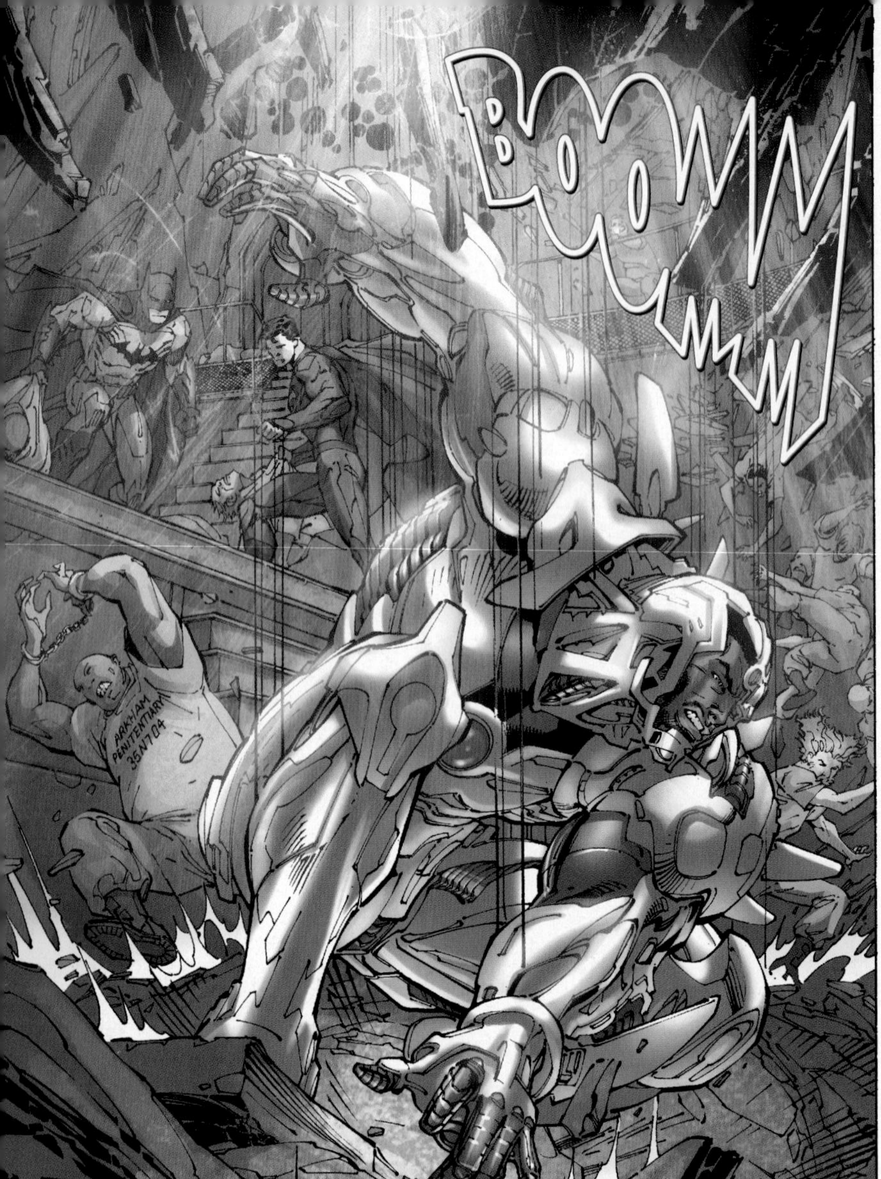
BOOOM
ARKHAM PENITENTIARY 35N704

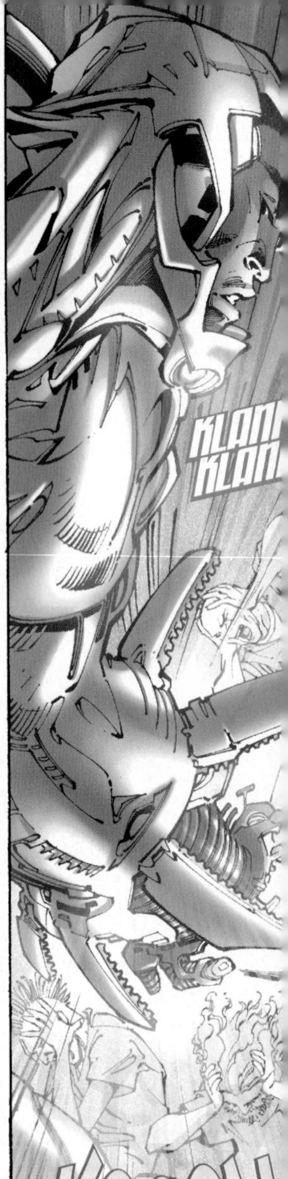
KLAN KLAN
KOOOM

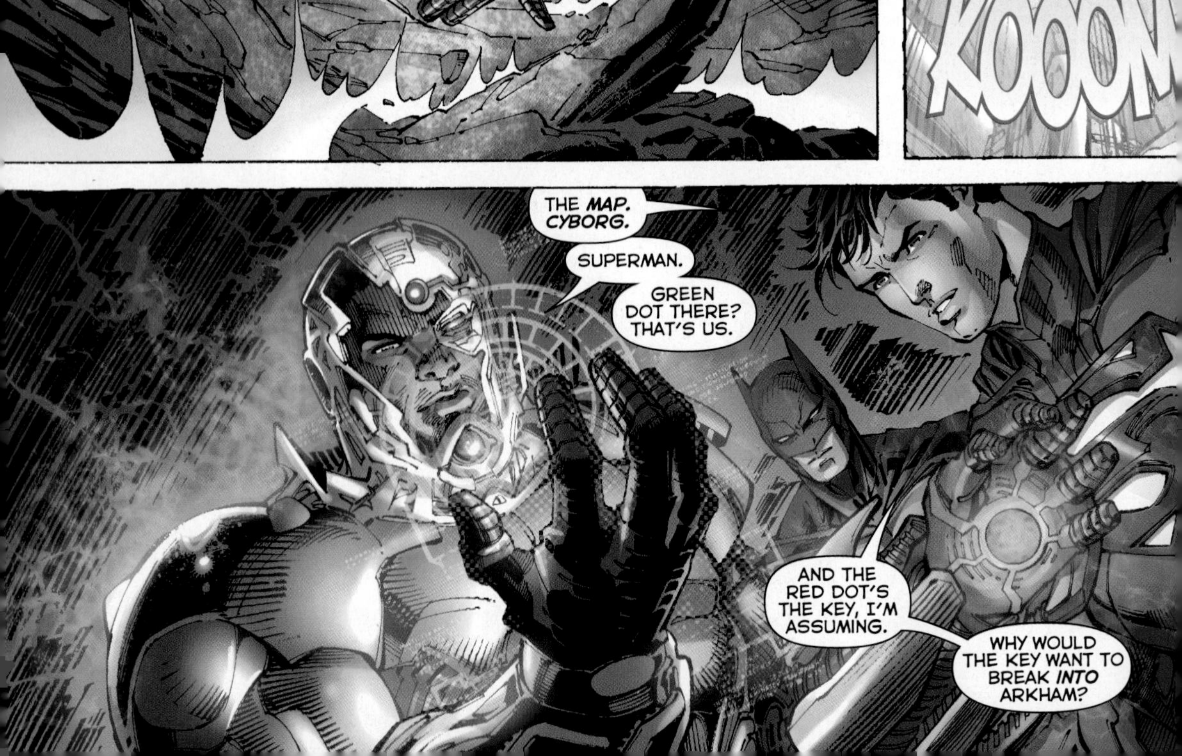
THE MAP. CYBORG.
SUPERMAN.
GREEN DOT THERE? THAT'S US.
AND THE RED DOT'S THE KEY, I'M ASSUMING.
WHY WOULD THE KEY WANT TO BREAK INTO ARKHAM?

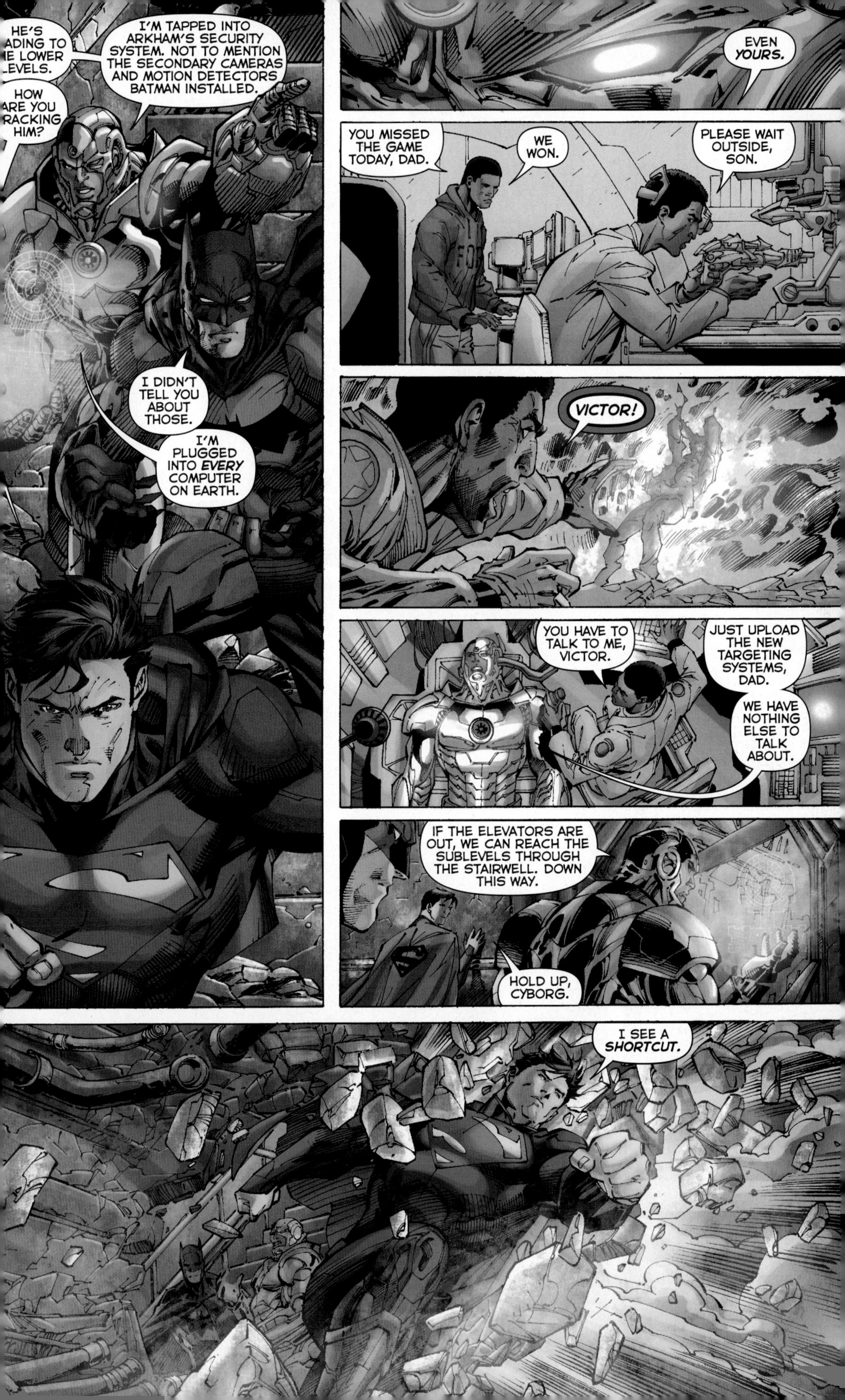
HE'S
ADING TO
E LOWER
LEVELS.
HOW
ARE YOU
RACKING
HIM?
I'M TAPPED INTO ARKHAM'S SECURITY SYSTEM. NOT TO MENTION THE SECONDARY CAMERAS AND MOTION DETECTORS BATMAN INSTALLED.
I DIDN'T TELL YOU ABOUT THOSE.
I'M PLUGGED INTO EVERY COMPUTER ON EARTH.
EVEN YOURS.
YOU MISSED THE GAME TODAY, DAD.
WE WON.
PLEASE WAIT OUTSIDE, SON.
VICTOR!
YOU HAVE TO TALK TO ME, VICTOR.
JUST UPLOAD THE NEW TARGETING SYSTEMS, DAD.
WE HAVE NOTHING ELSE TO TALK ABOUT.
IF THE ELEVATORS ARE OUT, WE CAN REACH THE SUBLEVELS THROUGH THE STAIRWELL. DOWN THIS WAY.
HOLD UP, CYBORG.
I SEE A SHORTCUT.

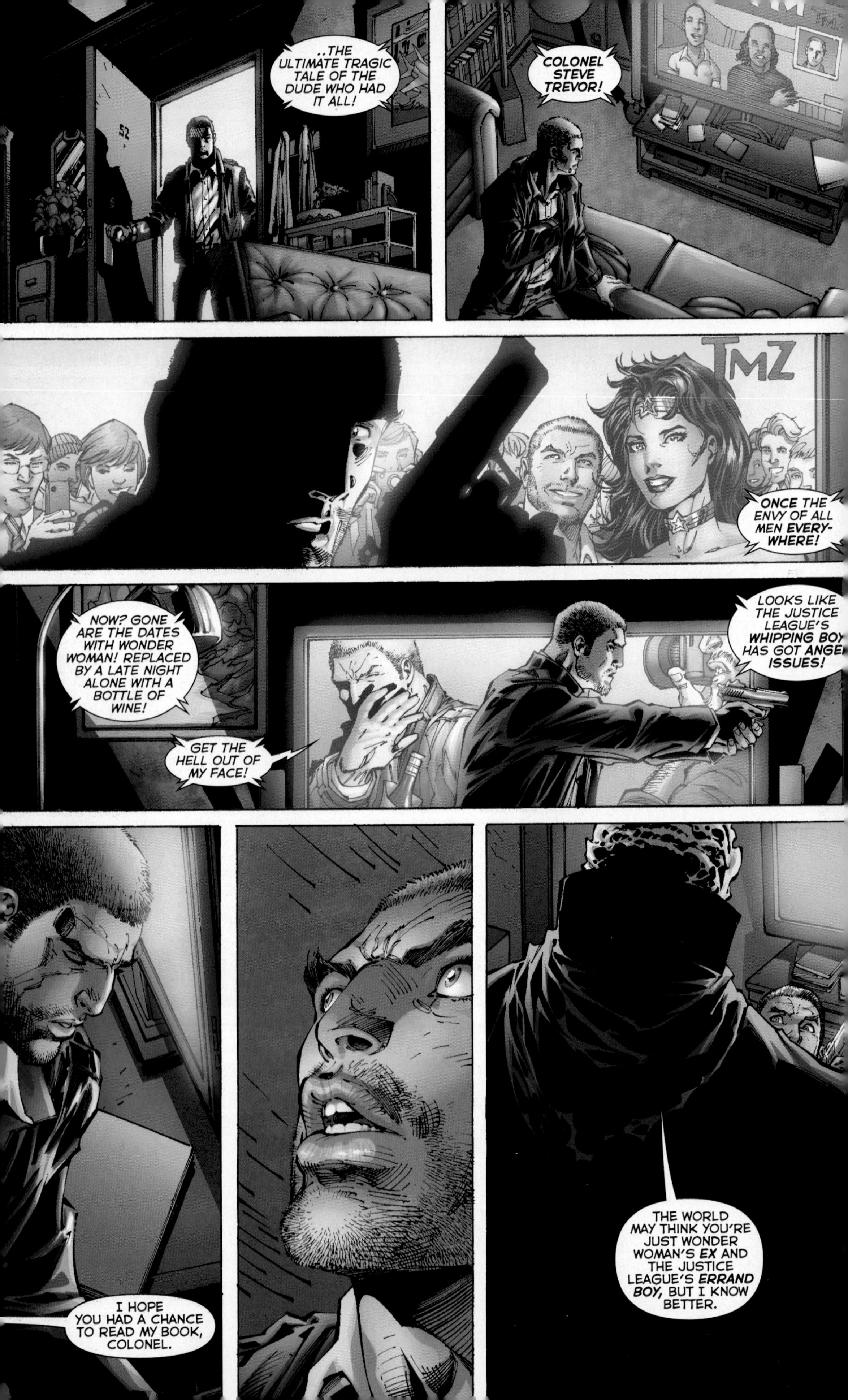
..THE ULTIMATE TRAGIC TALE OF THE DUDE WHO HAD IT ALL!
COLONEL STEVE TREVOR!
TMZ
ONCE THE ENVY OF ALL MEN EVERY-WHERE!
NOW? GONE ARE THE DATES WITH WONDER WOMAN! REPLACED BY A LATE NIGHT ALONE WITH A BOTTLE OF WINE!
LOOKS LIKE THE JUSTICE LEAGUE'S WHIPPING BOY HAS GOT ANGER ISSUES!
GET THE HELL OUT OF MY FACE!
I HOPE YOU HAD A CHANCE TO READ MY BOOK, COLONEL.
THE WORLD MAY THINK YOU'RE JUST WONDER WOMAN'S EX AND THE JUSTICE LEAGUE'S ERRAND BOY, BUT I KNOW BETTER.

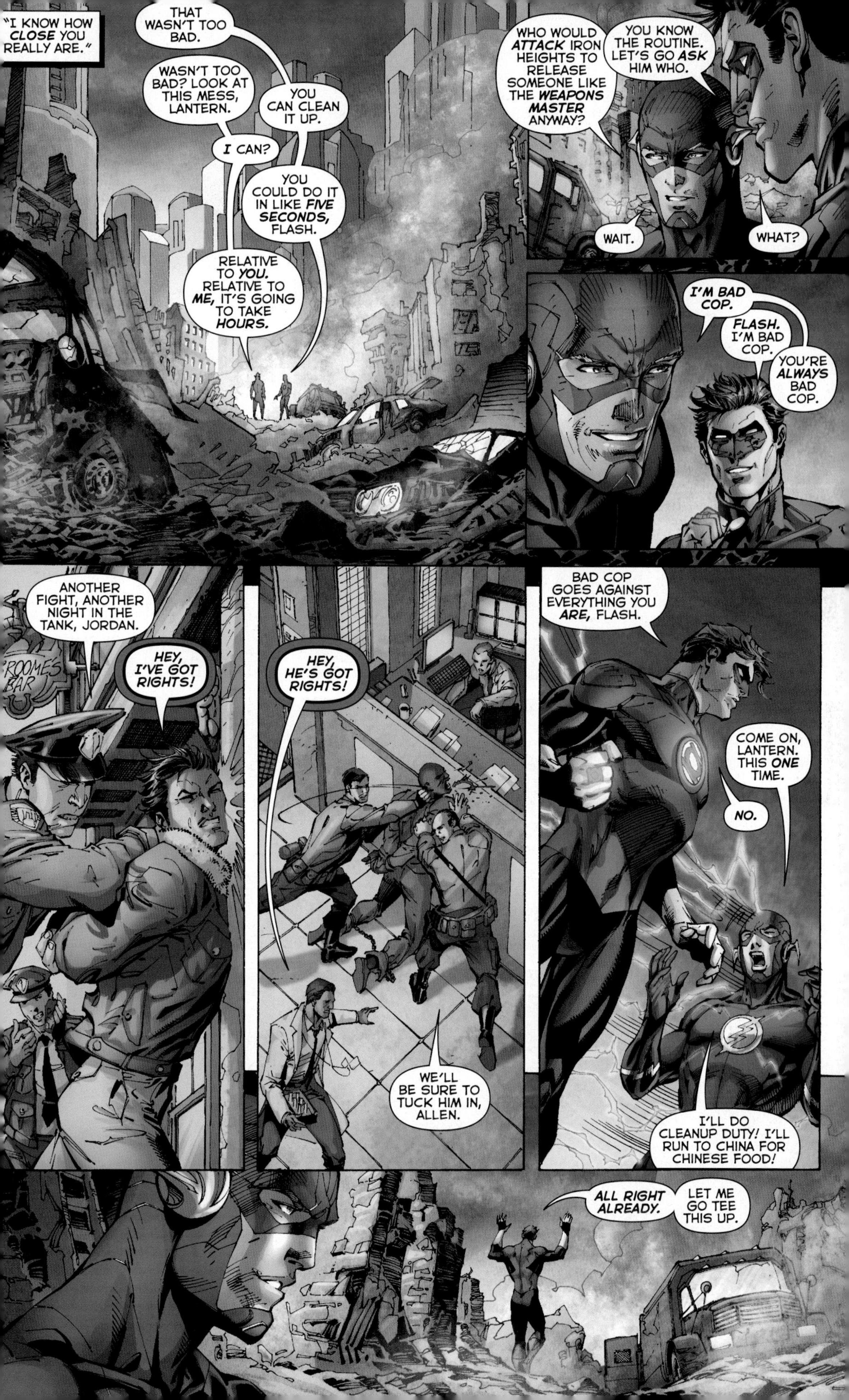

"I KNOW HOW CLOSE YOU REALLY ARE."
THAT WASN'T TOO BAD.
WASN'T TOO BAD? LOOK AT THIS MESS, LANTERN.
YOU CAN CLEAN IT UP.
I CAN?
YOU COULD DO IT IN LIKE FIVE SECONDS, FLASH.
RELATIVE TO YOU. RELATIVE TO ME, IT'S GOING TO TAKE HOURS.
WHO WOULD ATTACK IRON HEIGHTS TO RELEASE SOMEONE LIKE THE WEAPONS MASTER ANYWAY?
YOU KNOW THE ROUTINE. LET'S GO ASK HIM WHO.
WAIT.
WHAT?
I'M BAD COP.
FLASH. I'M BAD COP.
YOU'RE ALWAYS BAD COP.
ANOTHER FIGHT, ANOTHER NIGHT IN THE TANK, JORDAN.
HEY, I'VE GOT RIGHTS!
HEY, HE'S GOT RIGHTS!
WE'LL BE SURE TO TUCK HIM IN, ALLEN.
BAD COP GOES AGAINST EVERYTHING YOU ARE, FLASH.
COME ON, LANTERN. THIS ONE TIME.
NO.
I'LL DO CLEANUP DUTY! I'LL RUN TO CHINA FOR CHINESE FOOD!
ALL RIGHT ALREADY.
LET ME GO TEE THIS UP.

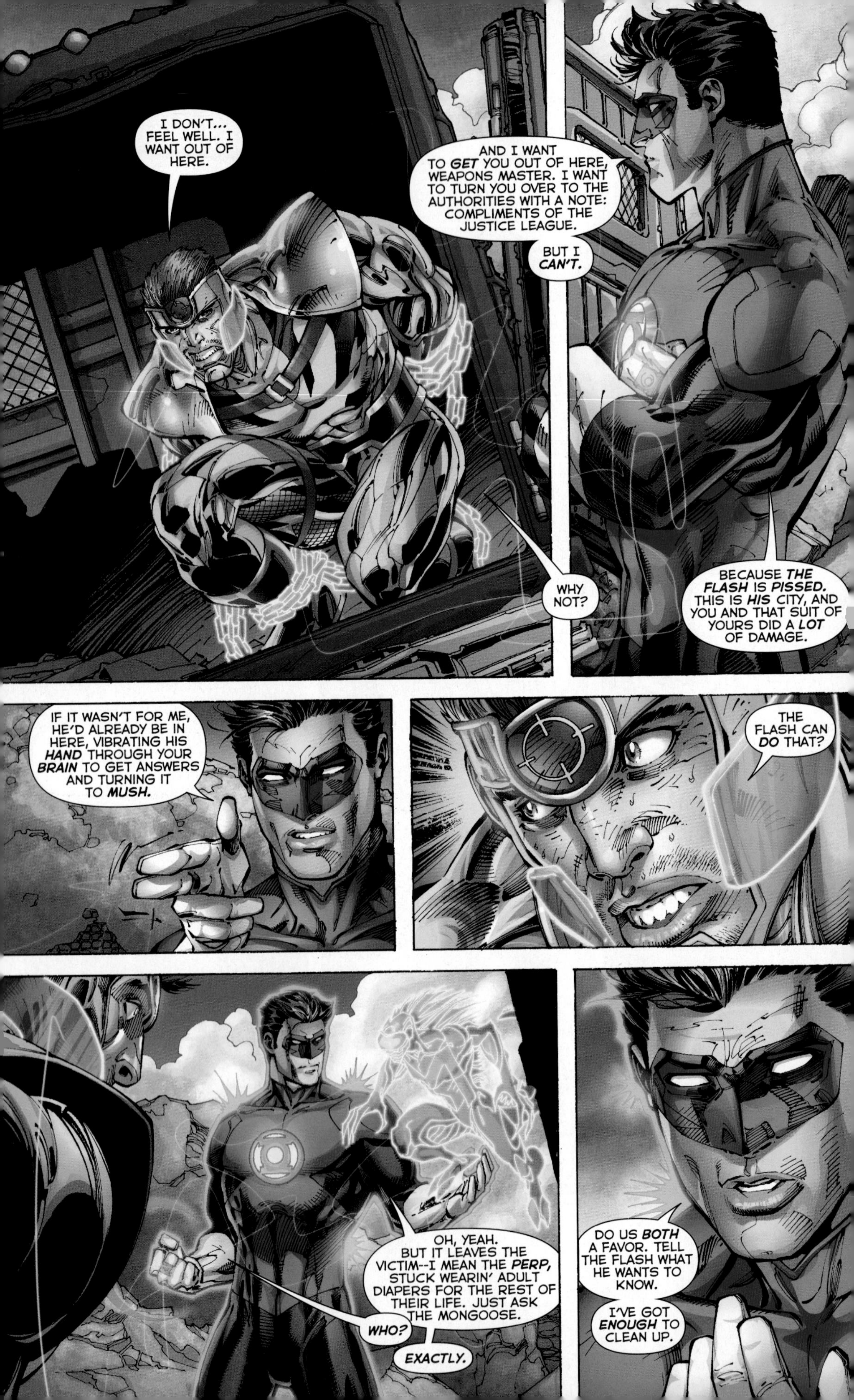

I DON'T... FEEL WELL. I WANT OUT OF HERE.
AND I WANT TO GET YOU OUT OF HERE, WEAPONS MASTER. I WANT TO TURN YOU OVER TO THE AUTHORITIES WITH A NOTE: COMPLIMENTS OF THE JUSTICE LEAGUE.
BUT I CAN'T.
WHY NOT?
BECAUSE THE FLASH IS PISSED. THIS IS HIS CITY, AND YOU AND THAT SUIT OF YOURS DID A LOT OF DAMAGE.
IF IT WASN'T FOR ME, HE'D ALREADY BE IN HERE, VIBRATING HIS HAND THROUGH YOUR BRAIN TO GET ANSWERS AND TURNING IT TO MUSH.
THE FLASH CAN DO THAT?
OH, YEAH. BUT IT LEAVES THE VICTIM--I MEAN THE PERP, STUCK WEARIN' ADULT DIAPERS FOR THE REST OF THEIR LIFE. JUST ASK THE MONGOOSE.
WHO?
EXACTLY.
DO US BOTH A FAVOR. TELL THE FLASH WHAT HE WANTS TO KNOW.
I'VE GOT ENOUGH TO CLEAN UP.

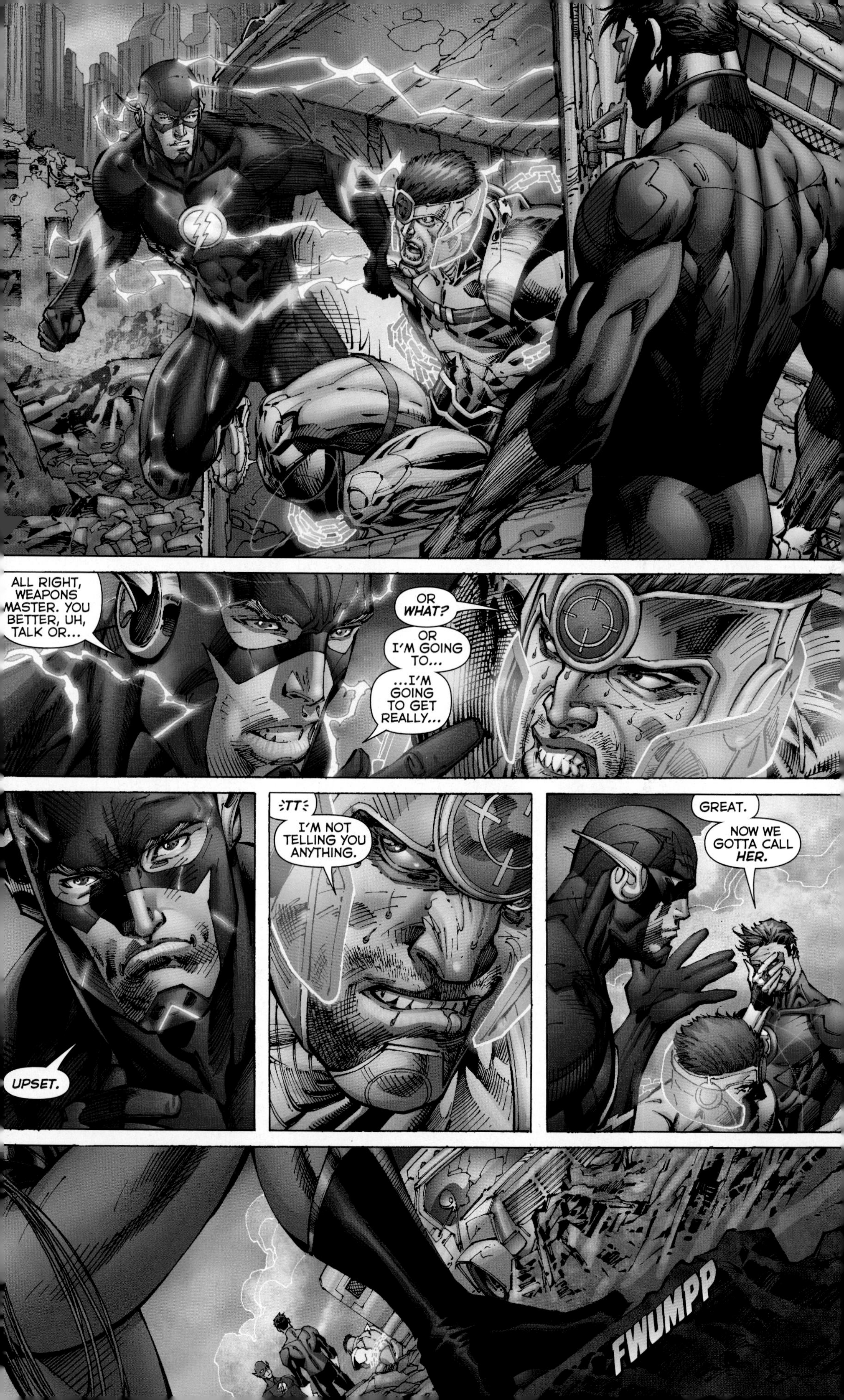
ALL RIGHT, WEAPONS MASTER. YOU BETTER, UH, TALK OR...
OR *WHAT?*
OR I'M GOING TO...
...I'M GOING TO GET REALLY...
UPSET.
TT
I'M NOT TELLING YOU ANYTHING.
GREAT.
NOW WE GOTTA CALL *HER.*
FWUMPP

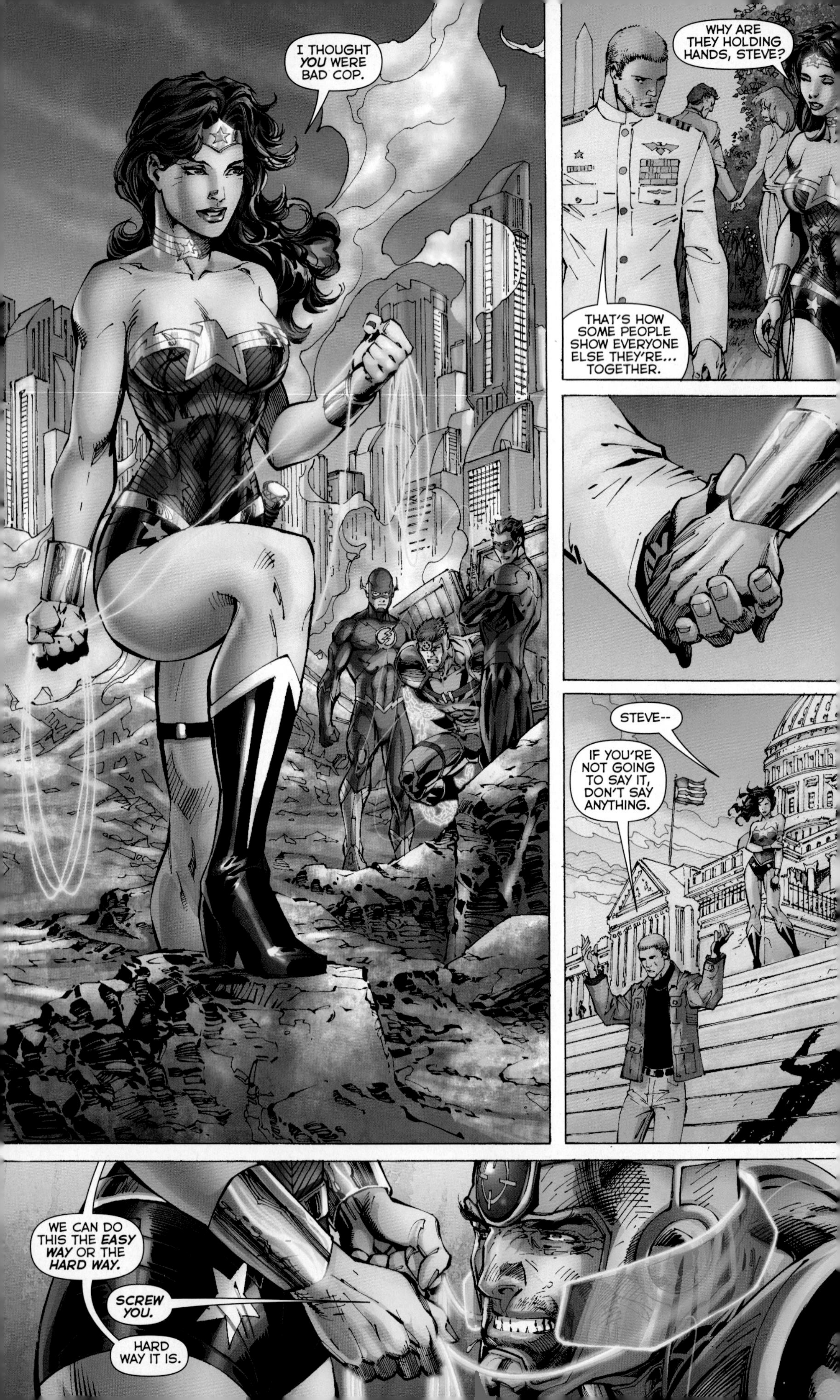
I THOUGHT *YOU* WERE BAD COP.
WHY ARE THEY HOLDING HANDS, STEVE?
THAT'S HOW SOME PEOPLE SHOW EVERYONE ELSE THEY'RE... TOGETHER.
STEVE--
IF YOU'RE NOT GOING TO SAY IT, DON'T SAY ANYTHING.
WE CAN DO THIS THE *EASY WAY* OR THE *HARD WAY.*
SCREW YOU.
HARD WAY IT IS.

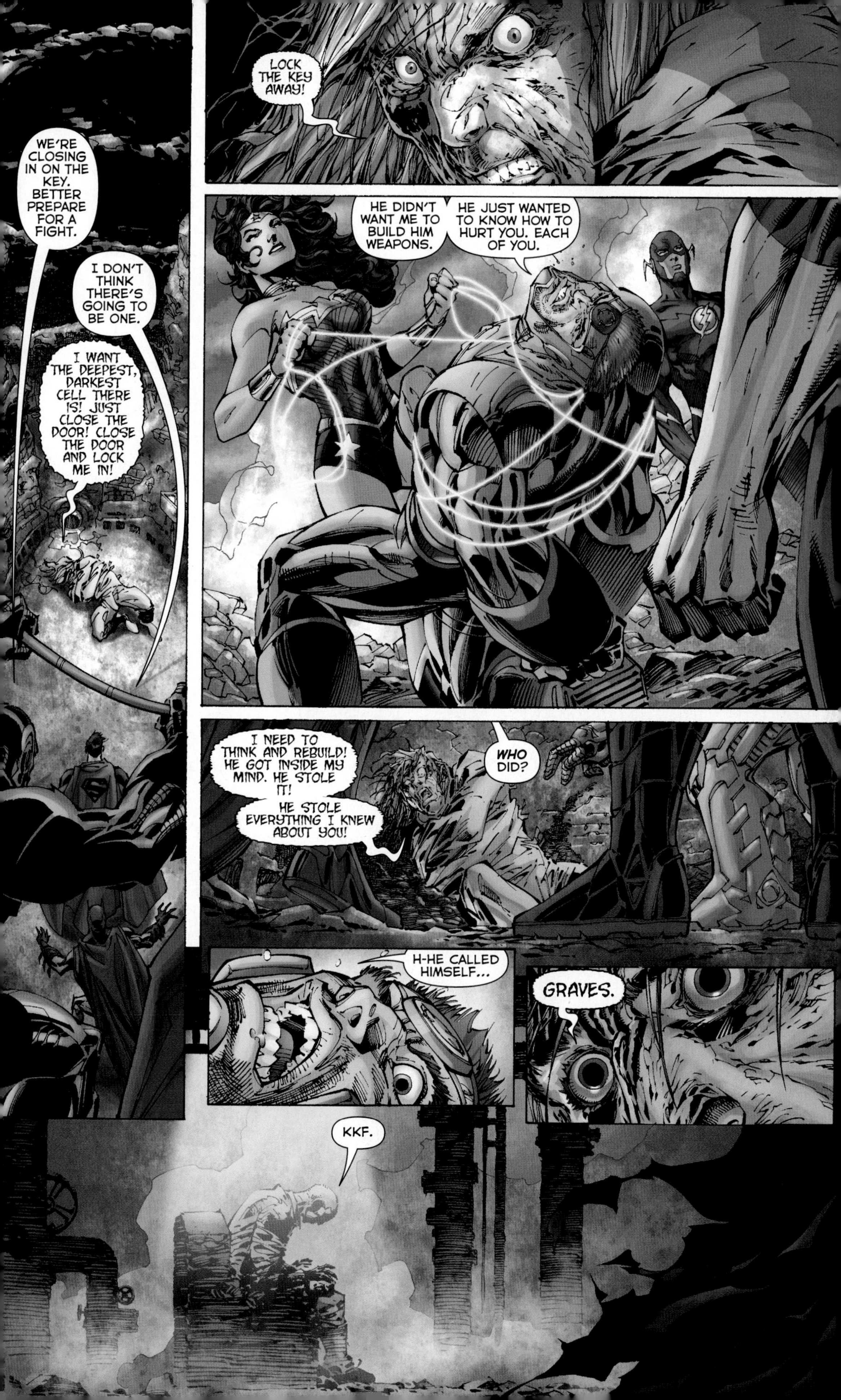
LOCK THE KEY AWAY!
WE'RE CLOSING IN ON THE KEY. BETTER PREPARE FOR A FIGHT.
I DON'T THINK THERE'S GOING TO BE ONE.
I WANT THE DEEPEST, DARKEST CELL THERE IS! JUST CLOSE THE DOOR! CLOSE THE DOOR AND LOCK ME IN!
HE DIDN'T WANT ME TO BUILD HIM WEAPONS.
HE JUST WANTED TO KNOW HOW TO HURT YOU. EACH OF YOU.
I NEED TO THINK AND REBUILD! HE GOT INSIDE MY MIND. HE STOLE IT!
HE STOLE EVERYTHING I KNEW ABOUT YOU!
WHO DID?
H-HE CALLED HIMSELF...
GRAVES.
KKF.

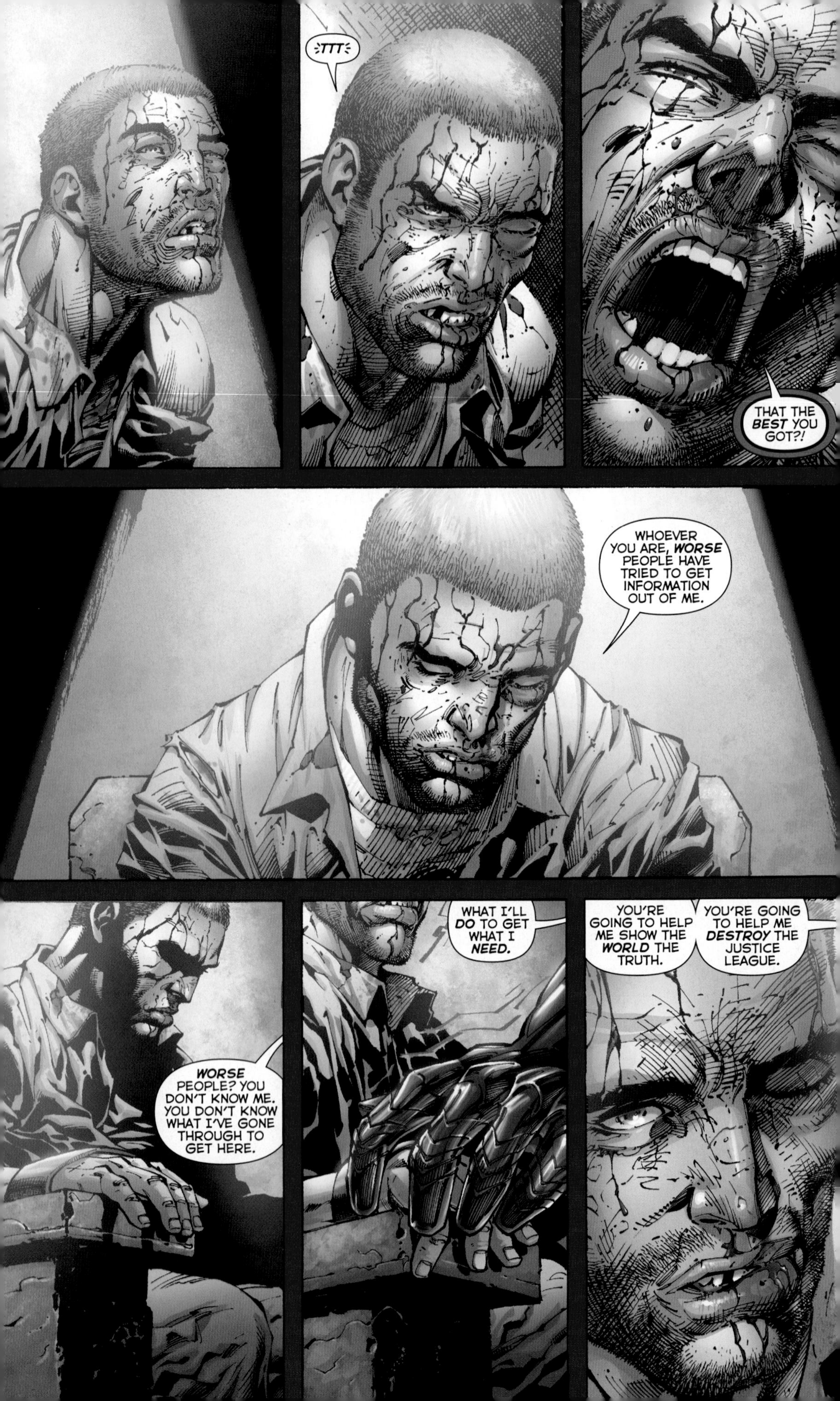
TTT
THAT THE BEST YOU GOT?!
WHOEVER YOU ARE, WORSE PEOPLE HAVE TRIED TO GET INFORMATION OUT OF ME.
WORSE PEOPLE? YOU DON'T KNOW ME. YOU DON'T KNOW WHAT I'VE GONE THROUGH TO GET HERE.
WHAT I'LL DO TO GET WHAT I NEED.
YOU'RE GOING TO HELP ME SHOW THE WORLD THE TRUTH.
YOU'RE GOING TO HELP ME DESTROY THE JUSTICE LEAGUE.

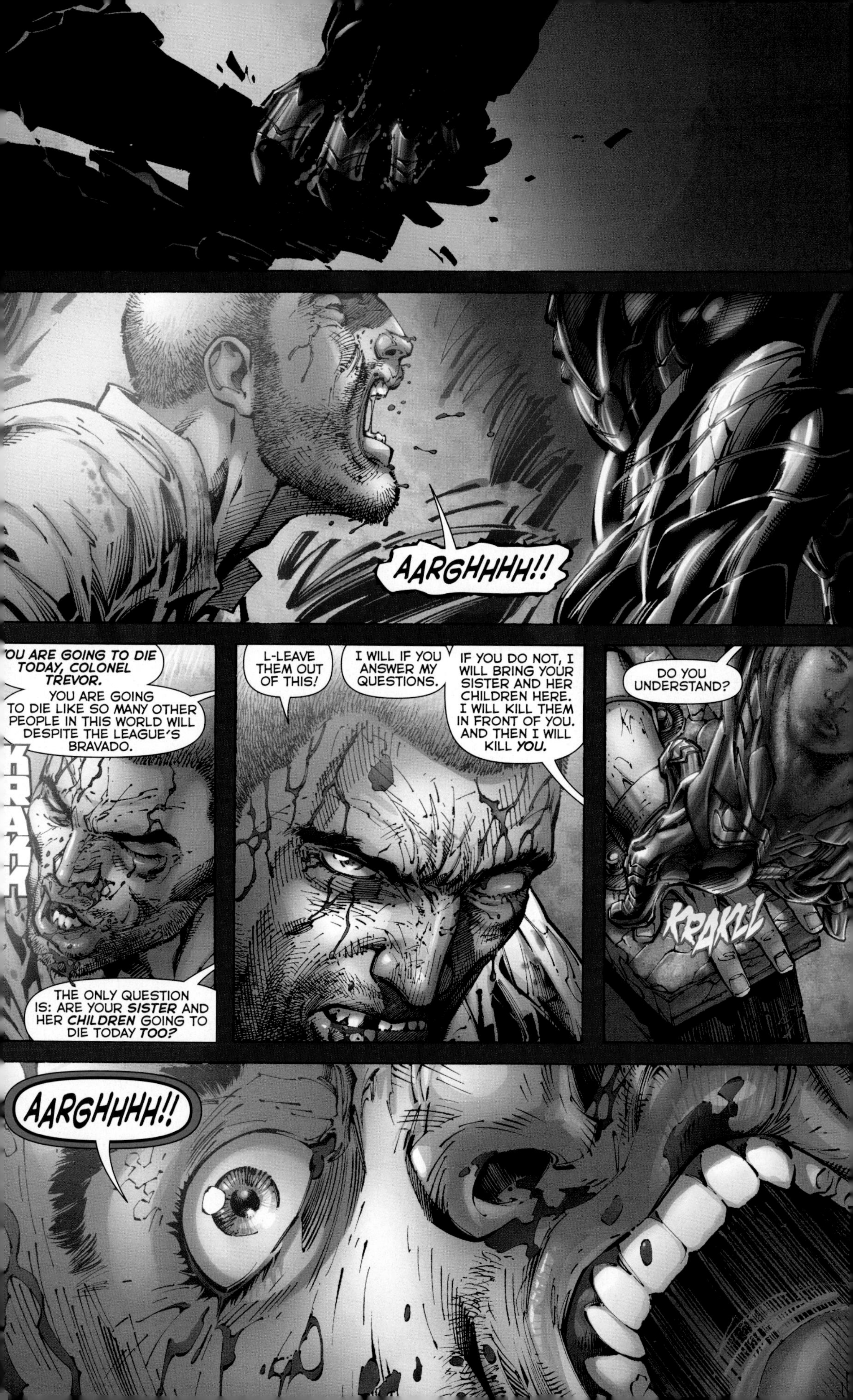
AARGHHHH!!
OU ARE GOING TO DIE TODAY, COLONEL TREVOR.
YOU ARE GOING TO DIE LIKE SO MANY OTHER PEOPLE IN THIS WORLD WILL DESPITE THE LEAGUE'S BRAVADO.
THE ONLY QUESTION IS: ARE YOUR SISTER AND HER CHILDREN GOING TO DIE TODAY TOO?
L-LEAVE THEM OUT OF THIS!
I WILL IF YOU ANSWER MY QUESTIONS.
IF YOU DO NOT, I WILL BRING YOUR SISTER AND HER CHILDREN HERE. I WILL KILL THEM IN FRONT OF YOU. AND THEN I WILL KILL YOU.
DO YOU UNDERSTAND?
KRAKLL
AARGHHHH!!

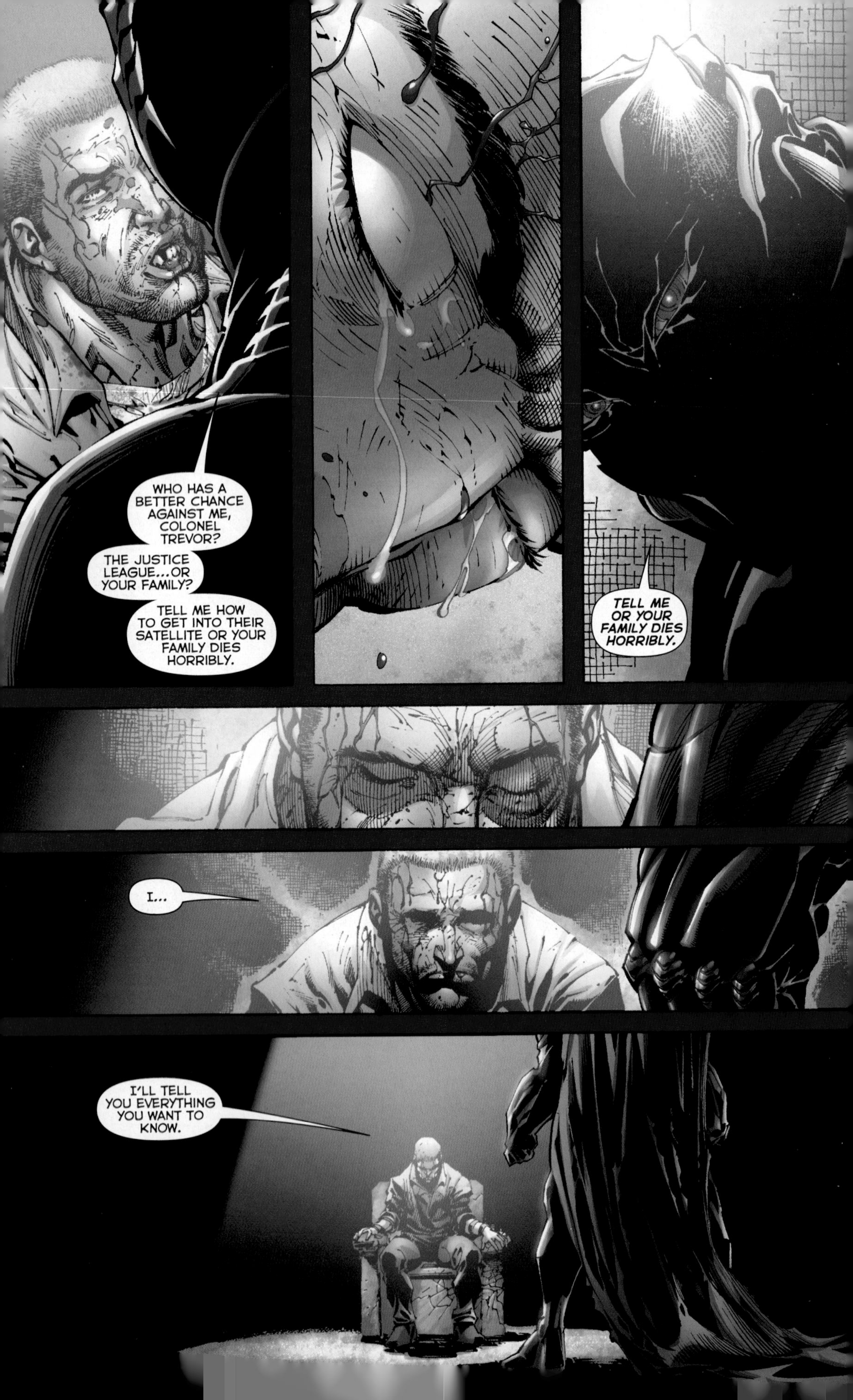
WHO HAS A BETTER CHANCE AGAINST ME, COLONEL TREVOR?
THE JUSTICE LEAGUE...OR YOUR FAMILY?
TELL ME HOW TO GET INTO THEIR SATELLITE OR YOUR FAMILY DIES HORRIBLY.
TELL ME OR YOUR FAMILY DIES HORRIBLY.
I...
I'LL TELL YOU EVERYTHING YOU WANT TO KNOW.

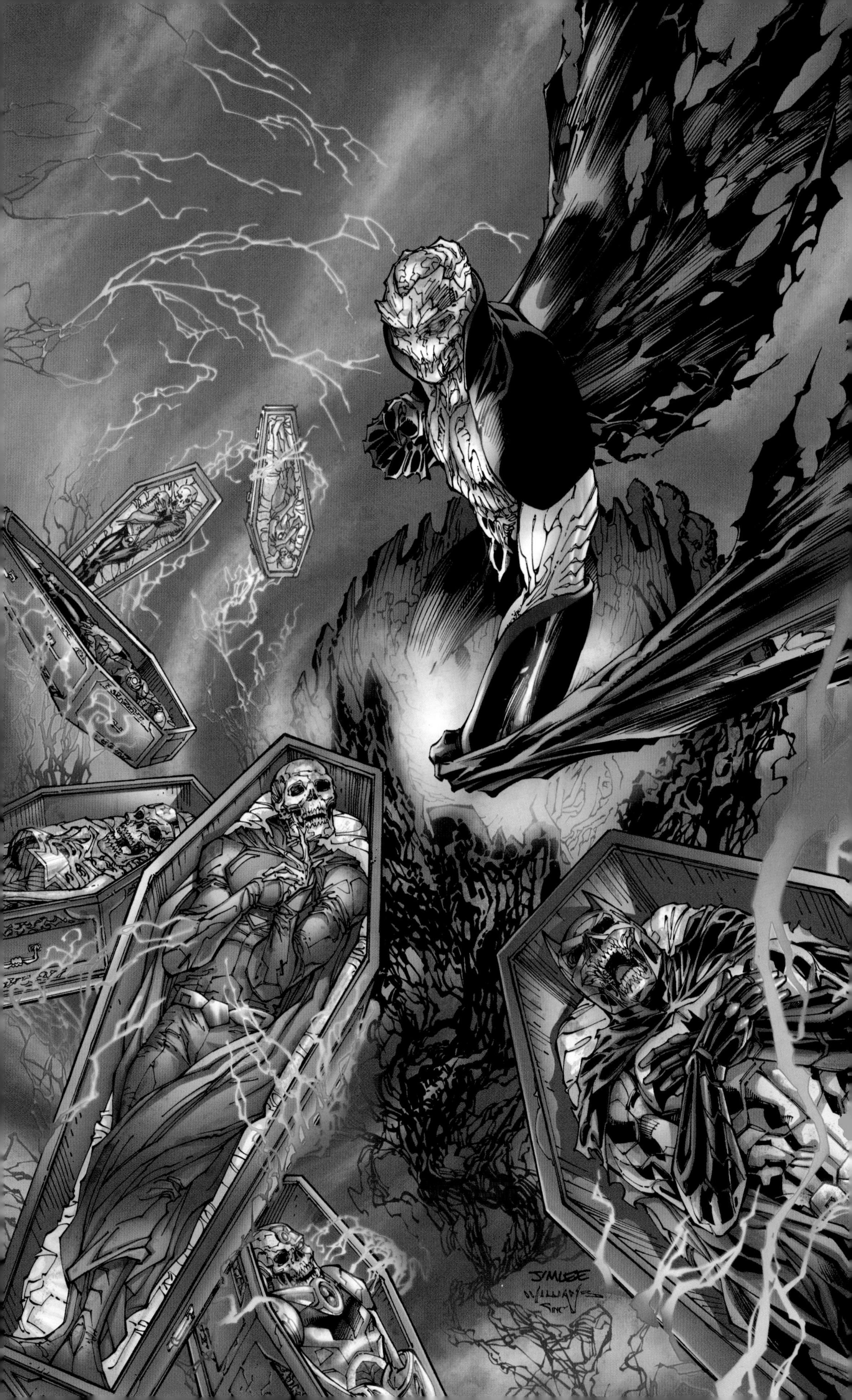

THE VILLAIN'S JOURNEY CHAPTER TWO: THE BELLY OF THE BEAST

GEOFF JOHNS writer **JIM LEE** penciller **SCOTT WILLIAMS, MARK IRWIN & JONATHAN GLAPION** inkers cover by **JIM LEE, SCOTT WILLIAMS & ALEX SINCLAIR**

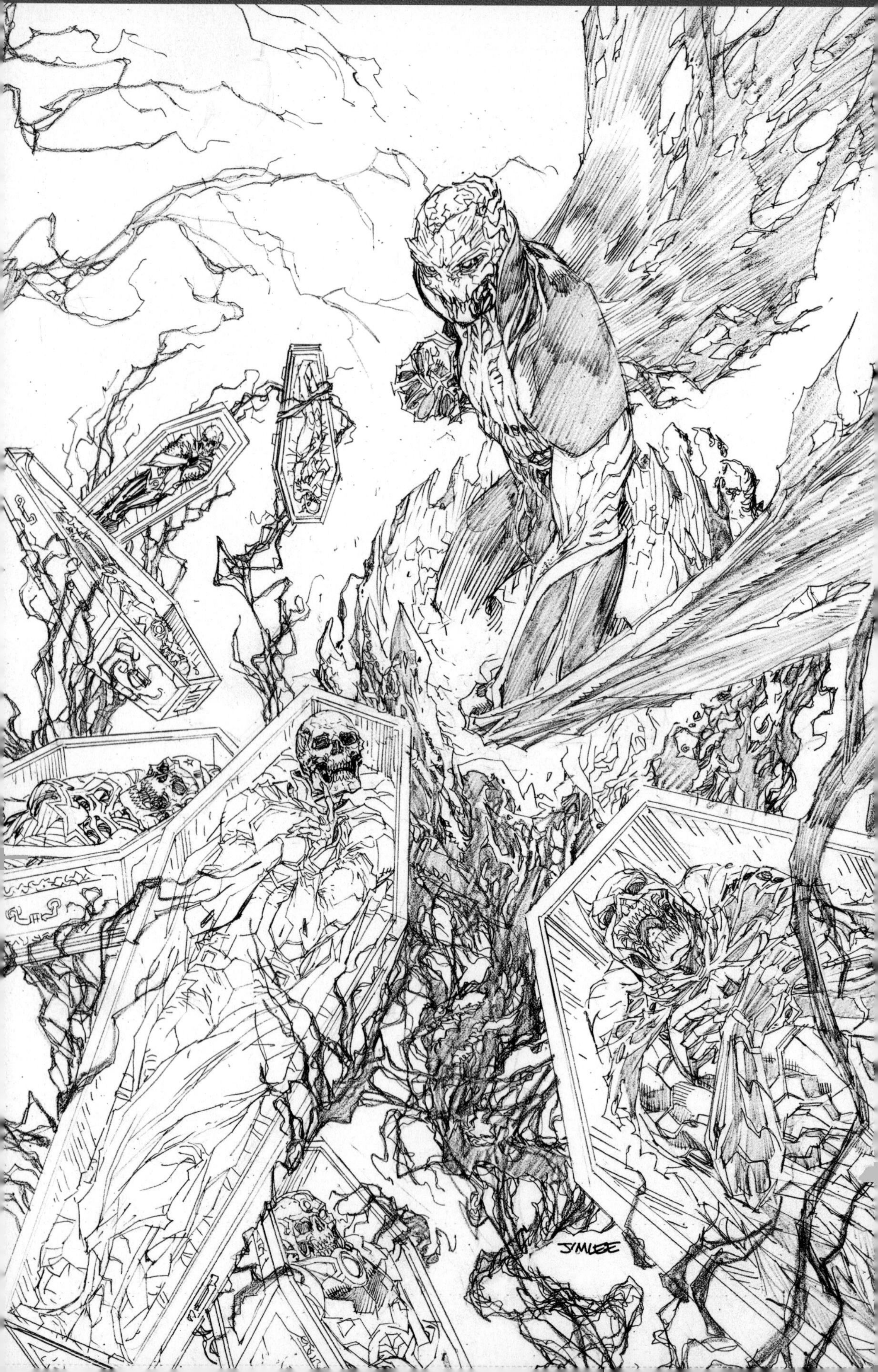
JIMLEE

David Graves
—world-renowned author of
JUSTICE LEAGUE: GODS AMONG MEN

as well as his cult series of mystery
non-fiction novels including THE SECRET
HISTORY OF ATLANTIS and his quest THE
SEARCH FOR MOUNT SUMERU...

KFF

Mount Sumeru and its surroundings are a probable nexus to the worlds of the afterlife in some respects. A place some consider a myth, but they're wrong

KAFFF
KFFF

FUMP

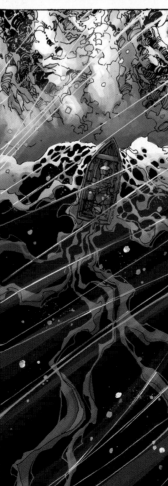

Only those walking the line of death could find their way

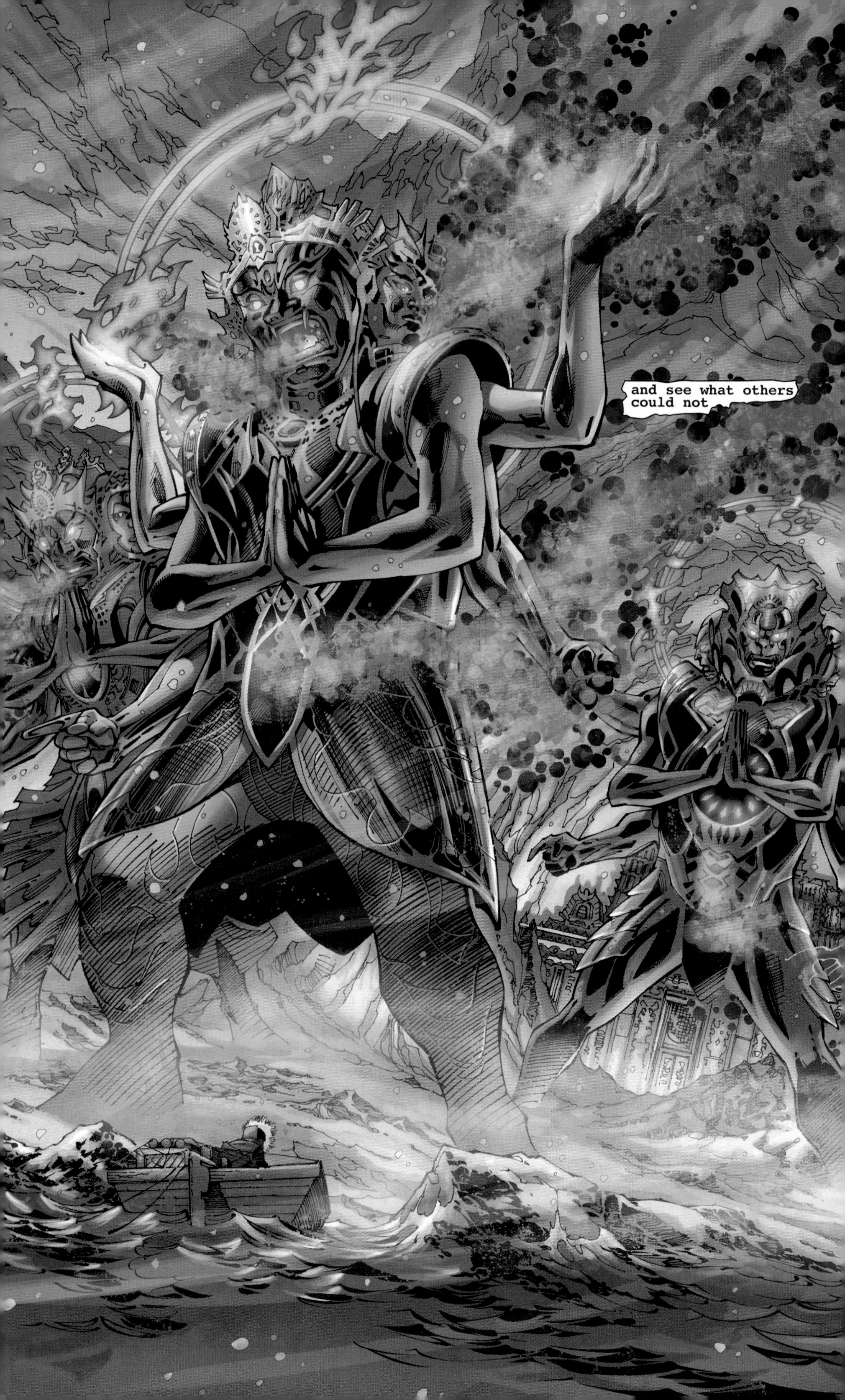
and see what others could not

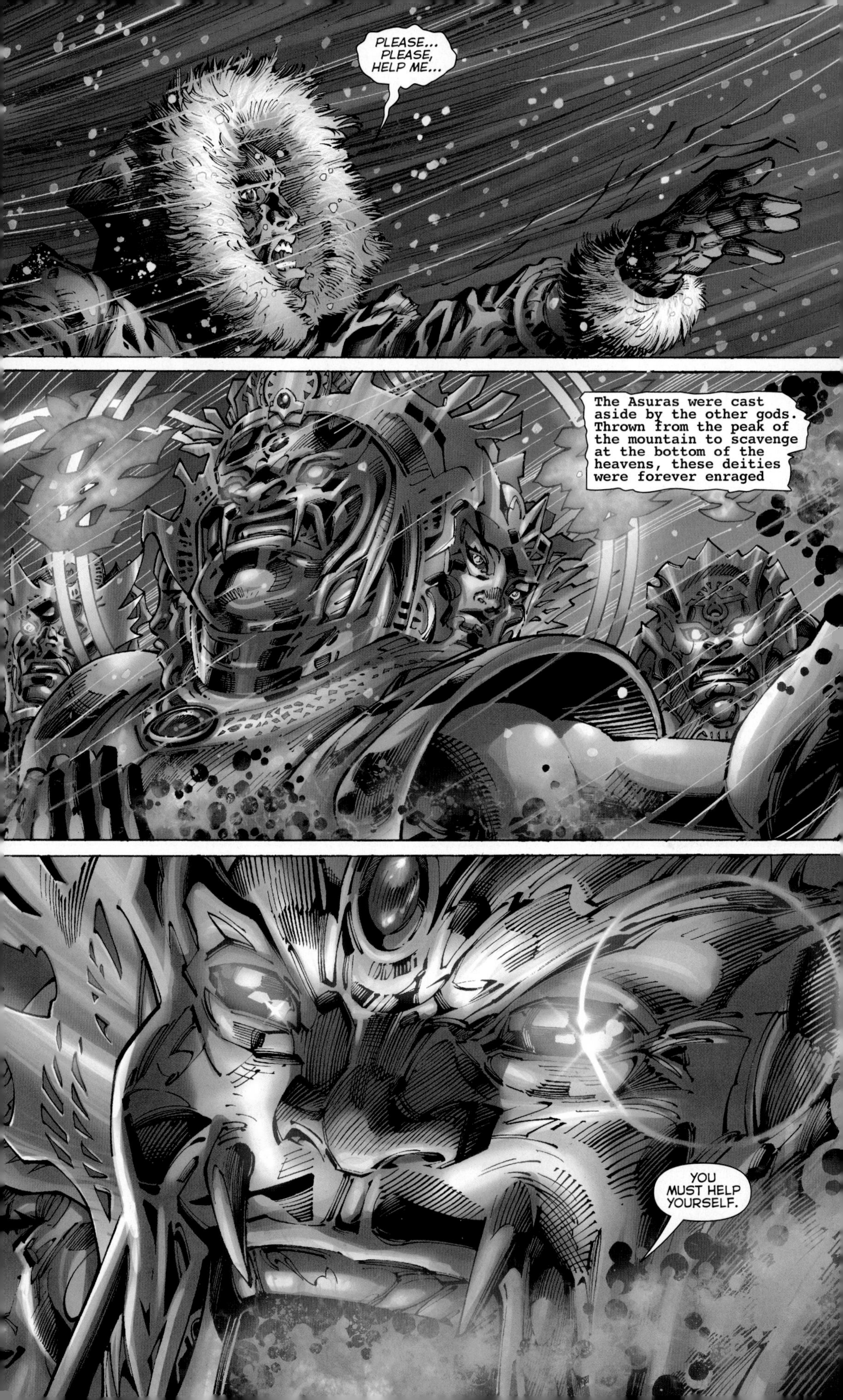
PLEASE... PLEASE, HELP ME...
The Asuras were cast aside by the other gods. Thrown from the peak of the mountain to scavenge at the bottom of the heavens, these deities were forever enraged
YOU MUST HELP YOURSELF.

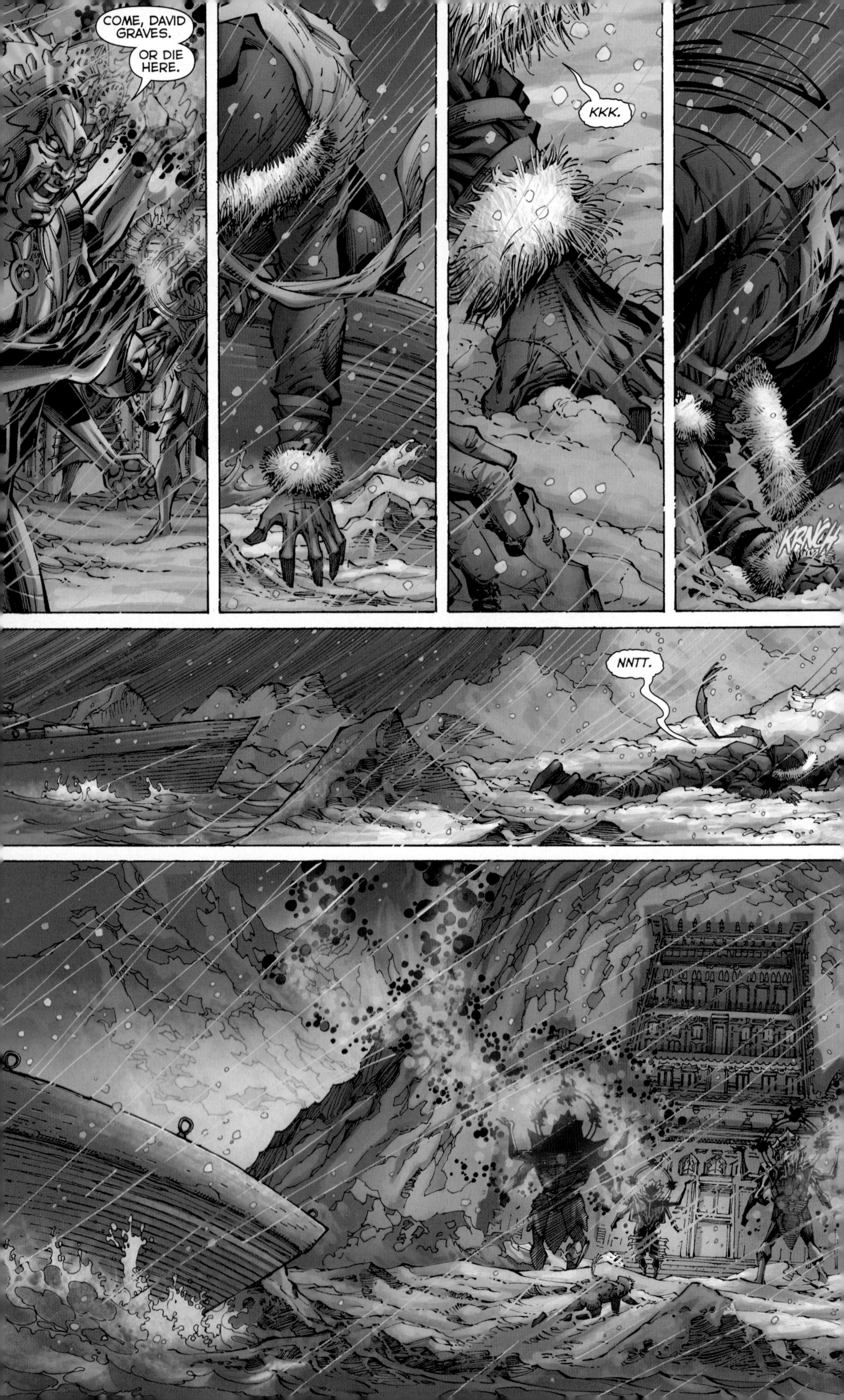

COME, DAVID GRAVES.
OR DIE HERE.
KKK.
KRNCH
NNTT.

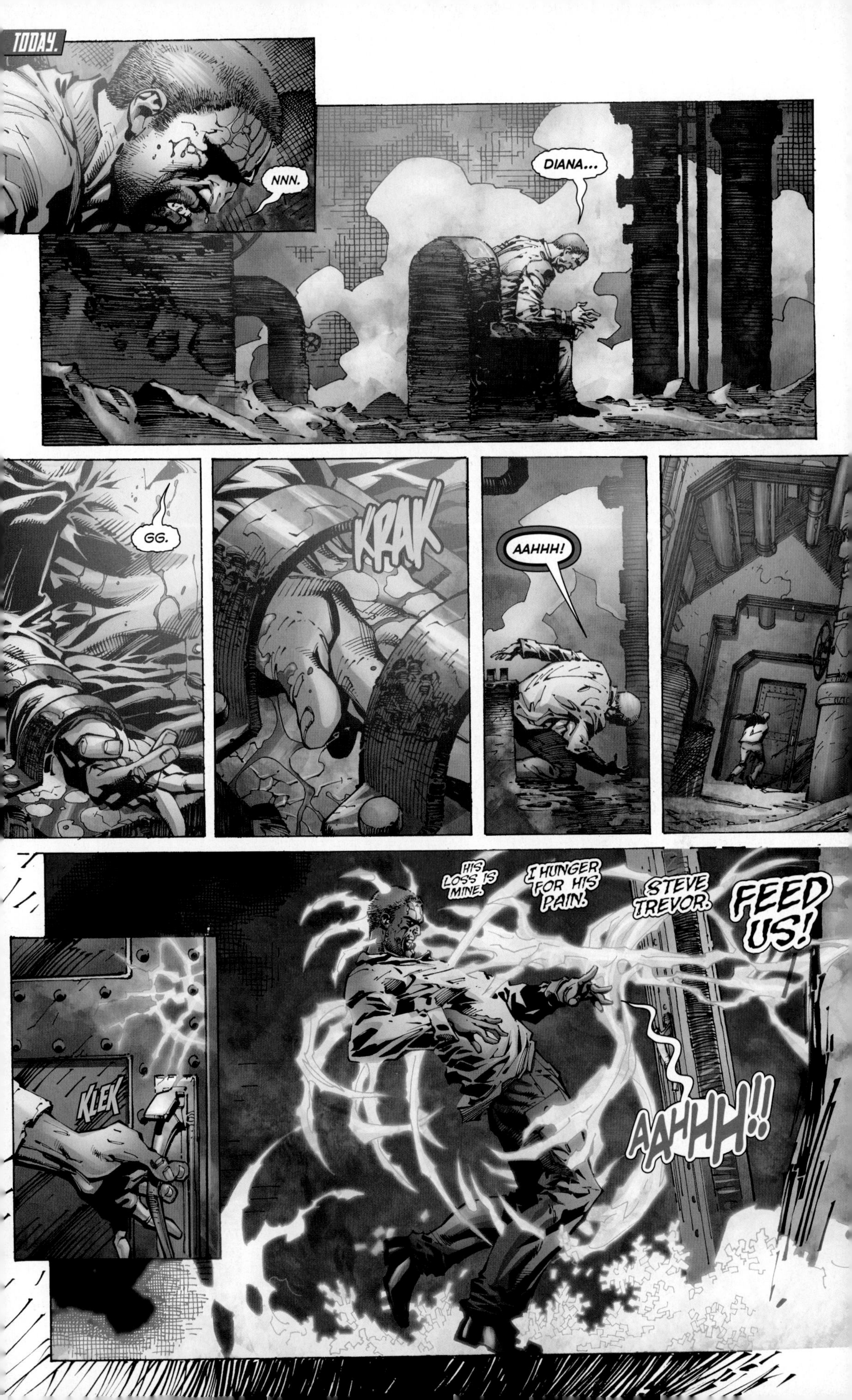
TODAY.
NNN.
DIANA...
GG.
KRAK
AAHHH!
KLEK
HIS LOSS IS MINE.
I HUNGER FOR HIS PAIN.
STEVE TREVOR.
FEED US!
AAHHH!!

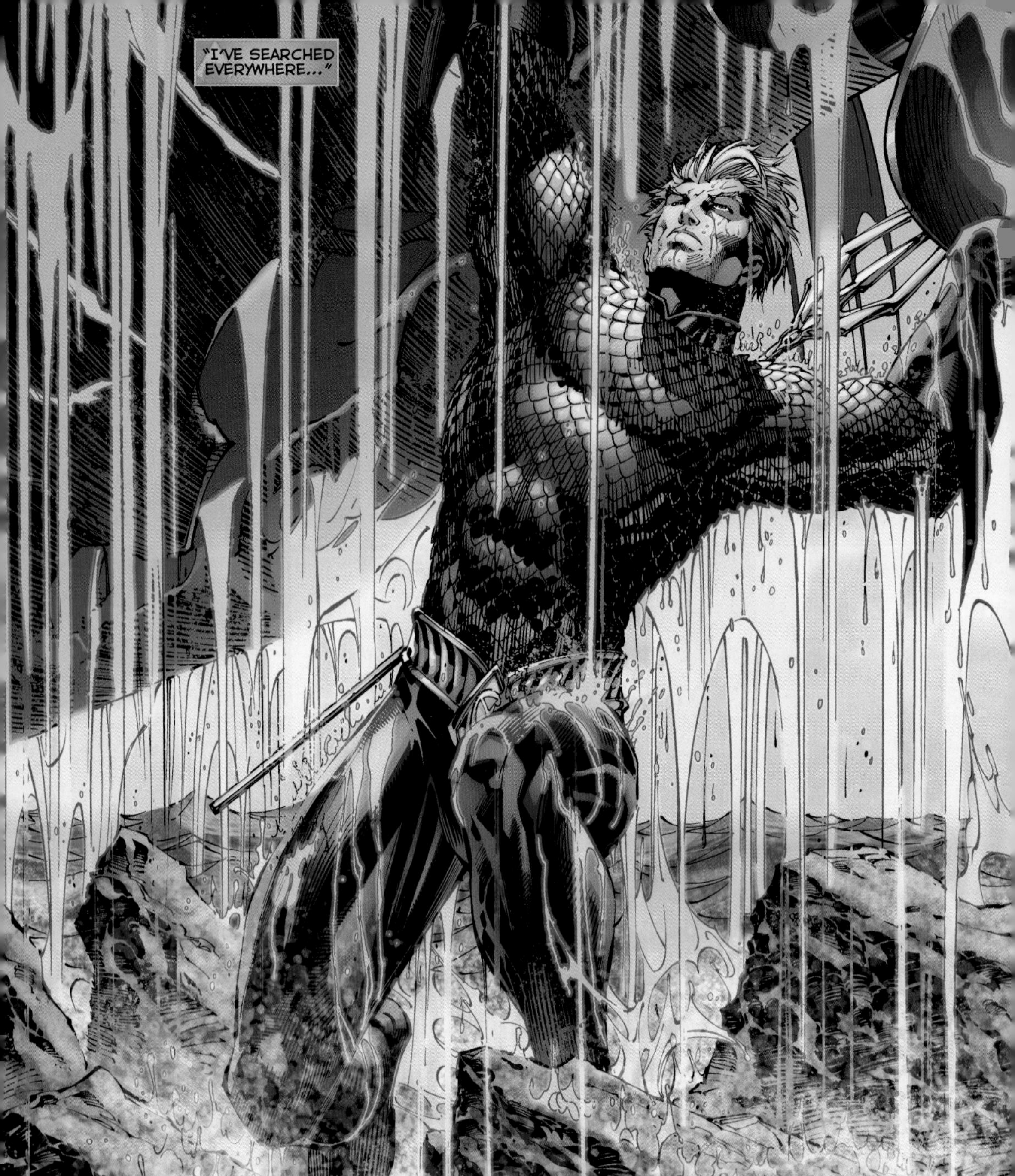
"I'VE SEARCHED EVERYWHERE..."

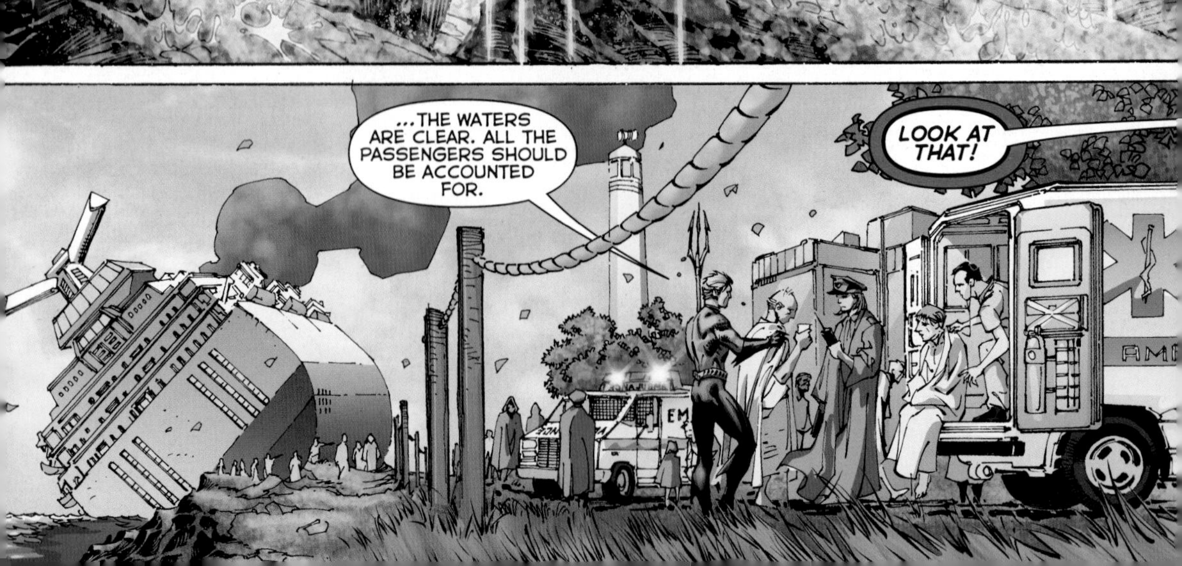
...THE WATERS ARE CLEAR. ALL THE PASSENGERS SHOULD BE ACCOUNTED FOR.
LOOK AT THAT!

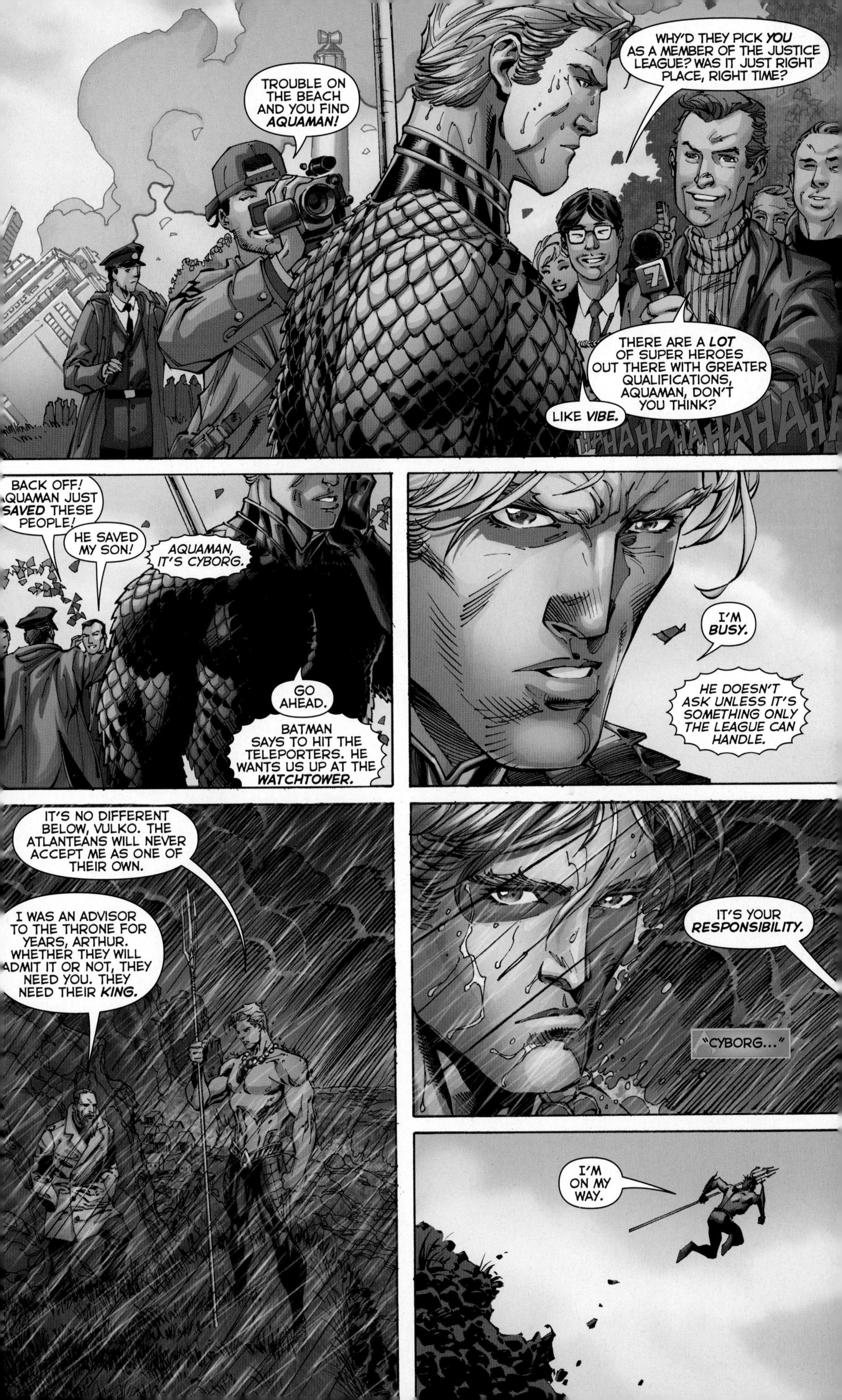
TROUBLE ON THE BEACH AND YOU FIND AQUAMAN!
WHY'D THEY PICK YOU AS A MEMBER OF THE JUSTICE LEAGUE? WAS IT JUST RIGHT PLACE, RIGHT TIME?
THERE ARE A LOT OF SUPER HEROES OUT THERE WITH GREATER QUALIFICATIONS, AQUAMAN, DON'T YOU THINK?
LIKE VIBE.
HAHAHAHAHAHAHAHA
BACK OFF! AQUAMAN JUST SAVED THESE PEOPLE!
HE SAVED MY SON!
AQUAMAN, IT'S CYBORG.
GO AHEAD.
BATMAN SAYS TO HIT THE TELEPORTERS. HE WANTS US UP AT THE WATCHTOWER.
I'M BUSY.
HE DOESN'T ASK UNLESS IT'S SOMETHING ONLY THE LEAGUE CAN HANDLE.
IT'S NO DIFFERENT BELOW, VULKO. THE ATLANTEANS WILL NEVER ACCEPT ME AS ONE OF THEIR OWN.
I WAS AN ADVISOR TO THE THRONE FOR YEARS, ARTHUR. WHETHER THEY WILL ADMIT IT OR NOT, THEY NEED YOU. THEY NEED THEIR KING.
IT'S YOUR RESPONSIBILITY.
"CYBORG..."
I'M ON MY WAY.

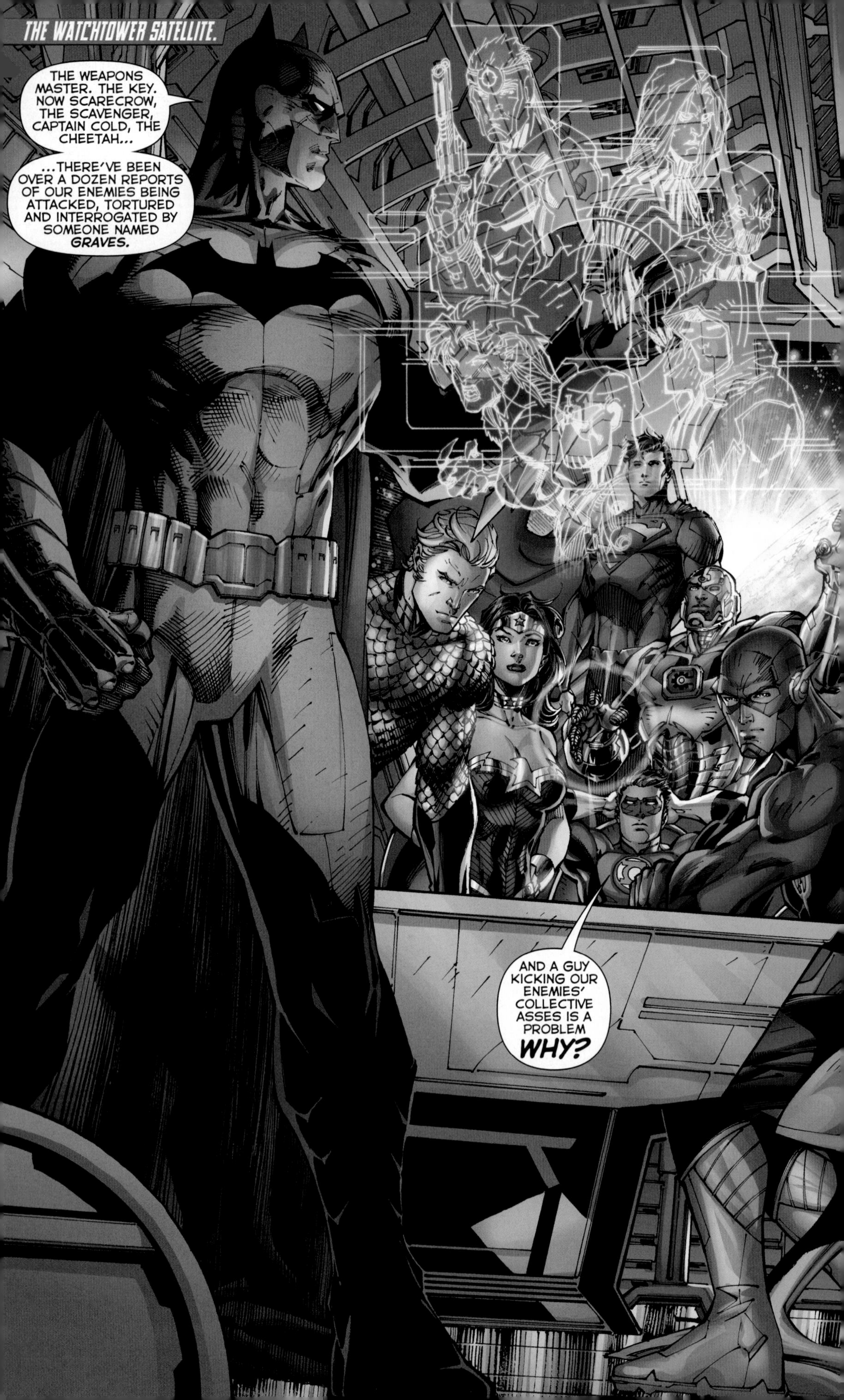
THE WATCHTOWER SATELLITE.
THE WEAPONS MASTER. THE KEY. NOW SCARECROW, THE SCAVENGER, CAPTAIN COLD, THE CHEETAH...
...THERE'VE BEEN OVER A DOZEN REPORTS OF OUR ENEMIES BEING ATTACKED, TORTURED AND INTERROGATED BY SOMEONE NAMED GRAVES.
AND A GUY KICKING OUR ENEMIES' COLLECTIVE ASSES IS A PROBLEM WHY?

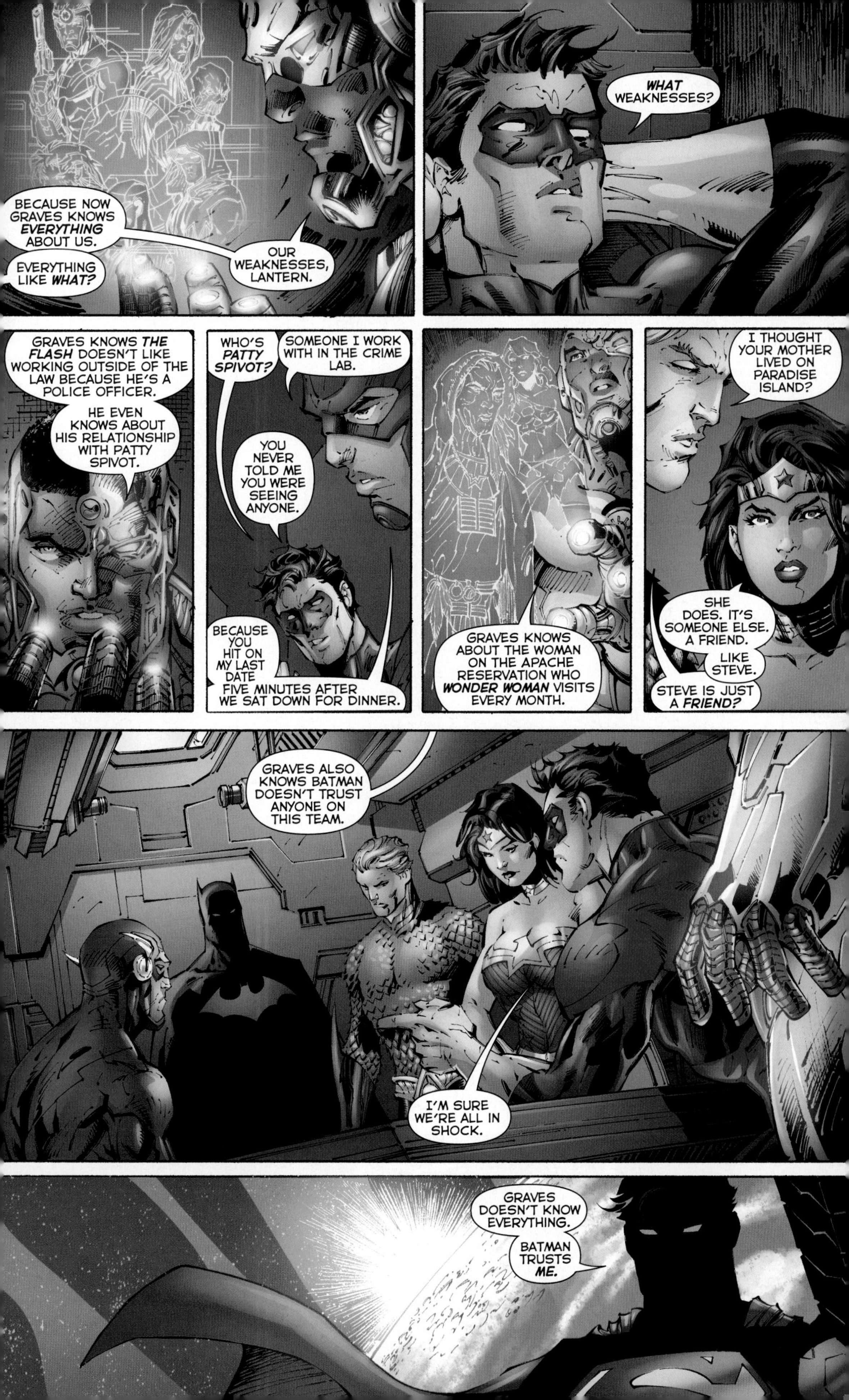
BECAUSE NOW GRAVES KNOWS EVERYTHING ABOUT US.
EVERYTHING LIKE WHAT?
OUR WEAKNESSES, LANTERN.
WHAT WEAKNESSES?
GRAVES KNOWS THE FLASH DOESN'T LIKE WORKING OUTSIDE OF THE LAW BECAUSE HE'S A POLICE OFFICER.
HE EVEN KNOWS ABOUT HIS RELATIONSHIP WITH PATTY SPIVOT.
WHO'S PATTY SPIVOT?
SOMEONE I WORK WITH IN THE CRIME LAB.
YOU NEVER TOLD ME YOU WERE SEEING ANYONE.
BECAUSE YOU HIT ON MY LAST DATE FIVE MINUTES AFTER WE SAT DOWN FOR DINNER.
GRAVES KNOWS ABOUT THE WOMAN ON THE APACHE RESERVATION WHO WONDER WOMAN VISITS EVERY MONTH.
I THOUGHT YOUR MOTHER LIVED ON PARADISE ISLAND?
SHE DOES. IT'S SOMEONE ELSE. A FRIEND.
LIKE STEVE.
STEVE IS JUST A FRIEND?
GRAVES ALSO KNOWS BATMAN DOESN'T TRUST ANYONE ON THIS TEAM.
I'M SURE WE'RE ALL IN SHOCK.
GRAVES DOESN'T KNOW EVERYTHING.
BATMAN TRUSTS ME.

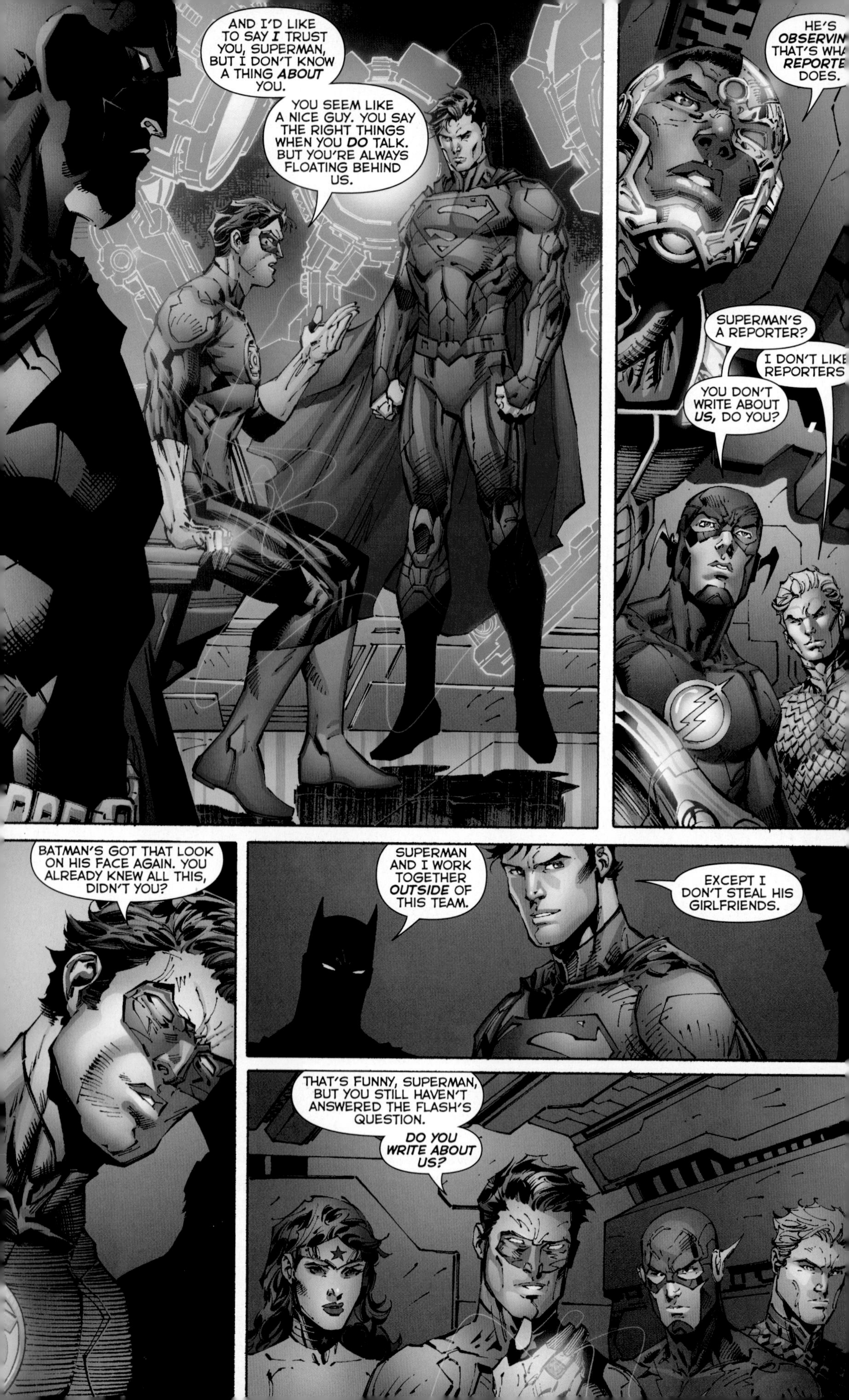
AND I'D LIKE TO SAY *I* TRUST YOU, SUPERMAN, BUT I DON'T KNOW A THING *ABOUT* YOU.
YOU SEEM LIKE A NICE GUY. YOU SAY THE RIGHT THINGS WHEN YOU *DO* TALK. BUT YOU'RE ALWAYS FLOATING BEHIND US.
HE'S *OBSERVIN* THAT'S WHA *REPORTE* DOES.
SUPERMAN'S A REPORTER?
I DON'T LIKE REPORTERS
YOU DON'T WRITE ABOUT *US,* DO YOU?
BATMAN'S GOT THAT LOOK ON HIS FACE AGAIN. YOU ALREADY KNEW ALL THIS, DIDN'T YOU?
SUPERMAN AND I WORK TOGETHER *OUTSIDE* OF THIS TEAM.
EXCEPT I DON'T STEAL HIS GIRLFRIENDS.
THAT'S FUNNY, SUPERMAN, BUT YOU STILL HAVEN'T ANSWERED THE FLASH'S QUESTION.
DO YOU WRITE ABOUT US?

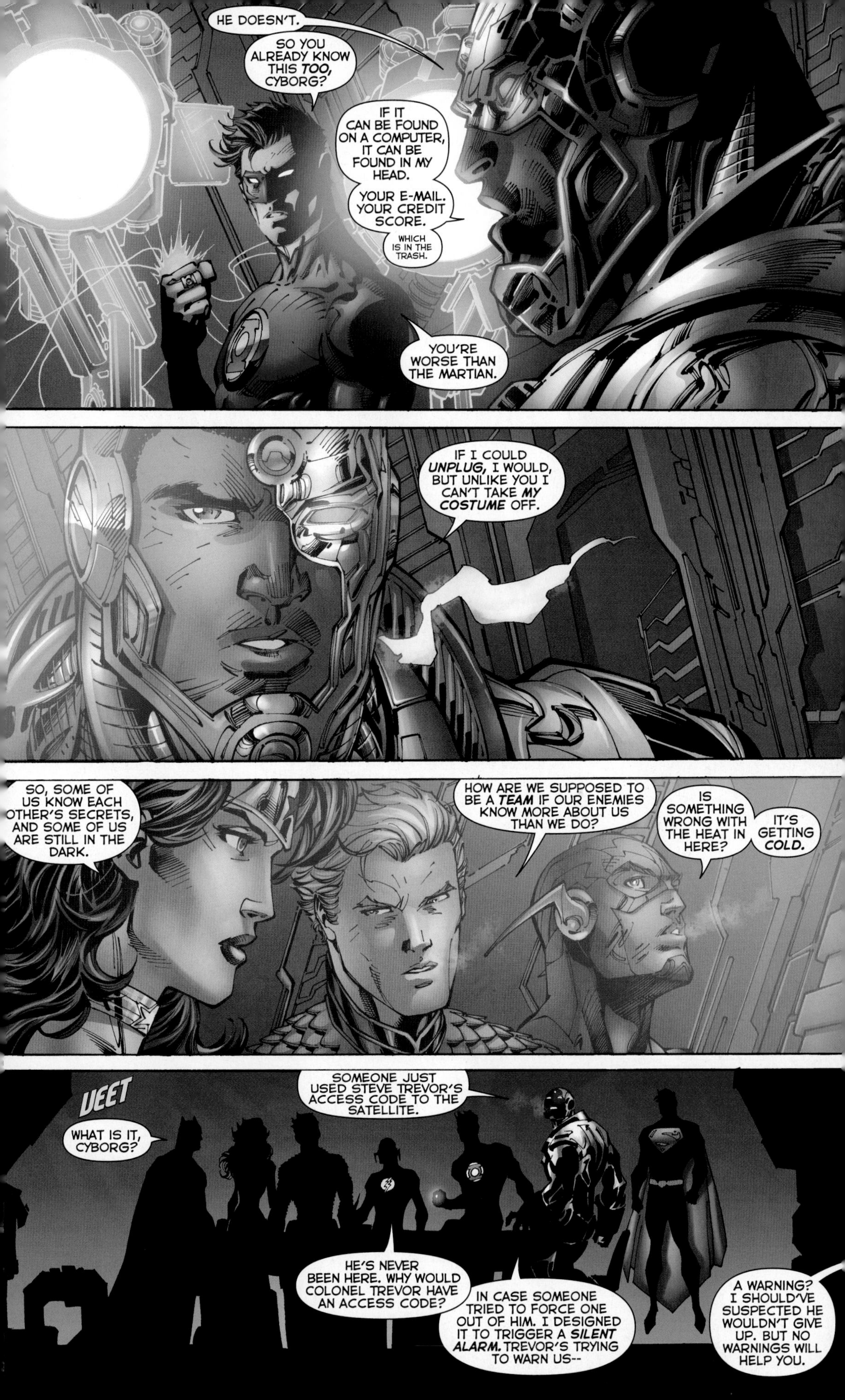
HE DOESN'T.
SO YOU ALREADY KNOW THIS TOO, CYBORG?
IF IT CAN BE FOUND ON A COMPUTER, IT CAN BE FOUND IN MY HEAD.
YOUR E-MAIL. YOUR CREDIT SCORE.
WHICH IS IN THE TRASH.
YOU'RE WORSE THAN THE MARTIAN.
IF I COULD UNPLUG, I WOULD, BUT UNLIKE YOU I CAN'T TAKE MY COSTUME OFF.
SO, SOME OF US KNOW EACH OTHER'S SECRETS, AND SOME OF US ARE STILL IN THE DARK.
HOW ARE WE SUPPOSED TO BE A TEAM IF OUR ENEMIES KNOW MORE ABOUT US THAN WE DO?
IS SOMETHING WRONG WITH THE HEAT IN HERE?
IT'S GETTING COLD.
VEET
WHAT IS IT, CYBORG?
SOMEONE JUST USED STEVE TREVOR'S ACCESS CODE TO THE SATELLITE.
HE'S NEVER BEEN HERE. WHY WOULD COLONEL TREVOR HAVE AN ACCESS CODE?
IN CASE SOMEONE TRIED TO FORCE ONE OUT OF HIM. I DESIGNED IT TO TRIGGER A SILENT ALARM. TREVOR'S TRYING TO WARN US--
A WARNING? I SHOULD'VE SUSPECTED HE WOULDN'T GIVE UP. BUT NO WARNINGS WILL HELP YOU.

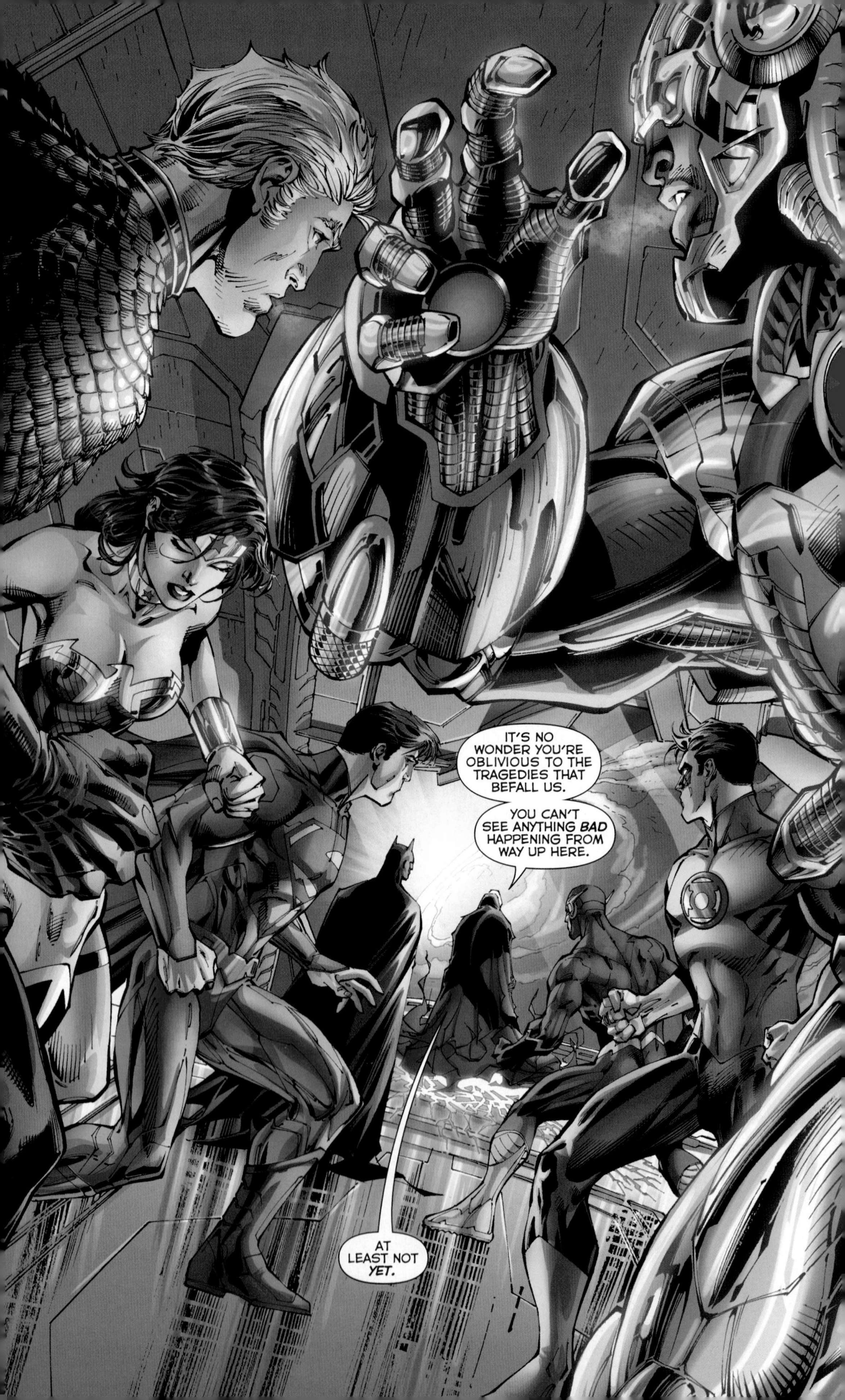
IT'S NO WONDER YOU'RE OBLIVIOUS TO THE TRAGEDIES THAT BEFALL US.
YOU CAN'T SEE ANYTHING *BAD* HAPPENING FROM WAY UP HERE.
AT LEAST NOT *YET.*

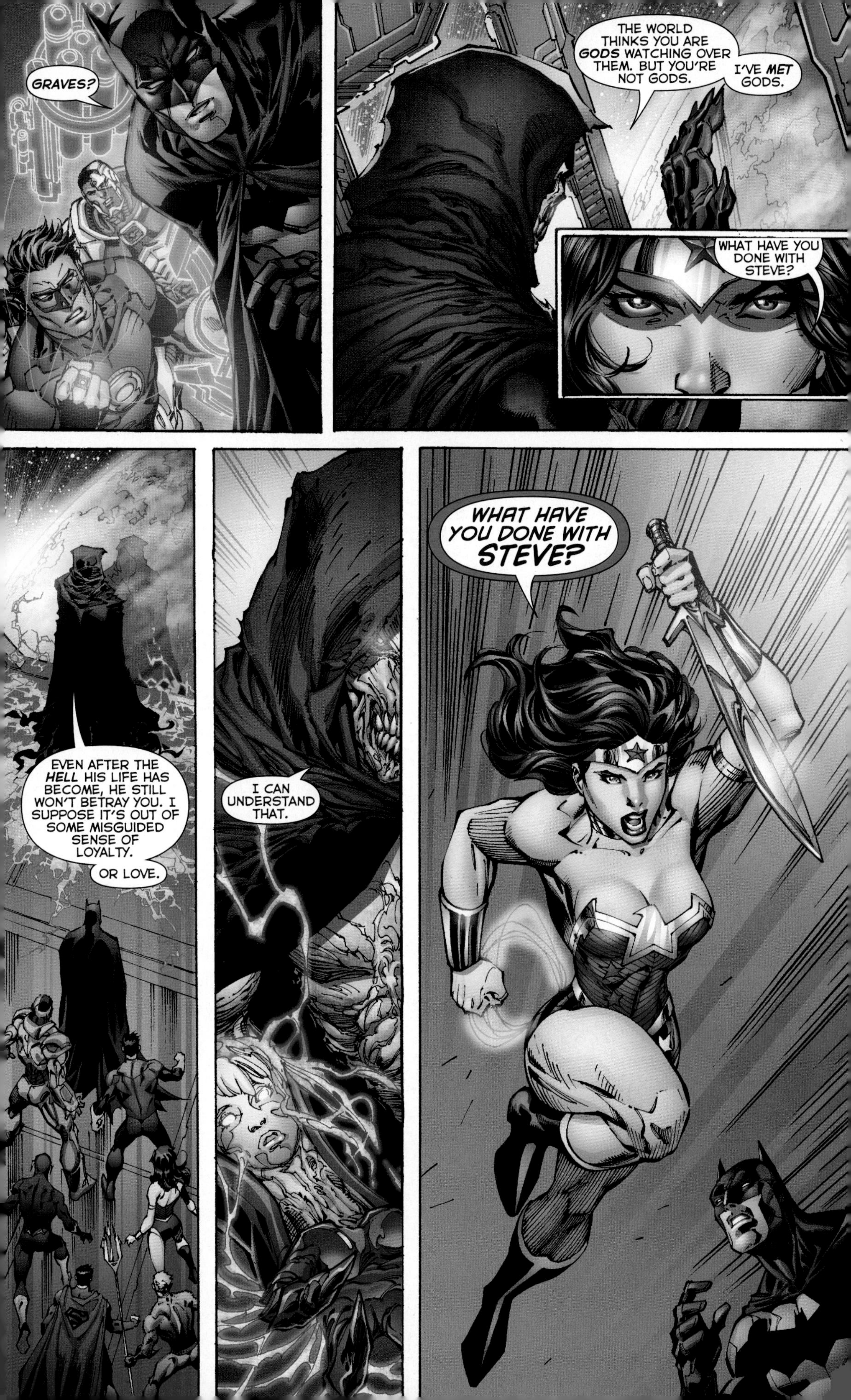
GRAVES?
THE WORLD THINKS YOU ARE GODS WATCHING OVER THEM. BUT YOU'RE NOT GODS.
I'VE MET GODS.
WHAT HAVE YOU DONE WITH STEVE?
EVEN AFTER THE HELL HIS LIFE HAS BECOME, HE STILL WON'T BETRAY YOU. I SUPPOSE IT'S OUT OF SOME MISGUIDED SENSE OF LOYALTY.
OR LOVE.
I CAN UNDERSTAND THAT.
WHAT HAVE YOU DONE WITH STEVE?

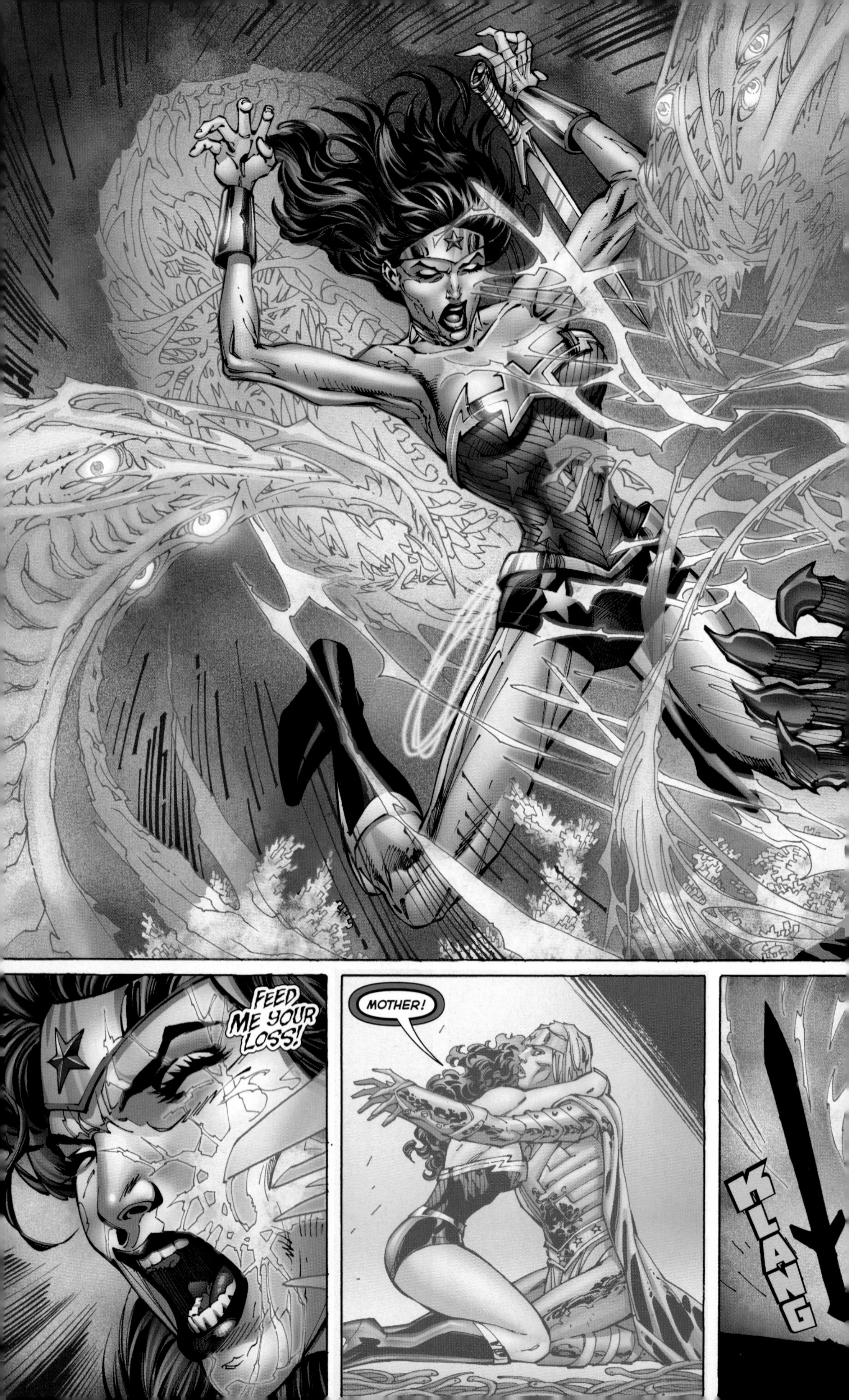
FEED ME YOUR LOSS!
MOTHER!
KLANG

YOU WILL NEVER KNOW, WONDER WOMAN.

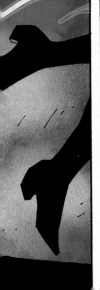

WONDER WOMAN?!

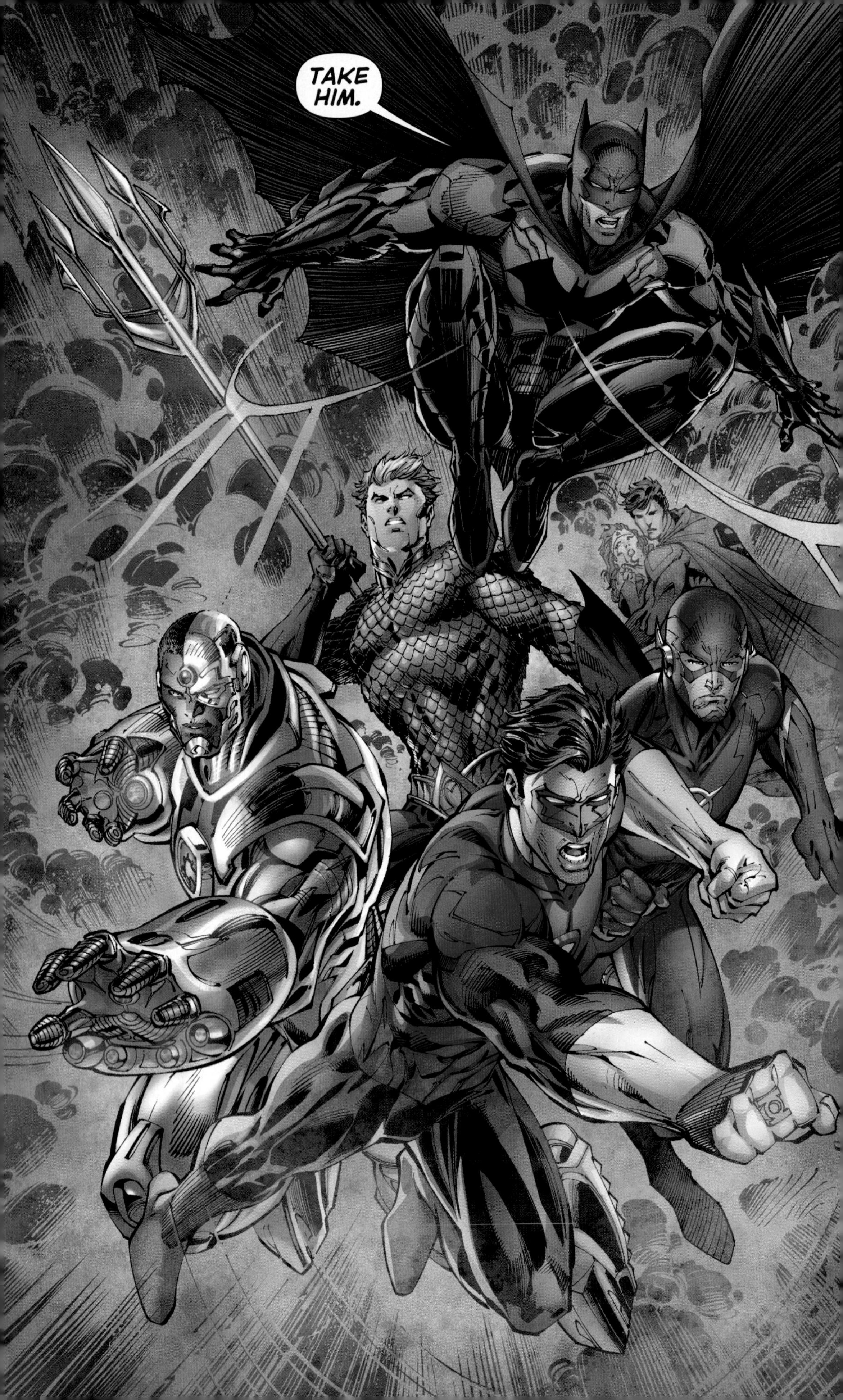
TAKE HIM.

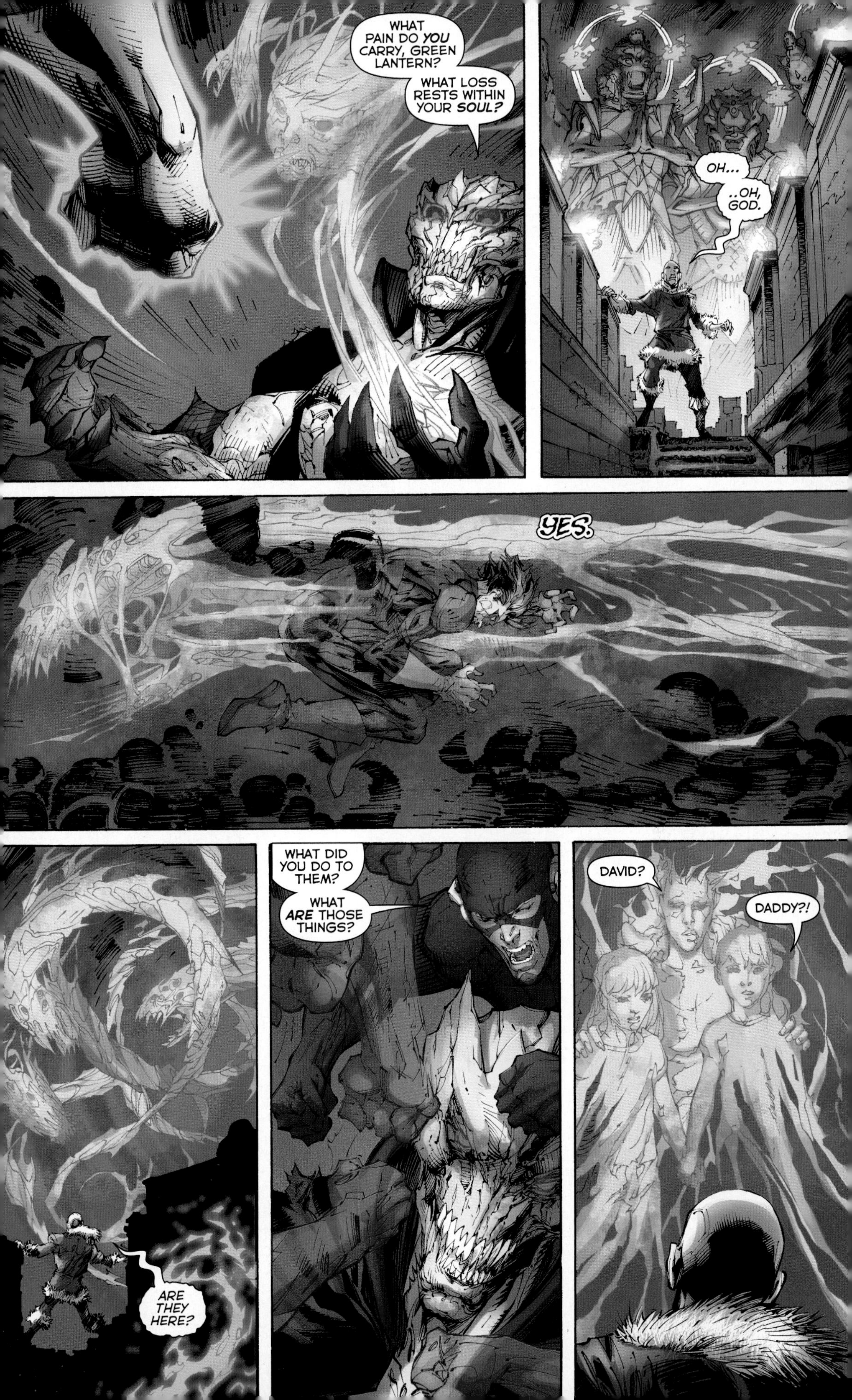
WHAT PAIN DO YOU CARRY, GREEN LANTERN?
WHAT LOSS RESTS WITHIN YOUR SOUL?
OH...
..OH, GOD.
YES.
ARE THEY HERE?
WHAT DID YOU DO TO THEM?
WHAT ARE THOSE THINGS?
DAVID?
DADDY?!

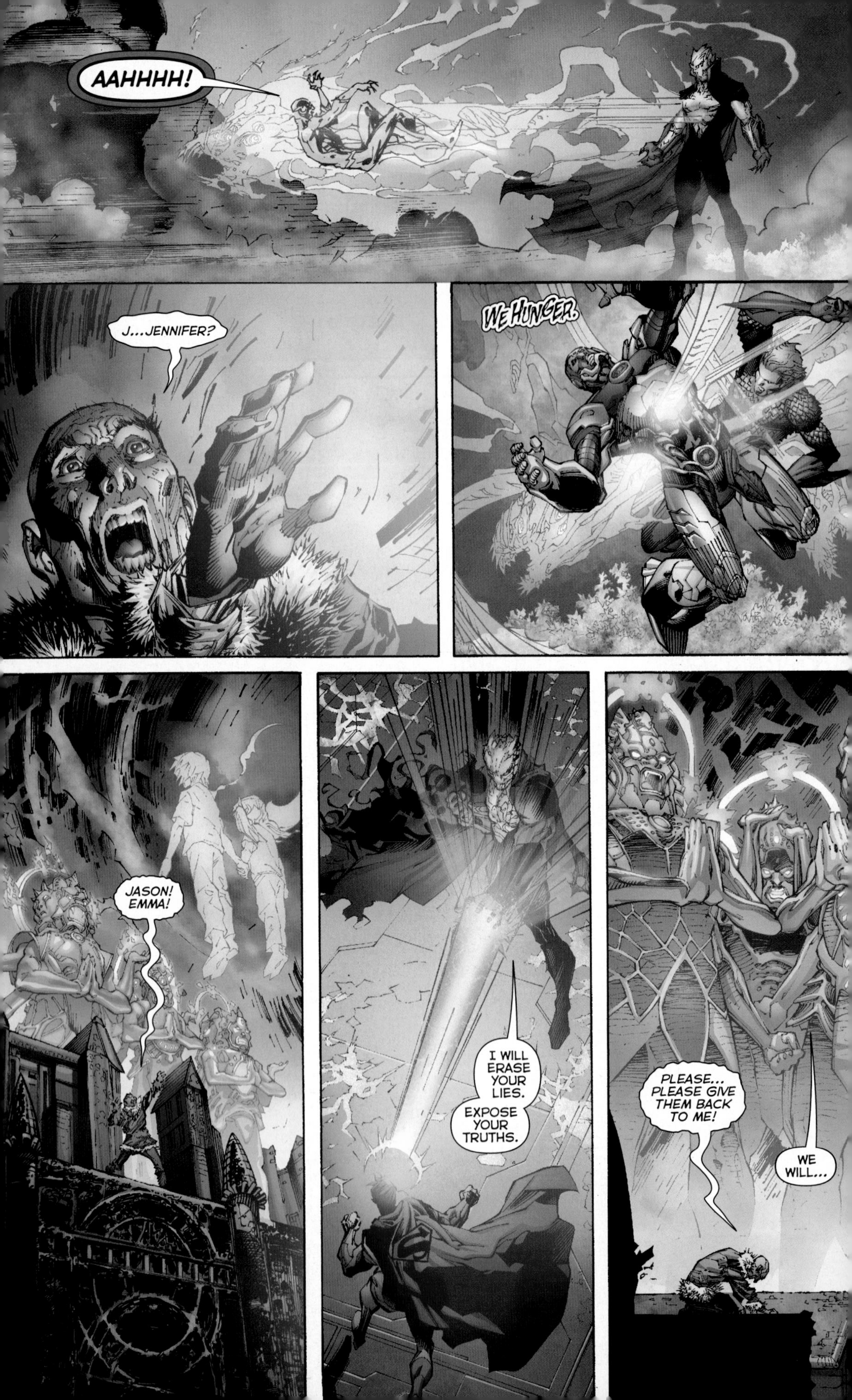
AAHHHH!
J...JENNIFER?
WE HUNGER.
JASON! EMMA!
I WILL ERASE YOUR LIES.
EXPOSE YOUR TRUTHS.
PLEASE... PLEASE GIVE THEM BACK TO ME!
WE WILL...

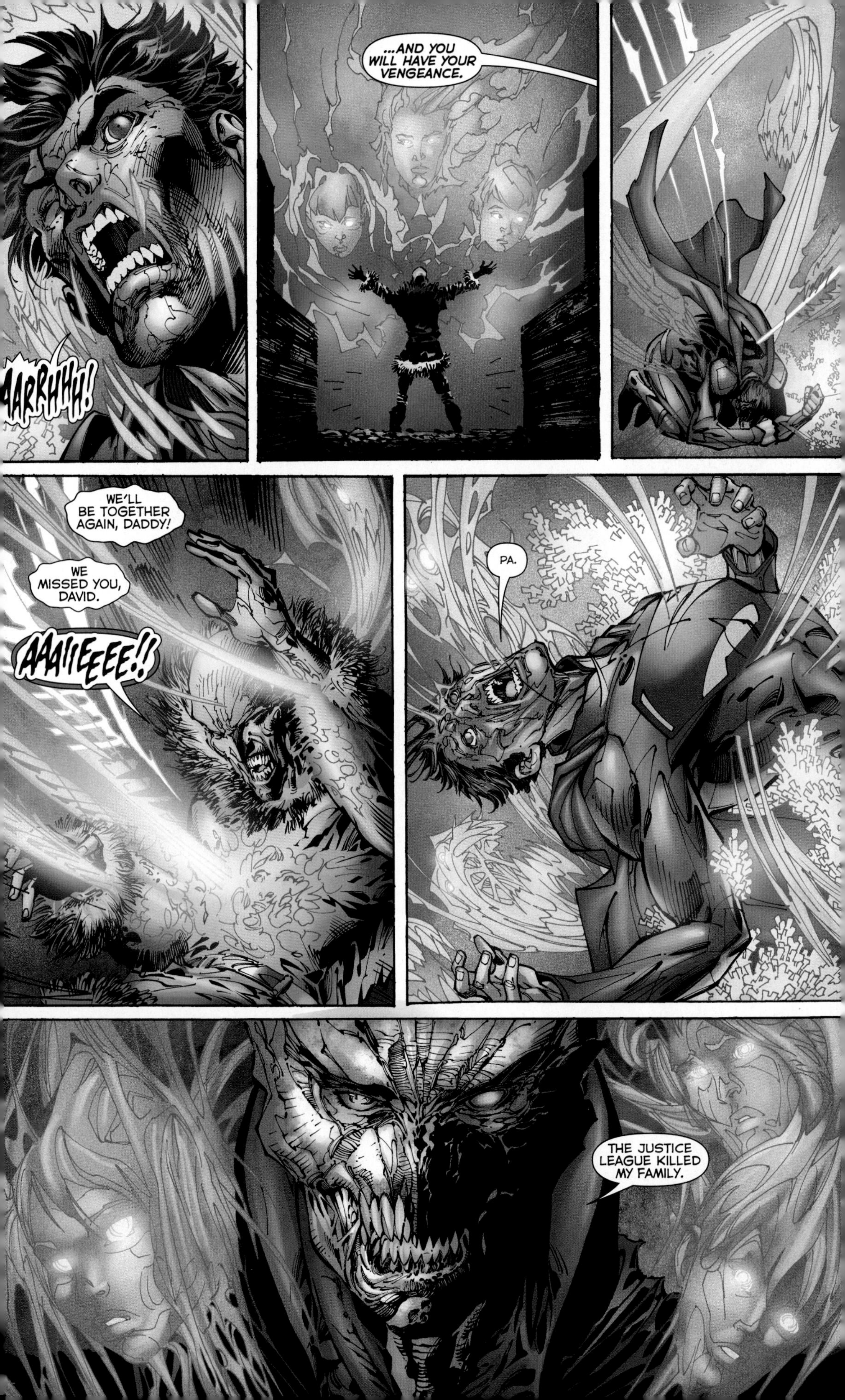
AARRHHH!
...AND YOU WILL HAVE YOUR VENGEANCE.
WE'LL BE TOGETHER AGAIN, DADDY!
WE MISSED YOU, DAVID.
AAAIIEEEE!!
PA.
THE JUSTICE LEAGUE KILLED MY FAMILY.

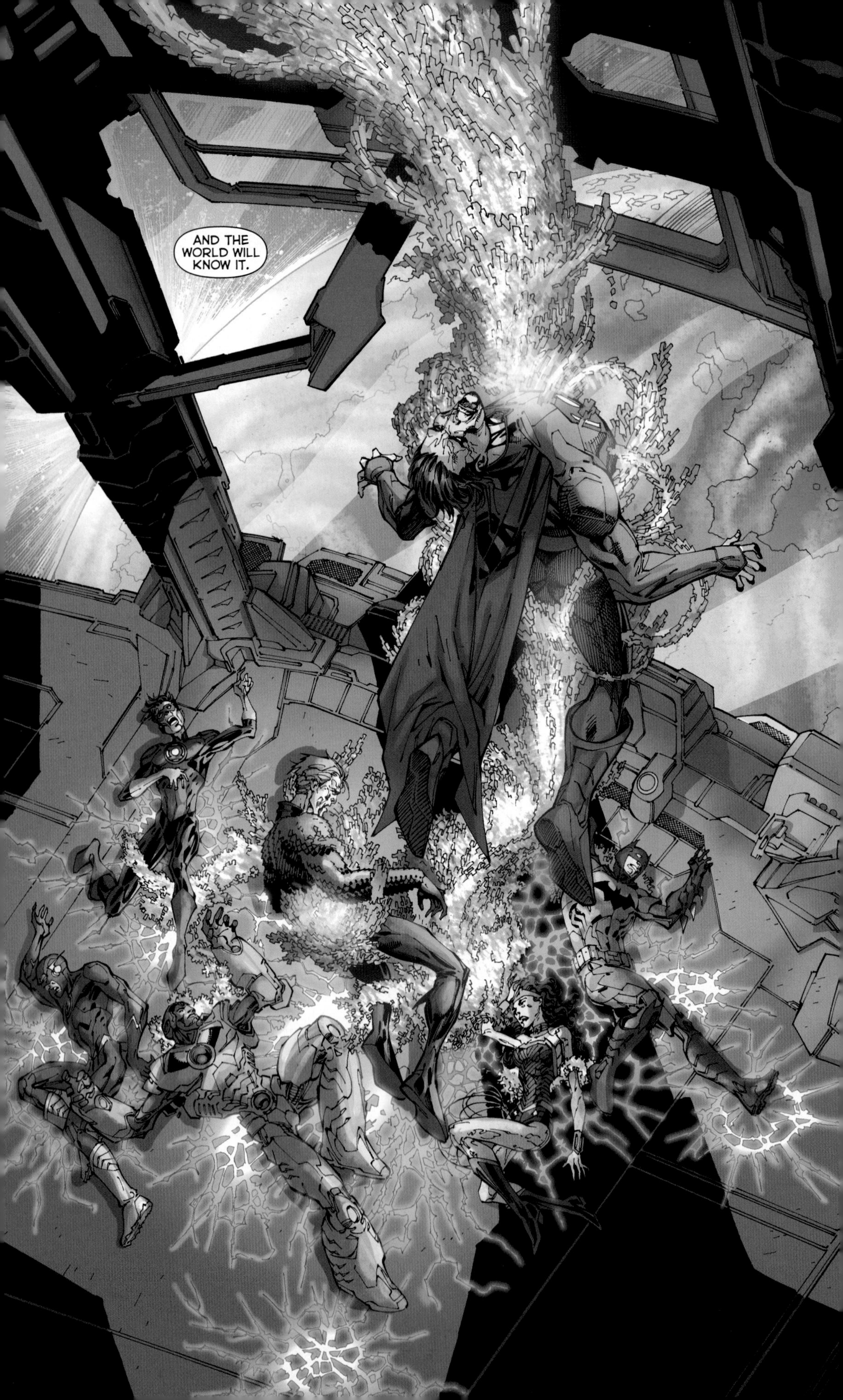
AND THE WORLD WILL KNOW IT.

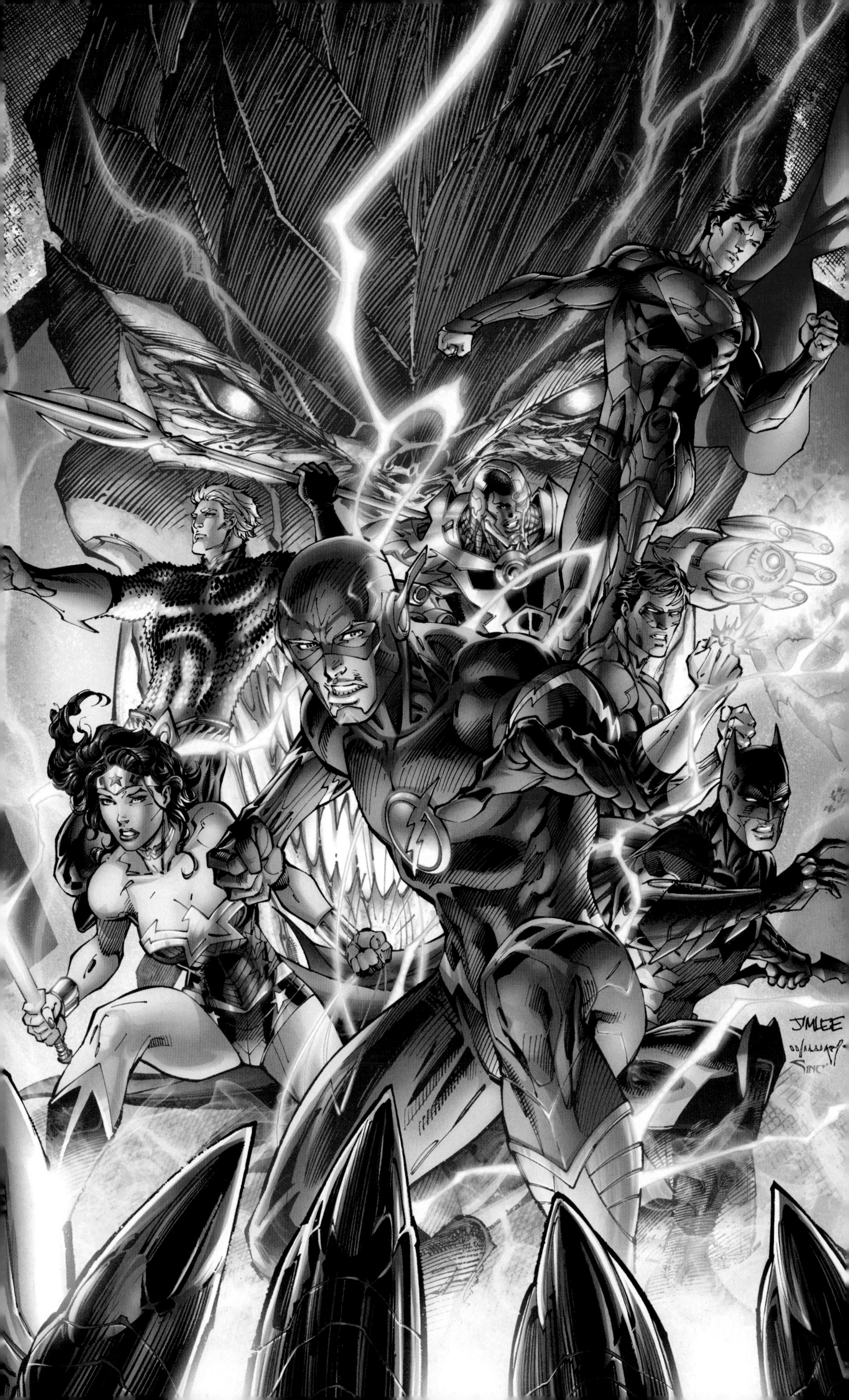
JIMLEE

THE VILLAIN'S JOURNEY CHAPTER THREE: ATONEMENT

GEOFF JOHNS writer **JIM LEE** penciller **SCOTT WILLIAMS & JONATHAN GLAPION** inkers cover by **JIM LEE, SCOTT WILLIAMS & ALEX SINCLAIR**

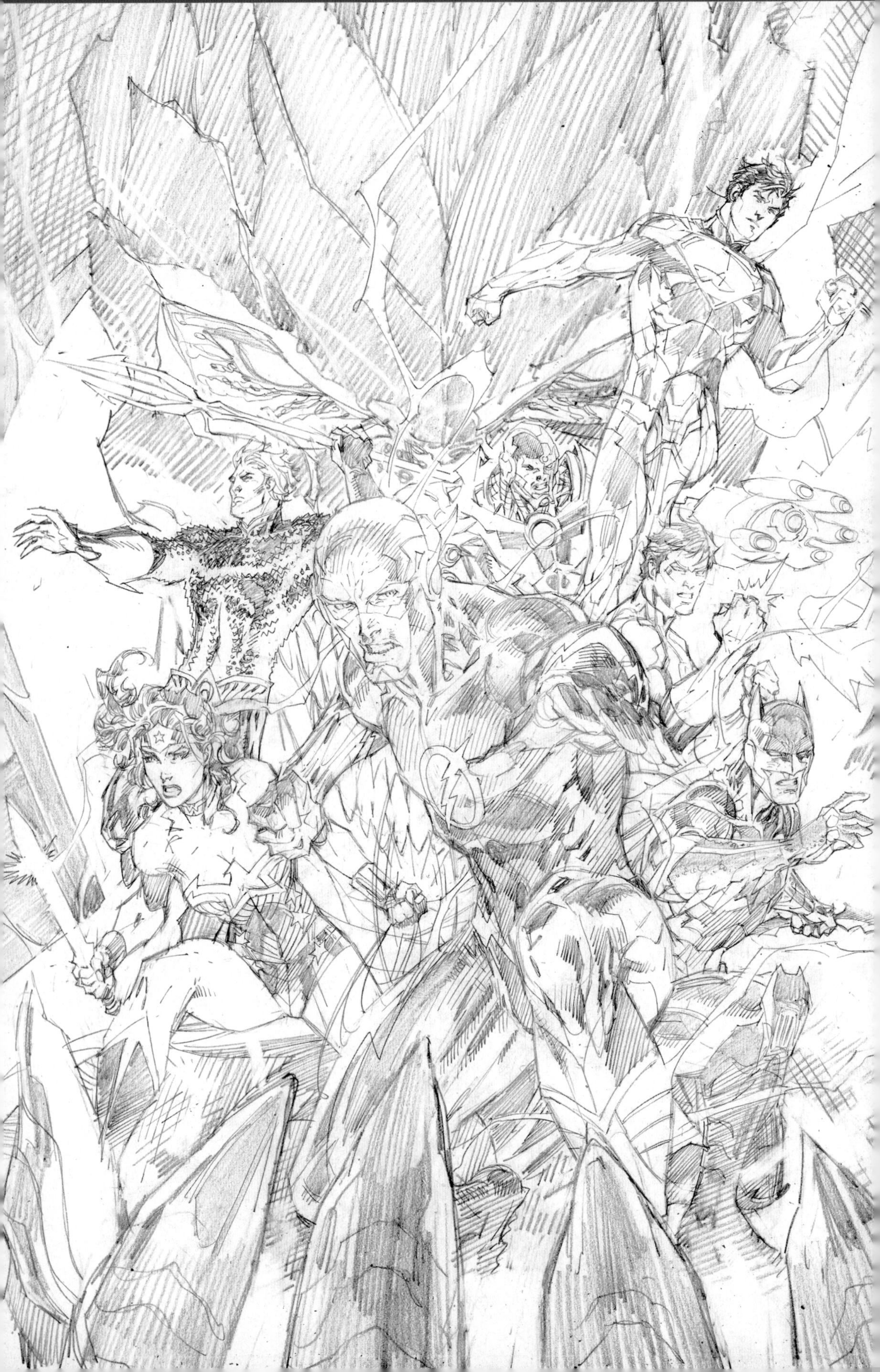

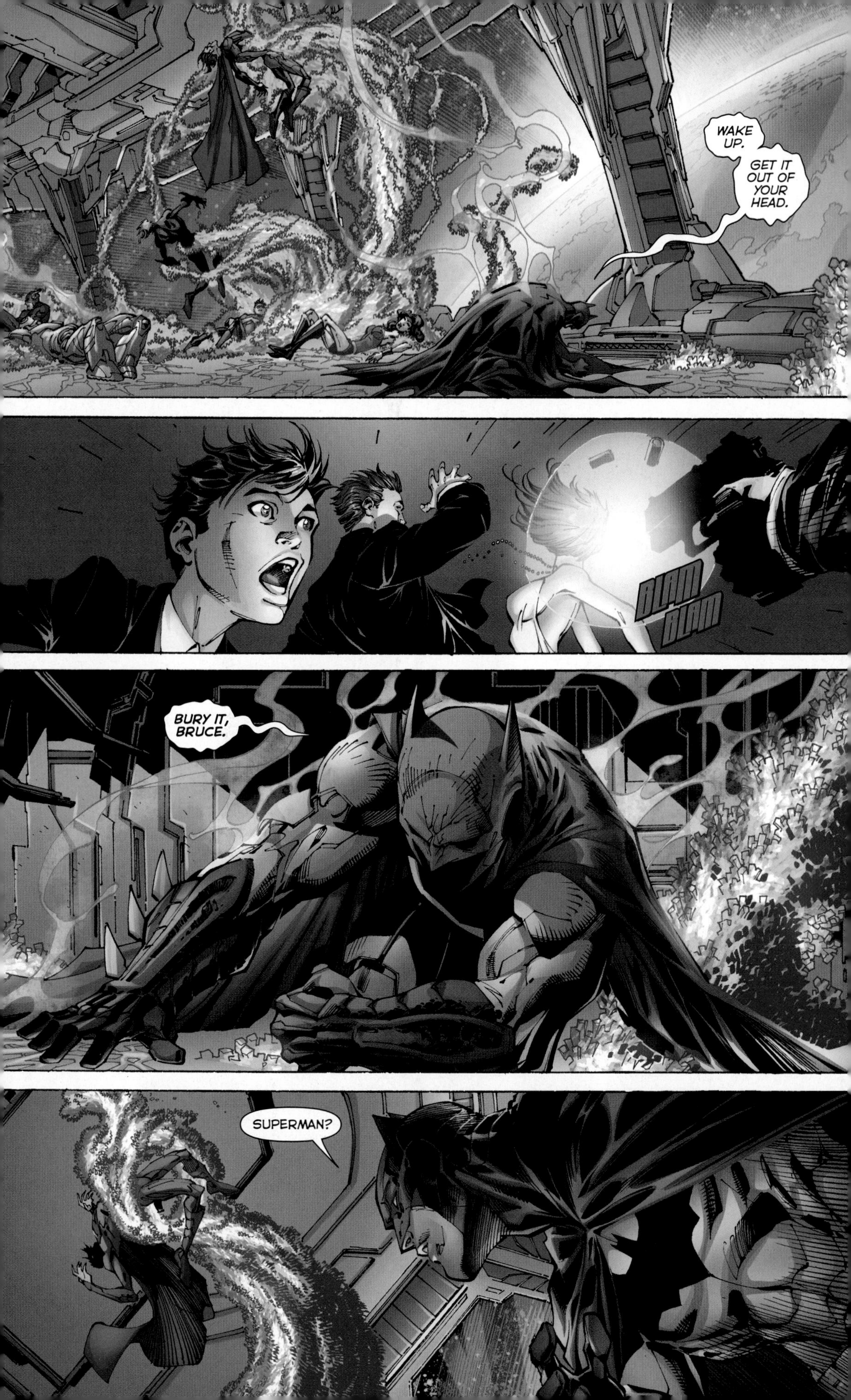
WAKE UP.
GET IT OUT OF YOUR HEAD.
BLAM BLAM
BURY IT, BRUCE.
SUPERMAN?

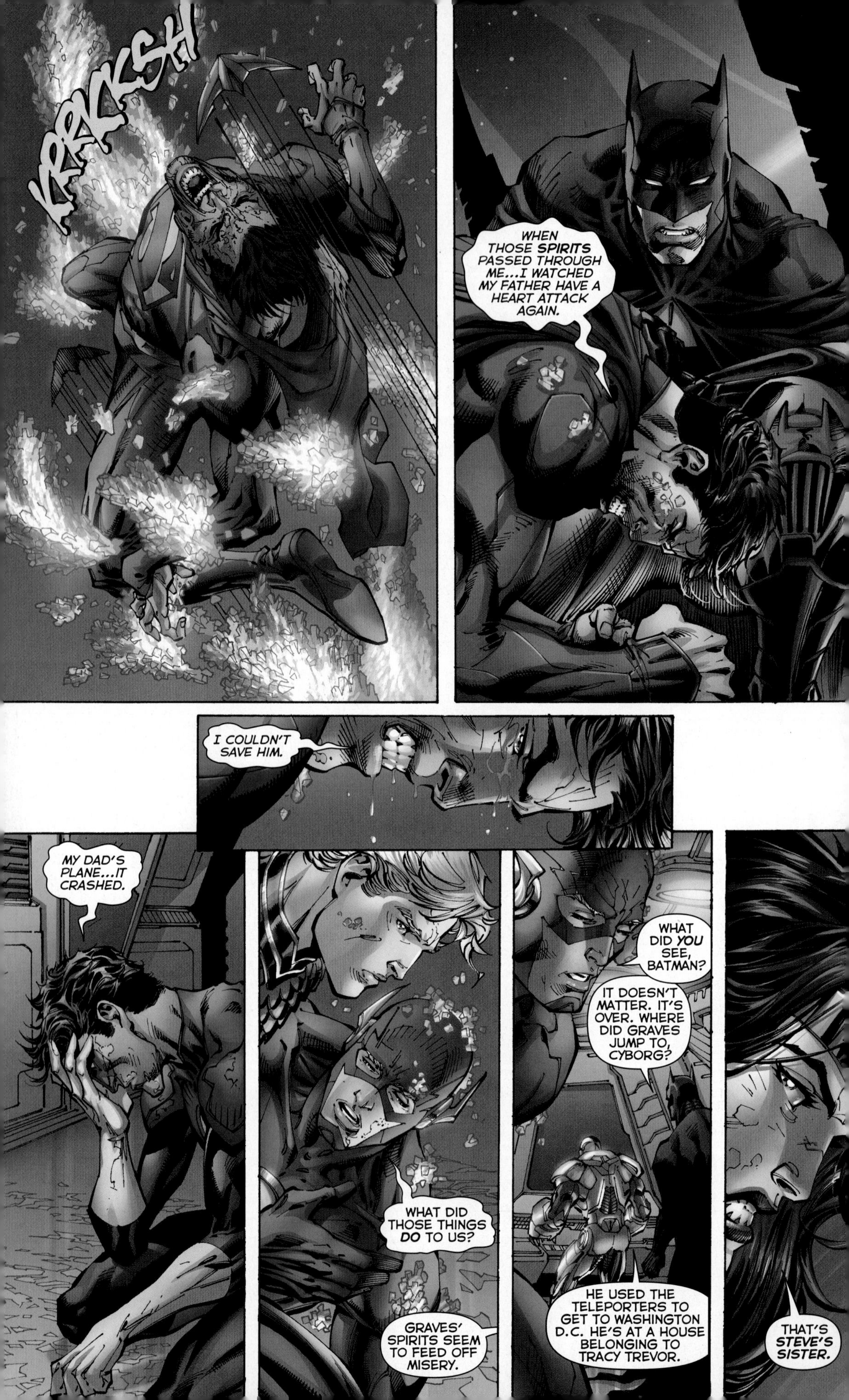
KRRKSH
WHEN THOSE SPIRITS PASSED THROUGH ME...I WATCHED MY FATHER HAVE A HEART ATTACK AGAIN.
I COULDN'T SAVE HIM.
MY DAD'S PLANE...IT CRASHED.
WHAT DID THOSE THINGS DO TO US?
GRAVES' SPIRITS SEEM TO FEED OFF MISERY.
WHAT DID YOU SEE, BATMAN?
IT DOESN'T MATTER. IT'S OVER. WHERE DID GRAVES JUMP TO, CYBORG?
HE USED THE TELEPORTERS TO GET TO WASHINGTON D.C. HE'S AT A HOUSE BELONGING TO TRACY TREVOR.
THAT'S STEVE'S SISTER.

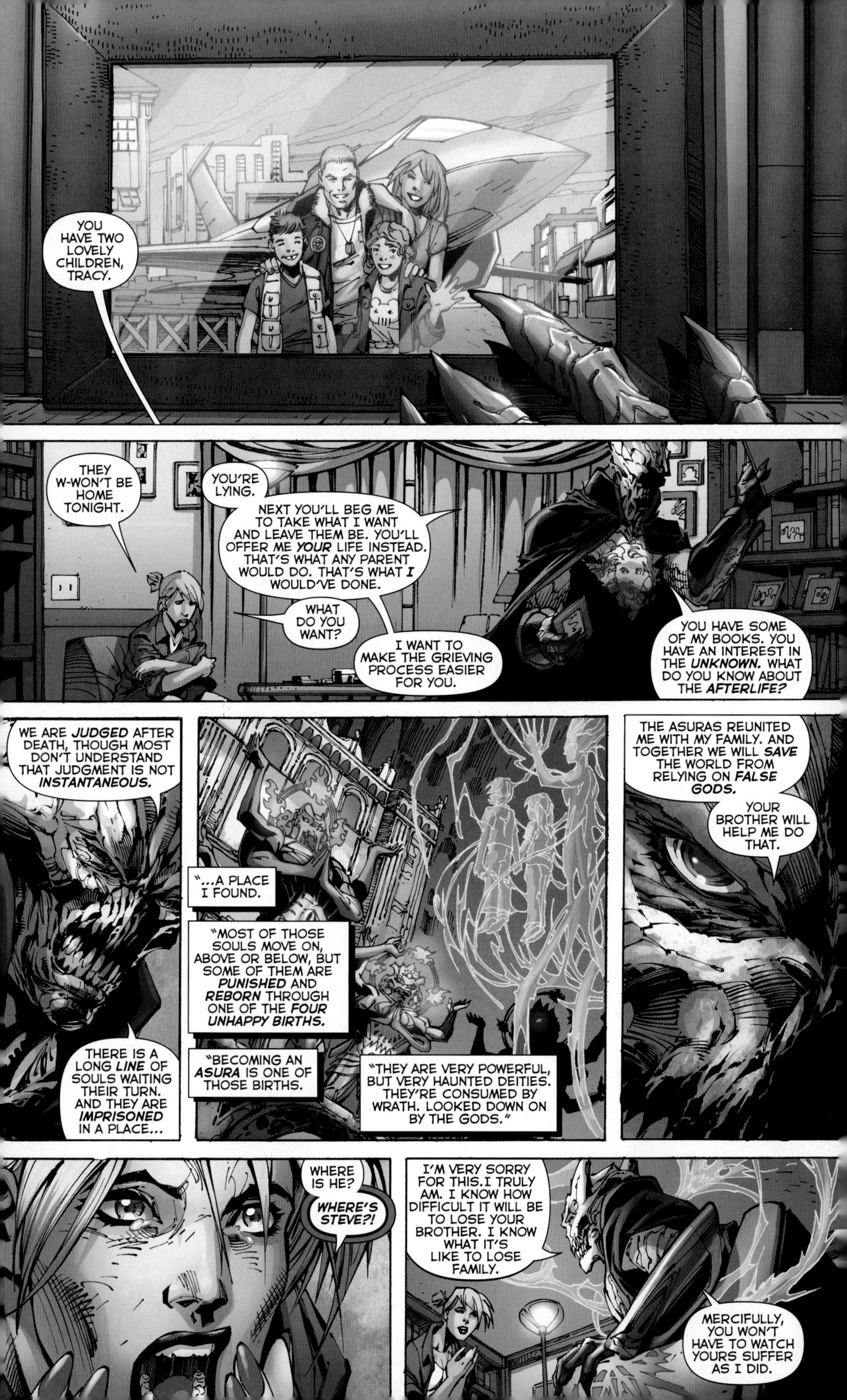
YOU HAVE TWO LOVELY CHILDREN, TRACY.
THEY W-WON'T BE HOME TONIGHT.
YOU'RE LYING.
NEXT YOU'LL BEG ME TO TAKE WHAT I WANT AND LEAVE THEM BE. YOU'LL OFFER ME YOUR LIFE INSTEAD. THAT'S WHAT ANY PARENT WOULD DO. THAT'S WHAT I WOULD'VE DONE.
WHAT DO YOU WANT?
I WANT TO MAKE THE GRIEVING PROCESS EASIER FOR YOU.
YOU HAVE SOME OF MY BOOKS. YOU HAVE AN INTEREST IN THE UNKNOWN. WHAT DO YOU KNOW ABOUT THE AFTERLIFE?
WE ARE JUDGED AFTER DEATH, THOUGH MOST DON'T UNDERSTAND THAT JUDGMENT IS NOT INSTANTANEOUS.
THERE IS A LONG LINE OF SOULS WAITING THEIR TURN. AND THEY ARE IMPRISONED IN A PLACE...
"...A PLACE I FOUND.
"MOST OF THOSE SOULS MOVE ON, ABOVE OR BELOW, BUT SOME OF THEM ARE PUNISHED AND REBORN THROUGH ONE OF THE FOUR UNHAPPY BIRTHS.
"BECOMING AN ASURA IS ONE OF THOSE BIRTHS.
"THEY ARE VERY POWERFUL, BUT VERY HAUNTED DEITIES. THEY'RE CONSUMED BY WRATH. LOOKED DOWN ON BY THE GODS."
THE ASURAS REUNITED ME WITH MY FAMILY. AND TOGETHER WE WILL SAVE THE WORLD FROM RELYING ON FALSE GODS.
YOUR BROTHER WILL HELP ME DO THAT.
WHERE IS HE?
WHERE'S STEVE?!
I'M VERY SORRY FOR THIS. I TRULY AM. I KNOW HOW DIFFICULT IT WILL BE TO LOSE YOUR BROTHER. I KNOW WHAT IT'S LIKE TO LOSE FAMILY.
MERCIFULLY, YOU WON'T HAVE TO WATCH YOURS SUFFER AS I DID.

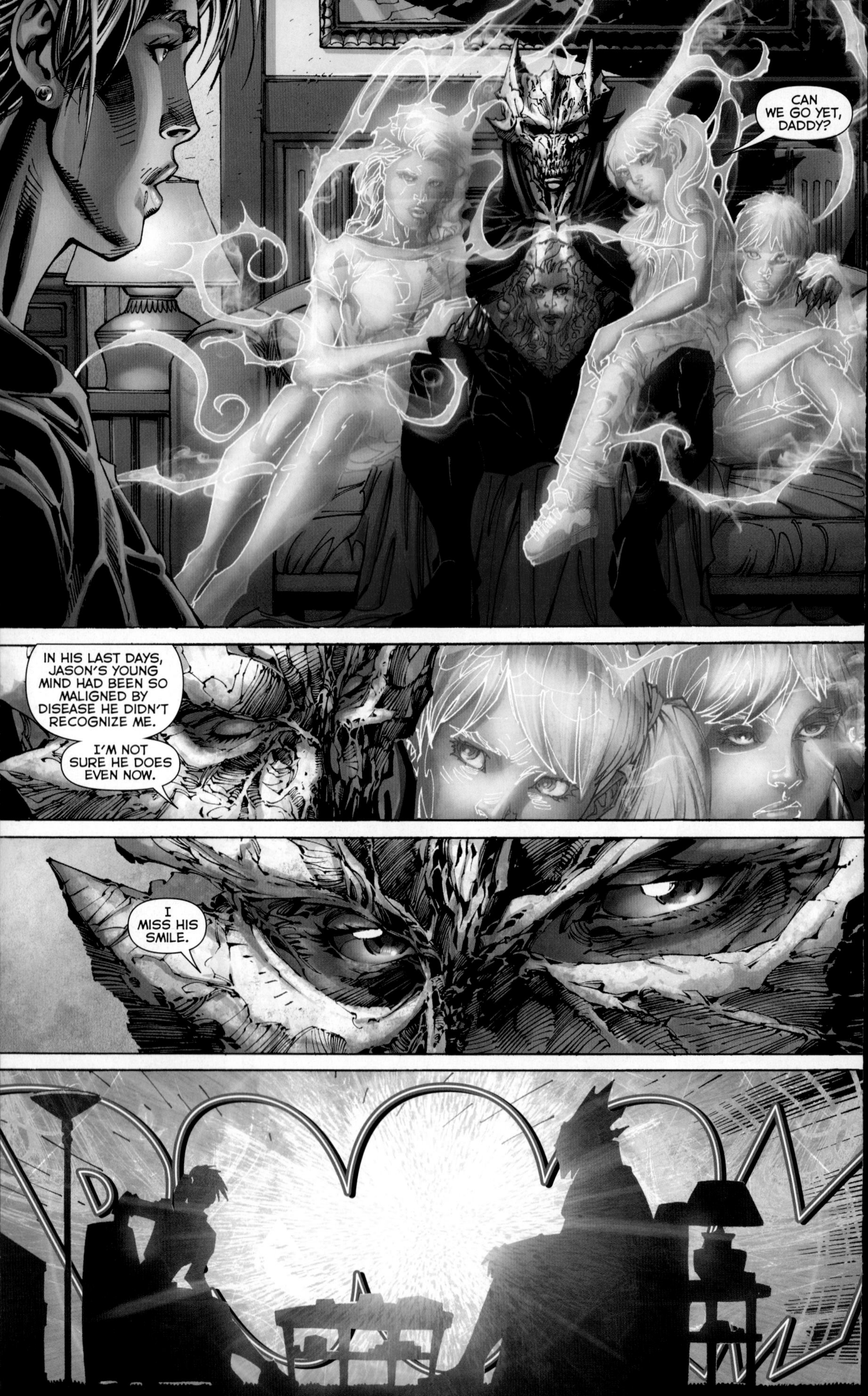
CAN WE GO YET, DADDY?
IN HIS LAST DAYS, JASON'S YOUNG MIND HAD BEEN SO MALIGNED BY DISEASE HE DIDN'T RECOGNIZE ME.
I'M NOT SURE HE DOES EVEN NOW.
I MISS HIS SMILE.

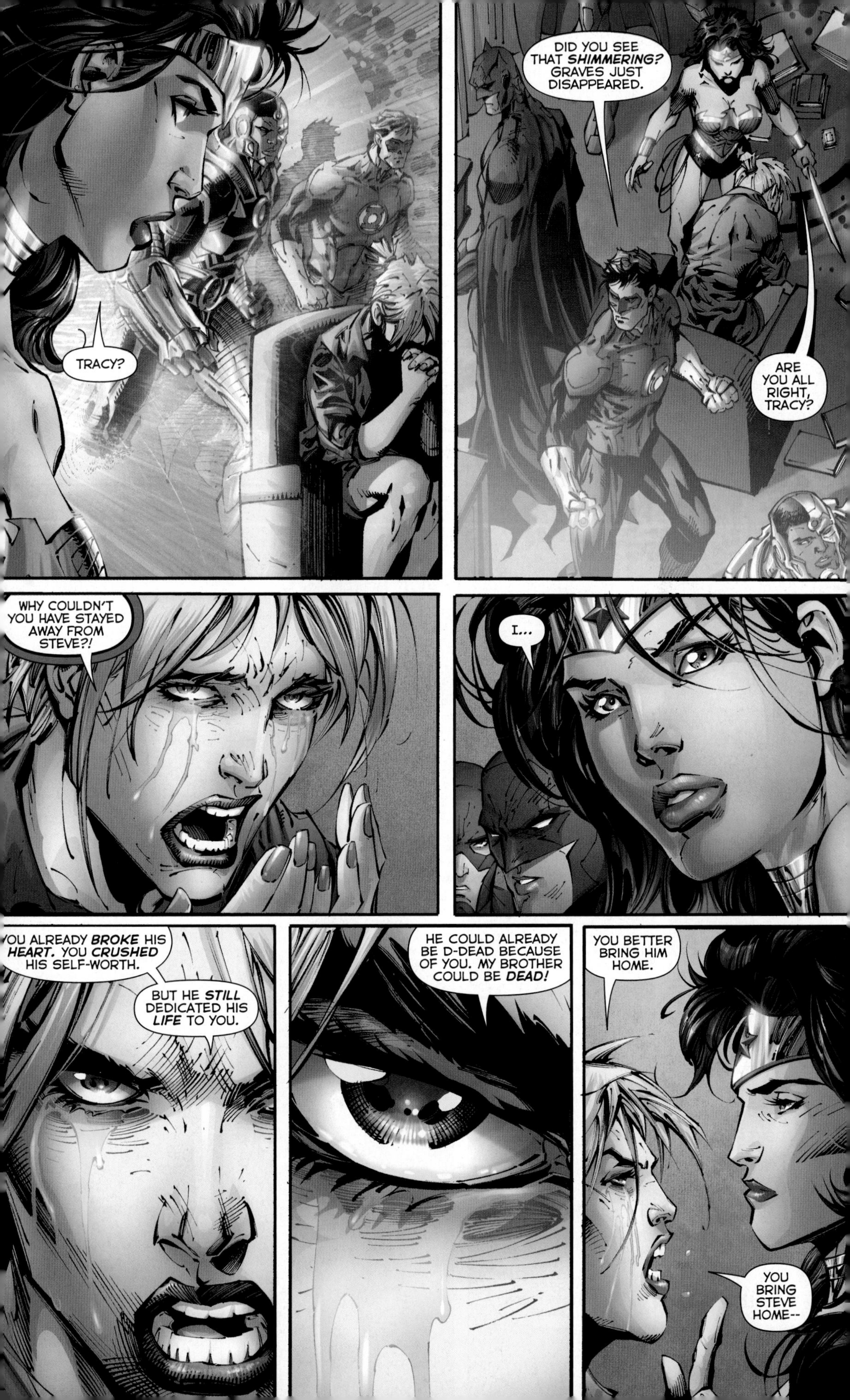
TRACY?
DID YOU SEE THAT SHIMMERING? GRAVES JUST DISAPPEARED.
ARE YOU ALL RIGHT, TRACY?
WHY COULDN'T YOU HAVE STAYED AWAY FROM STEVE?!
I...
YOU ALREADY BROKE HIS HEART. YOU CRUSHED HIS SELF-WORTH.
BUT HE STILL DEDICATED HIS LIFE TO YOU.
HE COULD ALREADY BE D-DEAD BECAUSE OF YOU. MY BROTHER COULD BE DEAD!
YOU BETTER BRING HIM HOME.
YOU BRING STEVE HOME--

"--OR I'LL HAUNT YOU FOR THE REST OF YOUR LIFE."

SHE'S JUST UPSET, WONDER WOMAN.

NO. SHE'S *RIGHT*, FLASH. THIS *IS* MY FAULT.

I SHOULD NEVER HAVE LET US GET AS CLOSE AS WE DID.

WE'LL FIND WHO HAS STEVE, DIANA.

WE ALREADY KNOW.

HIS NAME'S *DAVID GRAVES.*

WHO'S DAVID GRAVES?

THE AUTHOR. WE SAVED HIM AND HIS FAMILY DURING DARKSEID'S INVASION. THEN HE WROTE THE BOOK ABOUT US.

I DIDN'T FINISH IT.

BUT YOU KNOW IT CATAPULTED US INTO THE PUBLIC'S FAVOR.

US KICKING DARKSEID'S ROCKY *ASS* DID THAT. C'MON, SUPERMAN, YOU SOUND LIKE YOU *ADMIRE* THIS LUNATIC.

AS A *WRITER,* I DID.

DAVID GRAVES DISAPPEARED A FEW YEARS AGO AFTER HIS WIFE AND CHILDREN DIED. EVERYONE PRESUMED HE HA TOO. HE WAS TERMINAL.

WITH WHAT?

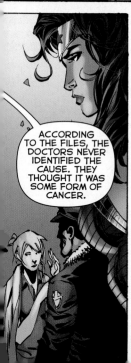

ACCORDING TO THE FILES, THE DOCTORS NEVER IDENTIFIED THE CAUSE. THEY THOUGHT IT WAS SOME FORM OF CANCER.

I HAVE HIS LAST KNOWN ADDRESS. A WRITING CABIN IN MAINE.

WHERE ARE YOU GOING, WONDER WOMAN?

TO GRAVES' CABIN.

I'M GOING TO FIND HIM--

--I'M GOING TO *CUT OFF HIS HEAD--*

--AND I'M GOING TO BRING STEVE *HOME.*

THIS IS A *LEAGUE* MISSION NOT A *WONDER WOMAN* ONE.

AND WE DON'T CUT OFF ANYONE'S HEAD.

I DO.

AND THE MORE YOU HOLD ME BACK, THE MORE LIKELY STEVE'S ALREADY DEAD.

THIS WASN'T JUST AN ATTACK ON YOU.

I NEED TO DO THIS *MYSELF.*

I CAN'T RISK STEVE'S LIFE.

SO YOU DON'T *TRUST* US TO HELP?

LANTERN, I HAVE THIS.

STEVE'S IMPORTANT TO ALL OF US, WONDER WOMAN.

SINCE WHEN?

SINCE WE KNOW HOW MUCH HE MEANS TO YOU. YOU MIGHT NOT SAY IT, BUT WE ALL KNOW WHY YOU CUT IT OFF...EVEN IF YOU DIDN'T WANT TO.

LET ME OUT OF HERE, LANTERN.

DON'T BE AS STUBBORN AS ME. GRAVES TOOK US *ALL* DOWN, WONDER WOMAN. YOU *NEED* BACK-UP.

LET ME OUT OF HERE.

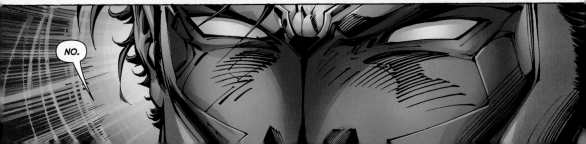

NO.

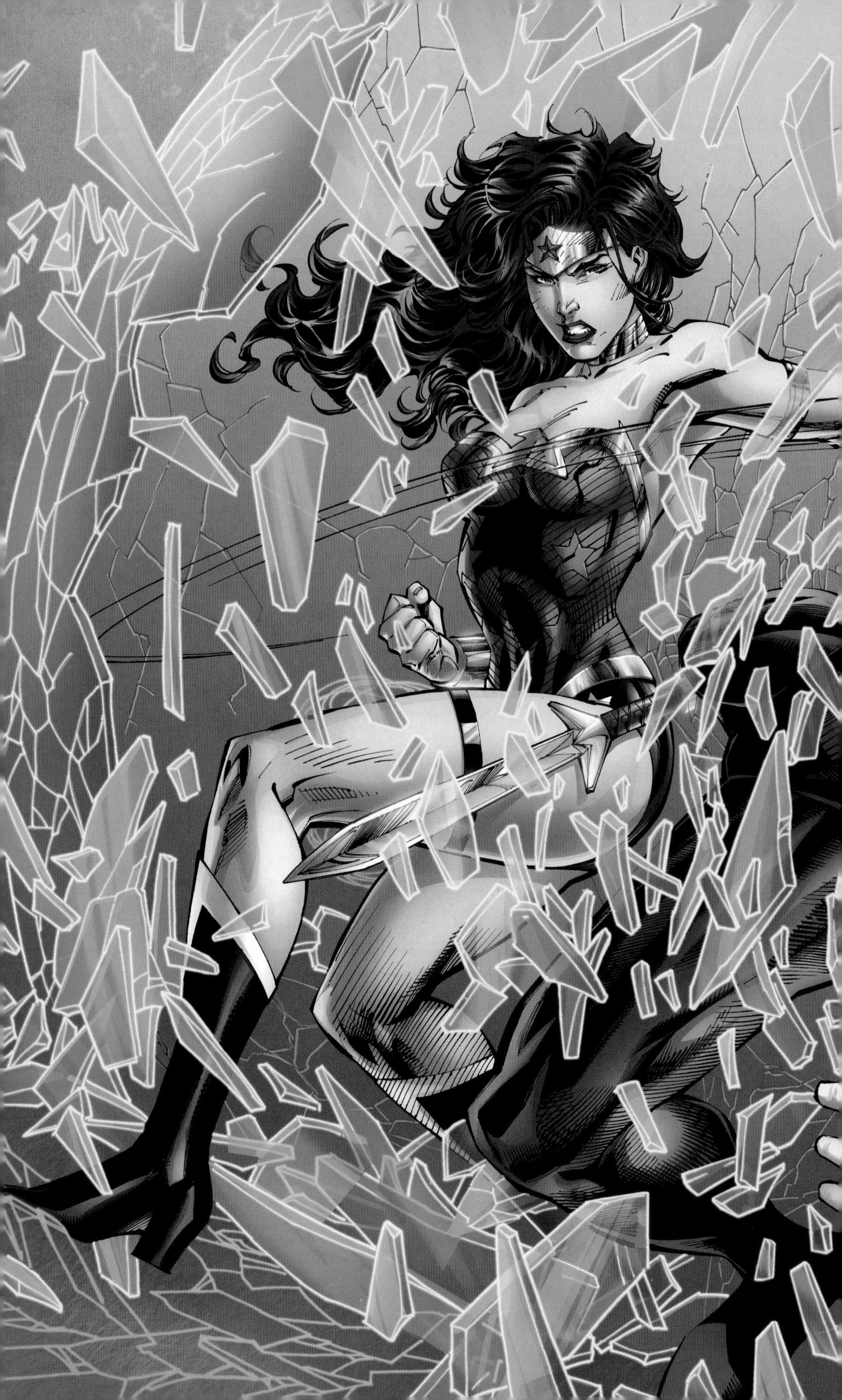

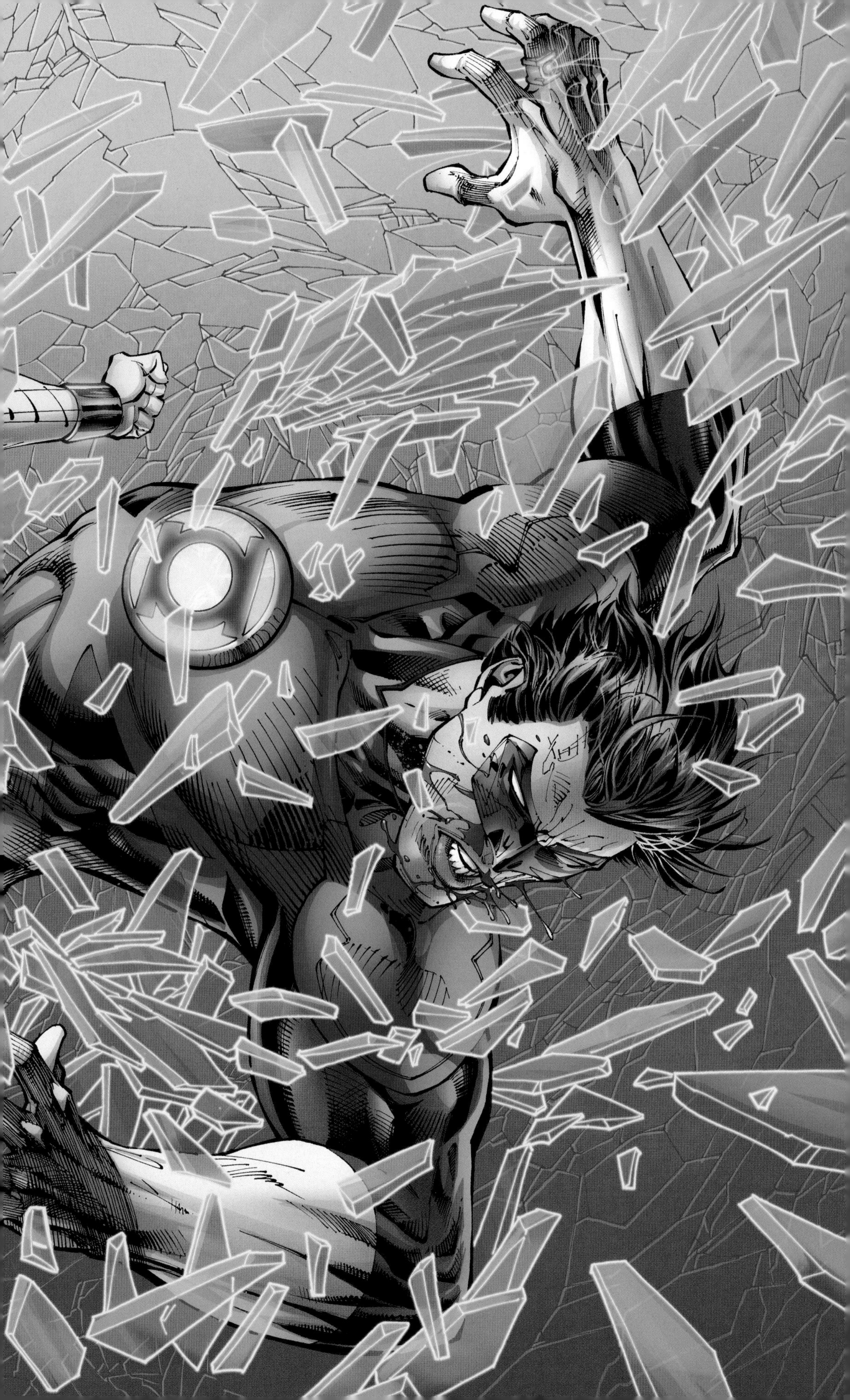

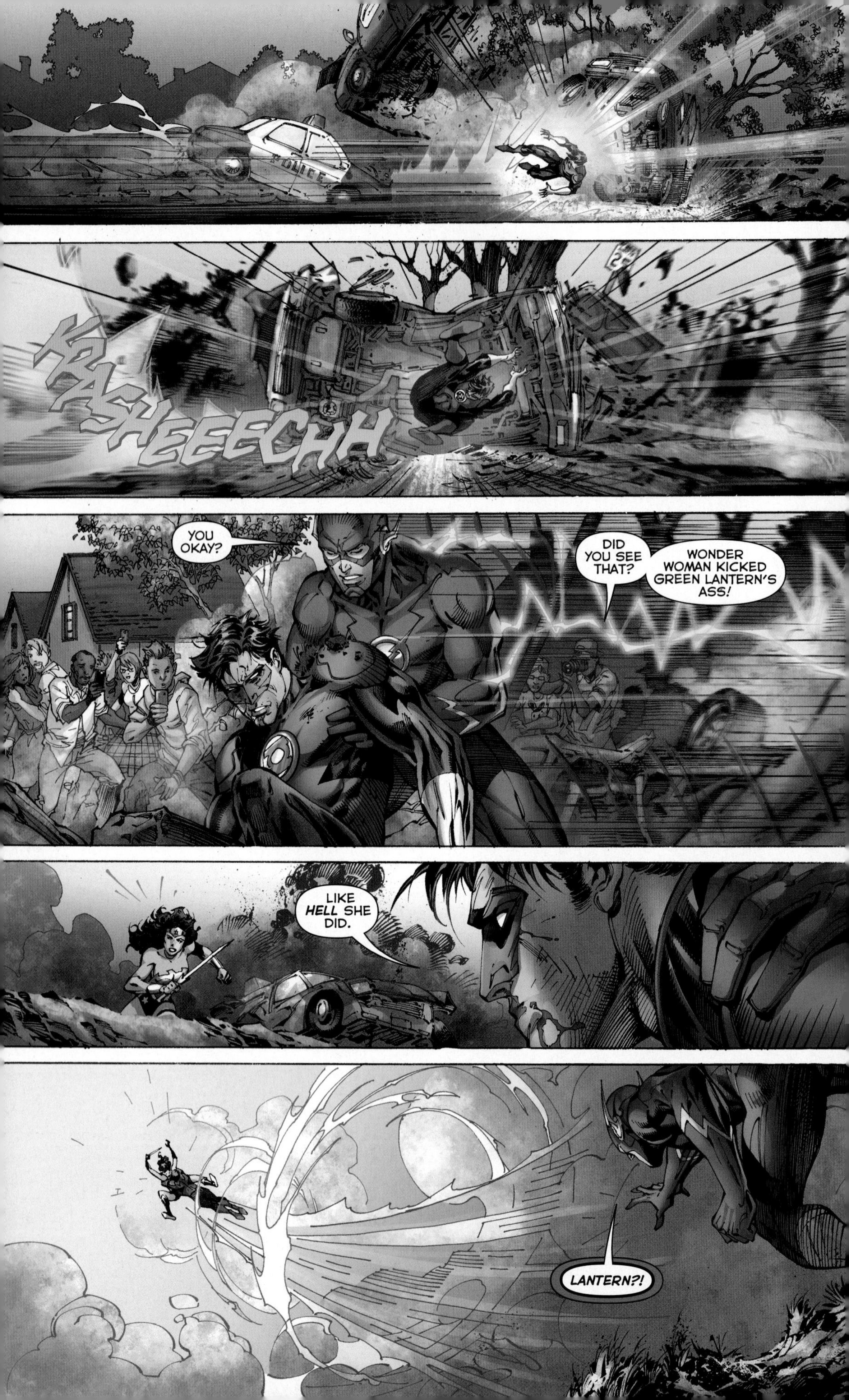
KRASHEEEECHH
YOU OKAY?
DID YOU SEE THAT?
WONDER WOMAN KICKED GREEN LANTERN'S ASS!
LIKE **HELL** SHE DID.
LANTERN?!

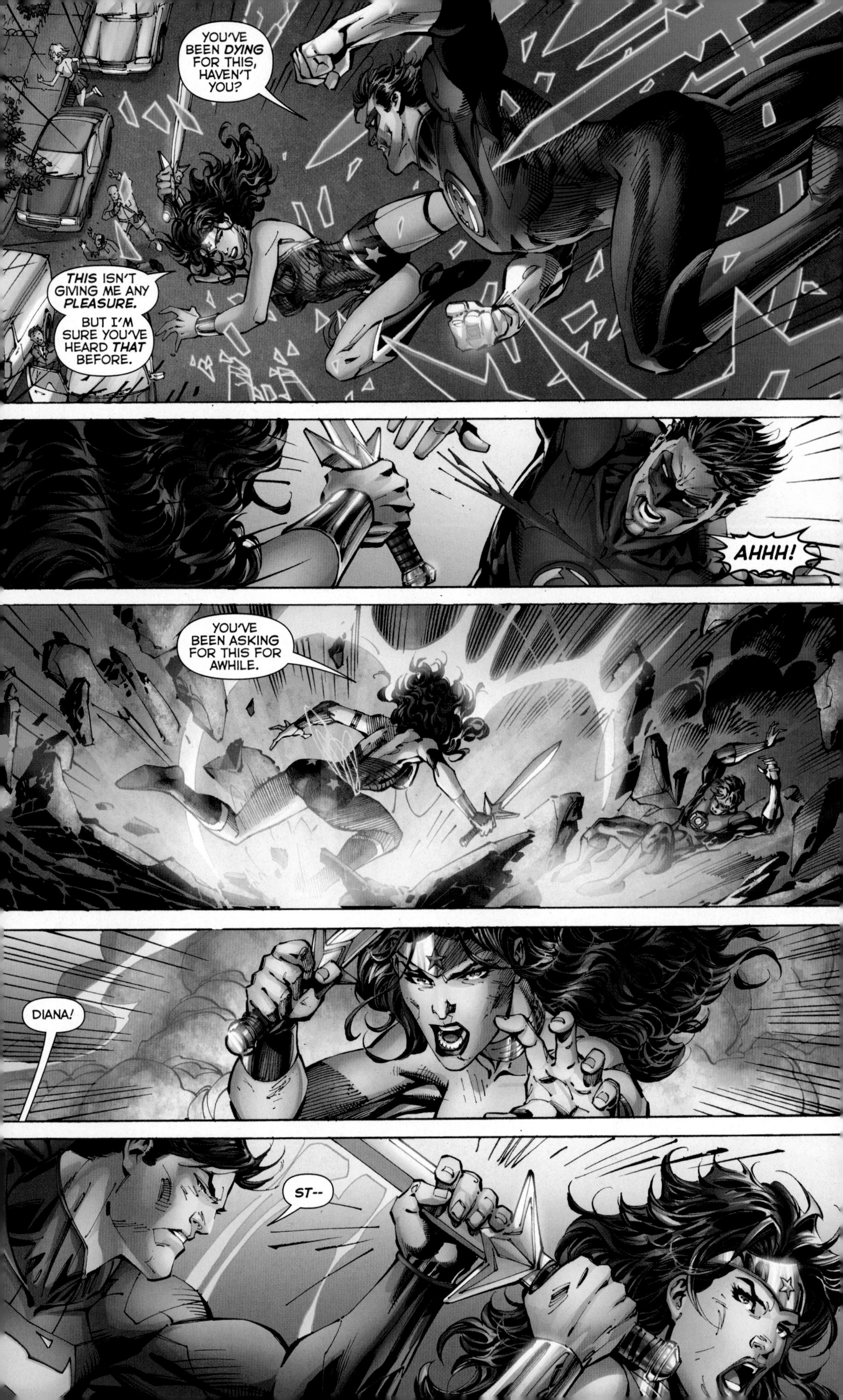
YOU'VE BEEN *DYING* FOR THIS, HAVEN'T YOU?
THIS ISN'T GIVING ME ANY *PLEASURE.*
BUT I'M SURE YOU'VE HEARD *THAT* BEFORE.
AHHH!
YOU'VE BEEN ASKING FOR THIS FOR AWHILE.
DIANA!
ST--

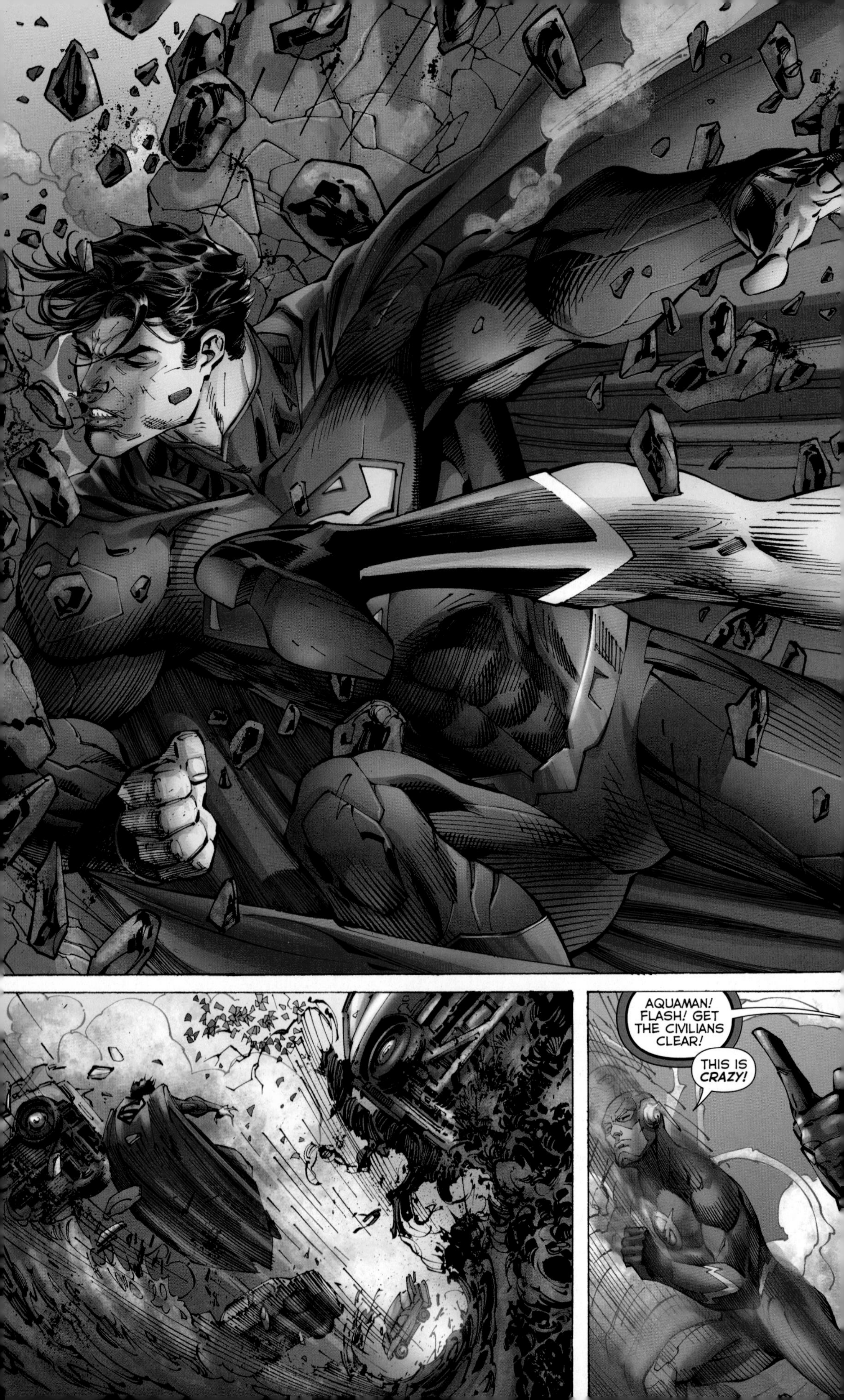
AQUAMAN! FLASH! GET THE CIVILIANS CLEAR!
THIS IS *CRAZY!*

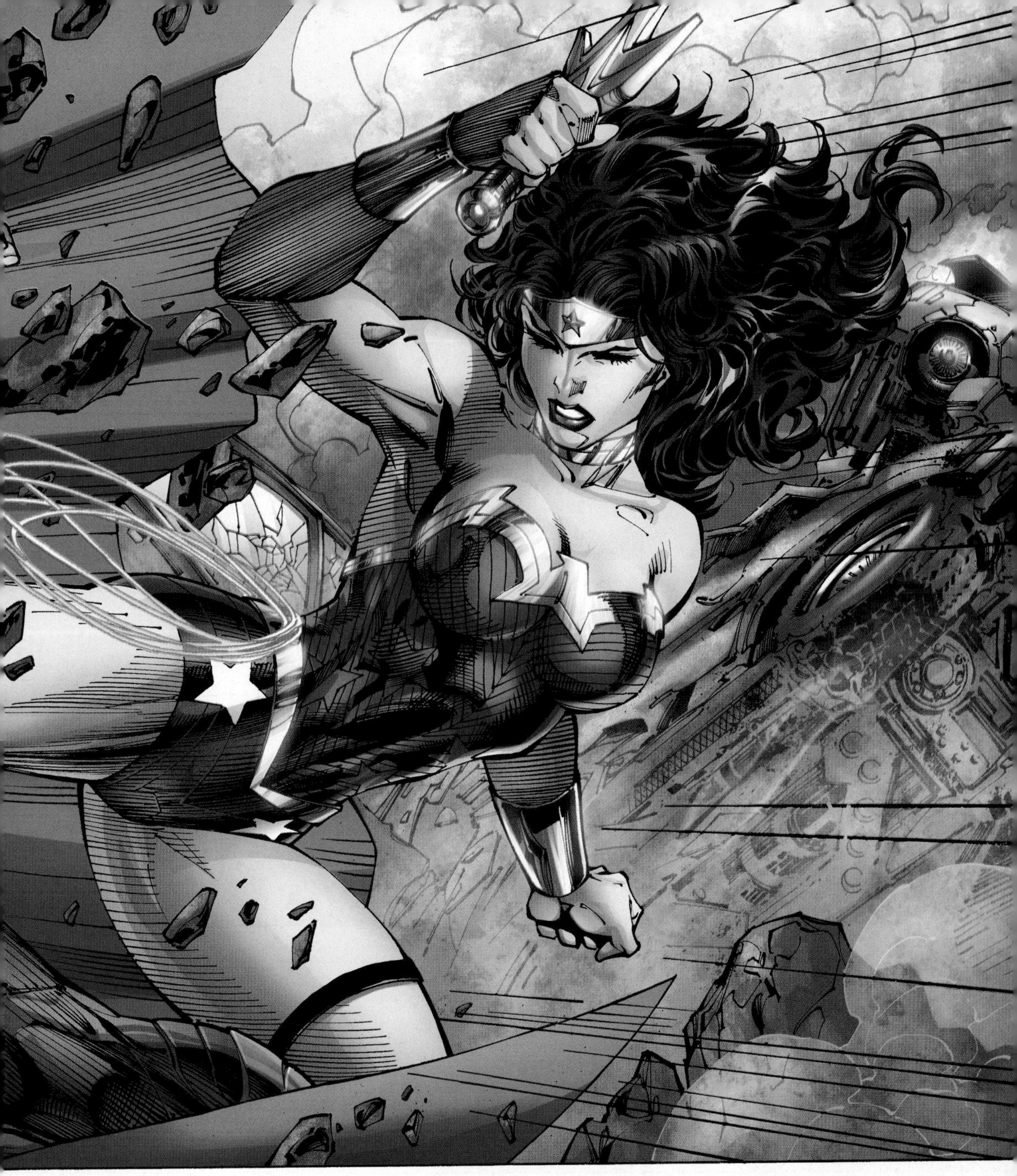

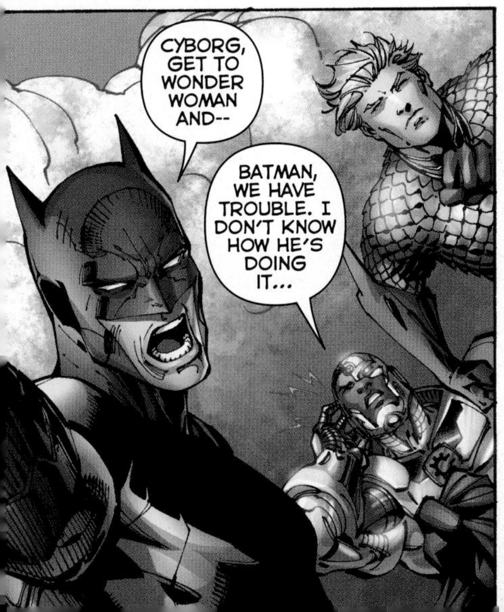
CYBORG, GET TO WONDER WOMAN AND--
BATMAN, WE HAVE TROUBLE. I DON'T KNOW HOW HE'S DOING IT...

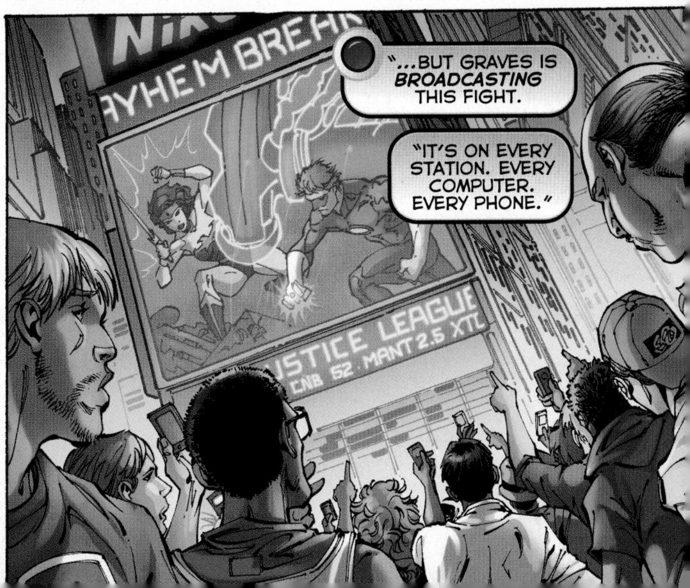
"...BUT GRAVES IS BROADCASTING THIS FIGHT.
"IT'S ON EVERY STATION. EVERY COMPUTER. EVERY PHONE."
JUSTICE LEAGUE

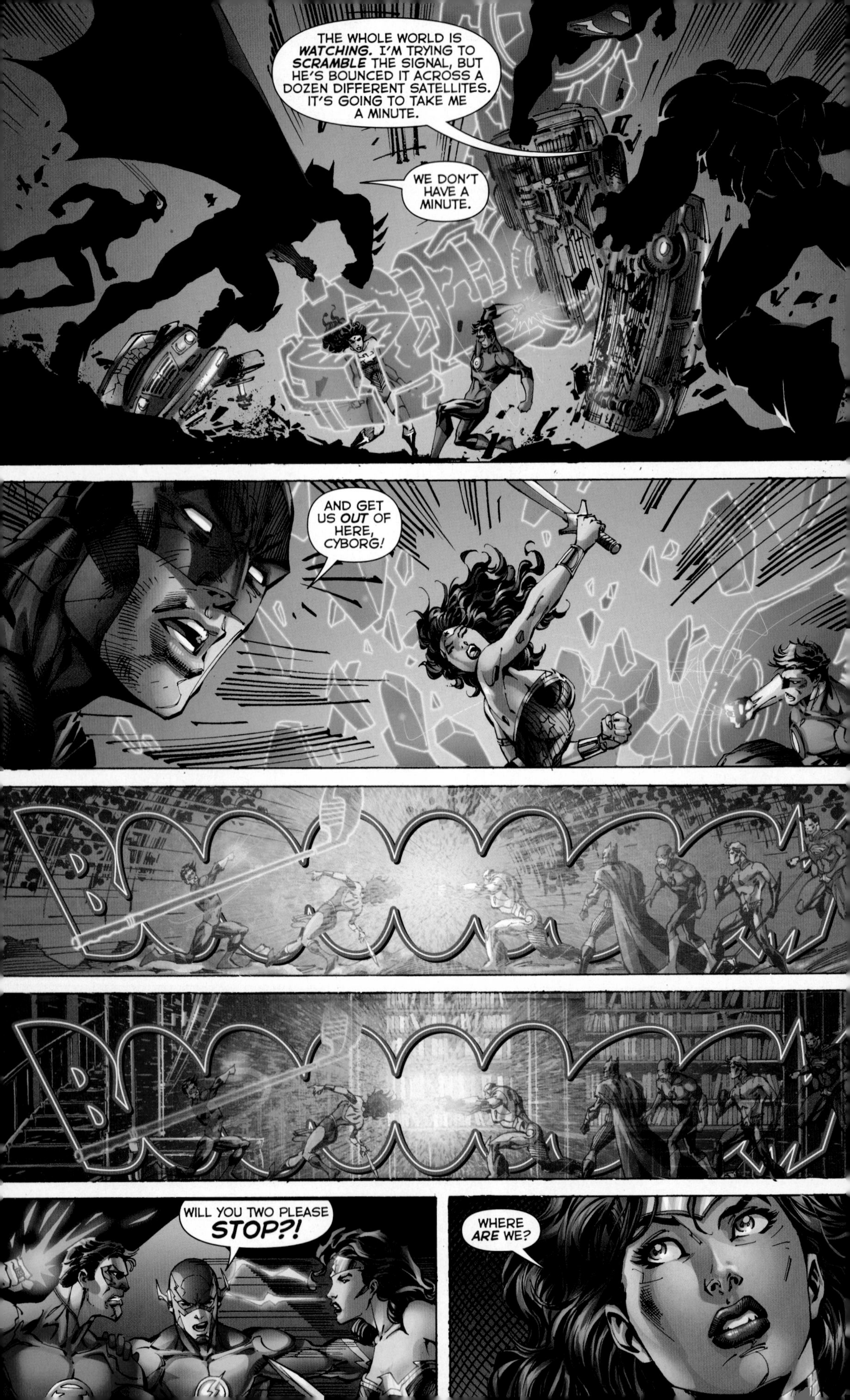
THE WHOLE WORLD IS WATCHING. I'M TRYING TO SCRAMBLE THE SIGNAL, BUT HE'S BOUNCED IT ACROSS A DOZEN DIFFERENT SATELLITES. IT'S GOING TO TAKE ME A MINUTE.
WE DON'T HAVE A MINUTE.
AND GET US OUT OF HERE, CYBORG!
WILL YOU TWO PLEASE STOP?!
WHERE ARE WE?

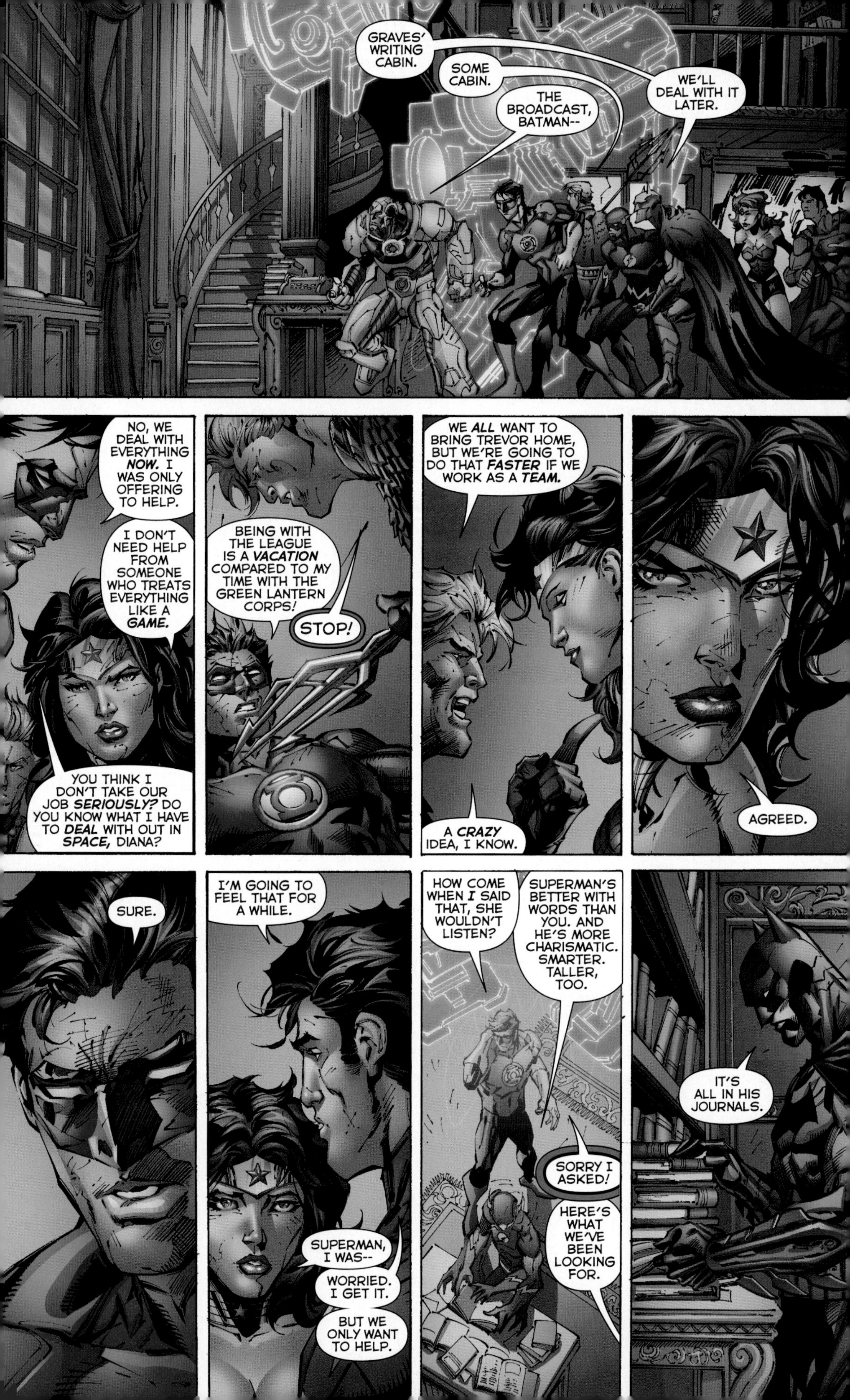
GRAVES' WRITING CABIN.
SOME CABIN.
THE BROADCAST, BATMAN--
WE'LL DEAL WITH IT LATER.
NO, WE DEAL WITH EVERYTHING NOW. I WAS ONLY OFFERING TO HELP.
I DON'T NEED HELP FROM SOMEONE WHO TREATS EVERYTHING LIKE A GAME.
YOU THINK I DON'T TAKE OUR JOB SERIOUSLY? DO YOU KNOW WHAT I HAVE TO DEAL WITH OUT IN SPACE, DIANA?
BEING WITH THE LEAGUE IS A VACATION COMPARED TO MY TIME WITH THE GREEN LANTERN CORPS!
STOP!
WE ALL WANT TO BRING TREVOR HOME, BUT WE'RE GOING TO DO THAT FASTER IF WE WORK AS A TEAM.
A CRAZY IDEA, I KNOW.
AGREED.
SURE.
I'M GOING TO FEEL THAT FOR A WHILE.
SUPERMAN, I WAS--
WORRIED. I GET IT.
BUT WE ONLY WANT TO HELP.
HOW COME WHEN I SAID THAT, SHE WOULDN'T LISTEN?
SUPERMAN'S BETTER WITH WORDS THAN YOU. AND HE'S MORE CHARISMATIC. SMARTER. TALLER, TOO.
SORRY I ASKED!
HERE'S WHAT WE'VE BEEN LOOKING FOR.
IT'S ALL IN HIS JOURNALS.

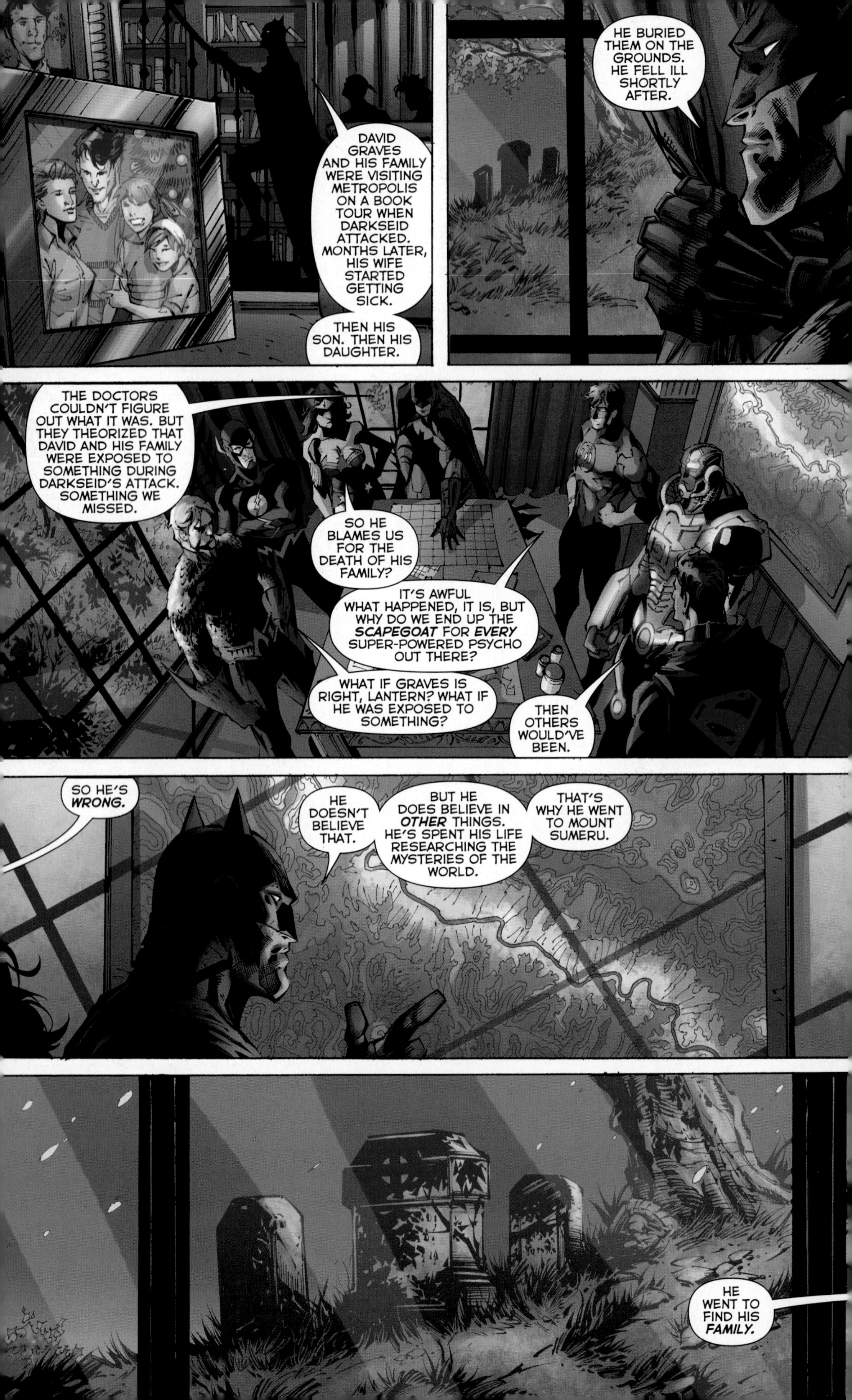
DAVID GRAVES AND HIS FAMILY WERE VISITING METROPOLIS ON A BOOK TOUR WHEN DARKSEID ATTACKED. MONTHS LATER, HIS WIFE STARTED GETTING SICK.
THEN HIS SON. THEN HIS DAUGHTER.
HE BURIED THEM ON THE GROUNDS. HE FELL ILL SHORTLY AFTER.
THE DOCTORS COULDN'T FIGURE OUT WHAT IT WAS. BUT THEY THEORIZED THAT DAVID AND HIS FAMILY WERE EXPOSED TO SOMETHING DURING DARKSEID'S ATTACK. SOMETHING WE MISSED.
SO HE BLAMES US FOR THE DEATH OF HIS FAMILY?
IT'S AWFUL WHAT HAPPENED, IT IS, BUT WHY DO WE END UP THE *SCAPEGOAT* FOR *EVERY* SUPER-POWERED PSYCHO OUT THERE?
WHAT IF GRAVES IS RIGHT, LANTERN? WHAT IF HE WAS EXPOSED TO SOMETHING?
THEN OTHERS WOULD'VE BEEN.
SO HE'S *WRONG.*
HE DOESN'T BELIEVE THAT.
BUT HE DOES BELIEVE IN *OTHER* THINGS. HE'S SPENT HIS LIFE RESEARCHING THE MYSTERIES OF THE WORLD.
THAT'S WHY HE WENT TO MOUNT SUMERU.
HE WENT TO FIND HIS *FAMILY.*

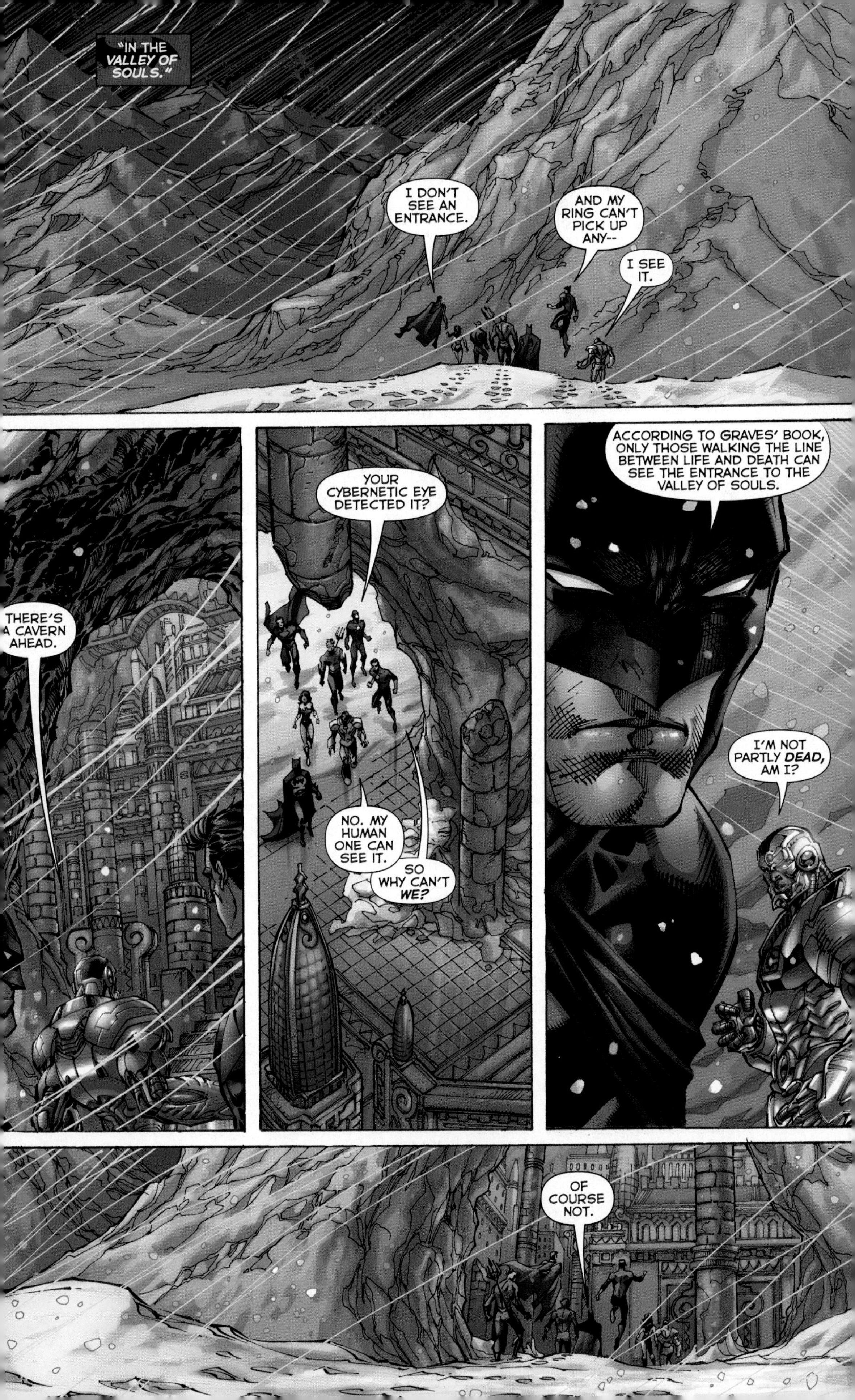
"IN THE VALLEY OF SOULS."
I DON'T SEE AN ENTRANCE.
AND MY RING CAN'T PICK UP ANY--
I SEE IT.
THERE'S A CAVERN AHEAD.
YOUR CYBERNETIC EYE DETECTED IT?
NO. MY HUMAN ONE CAN SEE IT.
SO WHY CAN'T WE?
ACCORDING TO GRAVES' BOOK, ONLY THOSE WALKING THE LINE BETWEEN LIFE AND DEATH CAN SEE THE ENTRANCE TO THE VALLEY OF SOULS.
I'M NOT PARTLY DEAD, AM I?
OF COURSE NOT.

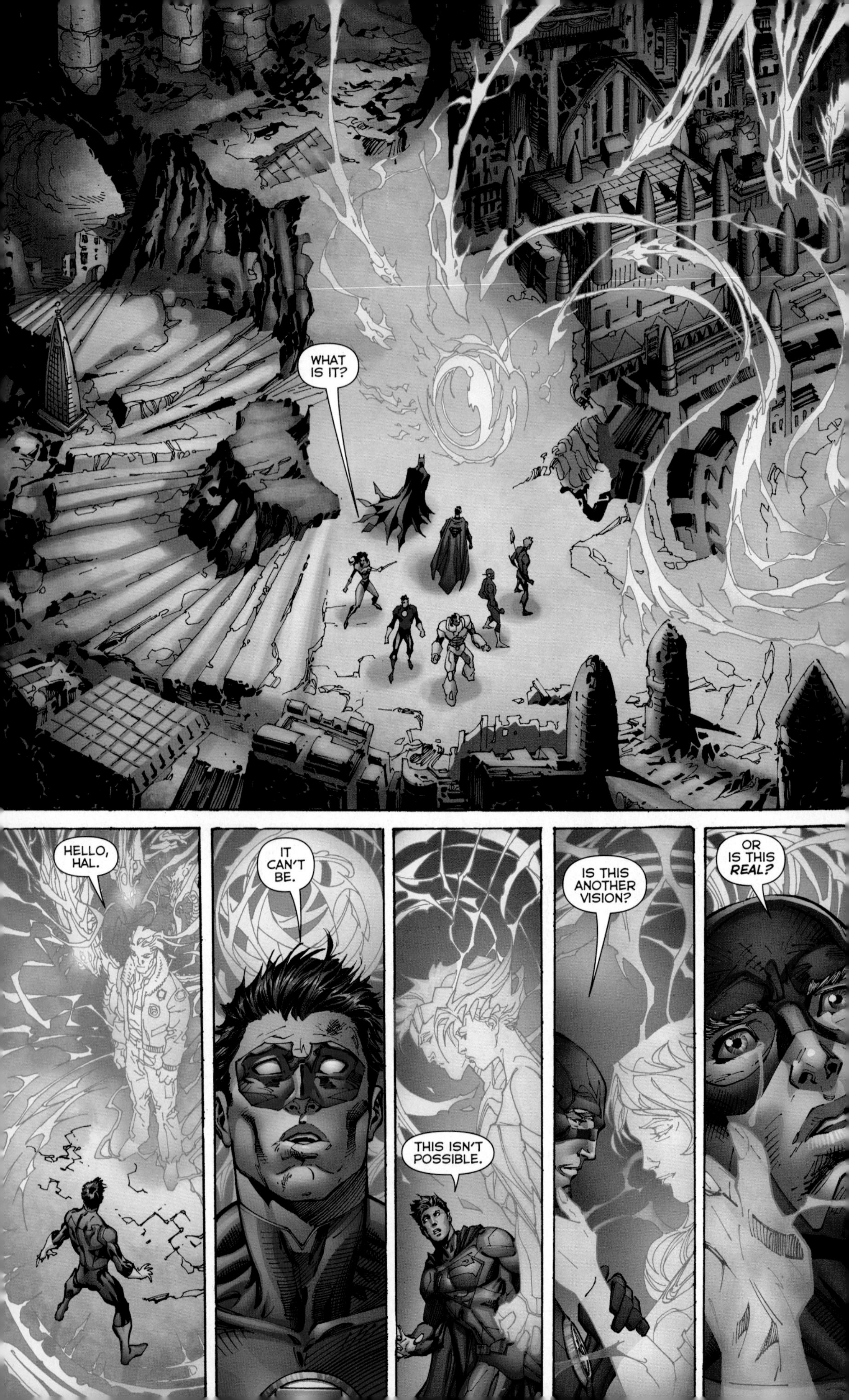
WHAT IS IT?
HELLO, HAL.
IT CAN'T BE.
THIS ISN'T POSSIBLE.
IS THIS ANOTHER VISION?
OR IS THIS *REAL?*

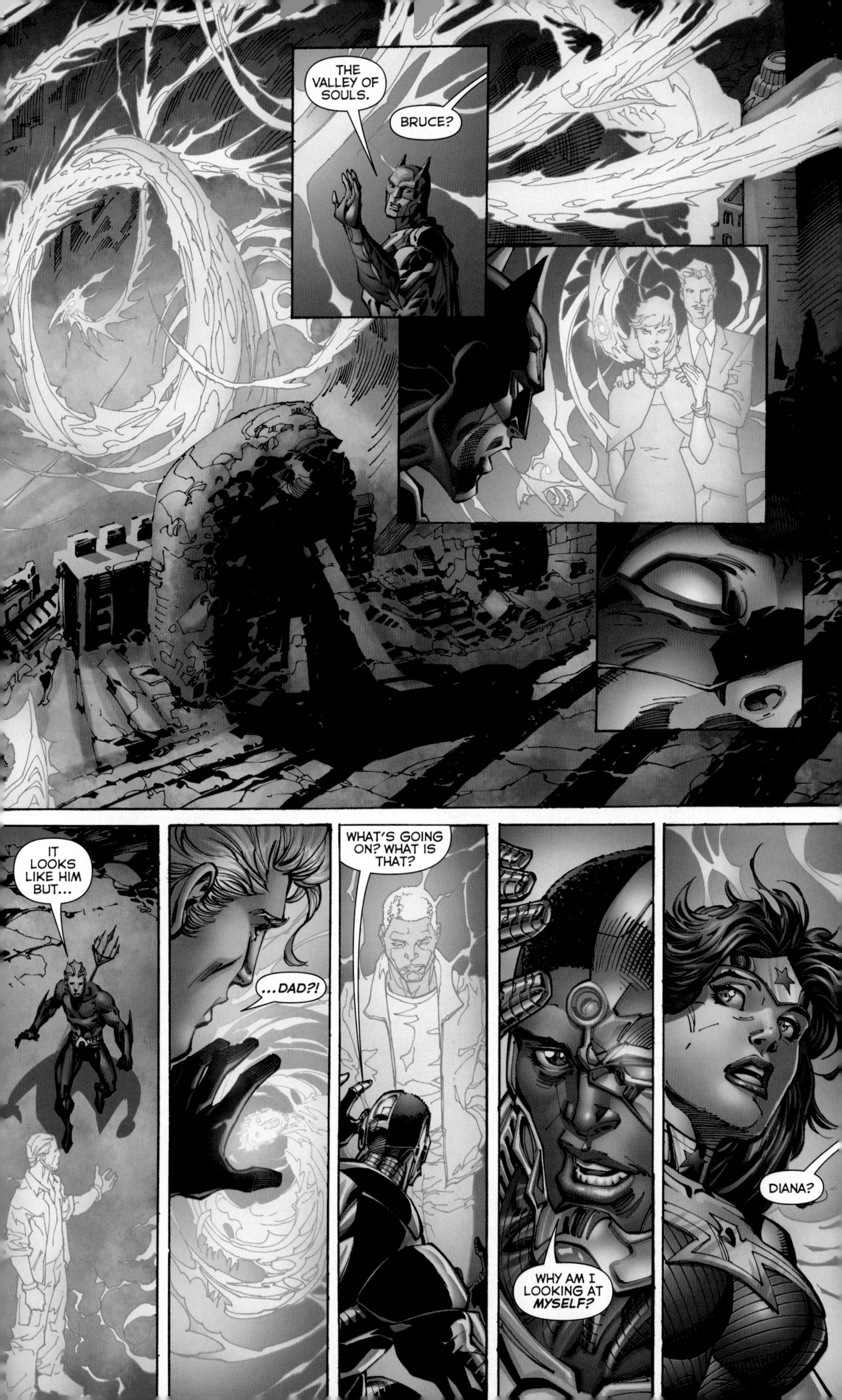
THE VALLEY OF SOULS.
BRUCE?
IT LOOKS LIKE HIM BUT...
...DAD?!
WHAT'S GOING ON? WHAT IS THAT?
WHY AM I LOOKING AT MYSELF?
DIANA?

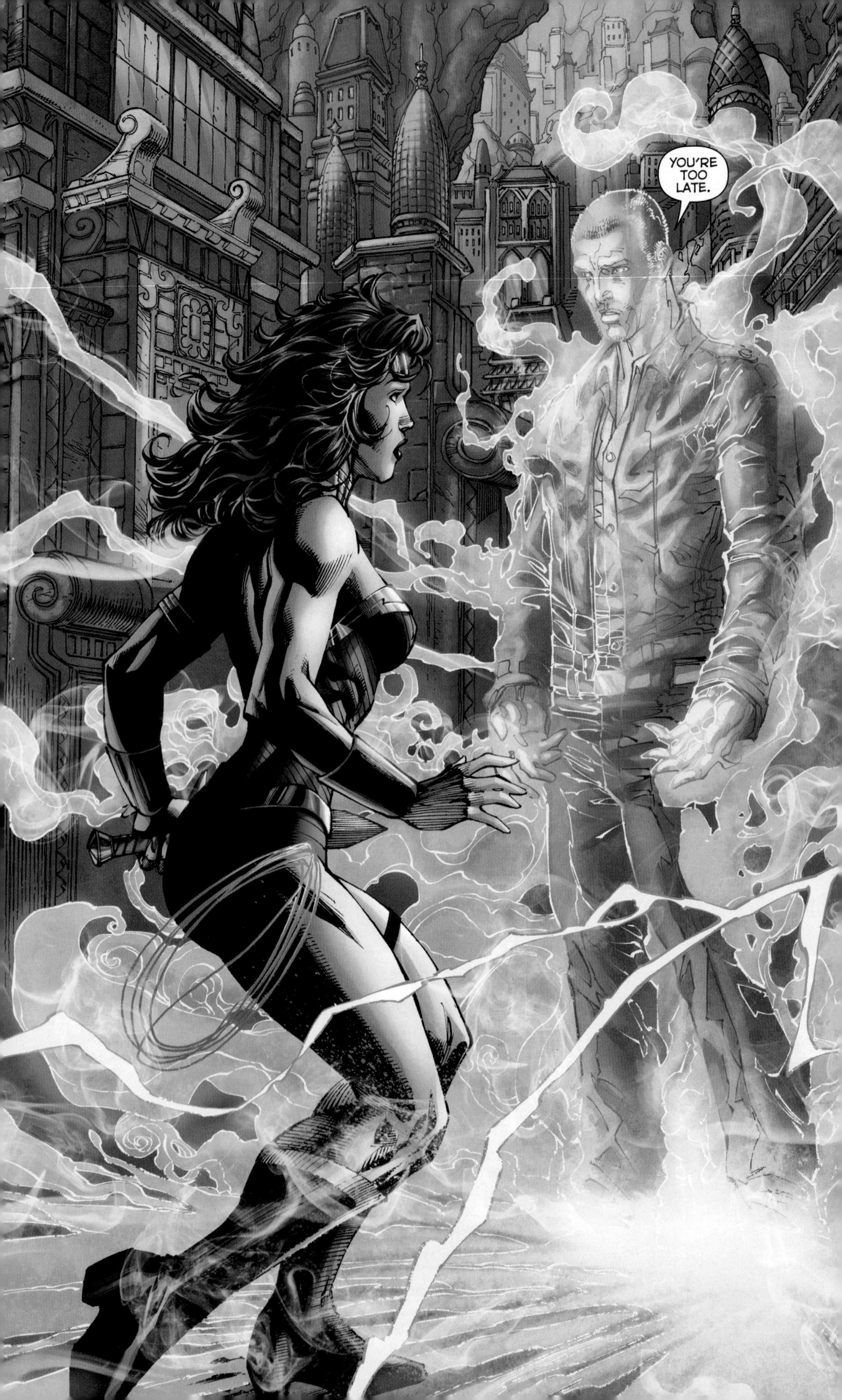
YOU'RE TOO LATE.

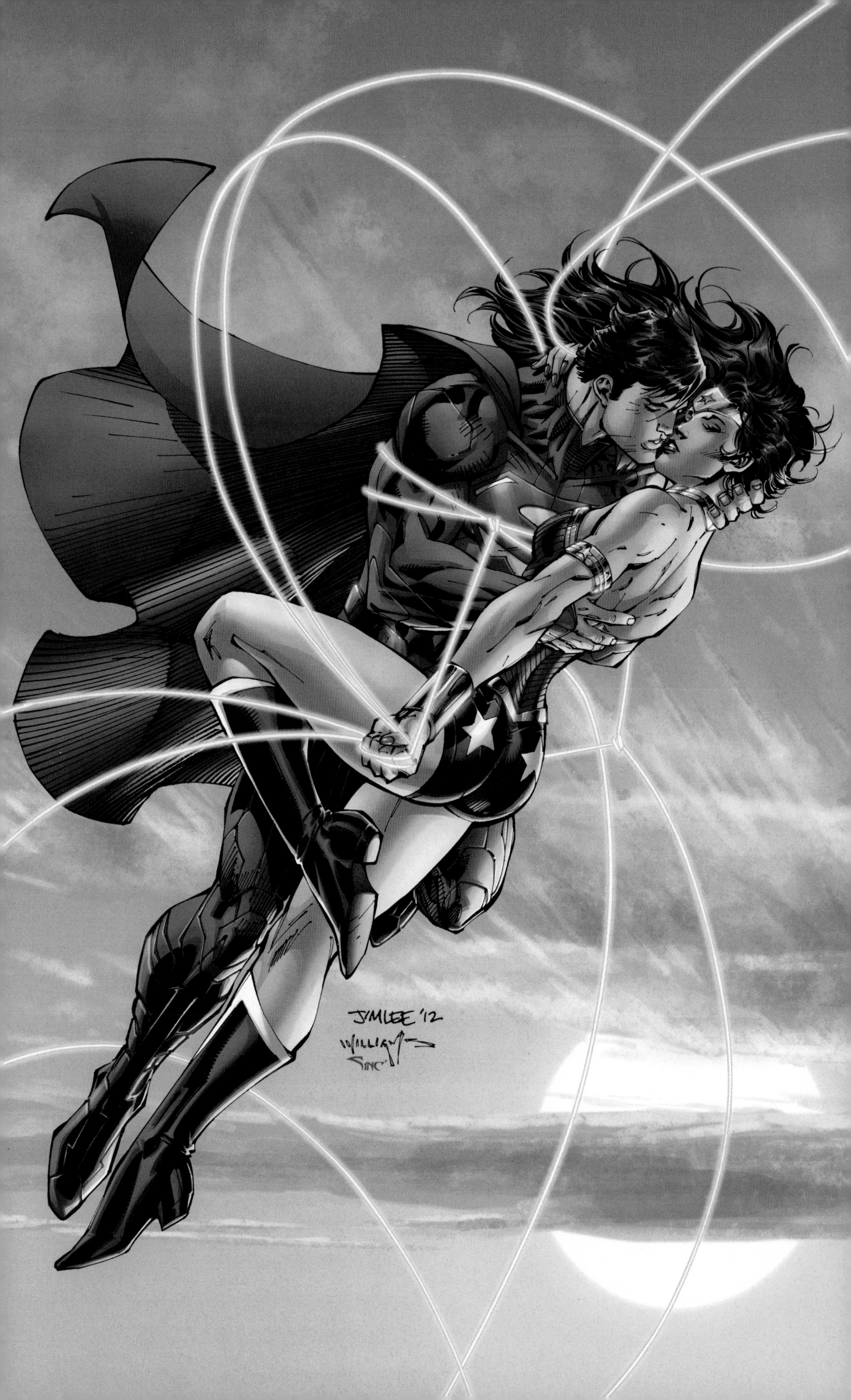
JIMLEE '12

THE VILLAIN'S JOURNEY CHAPTER FOUR: RESCUE FROM WITHIN

GEOFF JOHNS writer **JIM LEE** with **DAVID FINCH & IVAN REIS** pencillers **SCOTT WILLIAMS, SANDRA HOPE, JONATHAN GLAPION, MARK IRWIN, MATT BANNING, ROB HUNTER, JOE WEEMS, ALEX GARNER, TREVOR SCOTT, DAVID FINCH & JOE PRADO** inkers cover by **JIM LEE, SCOTT WILLIAMS & ALEX SINCLAIR**

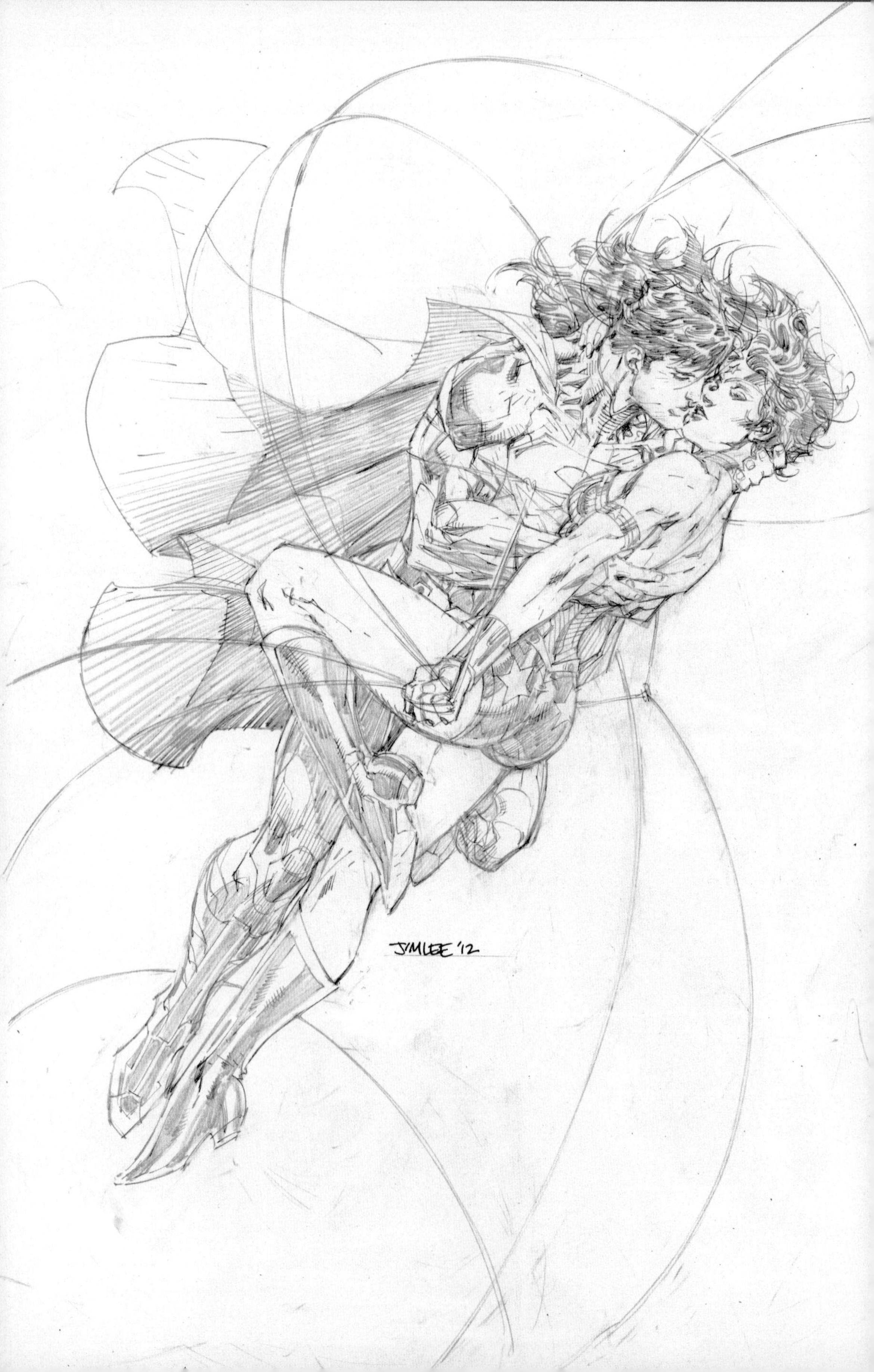
JIMLEE '12

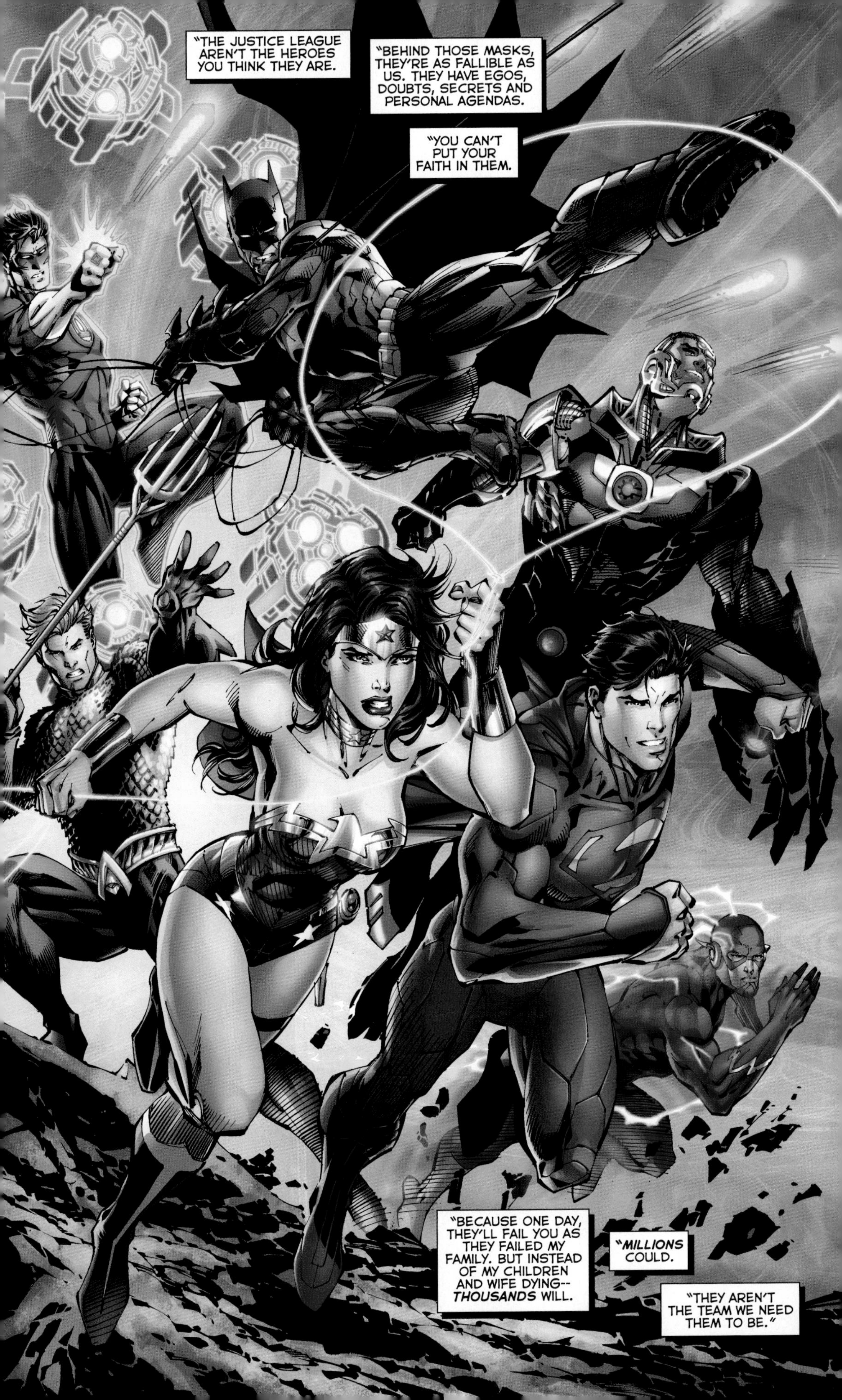
"THE JUSTICE LEAGUE AREN'T THE HEROES YOU THINK THEY ARE.
"BEHIND THOSE MASKS, THEY'RE AS FALLIBLE AS US. THEY HAVE EGOS, DOUBTS, SECRETS AND PERSONAL AGENDAS.
"YOU CAN'T PUT YOUR FAITH IN THEM.
"BECAUSE ONE DAY, THEY'LL FAIL YOU AS THEY FAILED MY FAMILY. BUT INSTEAD OF MY CHILDREN AND WIFE DYING-- *THOUSANDS* WILL.
"*MILLIONS* COULD.
"THEY AREN'T THE TEAM WE NEED THEM TO BE."

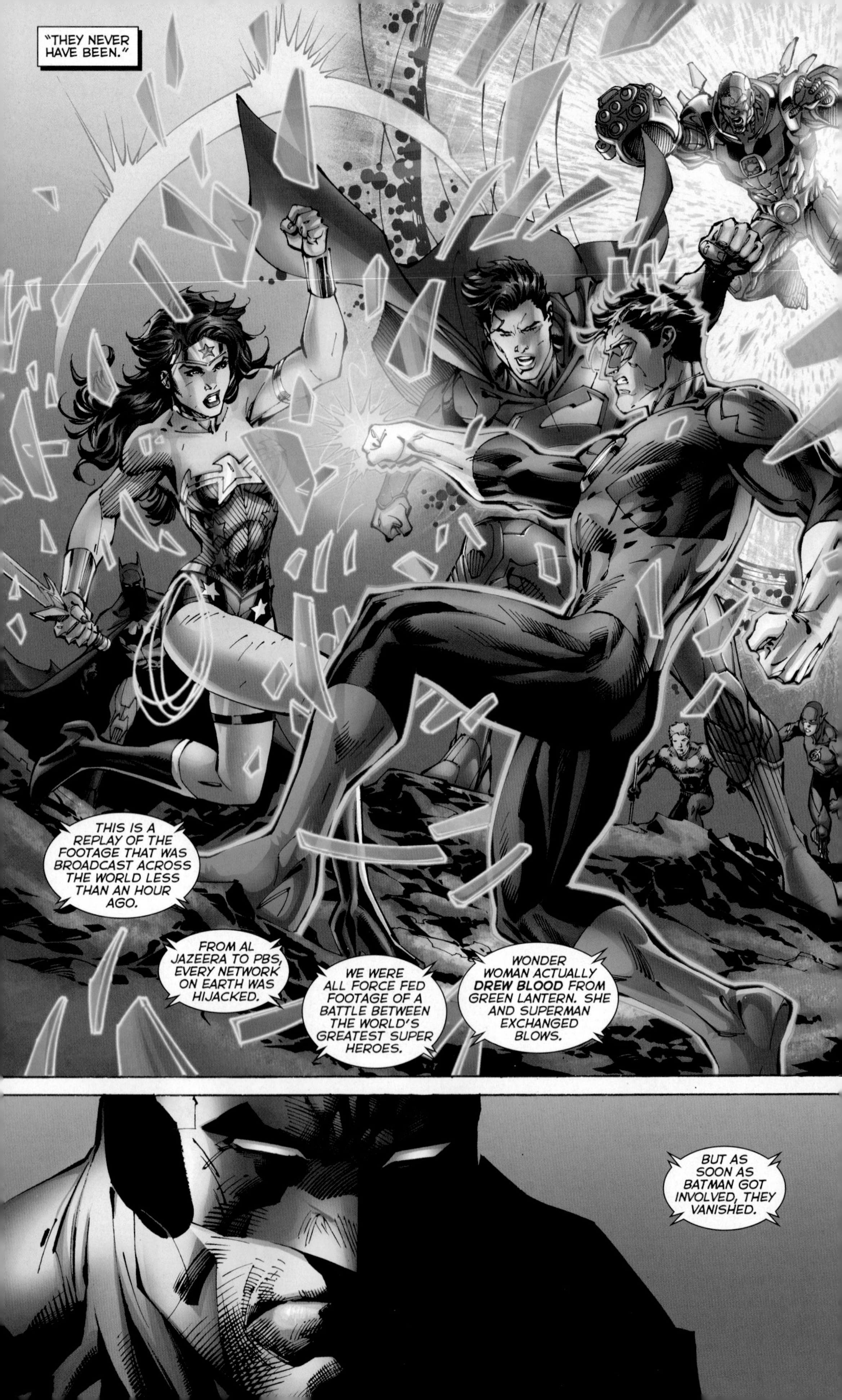
"THEY NEVER HAVE BEEN."
THIS IS A REPLAY OF THE FOOTAGE THAT WAS BROADCAST ACROSS THE WORLD LESS THAN AN HOUR AGO.
FROM AL JAZEERA TO PBS, EVERY NETWORK ON EARTH WAS HIJACKED.
WE WERE ALL FORCE FED FOOTAGE OF A BATTLE BETWEEN THE WORLD'S GREATEST SUPER HEROES.
WONDER WOMAN ACTUALLY DREW BLOOD FROM GREEN LANTERN. SHE AND SUPERMAN EXCHANGED BLOWS.
BUT AS SOON AS BATMAN GOT INVOLVED, THEY VANISHED.

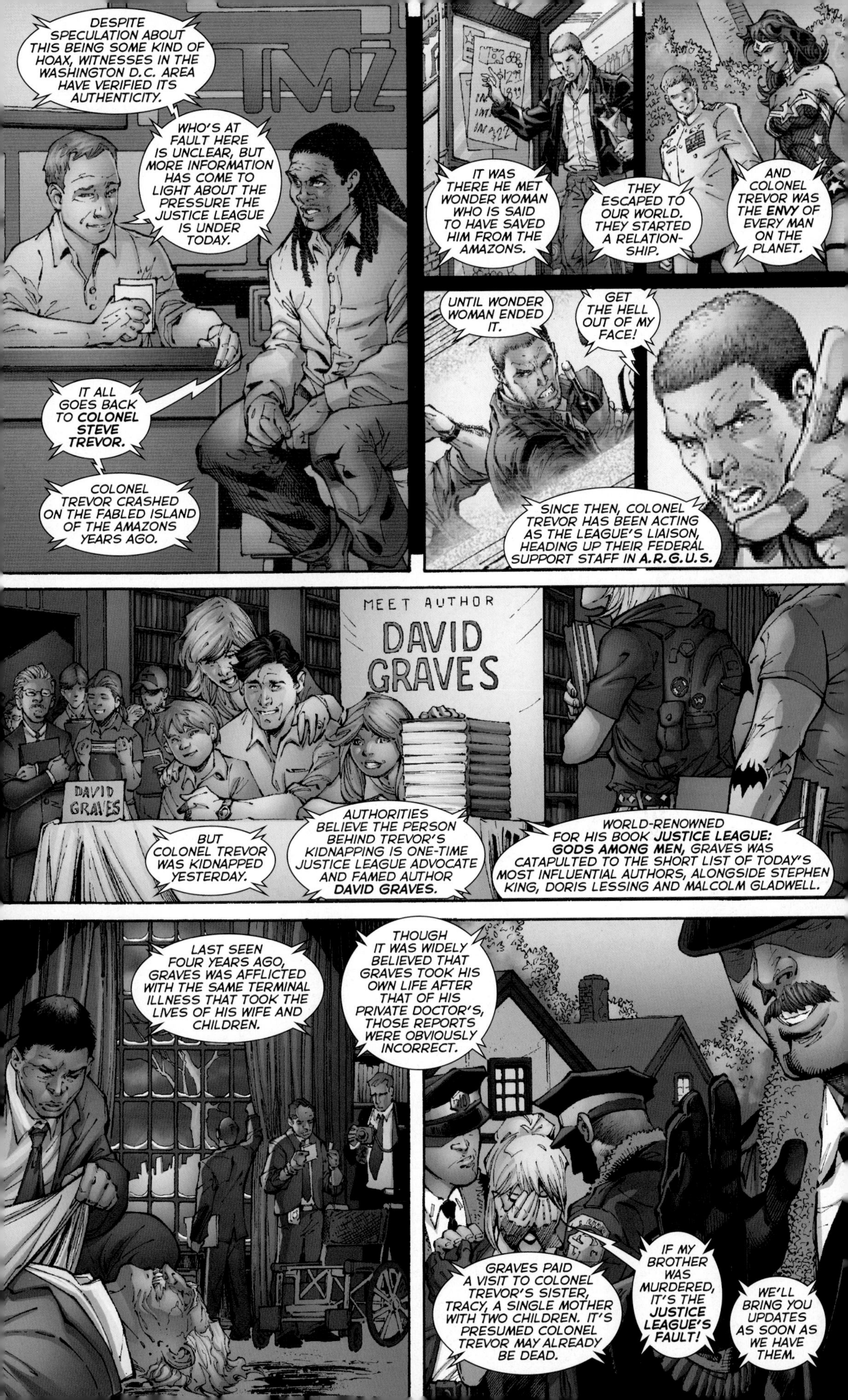
DESPITE SPECULATION ABOUT THIS BEING SOME KIND OF HOAX, WITNESSES IN THE WASHINGTON D.C. AREA HAVE VERIFIED ITS AUTHENTICITY.
WHO'S AT FAULT HERE IS UNCLEAR, BUT MORE INFORMATION HAS COME TO LIGHT ABOUT THE PRESSURE THE JUSTICE LEAGUE IS UNDER TODAY.
IT ALL GOES BACK TO **COLONEL STEVE TREVOR.**
COLONEL TREVOR CRASHED ON THE FABLED ISLAND OF THE AMAZONS YEARS AGO.
IT WAS THERE HE MET WONDER WOMAN WHO IS SAID TO HAVE SAVED HIM FROM THE AMAZONS.
THEY ESCAPED TO OUR WORLD. THEY STARTED A RELATION-SHIP.
AND COLONEL TREVOR WAS THE **ENVY** OF EVERY MAN ON THE PLANET.
UNTIL WONDER WOMAN ENDED IT.
GET THE HELL OUT OF MY FACE!
SINCE THEN, COLONEL TREVOR HAS BEEN ACTING AS THE LEAGUE'S LIAISON, HEADING UP THEIR FEDERAL SUPPORT STAFF IN **A.R.G.U.S.**
MEET AUTHOR
DAVID GRAVES
DAVID GRAVES
BUT COLONEL TREVOR WAS KIDNAPPED YESTERDAY.
AUTHORITIES BELIEVE THE PERSON BEHIND TREVOR'S KIDNAPPING IS ONE-TIME JUSTICE LEAGUE ADVOCATE AND FAMED AUTHOR **DAVID GRAVES.**
WORLD-RENOWNED FOR HIS BOOK **JUSTICE LEAGUE: GODS AMONG MEN,** GRAVES WAS CATAPULTED TO THE SHORT LIST OF TODAY'S MOST INFLUENTIAL AUTHORS, ALONGSIDE STEPHEN KING, DORIS LESSING AND MALCOLM GLADWELL.
LAST SEEN FOUR YEARS AGO, GRAVES WAS AFFLICTED WITH THE SAME TERMINAL ILLNESS THAT TOOK THE LIVES OF HIS WIFE AND CHILDREN.
THOUGH IT WAS WIDELY BELIEVED THAT GRAVES TOOK HIS OWN LIFE AFTER THAT OF HIS PRIVATE DOCTOR'S, THOSE REPORTS WERE OBVIOUSLY INCORRECT.
GRAVES PAID A VISIT TO COLONEL TREVOR'S SISTER, TRACY, A SINGLE MOTHER WITH TWO CHILDREN. IT'S PRESUMED COLONEL TREVOR MAY ALREADY BE DEAD.
IF MY BROTHER WAS MURDERED, IT'S THE **JUSTICE LEAGUE'S FAULT!**
WE'LL BRING YOU UPDATES AS SOON AS WE HAVE THEM.

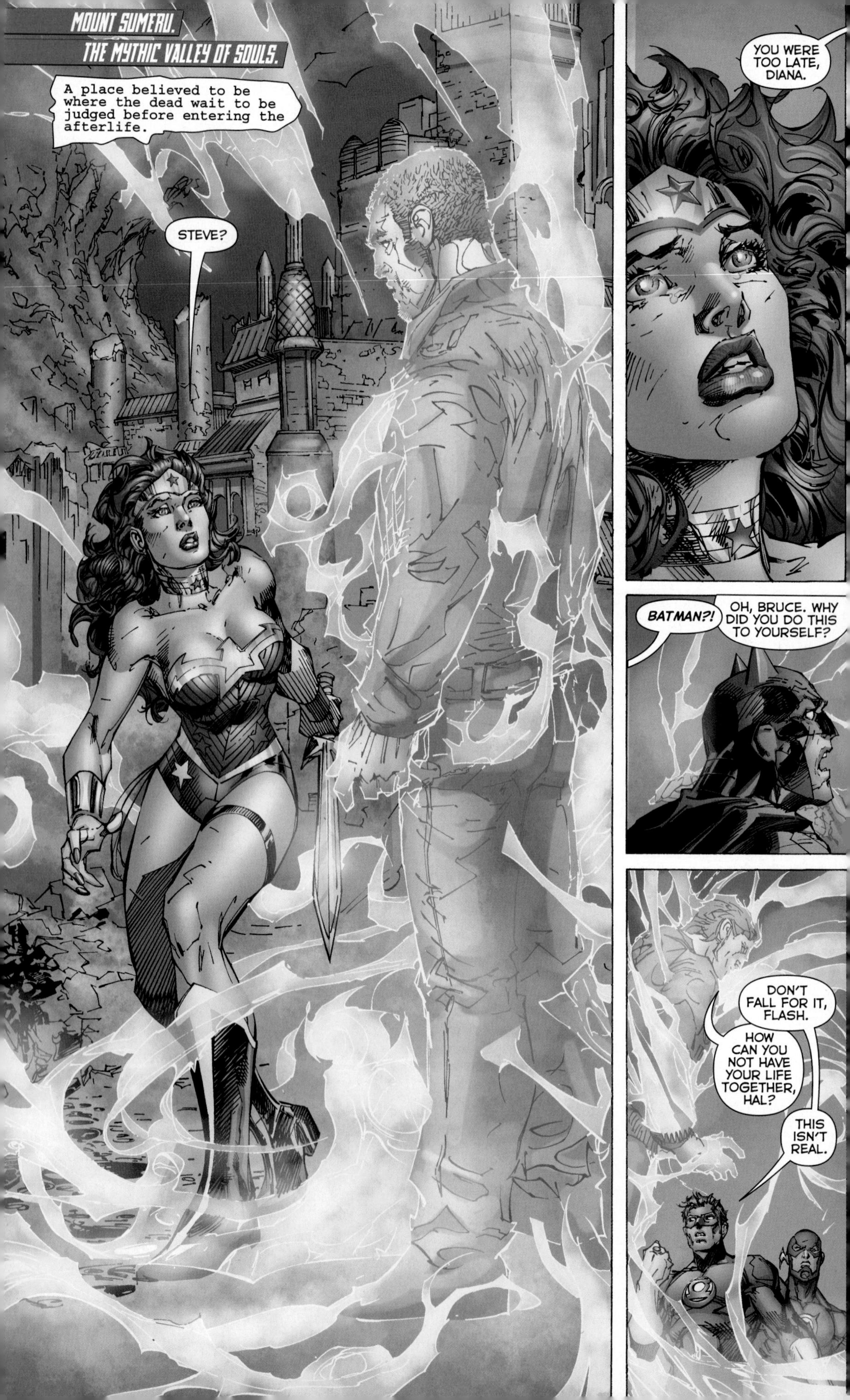
MOUNT SUMERU.
THE MYTHIC VALLEY OF SOULS.
A place believed to be where the dead wait to be judged before entering the afterlife.
STEVE?
YOU WERE TOO LATE, DIANA.
BATMAN?!
OH, BRUCE. WHY DID YOU DO THIS TO YOURSELF?
DON'T FALL FOR IT, FLASH.
HOW CAN YOU NOT HAVE YOUR LIFE TOGETHER, HAL?
THIS ISN'T REAL.

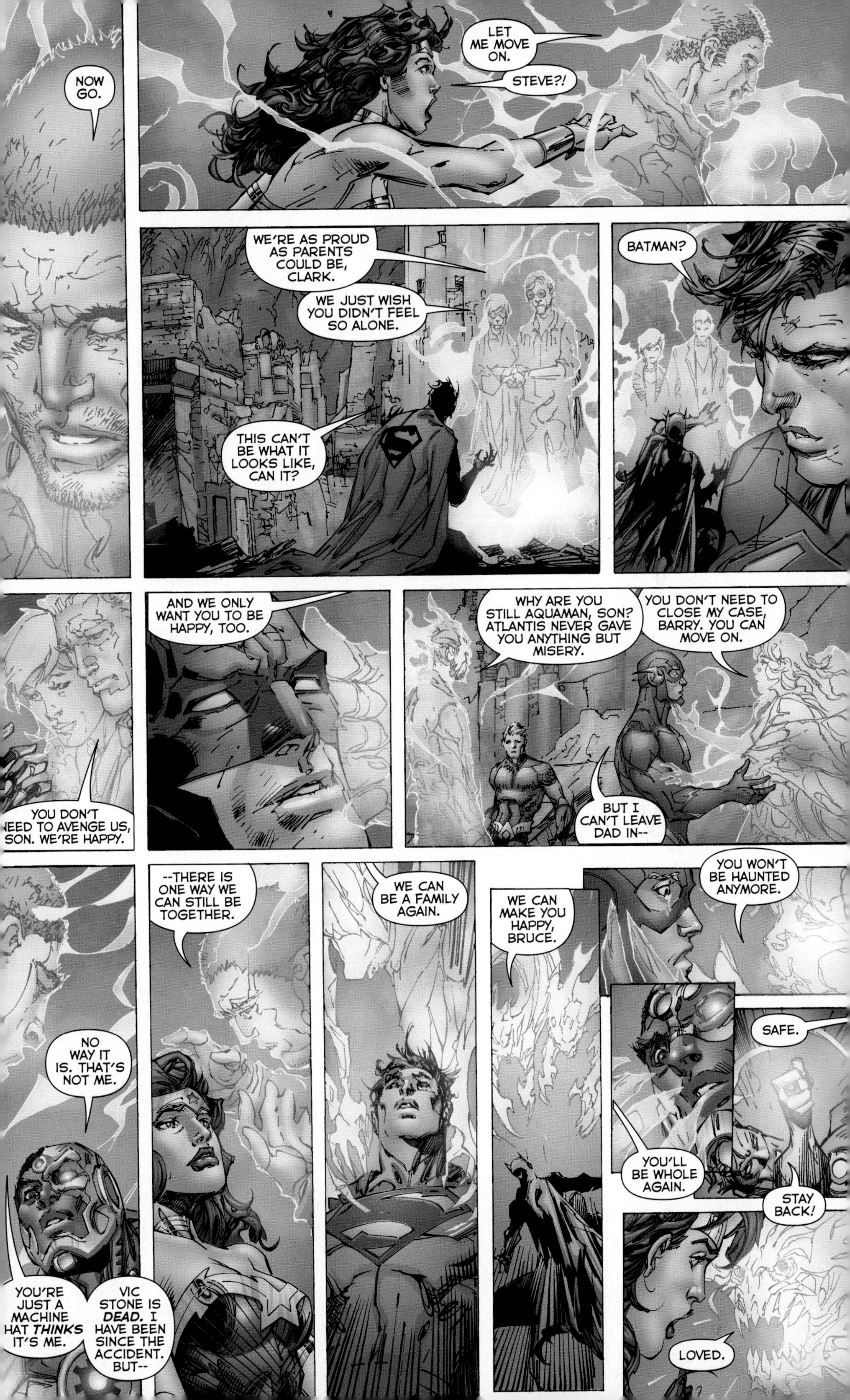
NOW GO.
LET ME MOVE ON.
STEVE?!
WE'RE AS PROUD AS PARENTS COULD BE, CLARK.
WE JUST WISH YOU DIDN'T FEEL SO ALONE.
THIS CAN'T BE WHAT IT LOOKS LIKE, CAN IT?
BATMAN?
AND WE ONLY WANT YOU TO BE HAPPY, TOO.
YOU DON'T NEED TO AVENGE US, SON. WE'RE HAPPY.
WHY ARE YOU STILL AQUAMAN, SON? ATLANTIS NEVER GAVE YOU ANYTHING BUT MISERY.
YOU DON'T NEED TO CLOSE MY CASE, BARRY. YOU CAN MOVE ON.
BUT I CAN'T LEAVE DAD IN--
NO WAY IT IS. THAT'S NOT ME.
YOU'RE JUST A MACHINE HAT *THINKS* IT'S ME.
VIC STONE IS *DEAD*. I HAVE BEEN SINCE THE ACCIDENT. BUT--
--THERE IS ONE WAY WE CAN STILL BE TOGETHER.
WE CAN BE A FAMILY AGAIN.
WE CAN MAKE YOU HAPPY, BRUCE.
YOU WON'T BE HAUNTED ANYMORE.
SAFE.
YOU'LL BE WHOLE AGAIN.
STAY BACK!
LOVED.

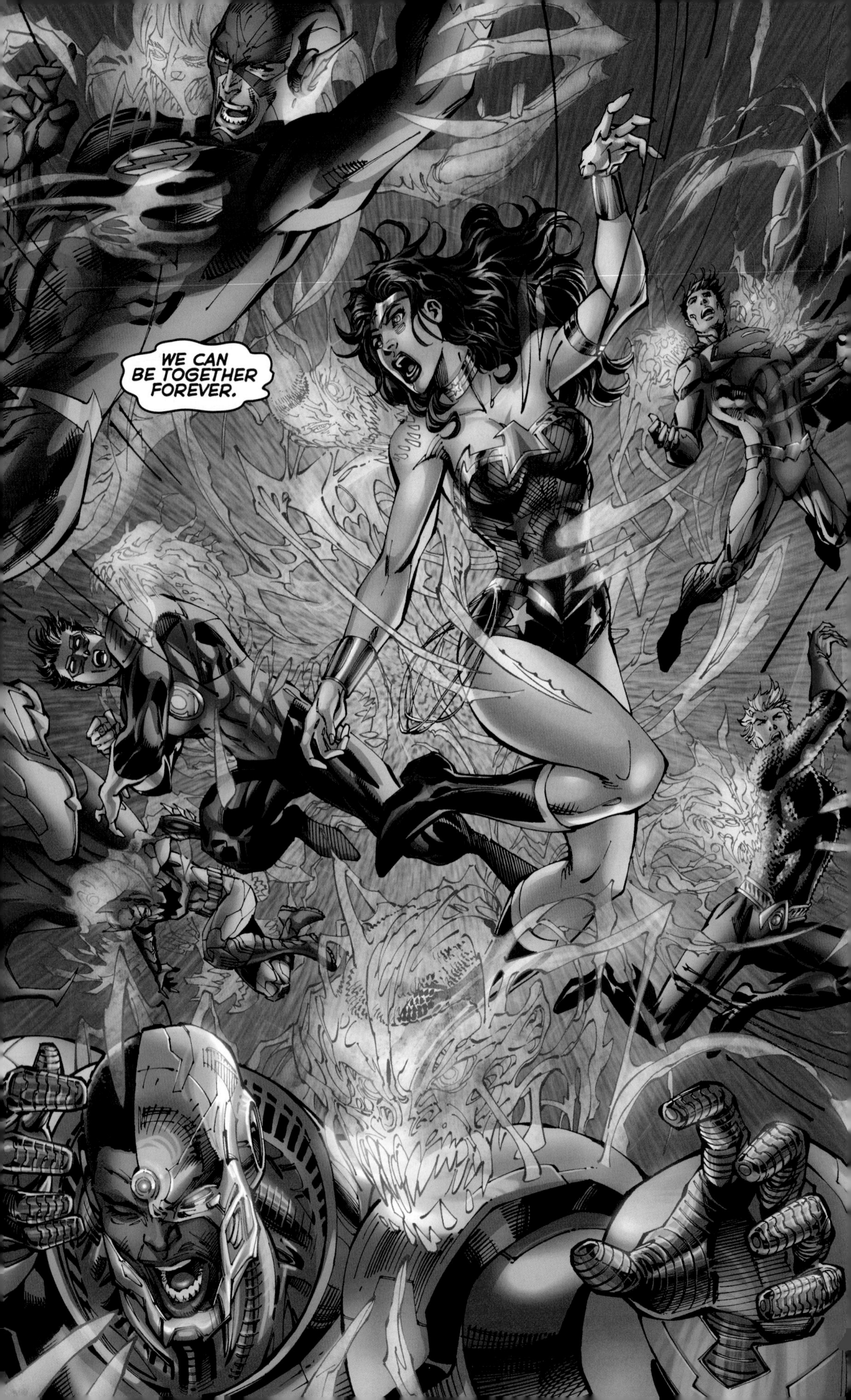
WE CAN BE TOGETHER FOREVER.

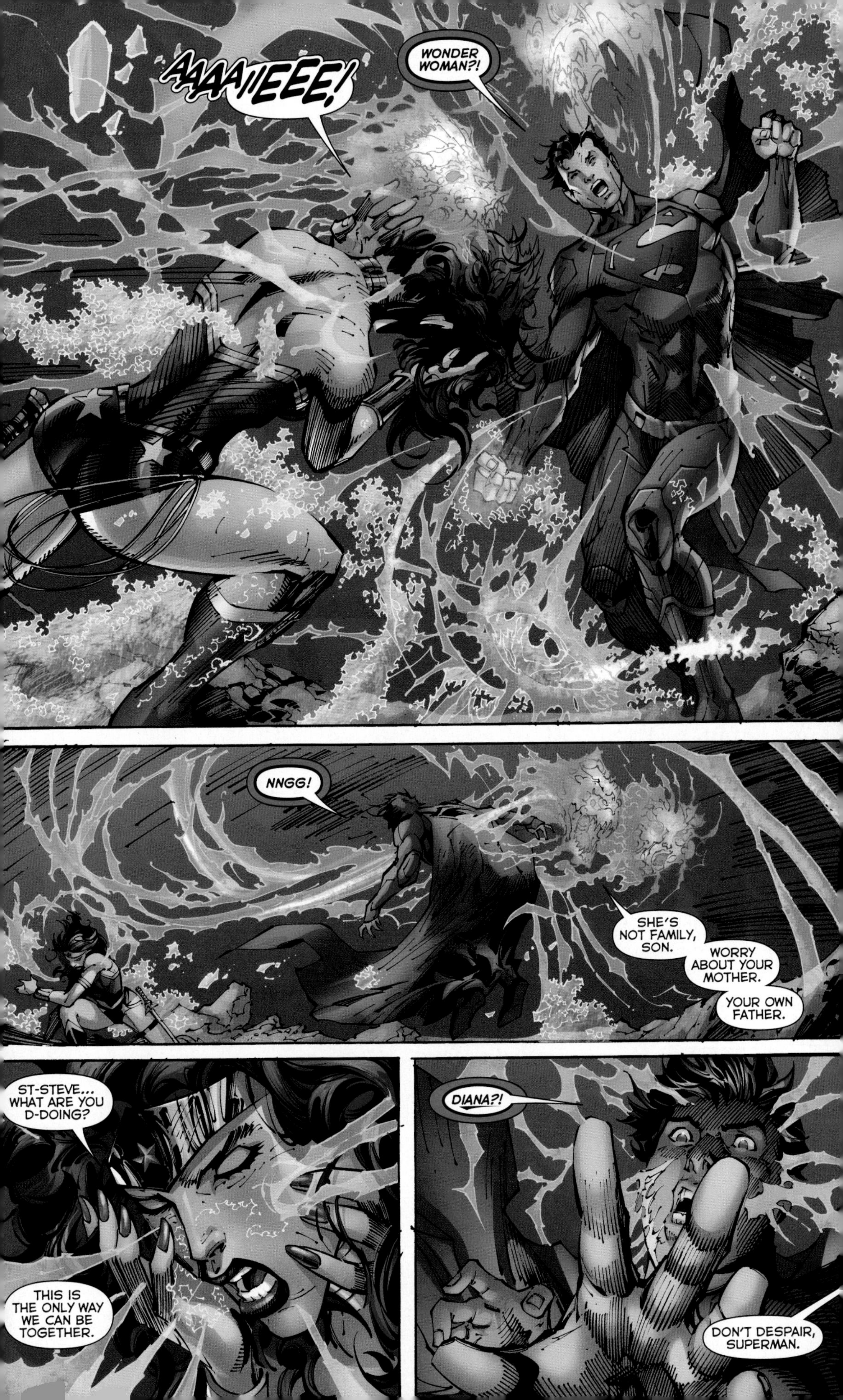

AAAAIIEEEE!
WONDER WOMAN?!
NNGG!
SHE'S NOT FAMILY, SON.
WORRY ABOUT YOUR MOTHER.
YOUR OWN FATHER.
ST-STEVE... WHAT ARE YOU D-DOING?
THIS IS THE ONLY WAY WE CAN BE TOGETHER.
DIANA?!
DON'T DESPAIR, SUPERMAN.

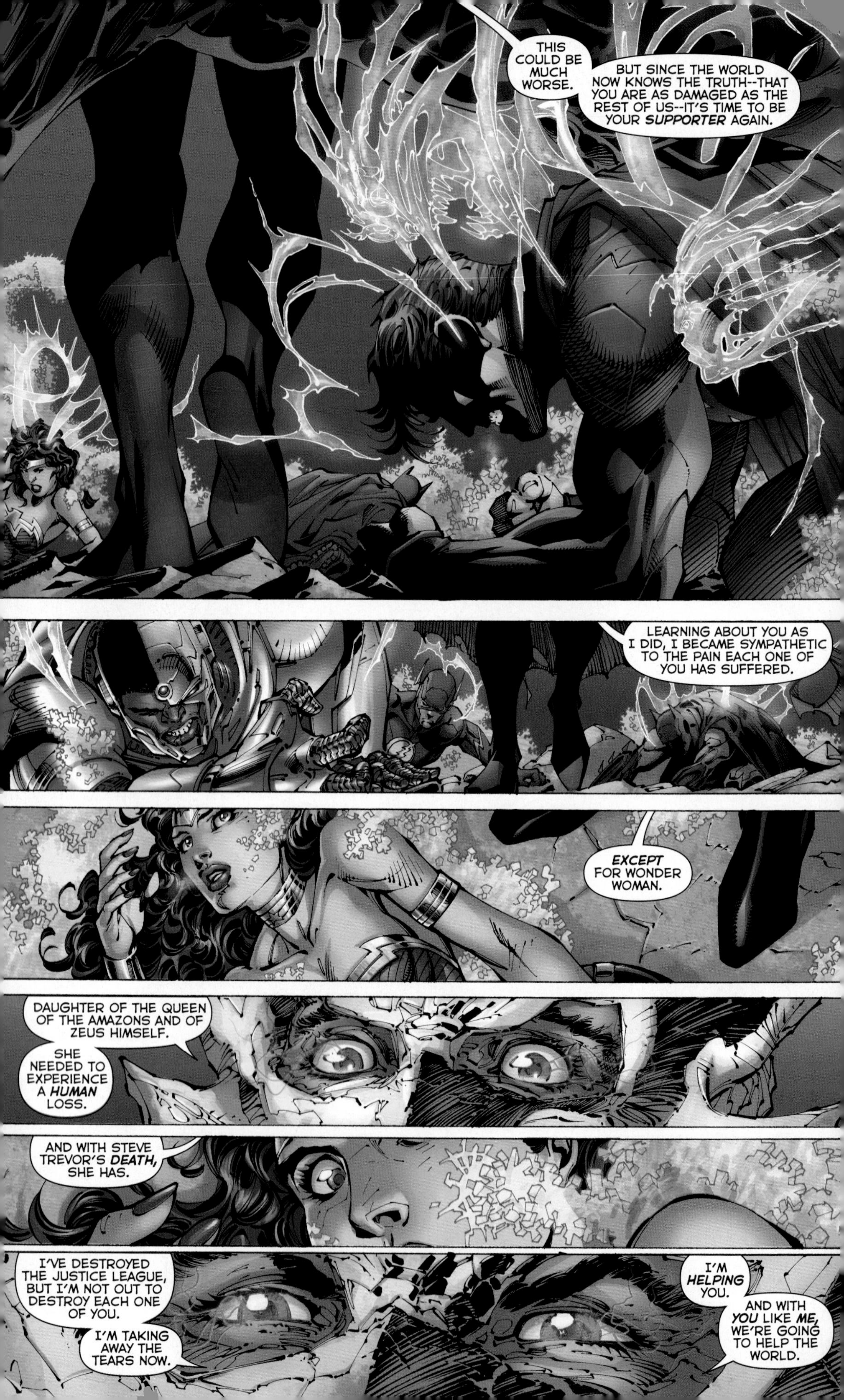

THIS COULD BE MUCH WORSE.
BUT SINCE THE WORLD NOW KNOWS THE TRUTH--THAT YOU ARE AS DAMAGED AS THE REST OF US--IT'S TIME TO BE YOUR *SUPPORTER* AGAIN.
LEARNING ABOUT YOU AS I DID, I BECAME SYMPATHETIC TO THE PAIN EACH ONE OF YOU HAS SUFFERED.
EXCEPT FOR WONDER WOMAN.
DAUGHTER OF THE QUEEN OF THE AMAZONS AND OF ZEUS HIMSELF.
SHE NEEDED TO EXPERIENCE A *HUMAN* LOSS.
AND WITH STEVE TREVOR'S *DEATH,* SHE HAS.
I'VE DESTROYED THE JUSTICE LEAGUE, BUT I'M NOT OUT TO DESTROY EACH ONE OF YOU.
I'M TAKING AWAY THE TEARS NOW.
I'M *HELPING* YOU.
AND WITH *YOU* LIKE *ME,* WE'RE GOING TO HELP THE WORLD.

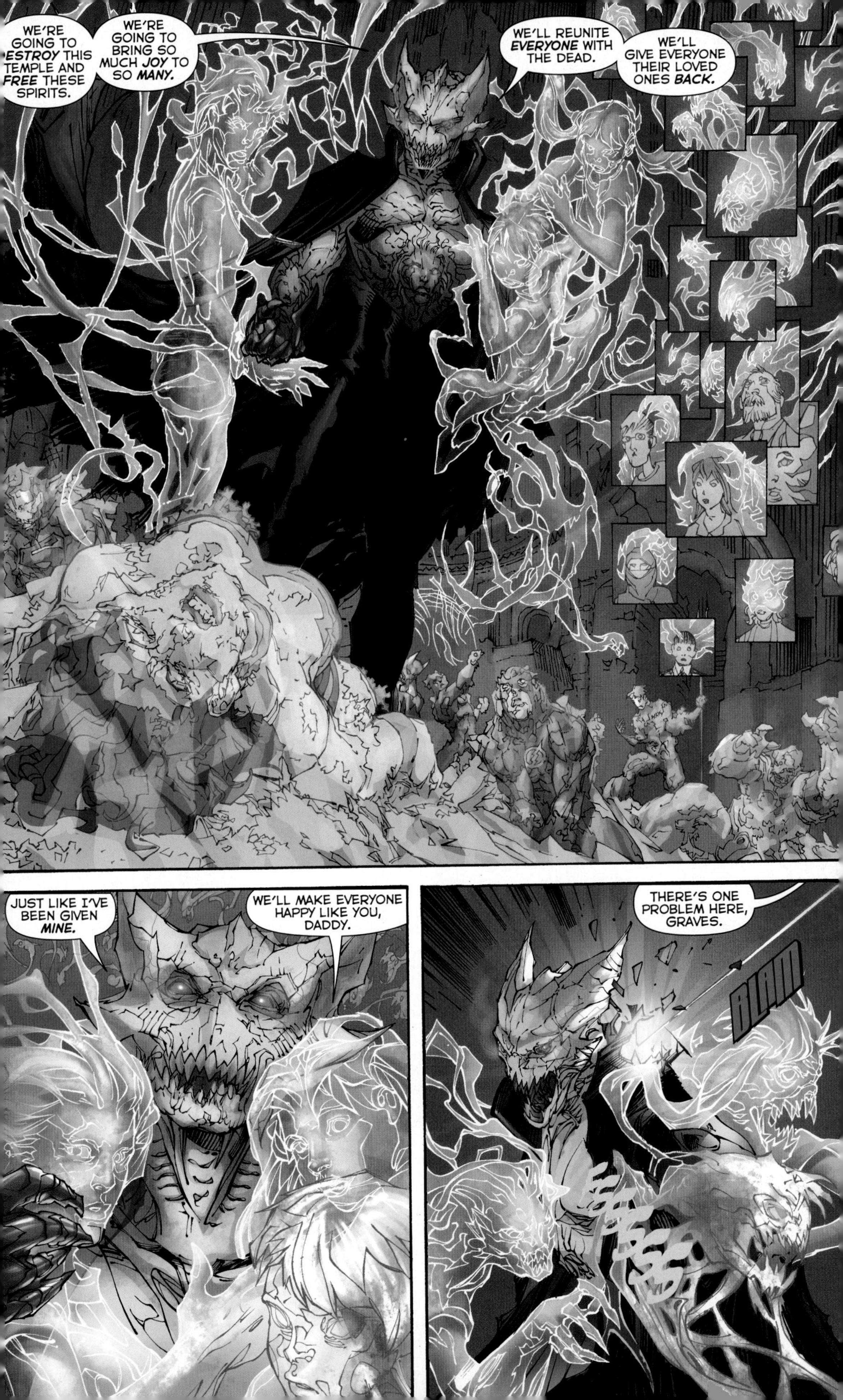
WE'RE GOING TO ESTROY THIS TEMPLE AND FREE THESE SPIRITS.
WE'RE GOING TO BRING SO MUCH JOY TO SO MANY.
WE'LL REUNITE EVERYONE WITH THE DEAD.
WE'LL GIVE EVERYONE THEIR LOVED ONES BACK.
JUST LIKE I'VE BEEN GIVEN MINE.
WE'LL MAKE EVERYONE HAPPY LIKE YOU, DADDY.
THERE'S ONE PROBLEM HERE, GRAVES.
BLAM

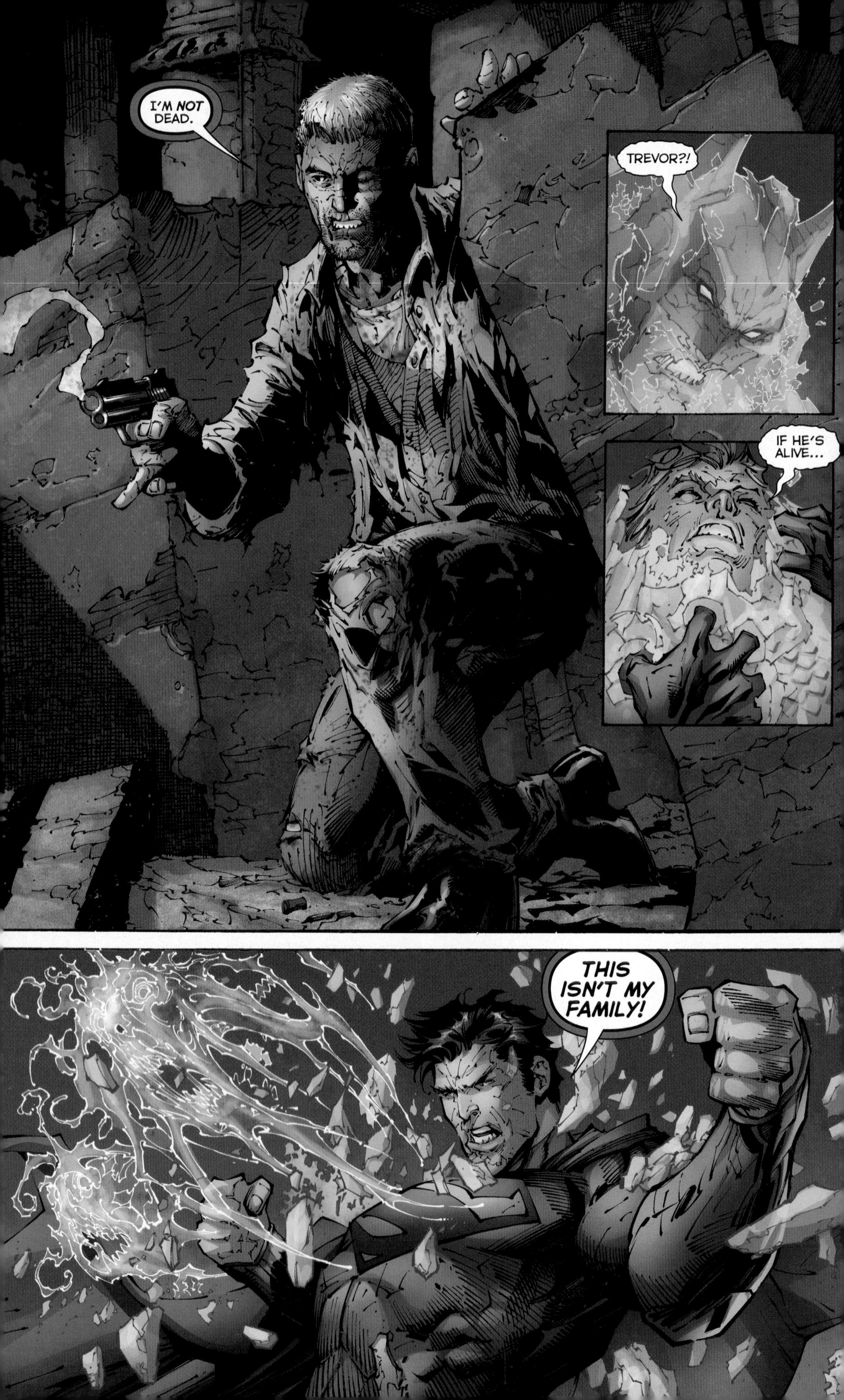
I'M NOT DEAD.
TREVOR?!
IF HE'S ALIVE...
THIS ISN'T MY FAMILY!

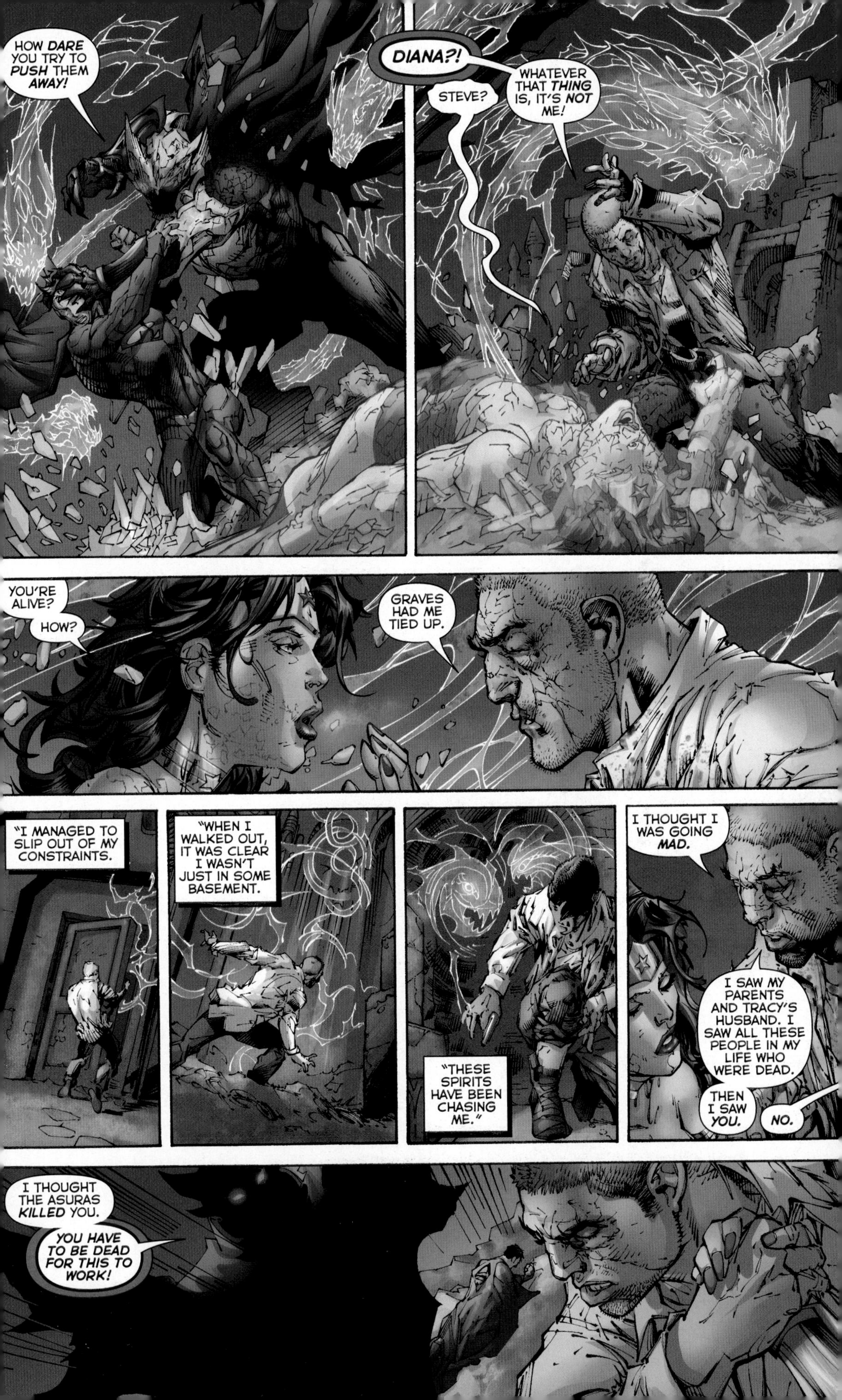

HOW DARE YOU TRY TO PUSH THEM AWAY!
DIANA?!
STEVE?
WHATEVER THAT THING IS, IT'S NOT ME!
YOU'RE ALIVE?
HOW?
GRAVES HAD ME TIED UP.
"I MANAGED TO SLIP OUT OF MY CONSTRAINTS.
"WHEN I WALKED OUT, IT WAS CLEAR I WASN'T JUST IN SOME BASEMENT.
"THESE SPIRITS HAVE BEEN CHASING ME."
I THOUGHT I WAS GOING MAD.
I SAW MY PARENTS AND TRACY'S HUSBAND. I SAW ALL THESE PEOPLE IN MY LIFE WHO WERE DEAD.
THEN I SAW YOU.
NO.
I THOUGHT THE ASURAS KILLED YOU.
YOU HAVE TO BE DEAD FOR THIS TO WORK!

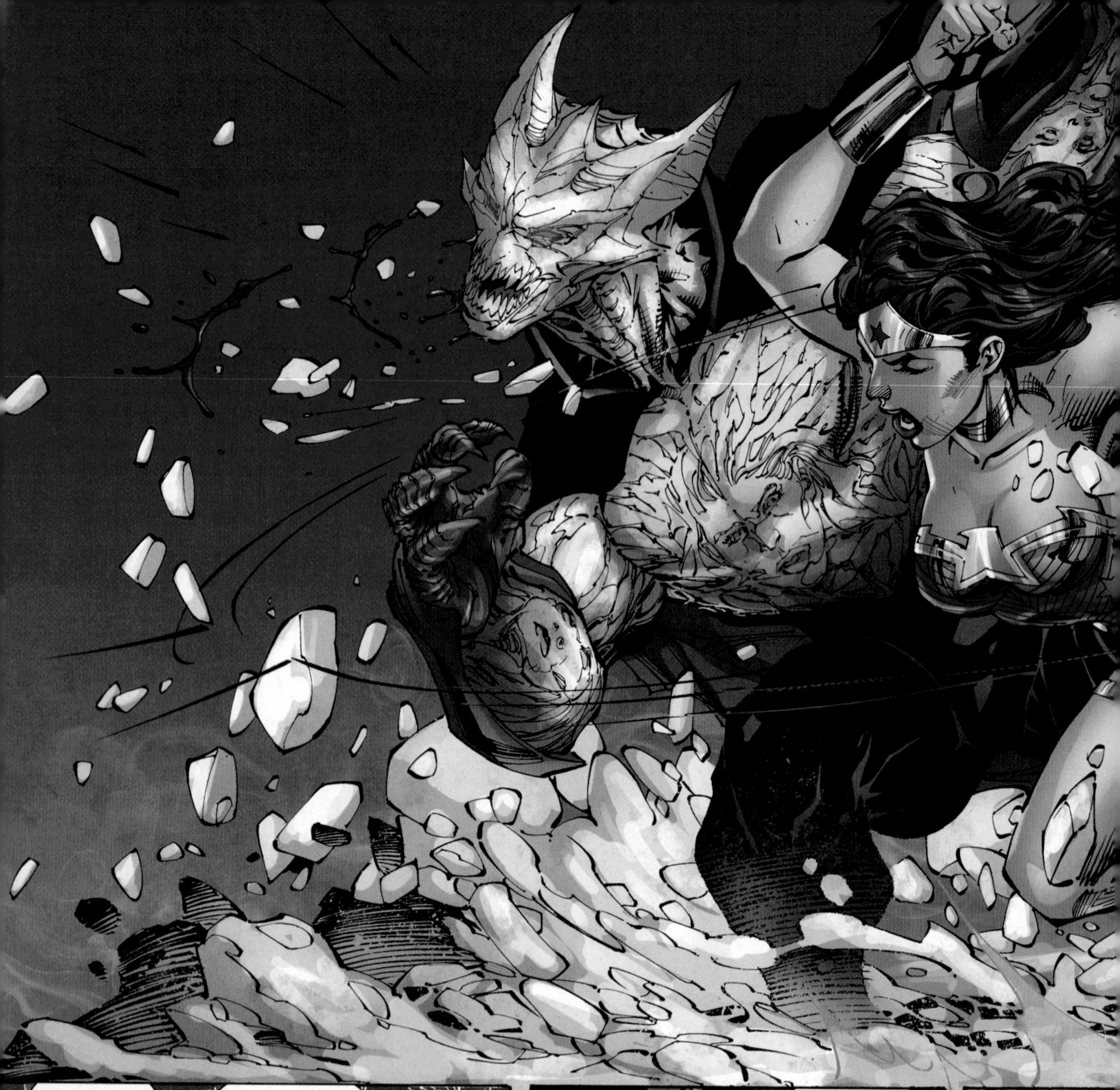
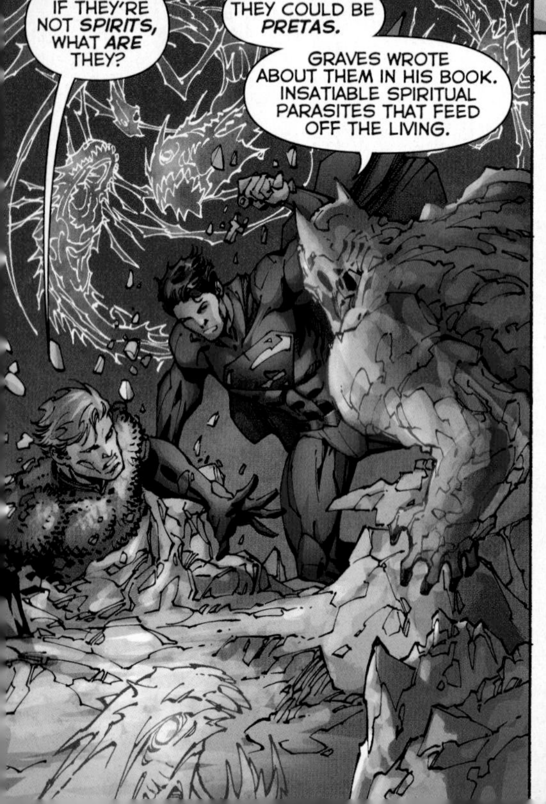
IF THEY'RE NOT *SPIRITS,* WHAT *ARE* THEY?
THEY COULD BE *PRETAS.*
GRAVES WROTE ABOUT THEM IN HIS BOOK. INSATIABLE SPIRITUAL PARASITES THAT FEED OFF THE LIVING.
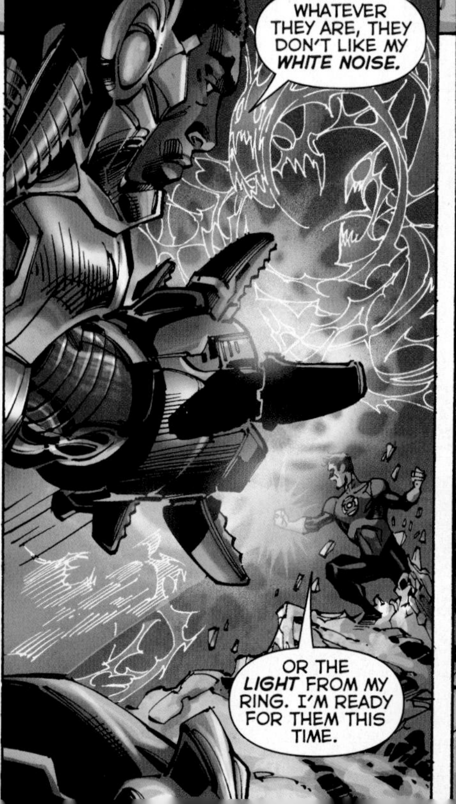
WHATEVER THEY ARE, THEY DON'T LIKE MY *WHITE NOISE.*
OR THE *LIGHT* FROM MY RING. I'M READY FOR THEM THIS TIME.
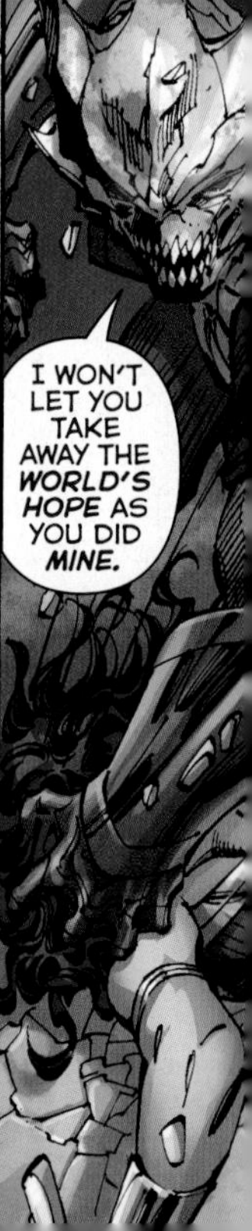
I WON'T LET YOU TAKE AWAY THE *WORLD'S HOPE* AS YOU DID *MINE.*

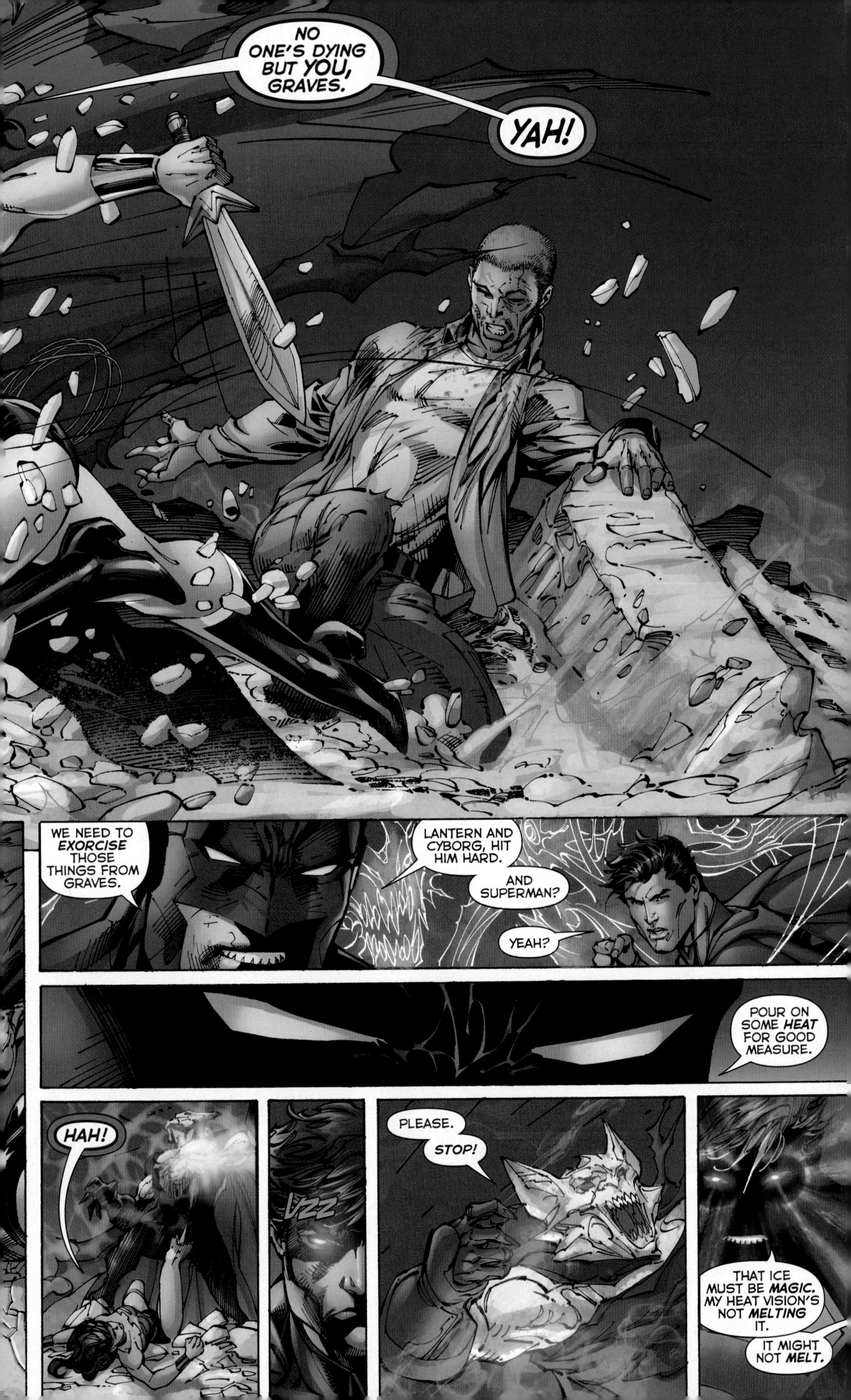
NO ONE'S DYING BUT YOU, GRAVES.
YAH!
WE NEED TO EXORCISE THOSE THINGS FROM GRAVES.
LANTERN AND CYBORG, HIT HIM HARD.
AND SUPERMAN?
YEAH?
POUR ON SOME HEAT FOR GOOD MEASURE.
HAH!
PLEASE.
STOP!
THAT ICE MUST BE MAGIC. MY HEAT VISION'S NOT MELTING IT.
IT MIGHT NOT MELT.

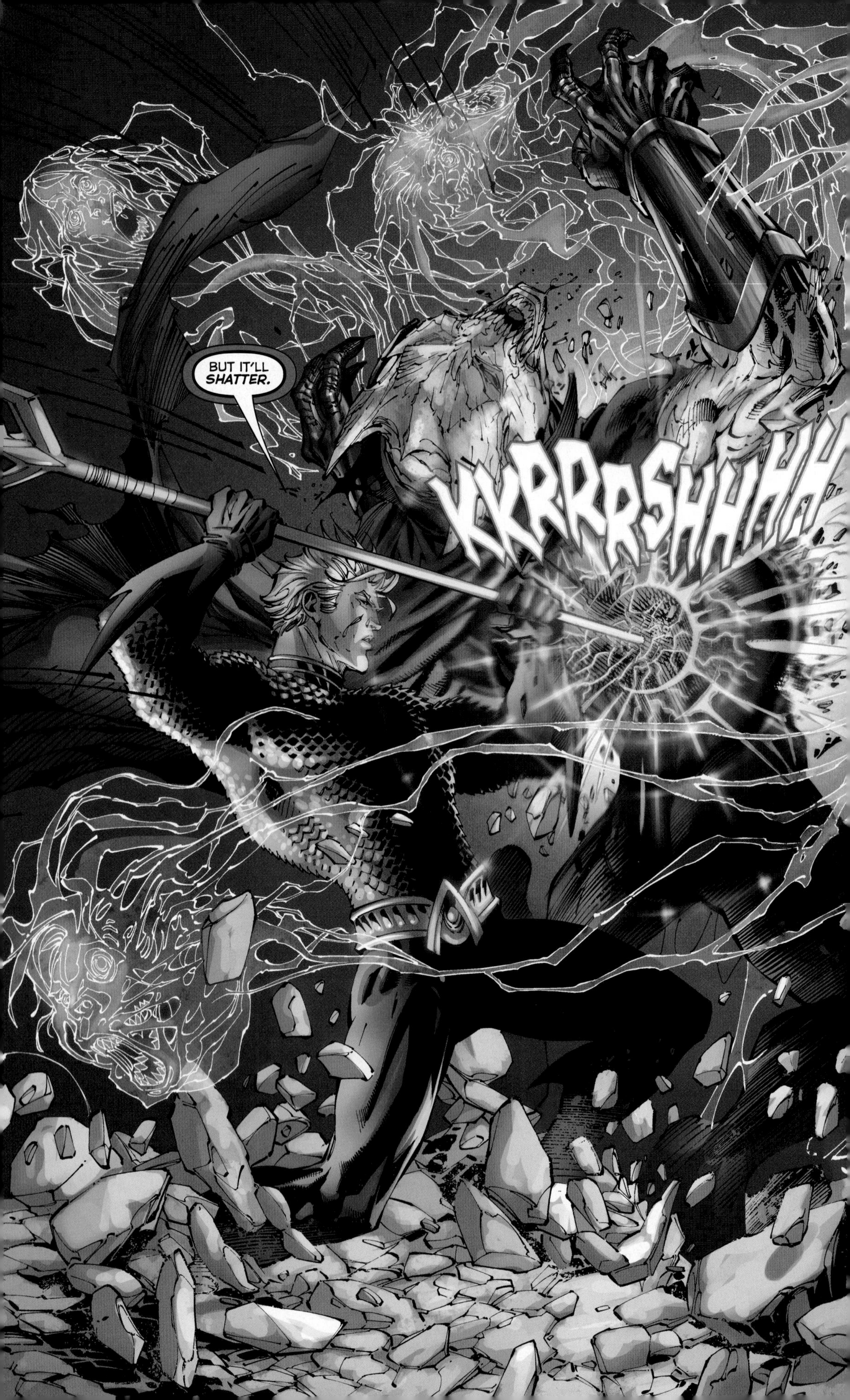
BUT IT'LL SHATTER.
KKRRRSHHHH

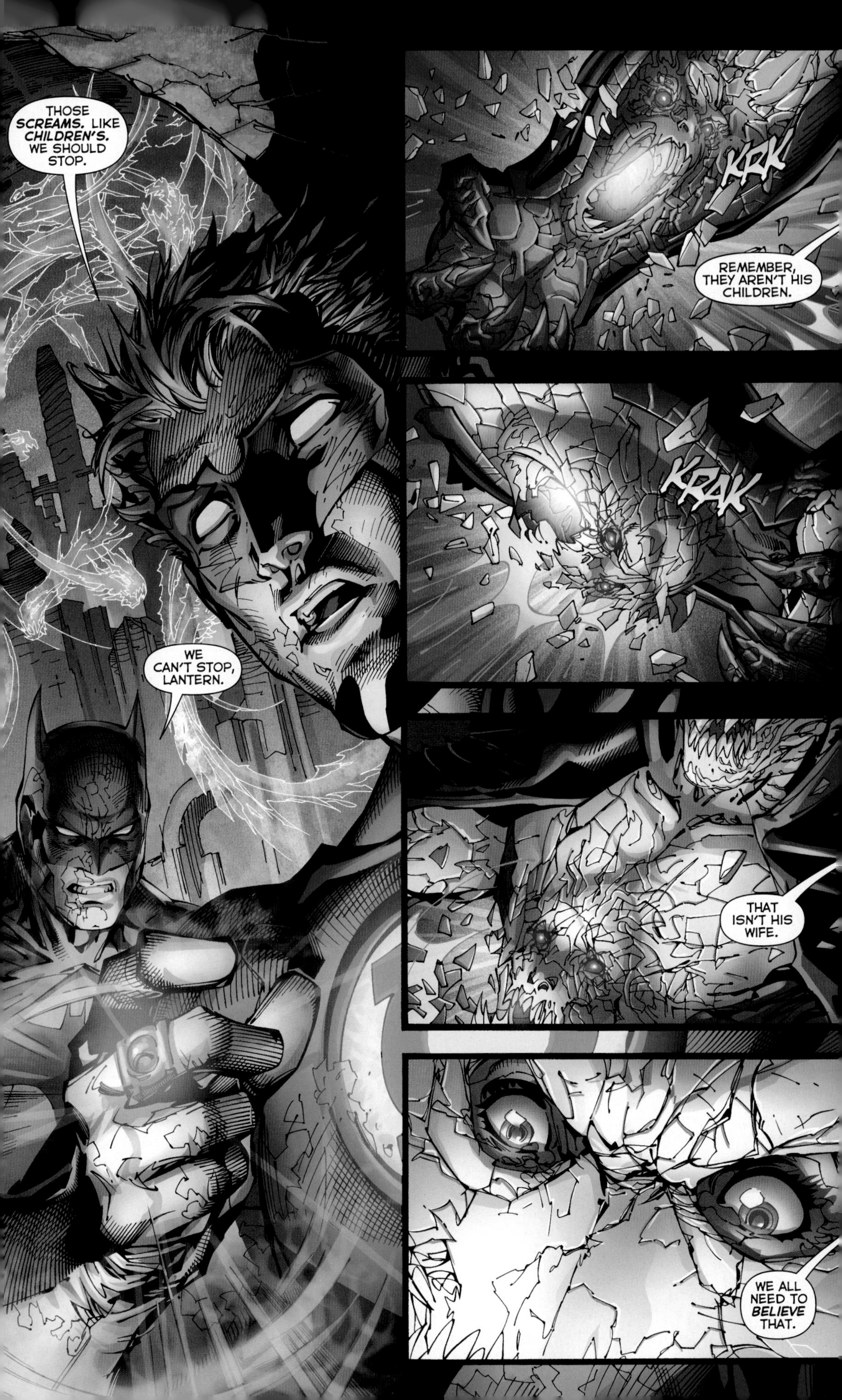
THOSE SCREAMS. LIKE CHILDREN'S. WE SHOULD STOP.
KRK
REMEMBER, THEY AREN'T HIS CHILDREN.
KRAK
WE CAN'T STOP, LANTERN.
THAT ISN'T HIS WIFE.
WE ALL NEED TO *BELIEVE* THAT.

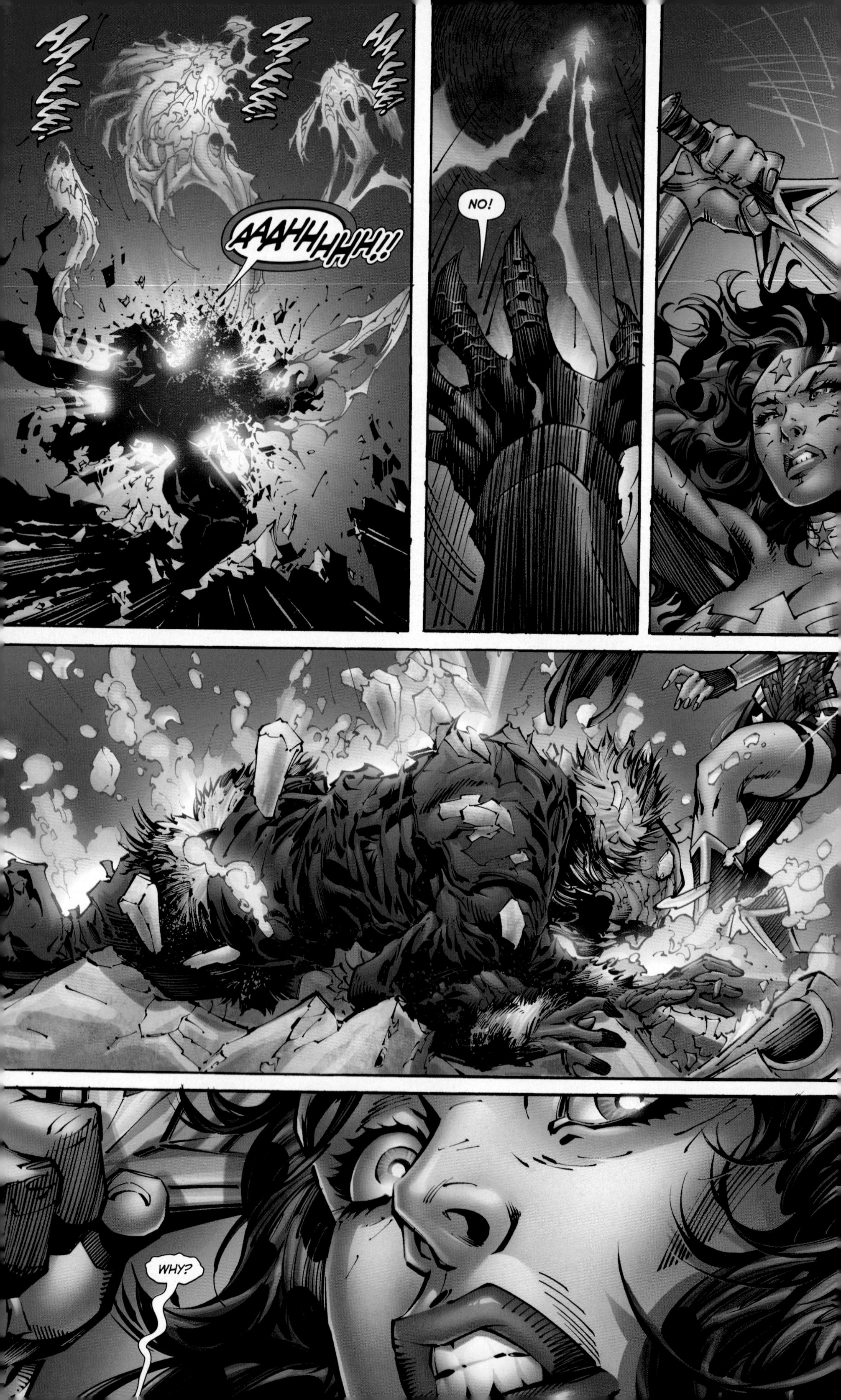
AAIEEEE!
AAIEEEE!
AAIEEEE!
AAAHHHHH!!
NO!
WHY?

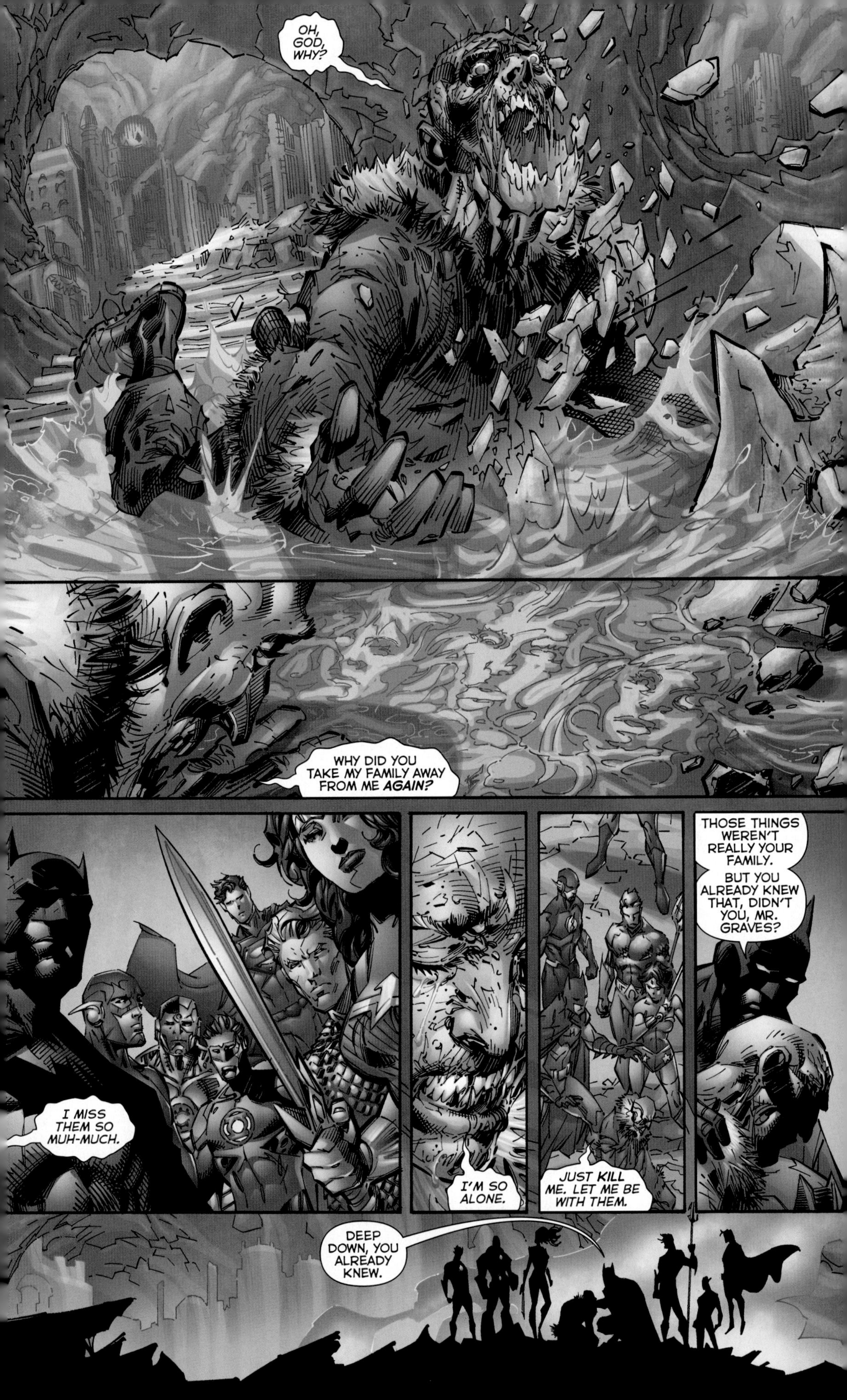
OH, GOD, WHY?
WHY DID YOU TAKE MY FAMILY AWAY FROM ME AGAIN?
I MISS THEM SO MUH-MUCH.
I'M SO ALONE.
JUST KILL ME. LET ME BE WITH THEM.
THOSE THINGS WEREN'T REALLY YOUR FAMILY.
BUT YOU ALREADY KNEW THAT, DIDN'T YOU, MR. GRAVES?
DEEP DOWN, YOU ALREADY KNEW.

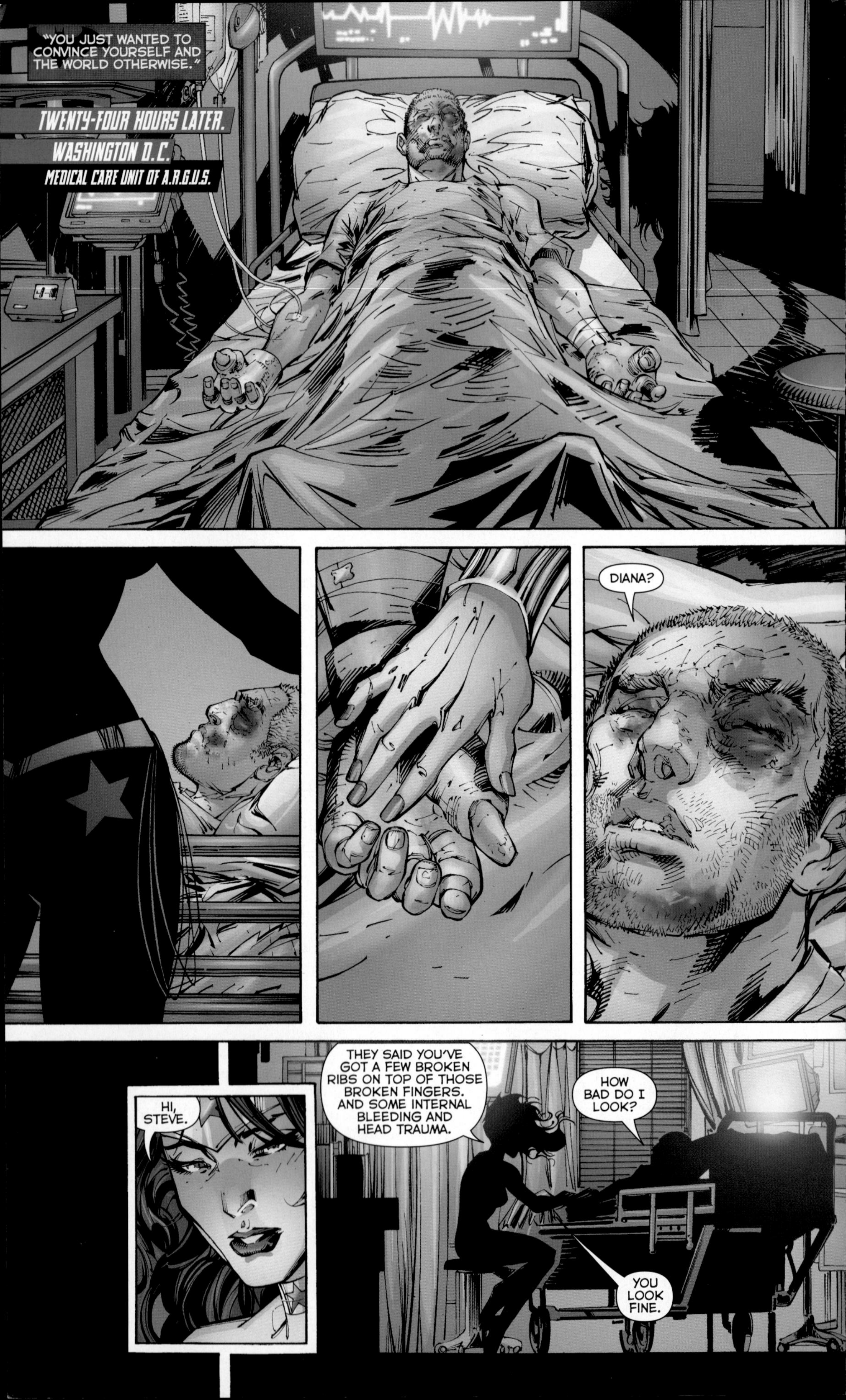
"YOU JUST WANTED TO CONVINCE YOURSELF AND THE WORLD OTHERWISE."
TWENTY-FOUR HOURS LATER.
WASHINGTON D.C.
MEDICAL CARE UNIT OF A.R.G.U.S.
DIANA?
HI, STEVE.
THEY SAID YOU'VE GOT A FEW BROKEN RIBS ON TOP OF THOSE BROKEN FINGERS. AND SOME INTERNAL BLEEDING AND HEAD TRAUMA.
HOW BAD DO I LOOK?
YOU LOOK FINE.

THIS WAS MY FAULT.

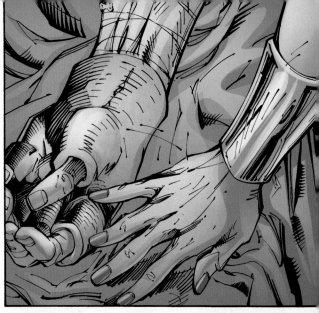

YOU'RE NOT DOING THIS *AGAIN*, ARE YOU?

I THOUGHT YOU WERE FAR ENOUGH AWAY, BUT I SHOULD'VE KNOWN BETTER. AFTER WHAT HAPPENED TO *BARBARA*--

WHAT HAPPENED TO *BARBARA MINERVA* WASN'T YOUR FAULT, EITHER. THE *CHEETAH*--

YOU NEARLY *DIED*, STEVE.

I'VE NEARLY DIED A HUNDRED TIMES, DIANA. I'M A GOVERNMENT AGENT.

AND I WAS OUT IN THE FIELD PROTECTING THE WORLD *LONG* BEFORE I MET YOU.

BUT *THIS* TIME YOU WERE TORTURED AND BEATEN AND ALMOST *KILLED* BECAUSE OF *OUR* RELATIONSHIP.

OUR *RELATIONSHIP? WHAT* RELATIONSHIP?! YOU *ENDED* IT. YOU THREW IT *AWAY*.

TOO CLOSE? THE ONLY TIME I'VE SEEN YOU IN OVER A *YEAR* IS ON A *COMPUTER*.

YOU'RE STILL TOO CLOSE.

WHY ARE YOU STILL WORKING WITH THE LEAGUE?

BECAUSE THE LEAGUE *NEEDS ME!*

I PROTECT THE LEAGUE FROM ALL THE RED TAPE AND FEAR MONGERING THAT FESTERS IN WASHINGTON!

JUST LIKE I'VE PROTECTED *YOU* FROM IT SINCE THE DAY YOU CAME HERE!

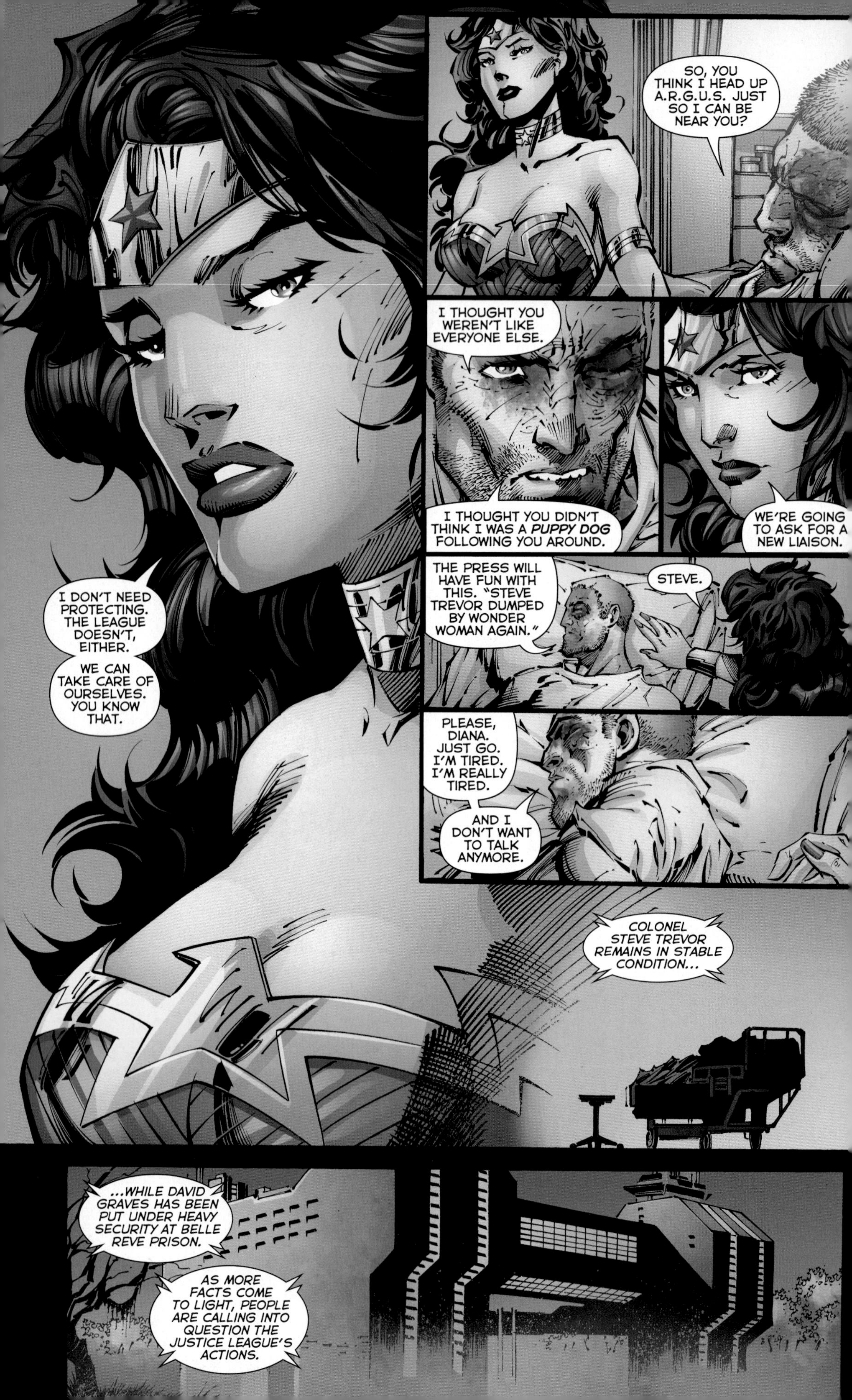
SO, YOU THINK I HEAD UP A.R.G.U.S. JUST SO I CAN BE NEAR YOU?
I THOUGHT YOU WEREN'T LIKE EVERYONE ELSE.
I THOUGHT YOU DIDN'T THINK I WAS A *PUPPY DOG* FOLLOWING YOU AROUND.
WE'RE GOING TO ASK FOR A NEW LIAISON.
THE PRESS WILL HAVE FUN WITH THIS. "STEVE TREVOR DUMPED BY WONDER WOMAN AGAIN."
STEVE.
PLEASE, DIANA. JUST GO. I'M TIRED. I'M REALLY TIRED.
AND I DON'T WANT TO TALK ANYMORE.
I DON'T NEED PROTECTING. THE LEAGUE DOESN'T, EITHER.
WE CAN TAKE CARE OF OURSELVES. YOU KNOW THAT.
COLONEL STEVE TREVOR REMAINS IN STABLE CONDITION...
...WHILE DAVID GRAVES HAS BEEN PUT UNDER HEAVY SECURITY AT BELLE REVE PRISON.
AS MORE FACTS COME TO LIGHT, PEOPLE ARE CALLING INTO QUESTION THE JUSTICE LEAGUE'S ACTIONS.

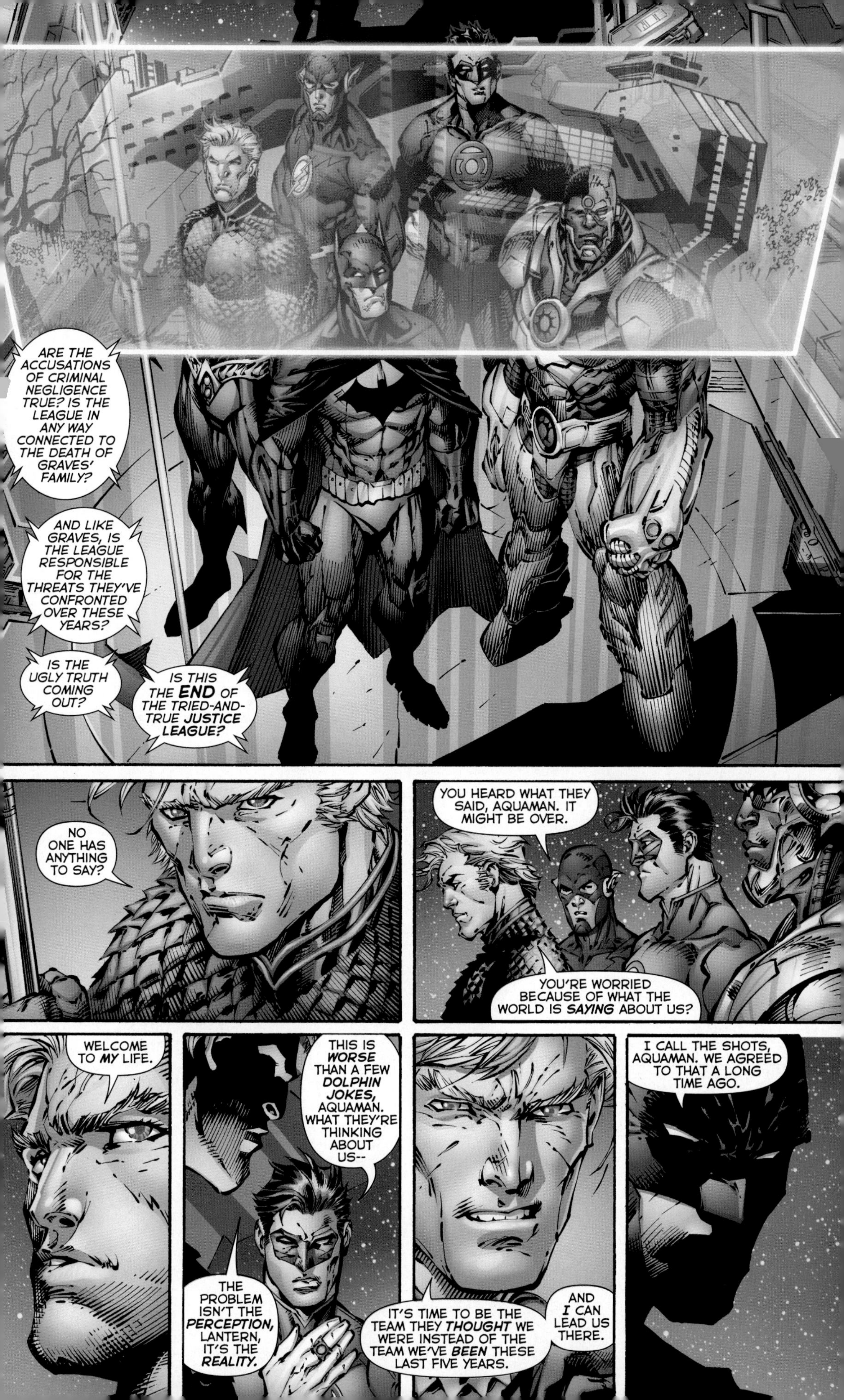
ARE THE ACCUSATIONS OF CRIMINAL NEGLIGENCE TRUE? IS THE LEAGUE IN ANY WAY CONNECTED TO THE DEATH OF GRAVES' FAMILY?
AND LIKE GRAVES, IS THE LEAGUE RESPONSIBLE FOR THE THREATS THEY'VE CONFRONTED OVER THESE YEARS?
IS THE UGLY TRUTH COMING OUT?
IS THIS THE **END** OF THE TRIED-AND-TRUE **JUSTICE LEAGUE?**
NO ONE HAS ANYTHING TO SAY?
YOU HEARD WHAT THEY SAID, AQUAMAN. IT MIGHT BE OVER.
YOU'RE WORRIED BECAUSE OF WHAT THE WORLD IS ***SAYING*** ABOUT US?
WELCOME TO ***MY*** LIFE.
THIS IS ***WORSE*** THAN A FEW ***DOLPHIN JOKES***, AQUAMAN. WHAT THEY'RE THINKING ABOUT US--
THE PROBLEM ISN'T THE ***PERCEPTION***, LANTERN, IT'S THE ***REALITY.***
IT'S TIME TO BE THE TEAM THEY ***THOUGHT*** WE WERE INSTEAD OF THE TEAM WE'VE ***BEEN*** THESE LAST FIVE YEARS.
AND ***I*** CAN LEAD US THERE.
I CALL THE SHOTS, AQUAMAN. WE AGREED TO THAT A LONG TIME AGO.

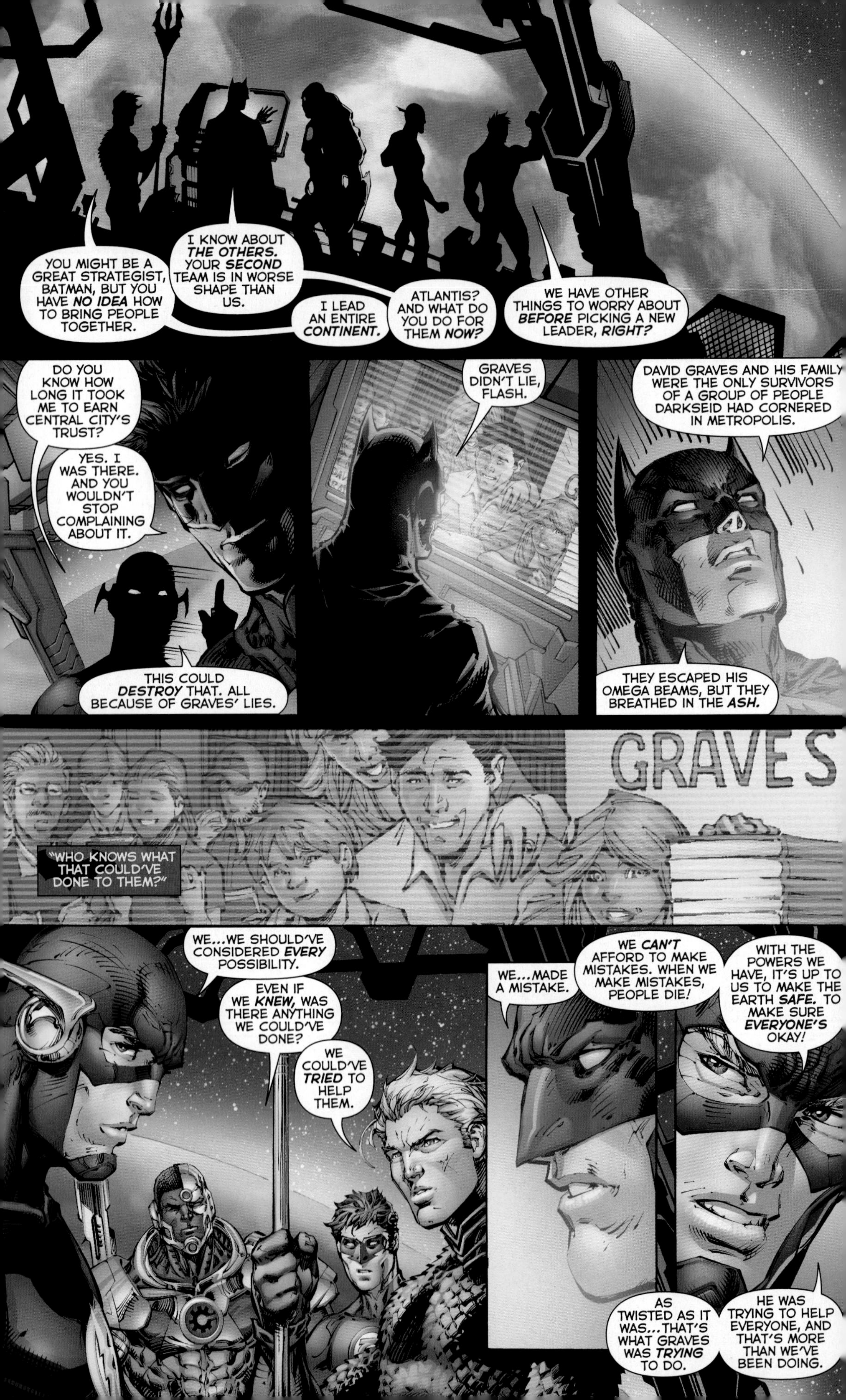
YOU MIGHT BE A GREAT STRATEGIST, BATMAN, BUT YOU HAVE NO IDEA HOW TO BRING PEOPLE TOGETHER.
I KNOW ABOUT THE OTHERS. YOUR SECOND TEAM IS IN WORSE SHAPE THAN US.
I LEAD AN ENTIRE CONTINENT.
ATLANTIS? AND WHAT DO YOU DO FOR THEM NOW?
WE HAVE OTHER THINGS TO WORRY ABOUT BEFORE PICKING A NEW LEADER, RIGHT?
DO YOU KNOW HOW LONG IT TOOK ME TO EARN CENTRAL CITY'S TRUST?
YES. I WAS THERE. AND YOU WOULDN'T STOP COMPLAINING ABOUT IT.
THIS COULD DESTROY THAT. ALL BECAUSE OF GRAVES' LIES.
GRAVES DIDN'T LIE, FLASH.
DAVID GRAVES AND HIS FAMILY WERE THE ONLY SURVIVORS OF A GROUP OF PEOPLE DARKSEID HAD CORNERED IN METROPOLIS.
THEY ESCAPED HIS OMEGA BEAMS, BUT THEY BREATHED IN THE ASH.
GRAVES
"WHO KNOWS WHAT THAT COULD'VE DONE TO THEM?"
WE...WE SHOULD'VE CONSIDERED EVERY POSSIBILITY.
EVEN IF WE KNEW, WAS THERE ANYTHING WE COULD'VE DONE?
WE COULD'VE TRIED TO HELP THEM.
WE...MADE A MISTAKE.
WE CAN'T AFFORD TO MAKE MISTAKES. WHEN WE MAKE MISTAKES, PEOPLE DIE!
WITH THE POWERS WE HAVE, IT'S UP TO US TO MAKE THE EARTH SAFE. TO MAKE SURE EVERYONE'S OKAY!
AS TWISTED AS IT WAS...THAT'S WHAT GRAVES WAS TRYING TO DO.
HE WAS TRYING TO HELP EVERYONE, AND THAT'S MORE THAN WE'VE BEEN DOING.

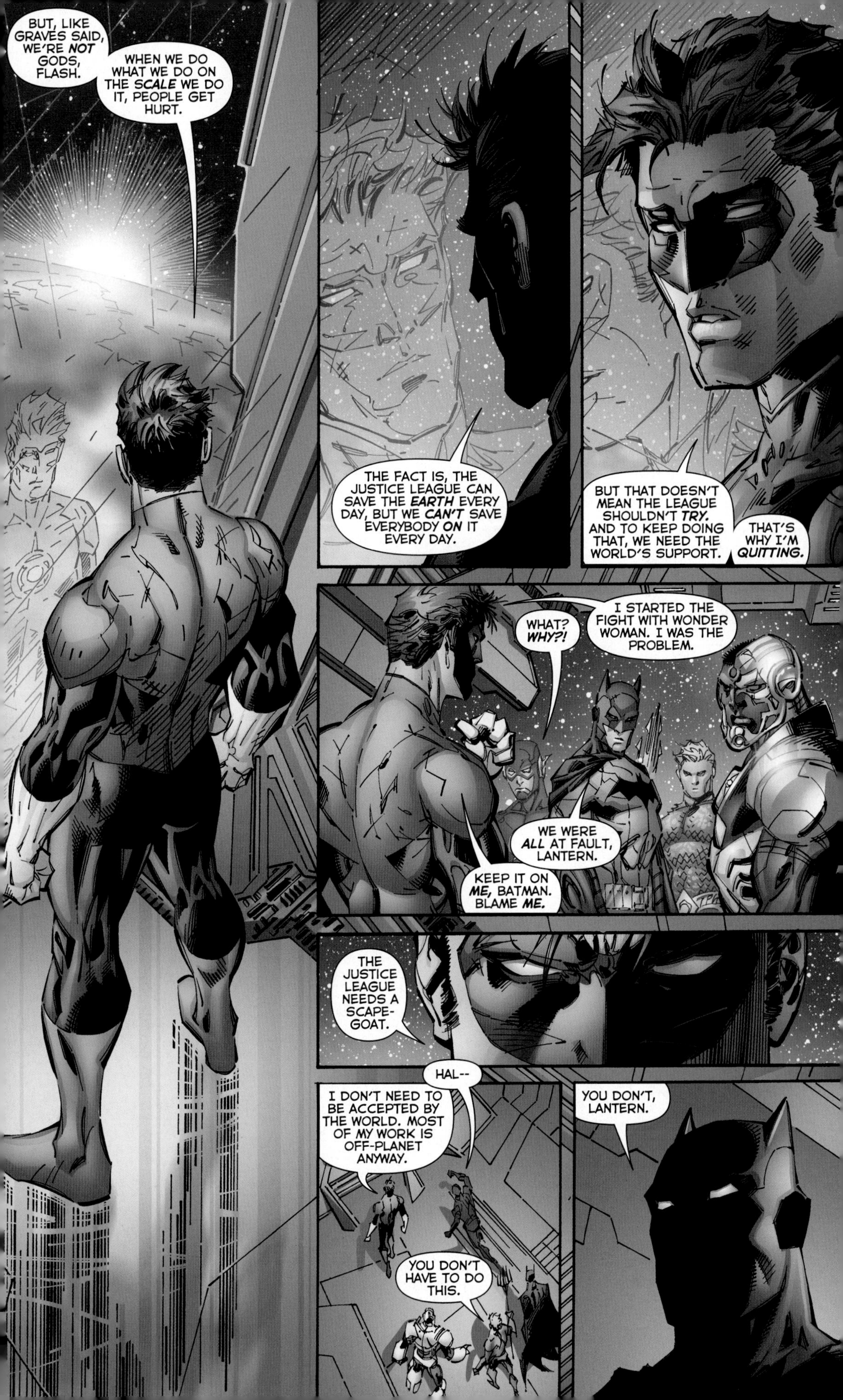
BUT, LIKE GRAVES SAID, WE'RE NOT GODS, FLASH.
WHEN WE DO WHAT WE DO ON THE SCALE WE DO IT, PEOPLE GET HURT.
THE FACT IS, THE JUSTICE LEAGUE CAN SAVE THE EARTH EVERY DAY, BUT WE CAN'T SAVE EVERYBODY ON IT EVERY DAY.
BUT THAT DOESN'T MEAN THE LEAGUE SHOULDN'T TRY. AND TO KEEP DOING THAT, WE NEED THE WORLD'S SUPPORT.
THAT'S WHY I'M QUITTING.
WHAT? WHY?!
I STARTED THE FIGHT WITH WONDER WOMAN. I WAS THE PROBLEM.
WE WERE ALL AT FAULT, LANTERN.
KEEP IT ON ME, BATMAN. BLAME ME.
THE JUSTICE LEAGUE NEEDS A SCAPE-GOAT.
HAL--
I DON'T NEED TO BE ACCEPTED BY THE WORLD. MOST OF MY WORK IS OFF-PLANET ANYWAY.
YOU DON'T HAVE TO DO THIS.
YOU DON'T, LANTERN.

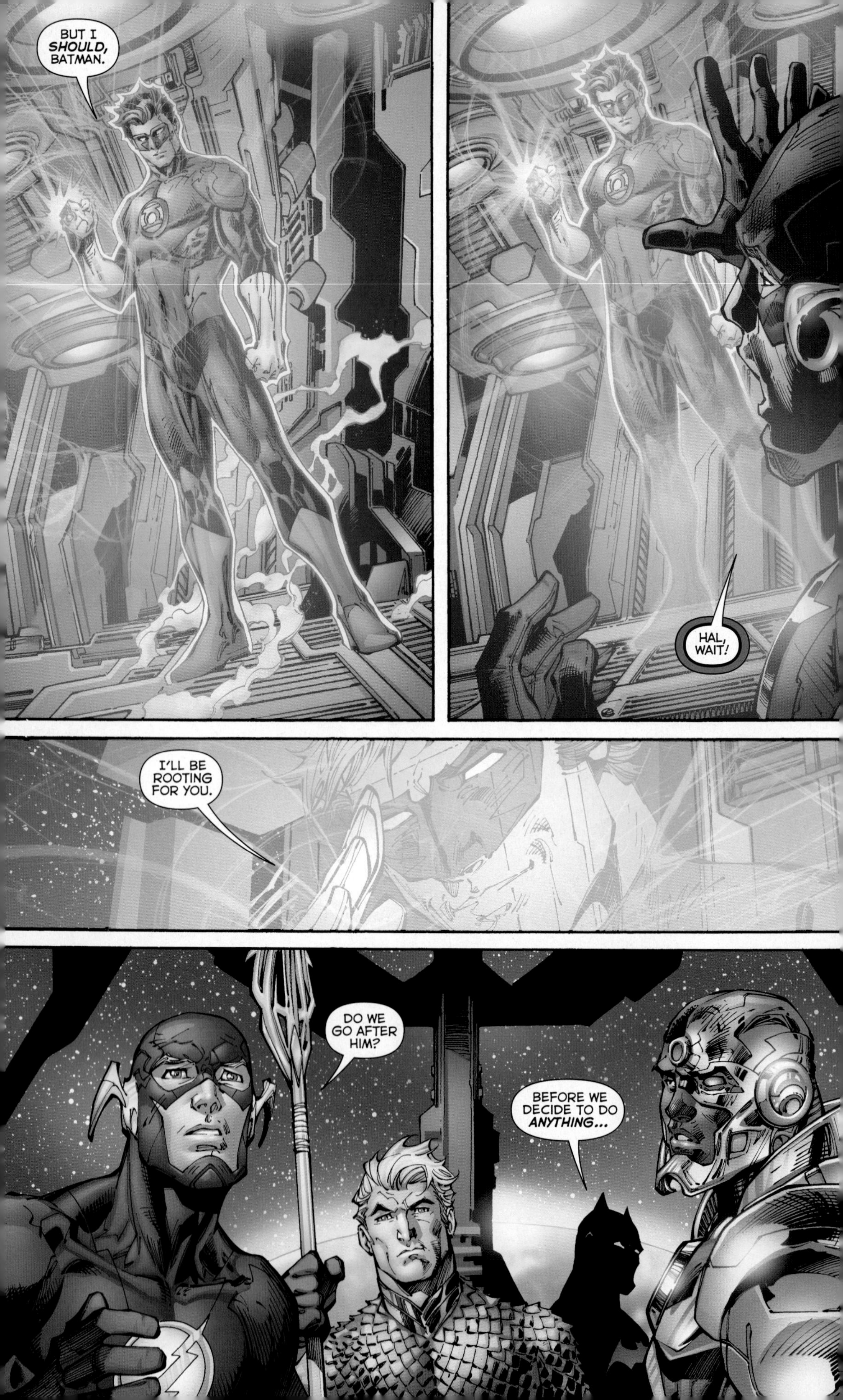
BUT I SHOULD, BATMAN.
HAL, WAIT!
I'LL BE ROOTING FOR YOU.
DO WE GO AFTER HIM?
BEFORE WE DECIDE TO DO ANYTHING...

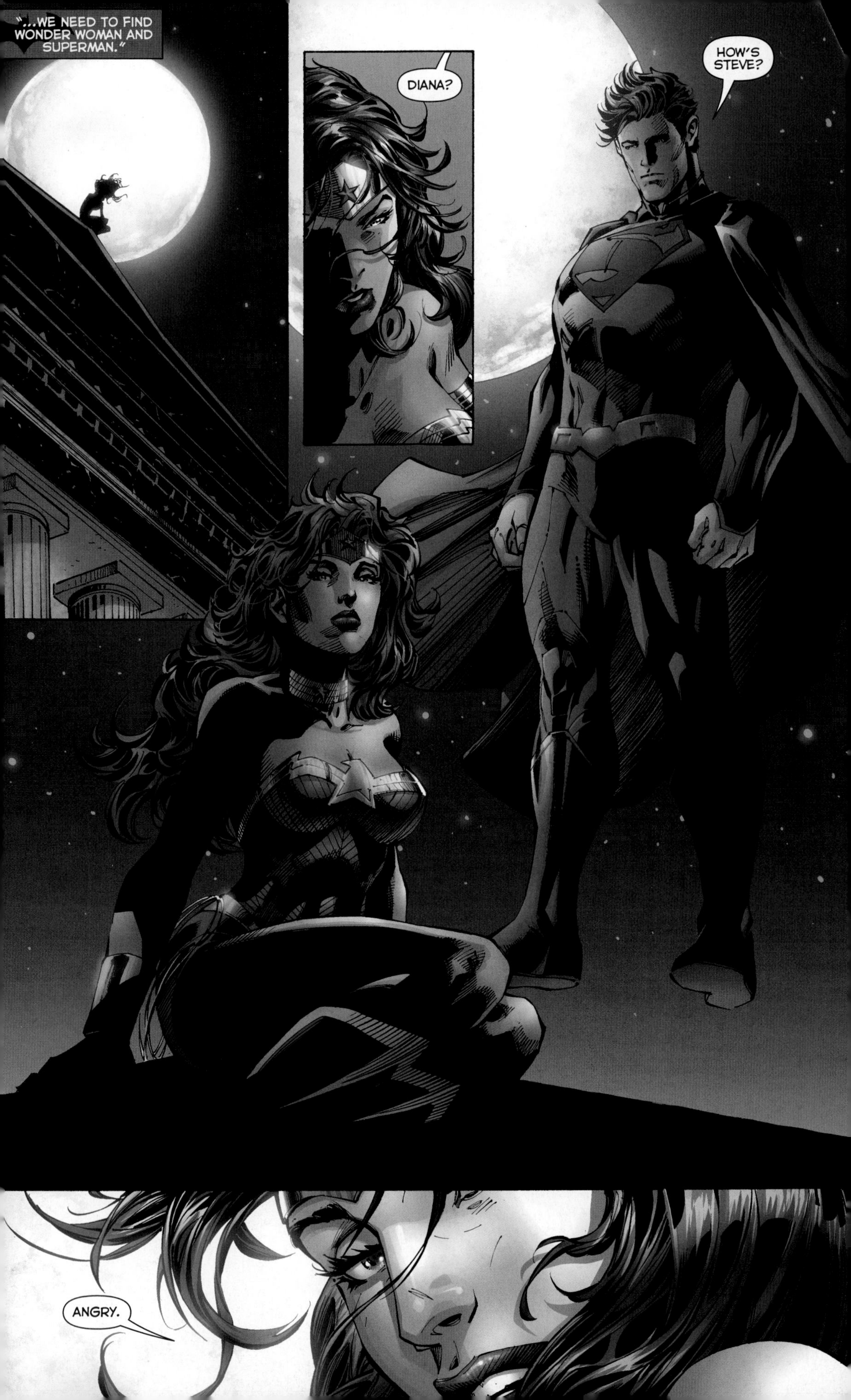
"...WE NEED TO FIND WONDER WOMAN AND SUPERMAN."
DIANA?
HOW'S STEVE?
ANGRY.

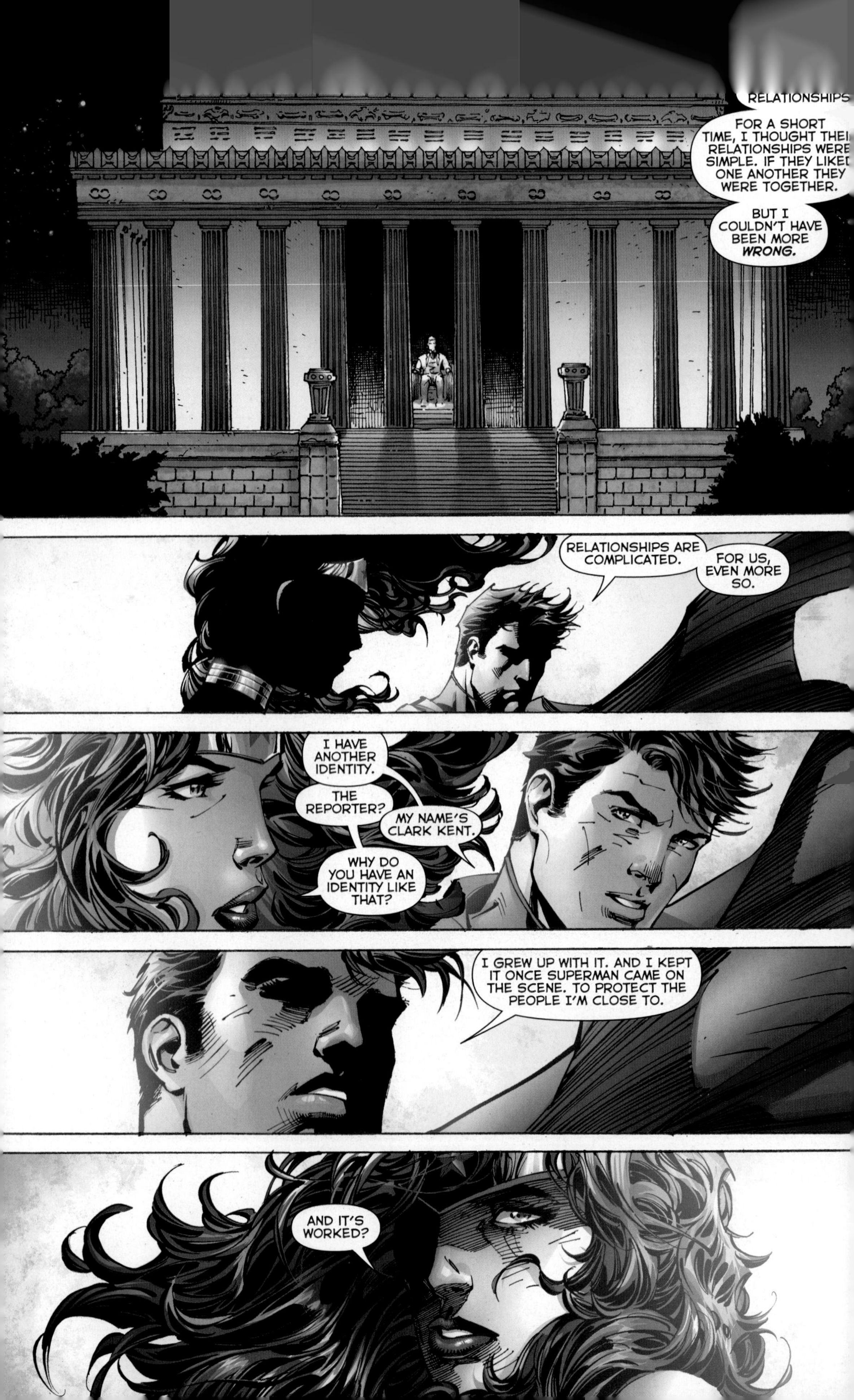

RELATIONSHIPS
FOR A SHORT TIME, I THOUGHT THEI RELATIONSHIPS WERE SIMPLE. IF THEY LIKED ONE ANOTHER THEY WERE TOGETHER.
BUT I COULDN'T HAVE BEEN MORE WRONG.
RELATIONSHIPS ARE COMPLICATED.
FOR US, EVEN MORE SO.
I HAVE ANOTHER IDENTITY.
MY NAME'S CLARK KENT.
THE REPORTER?
WHY DO YOU HAVE AN IDENTITY LIKE THAT?
I GREW UP WITH IT. AND I KEPT IT ONCE SUPERMAN CAME ON THE SCENE. TO PROTECT THE PEOPLE I'M CLOSE TO.
AND IT'S WORKED?

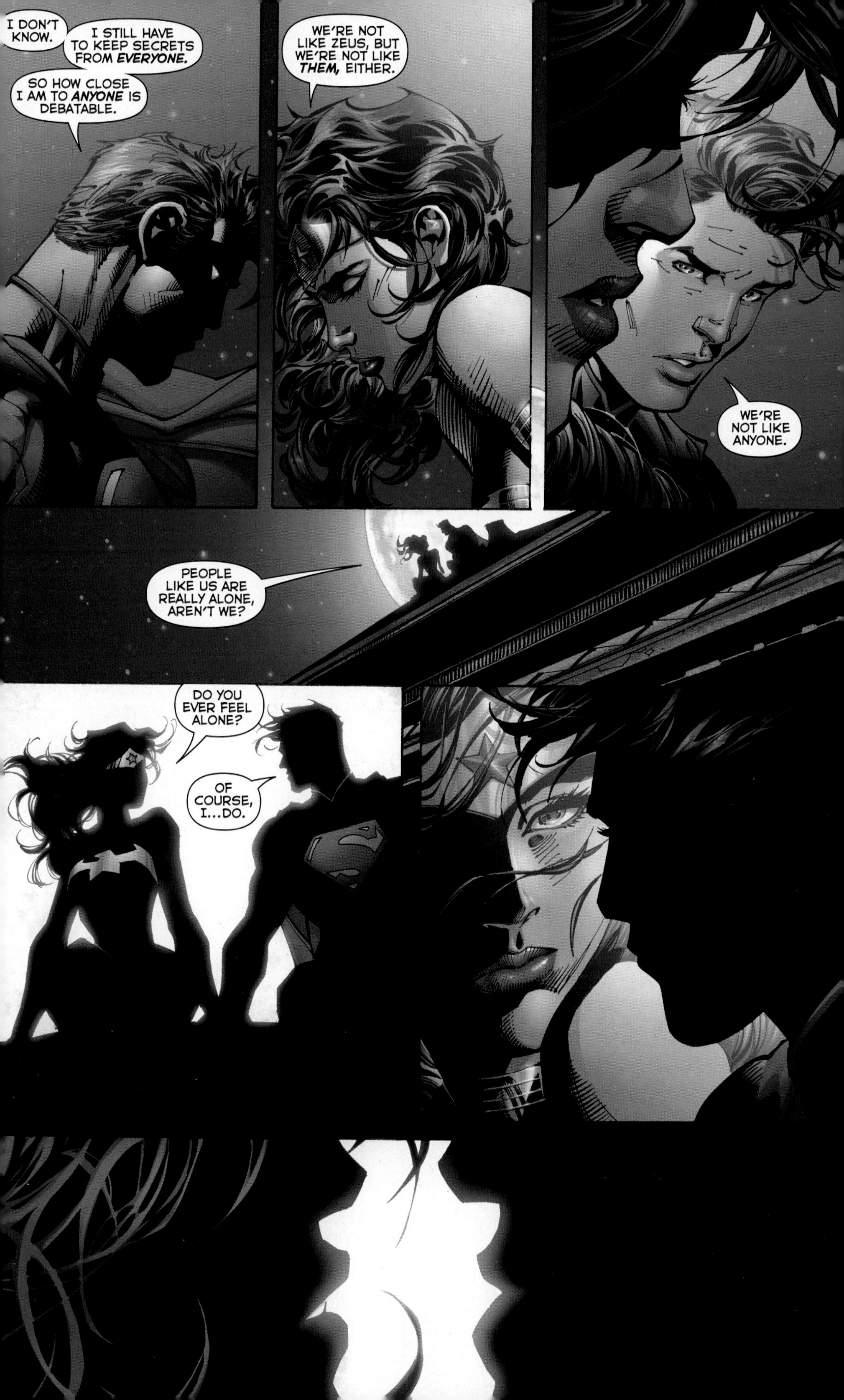

I DON'T KNOW.
I STILL HAVE TO KEEP SECRETS FROM **EVERYONE.**
SO HOW CLOSE I AM TO **ANYONE** IS DEBATABLE.
WE'RE NOT LIKE ZEUS, BUT WE'RE NOT LIKE **THEM,** EITHER.
WE'RE NOT LIKE ANYONE.
PEOPLE LIKE US ARE REALLY ALONE, AREN'T WE?
DO YOU EVER FEEL ALONE?
OF COURSE, I...DO.

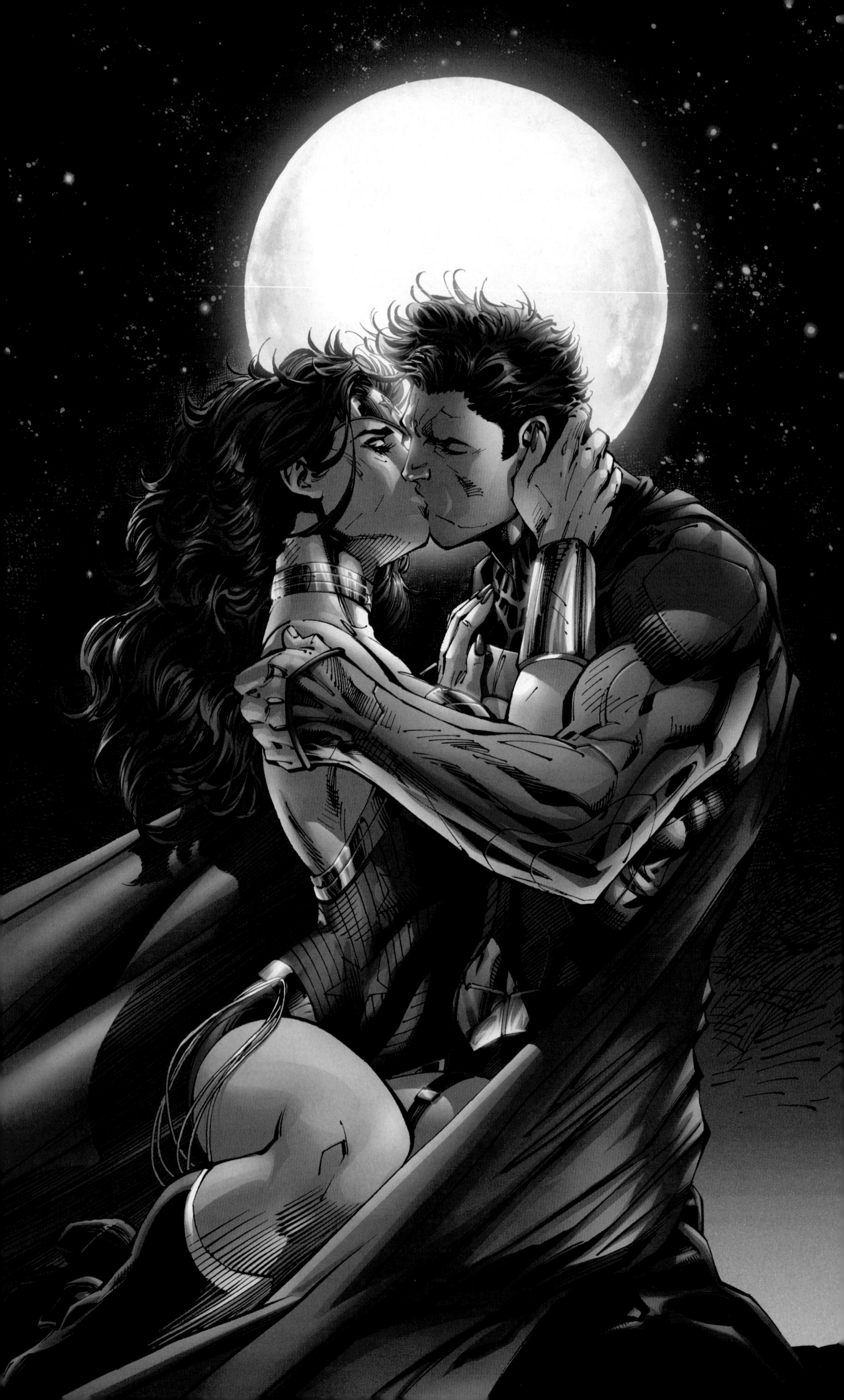

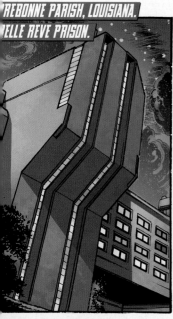

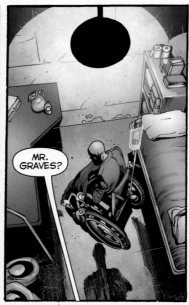

REBONNE PARISH, LOUISIANA.
ELLE REVE PRISON.
MR. GRAVES?
WHATEVER METAMORPHOSIS YOU WENT THROUGH, IT APPEARS TO HAVE SLOWED DOWN THE DISEASE THAT WAS KILLING YOU.
YOU'LL DIE SOONER THAN MOST, BUT NOT YET.
I'M TOLD YOU PREFER WRITING ON A TYPEWRITER.
WHO ARE YOU?
MY NAME IS AMANDA WALLER AND I BELIEVE IN YOU.
I WANT YOU TO WRITE A BOOK FOR ME, MR. GRAVES.
I WAS THINKING IT'D BE TITLED, "HOW TO DESTROY THE JUSTICE LEAGUE," BUT YOU'RE THE WRITER.
FINISH THE BOOK FOR ME, AND I'LL TAKE CARE OF THE REST.
ZZZK
TKTKTKTKTK
TK
THE VILLAIN'S JOURNEY
By David Graves

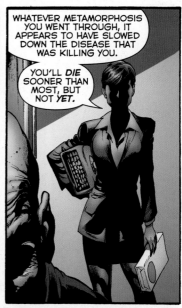

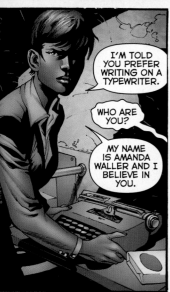

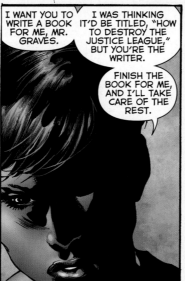

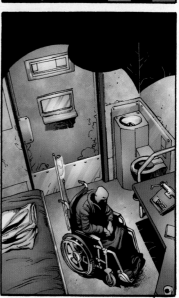

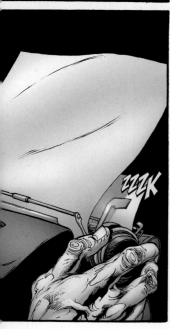

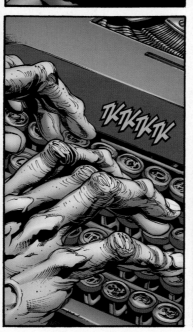

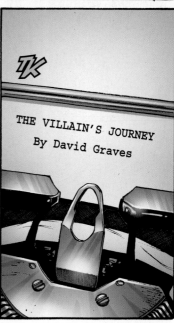

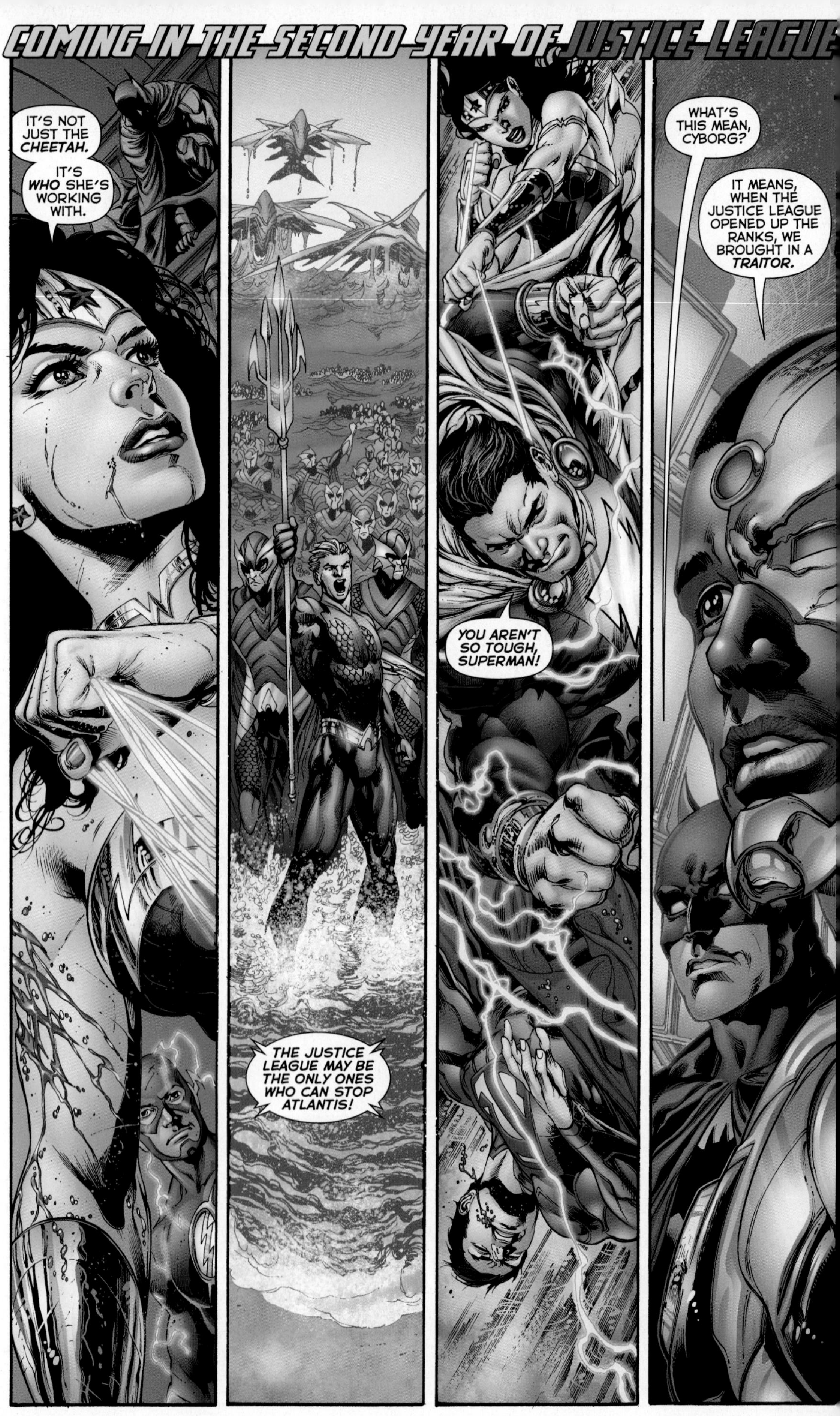
COMING IN THE SECOND YEAR OF JUSTICE LEAGUE
IT'S NOT JUST THE CHEETAH.
IT'S WHO SHE'S WORKING WITH.
THE JUSTICE LEAGUE MAY BE THE ONLY ONES WHO CAN STOP ATLANTIS!
YOU AREN'T SO TOUGH, SUPERMAN!
WHAT'S THIS MEAN, CYBORG?
IT MEANS, WHEN THE JUSTICE LEAGUE OPENED UP THE RANKS, WE BROUGHT IN A TRAITOR.

AND COMING IN 2013

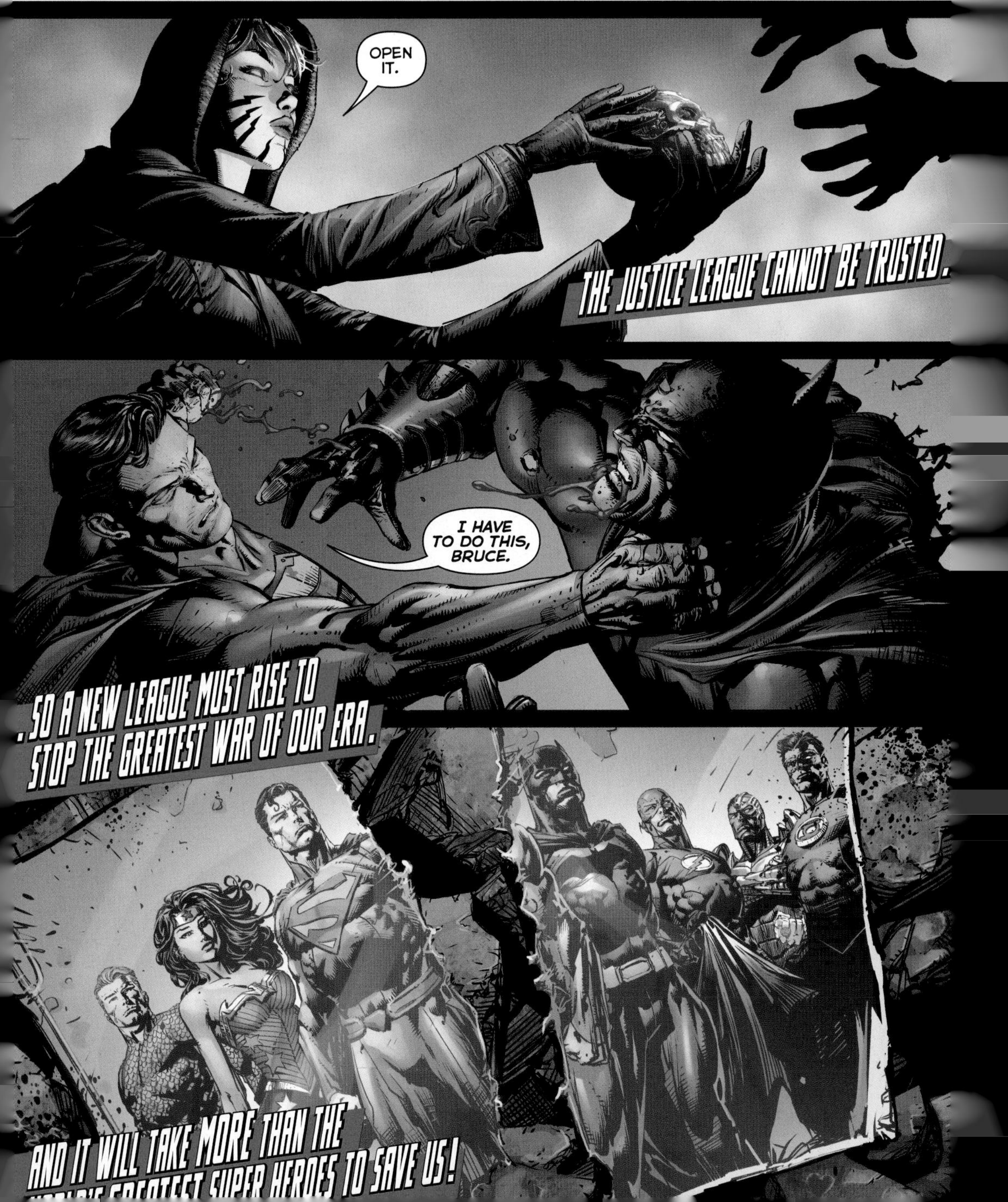
OPEN IT.
THE JUSTICE LEAGUE CANNOT BE TRUSTED.
I HAVE TO DO THIS, BRUCE.
...SO A NEW LEAGUE MUST RISE TO STOP THE GREATEST WAR OF OUR ERA.
AND IT WILL TAKE MORE THAN THE
GREATEST SUPER HEROES TO SAVE US!

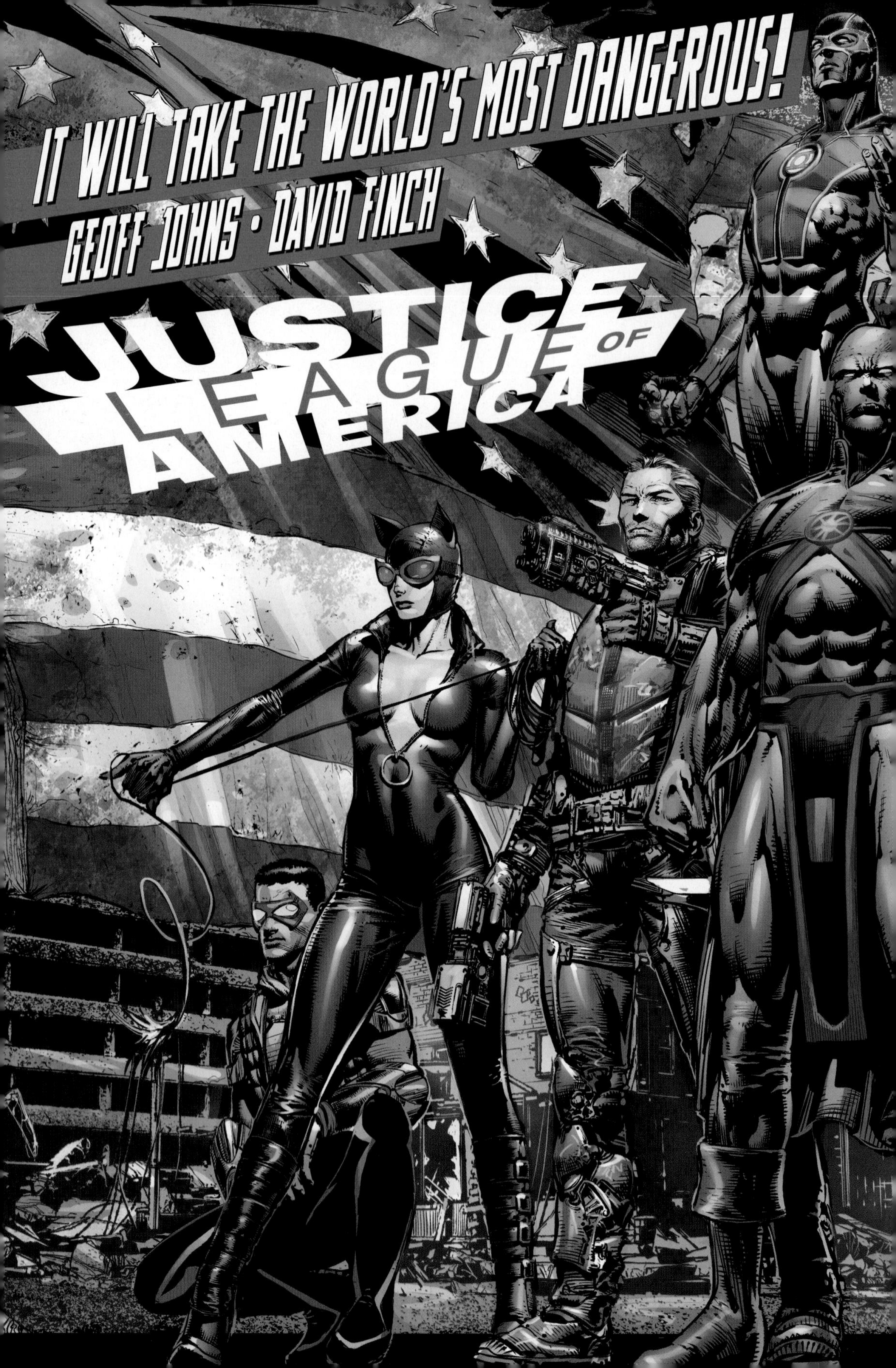
IT WILL TAKE THE WORLD'S MOST DANGEROUS!
GEOFF JOHNS · DAVID FINCH
JUSTICE LEAGUE OF AMERICA

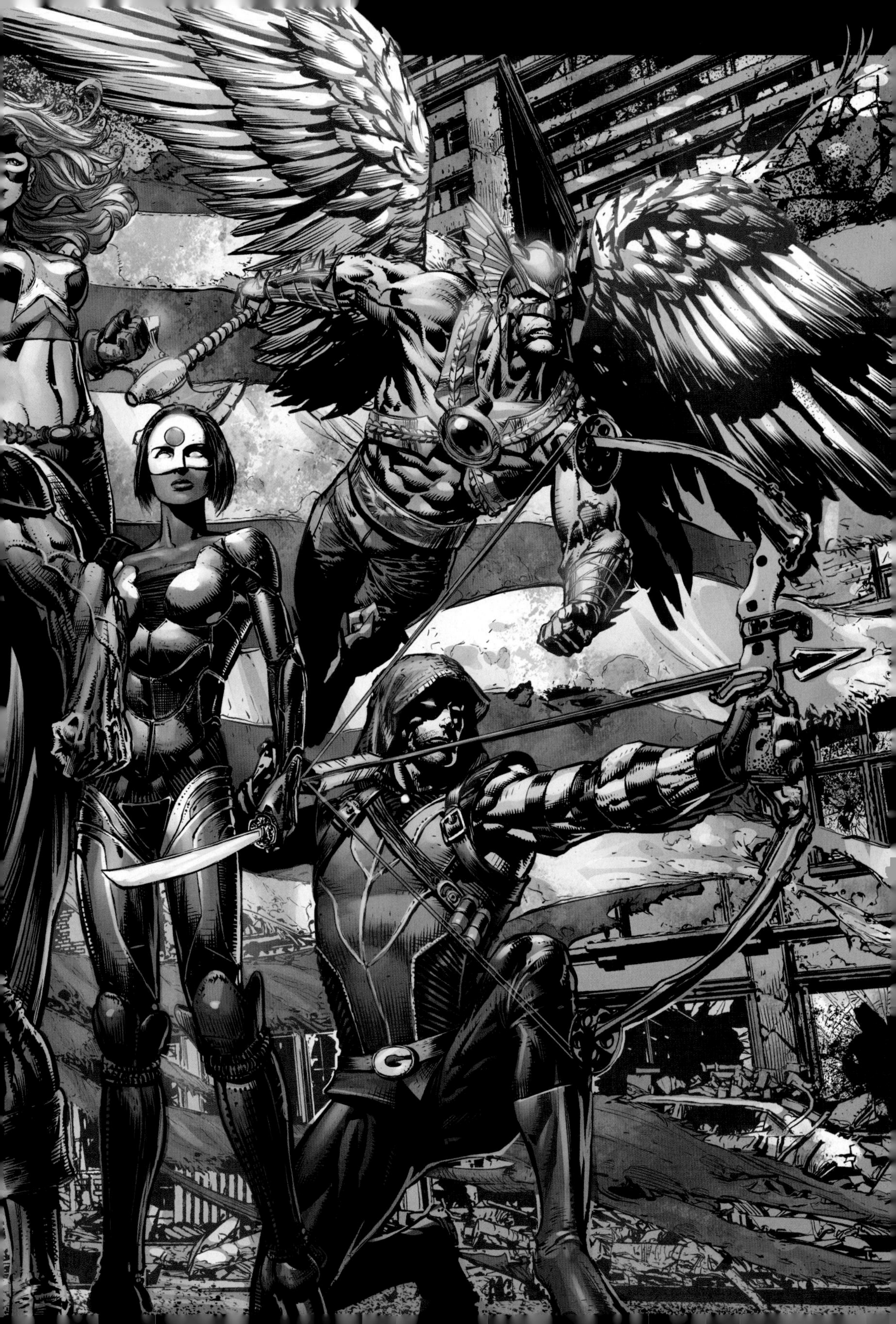

EPILOGUE: QUESTIONS

GEOFF JOHNS writer
ETHAN VAN SCIVER artist

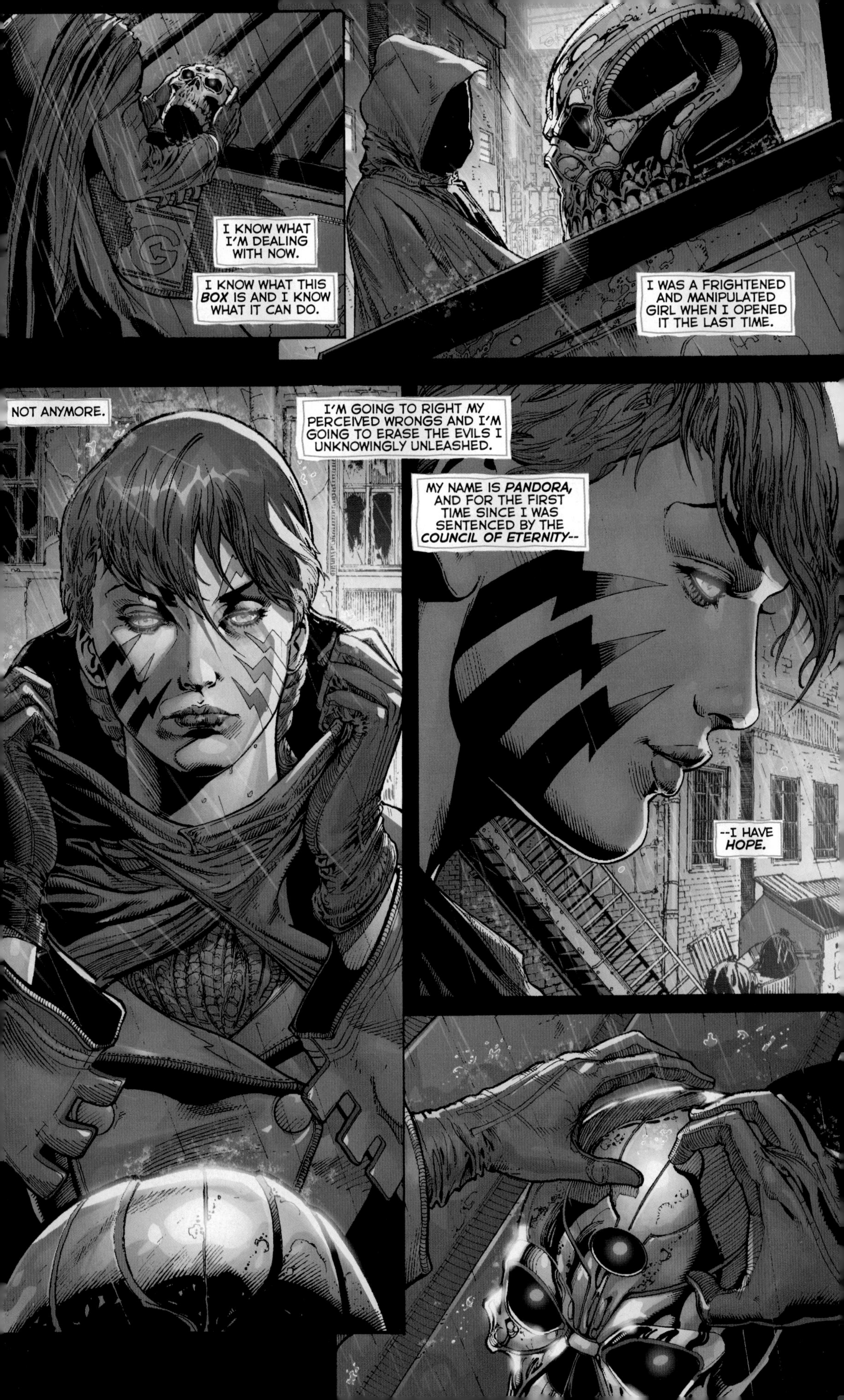
I KNOW WHAT I'M DEALING WITH NOW.
I KNOW WHAT THIS BOX IS AND I KNOW WHAT IT CAN DO.
I WAS A FRIGHTENED AND MANIPULATED GIRL WHEN I OPENED IT THE LAST TIME.
NOT ANYMORE.
I'M GOING TO RIGHT MY PERCEIVED WRONGS AND I'M GOING TO ERASE THE EVILS I UNKNOWINGLY UNLEASHED.
MY NAME IS PANDORA, AND FOR THE FIRST TIME SINCE I WAS SENTENCED BY THE COUNCIL OF ETERNITY--
--I HAVE HOPE.

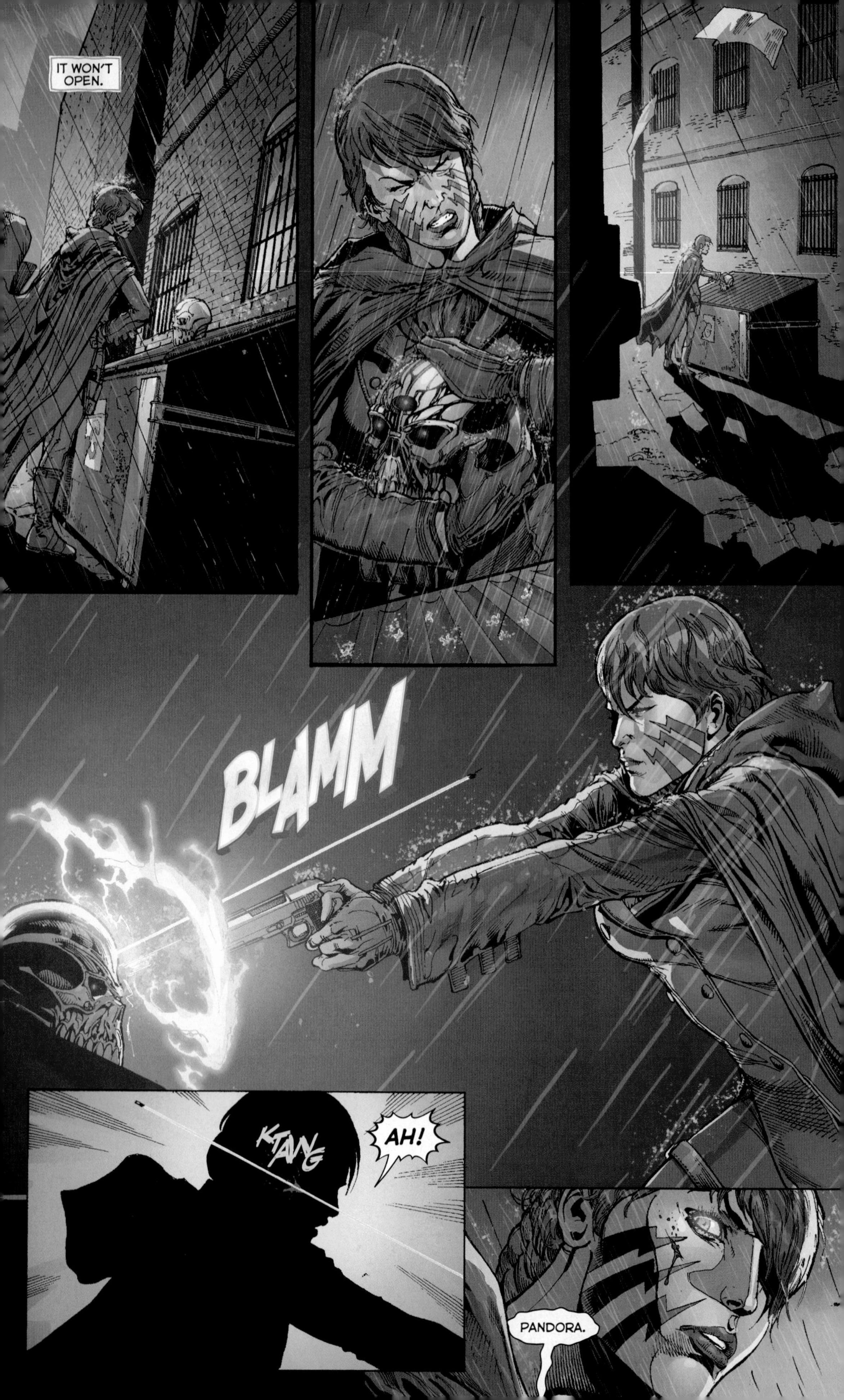
IT WON'T OPEN.
BLAMM
KTANG
AH!
PANDORA.

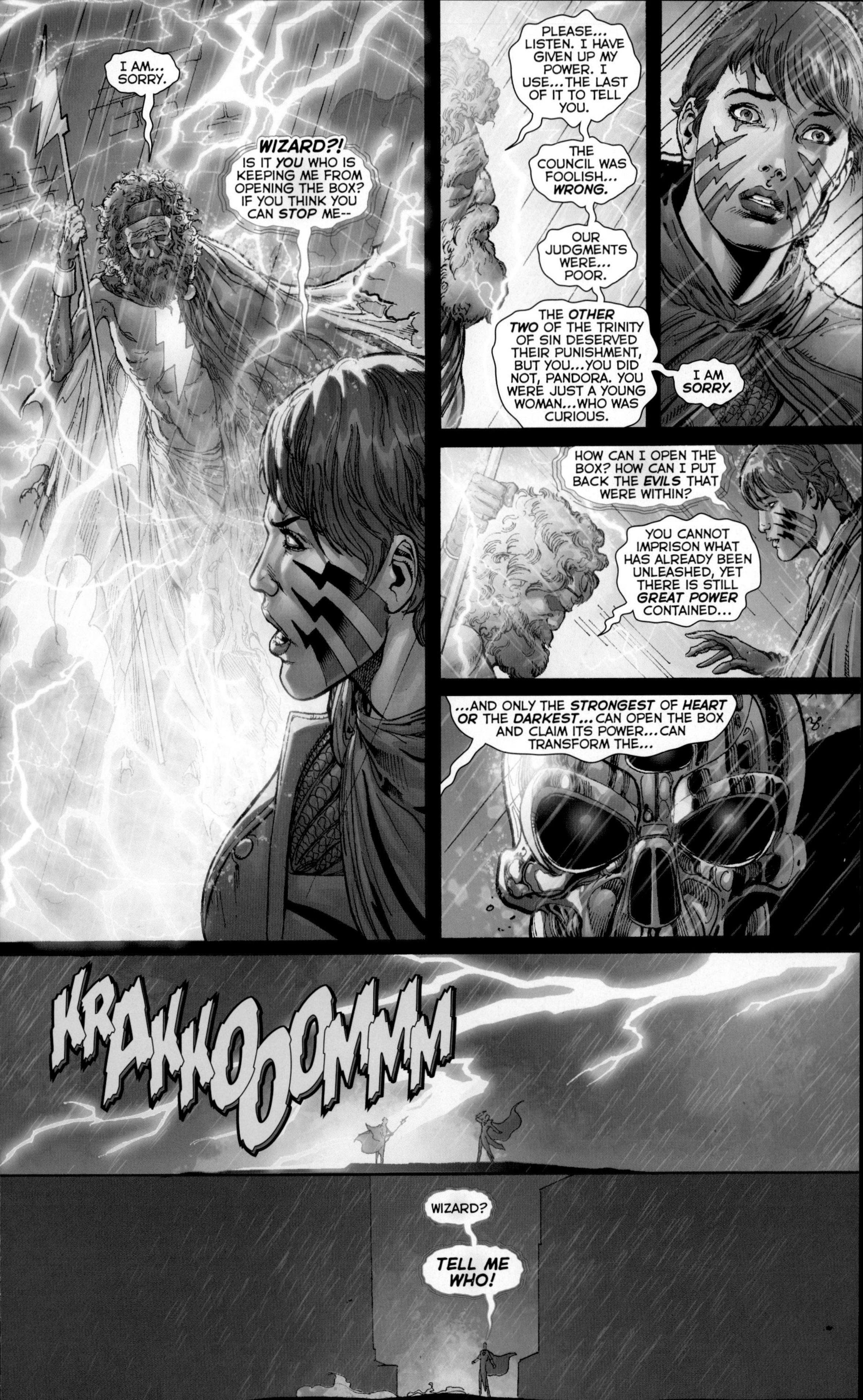
I AM... SORRY.
WIZARD?! IS IT YOU WHO IS KEEPING ME FROM OPENING THE BOX? IF YOU THINK YOU CAN STOP ME--
PLEASE... LISTEN. I HAVE GIVEN UP MY POWER. I USE...THE LAST OF IT TO TELL YOU.
THE COUNCIL WAS FOOLISH... WRONG.
OUR JUDGMENTS WERE... POOR.
THE OTHER TWO OF THE TRINITY OF SIN DESERVED THEIR PUNISHMENT, BUT YOU...YOU DID NOT, PANDORA. YOU WERE JUST A YOUNG WOMAN...WHO WAS CURIOUS.
I AM SORRY.
HOW CAN I OPEN THE BOX? HOW CAN I PUT BACK THE EVILS THAT WERE WITHIN?
YOU CANNOT IMPRISON WHAT HAS ALREADY BEEN UNLEASHED, YET THERE IS STILL GREAT POWER CONTAINED...
...AND ONLY THE STRONGEST OF HEART OR THE DARKEST...CAN OPEN THE BOX AND CLAIM ITS POWER...CAN TRANSFORM THE...
KRAKKOOOMMM
WIZARD?
TELL ME WHO!

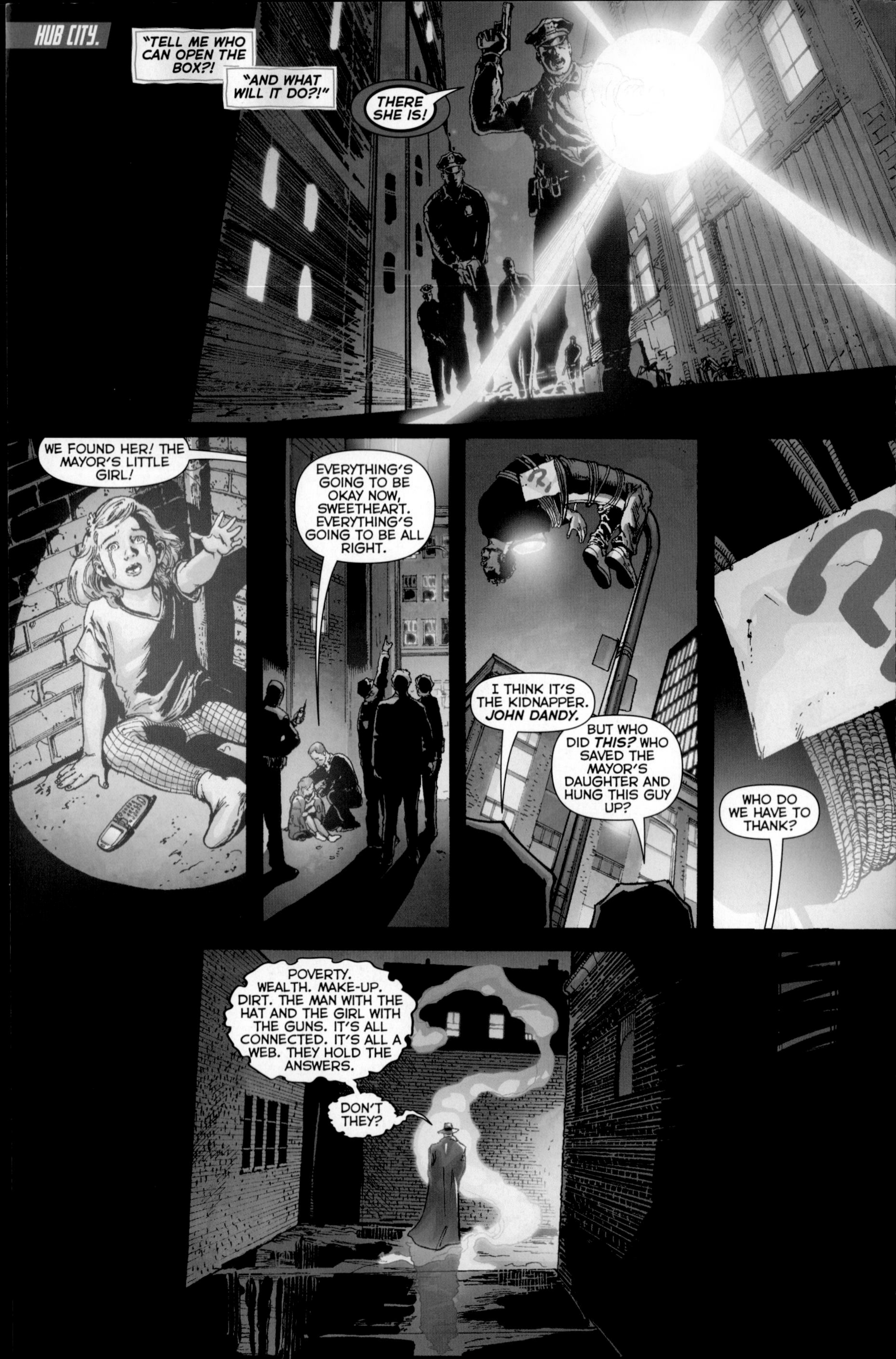
HUB CITY.
"TELL ME WHO CAN OPEN THE BOX?!
"AND WHAT WILL IT DO?!"
THERE SHE IS!
WE FOUND HER! THE MAYOR'S LITTLE GIRL!
EVERYTHING'S GOING TO BE OKAY NOW, SWEETHEART. EVERYTHING'S GOING TO BE ALL RIGHT.
I THINK IT'S THE KIDNAPPER. JOHN DANDY.
BUT WHO DID THIS? WHO SAVED THE MAYOR'S DAUGHTER AND HUNG THIS GUY UP?
WHO DO WE HAVE TO THANK?
POVERTY. WEALTH. MAKE-UP. DIRT. THE MAN WITH THE HAT AND THE GIRL WITH THE GUNS. IT'S ALL CONNECTED. IT'S ALL A WEB. THEY HOLD THE ANSWERS.
DON'T THEY?

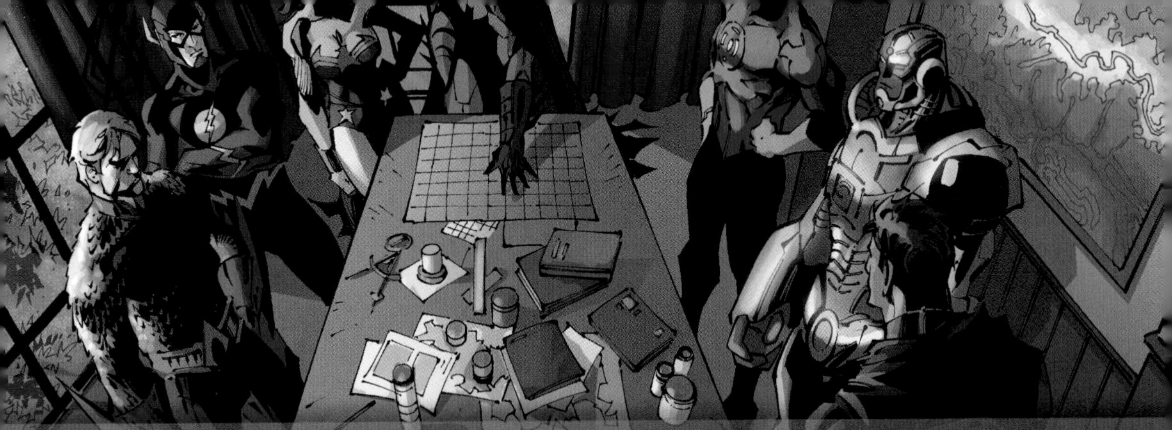

VARIANT COVER GALLERY

JUSTICE LEAGUE 7 combo pack
By Jim Lee, Scott Williams & Alex Sinclair

JUSTICE LEAGUE 7
by Gary Frank & Brad Anderson

JUSTICE LEAGUE 8 combo pack
By Jim Lee, Scott Williams & Alex Sinclair

JUSTICE LEAGUE 8
by Mike Choi & Marcelo Maiolo

JUSTICE LEAGUE 9 combo pack
By Jim Lee, Scott Williams & Alex Sinclair

JUSTICE LEAGUE 9
By Carlos D'Anda & Gabe Eltaeb

JUSTICE LEAGUE 10 combo pack
By Jim Lee, Scott Williams & Alex Sinclair

JUSTICE LEAGUE 10 combo pack
By Cully Hamner

JUSTICE LEAGUE 11 combo pack
By Jim Lee, Scott Williams & Alex Sinclair

JUSTICE LEAGUE 11
By Bryan Hitch & Paul Mounts

JUSTICE LEAGUE 11 Fan Expo Canada exclusive
By Jim Lee, Scott Williams & Alex Sinclair

JUSTICE LEAGUE 12
By Jim Lee, Scott Williams & Alex Sinclair

JUSTICE LEAGUE 12 combo pack
By Jim Lee, Scott Williams & Alex Sinclair

JUSTICE LEAGUE 12—second printing
By Jim Lee, Scott Williams & Alex Sinclair

JUSTICE LEAGUE 12 New York Comic Con exclusive
By Jim Lee, Scott Williams & Alex Sinclair

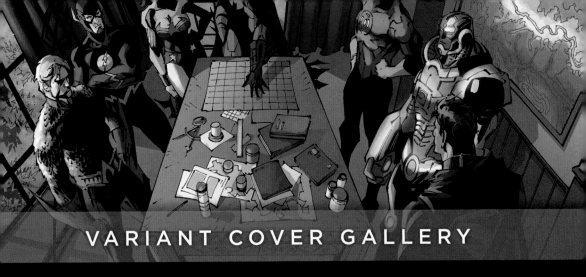

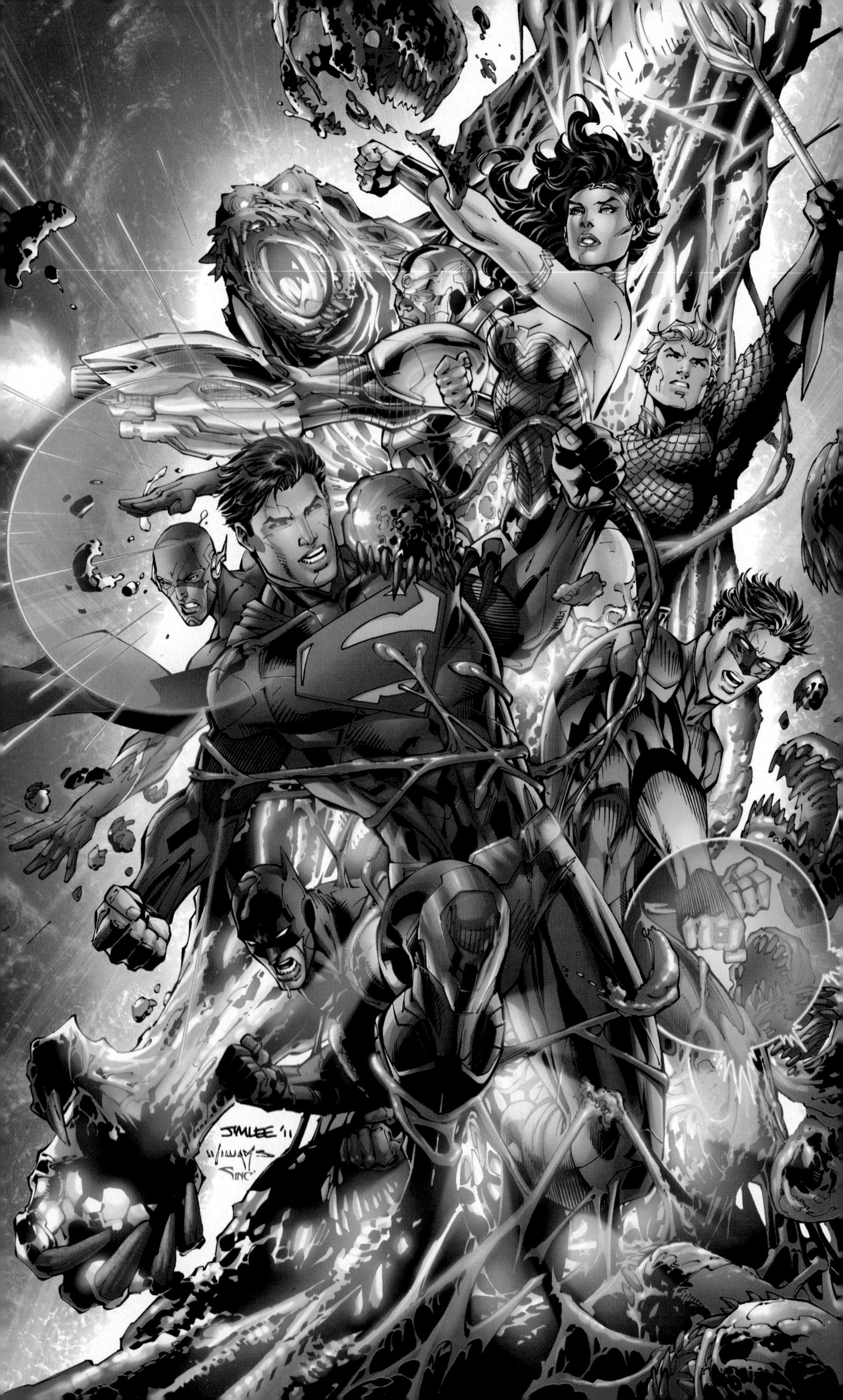
JIMLEE '11
SINC'

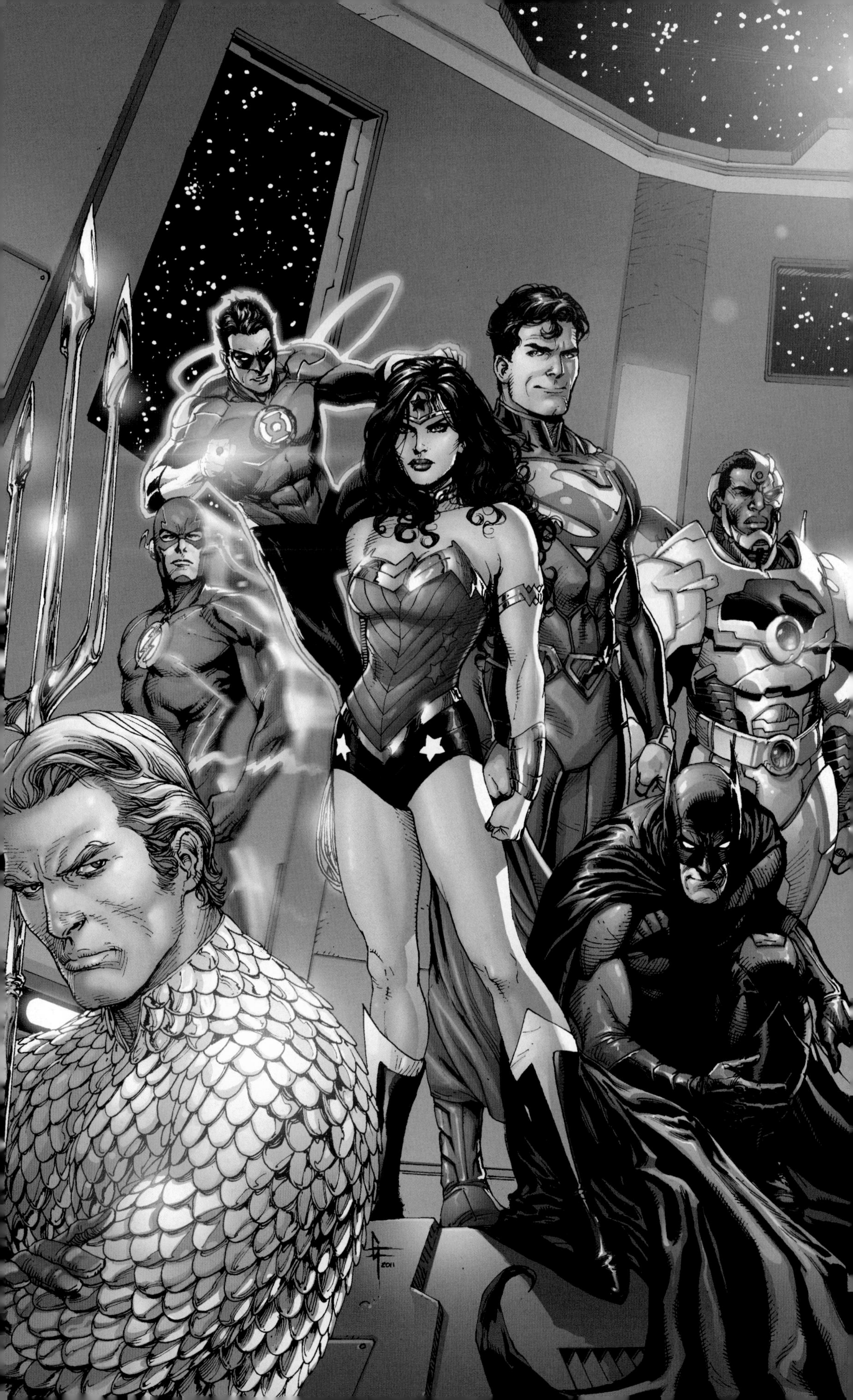

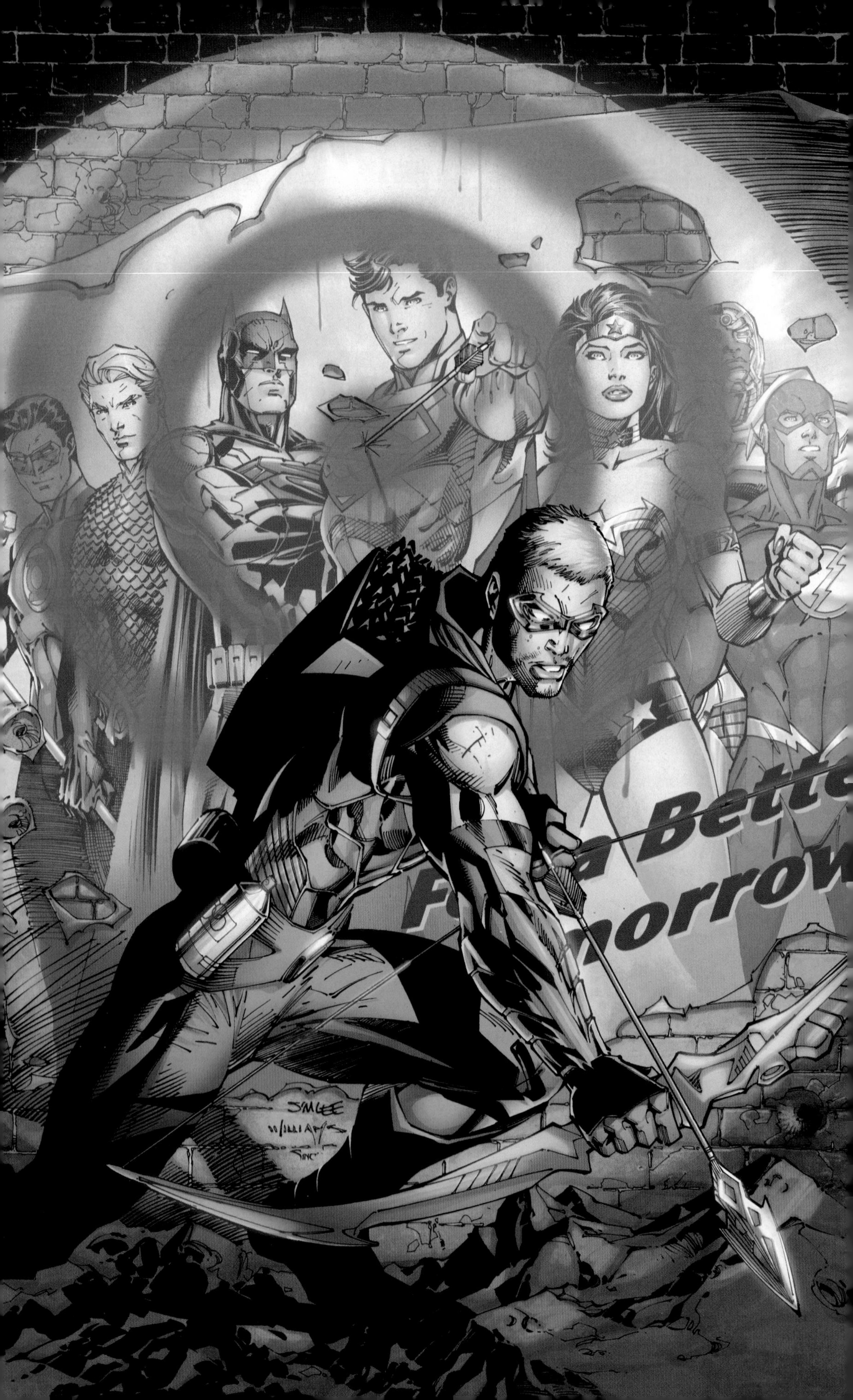

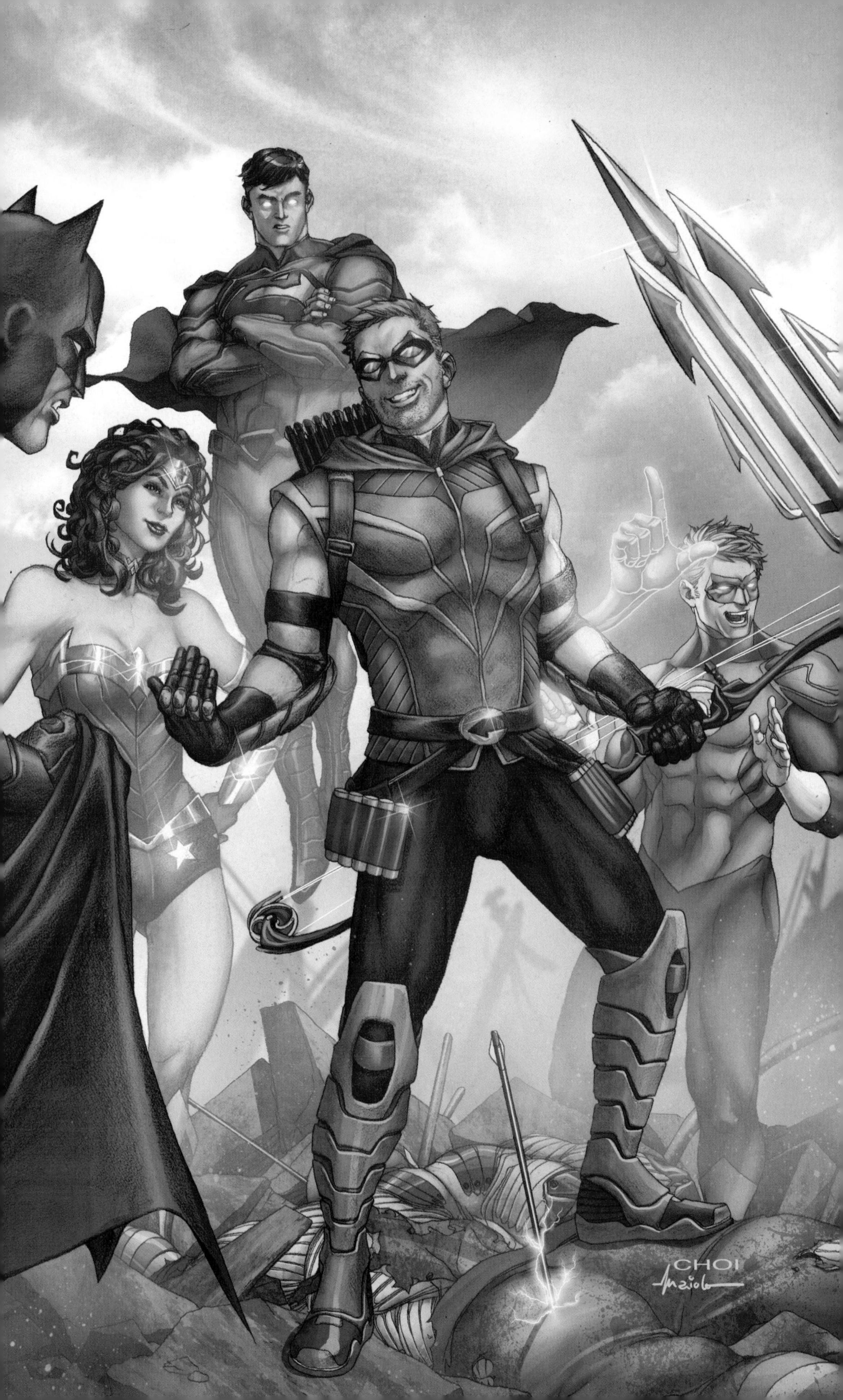
CHOI

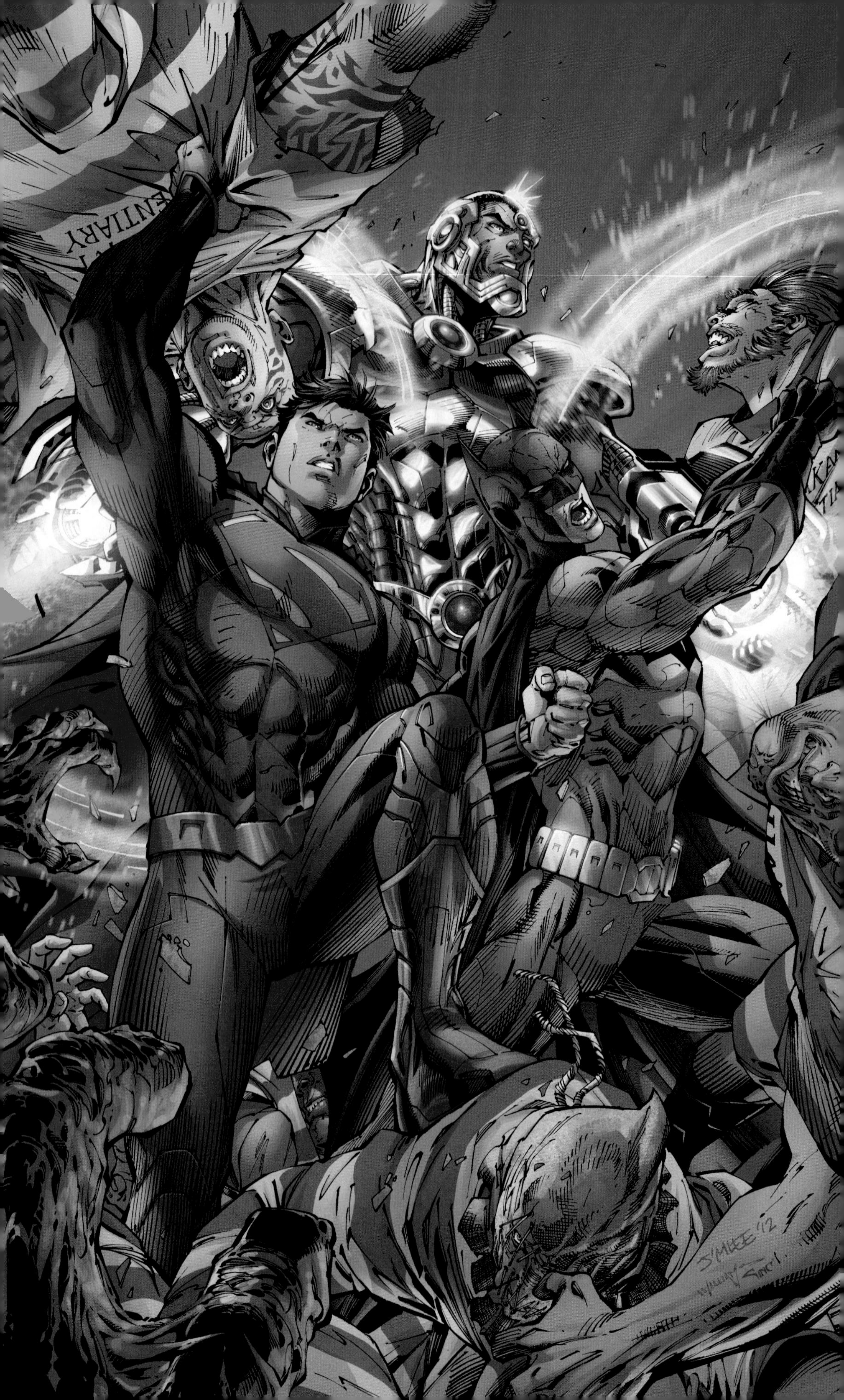

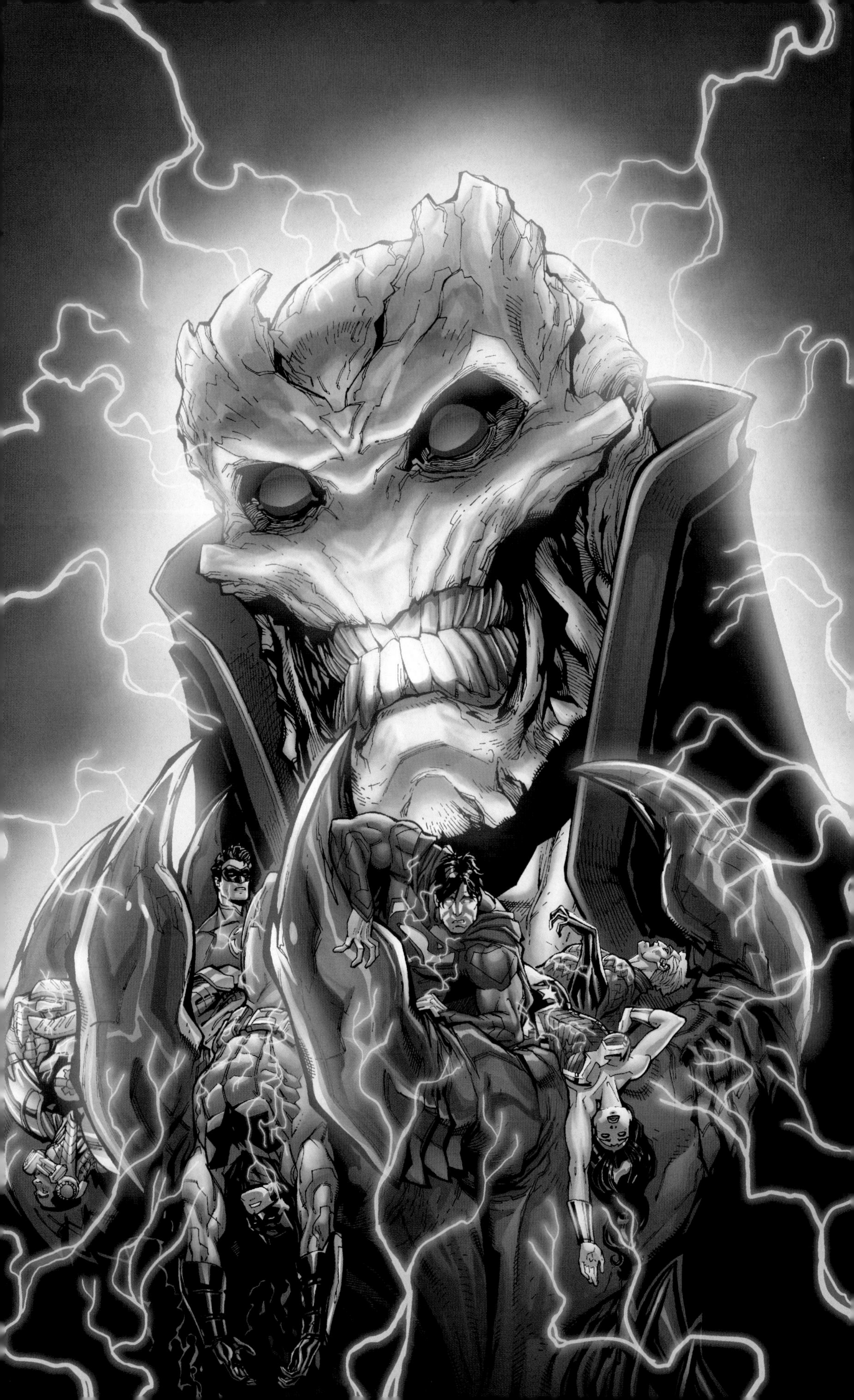

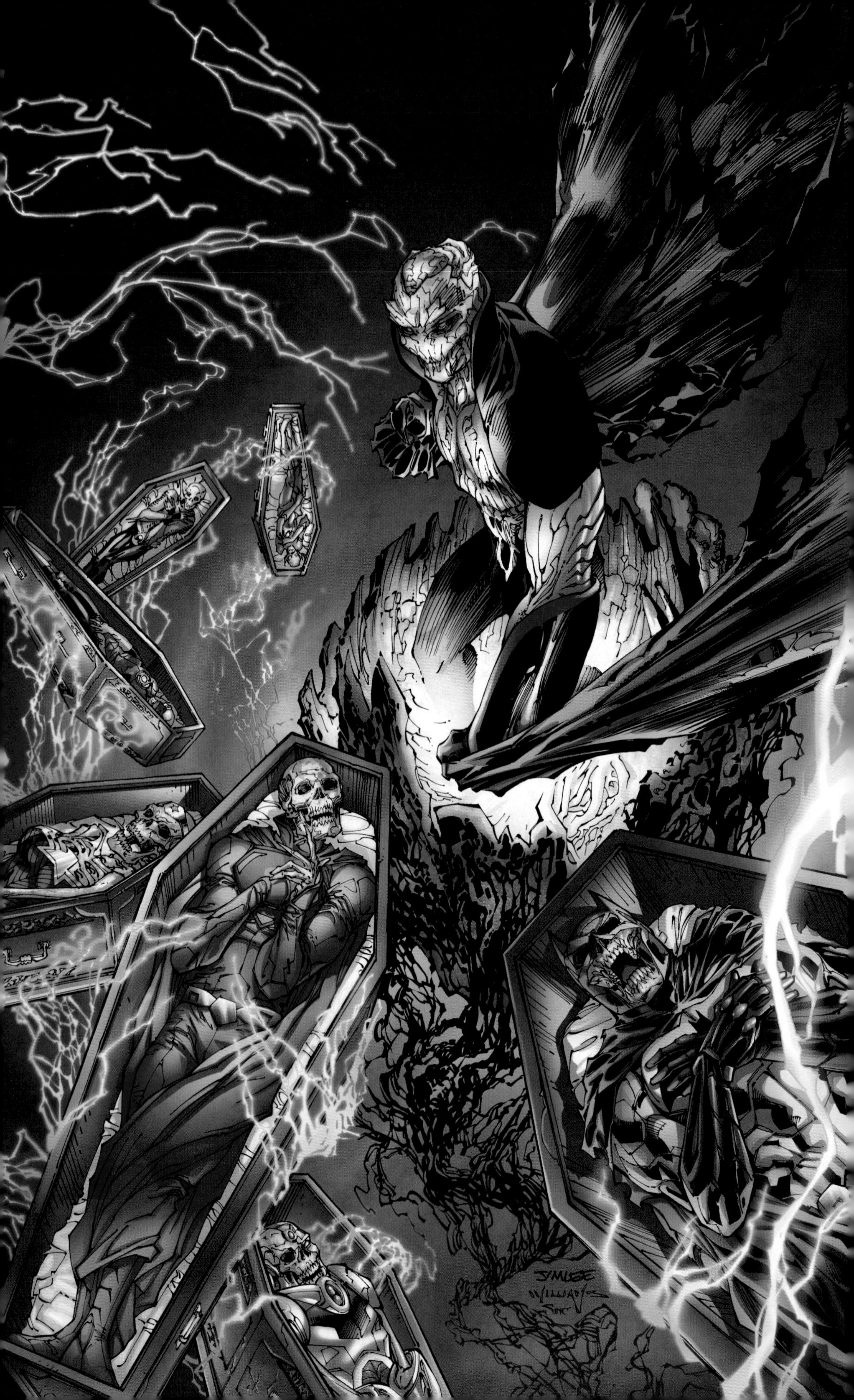

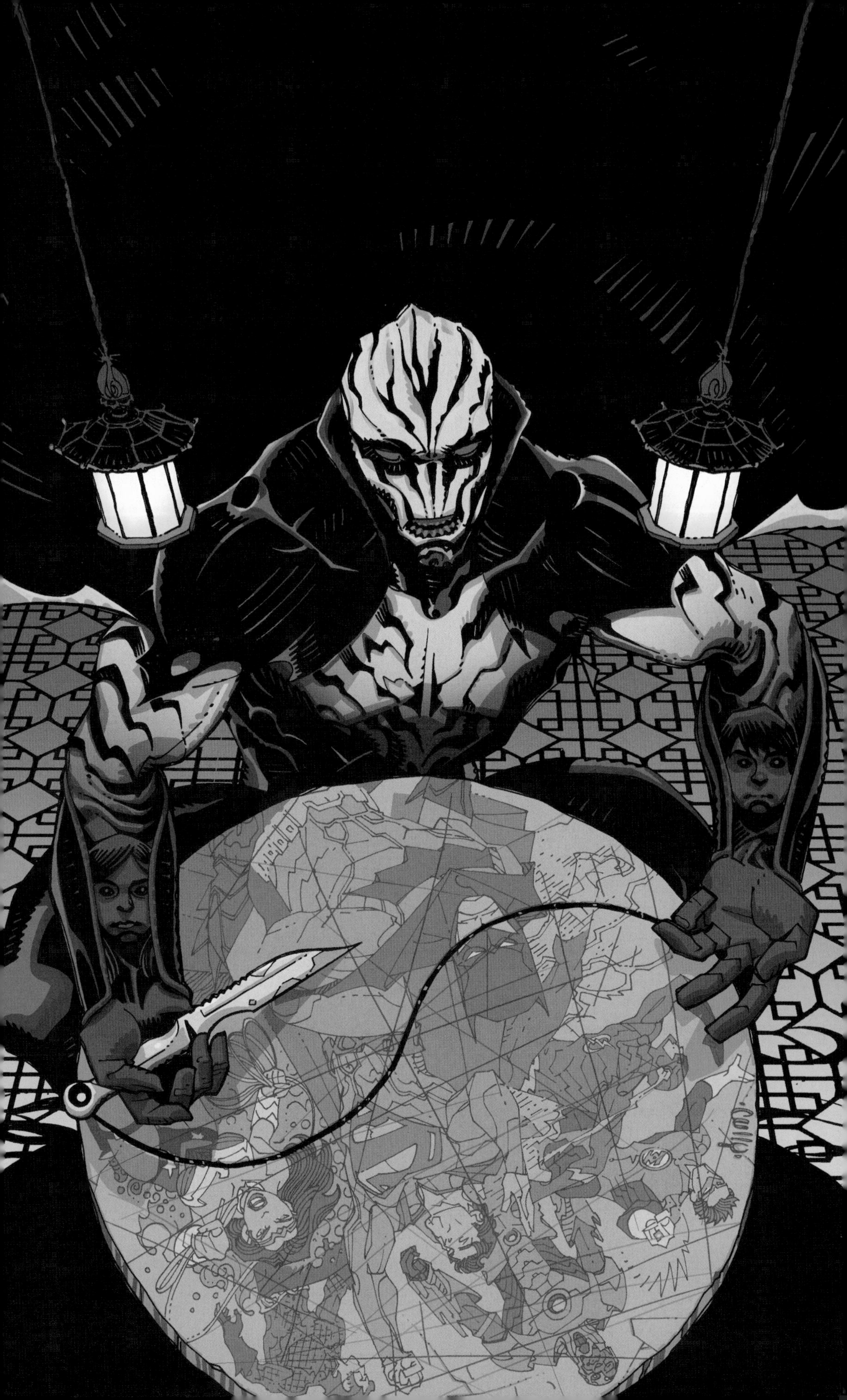

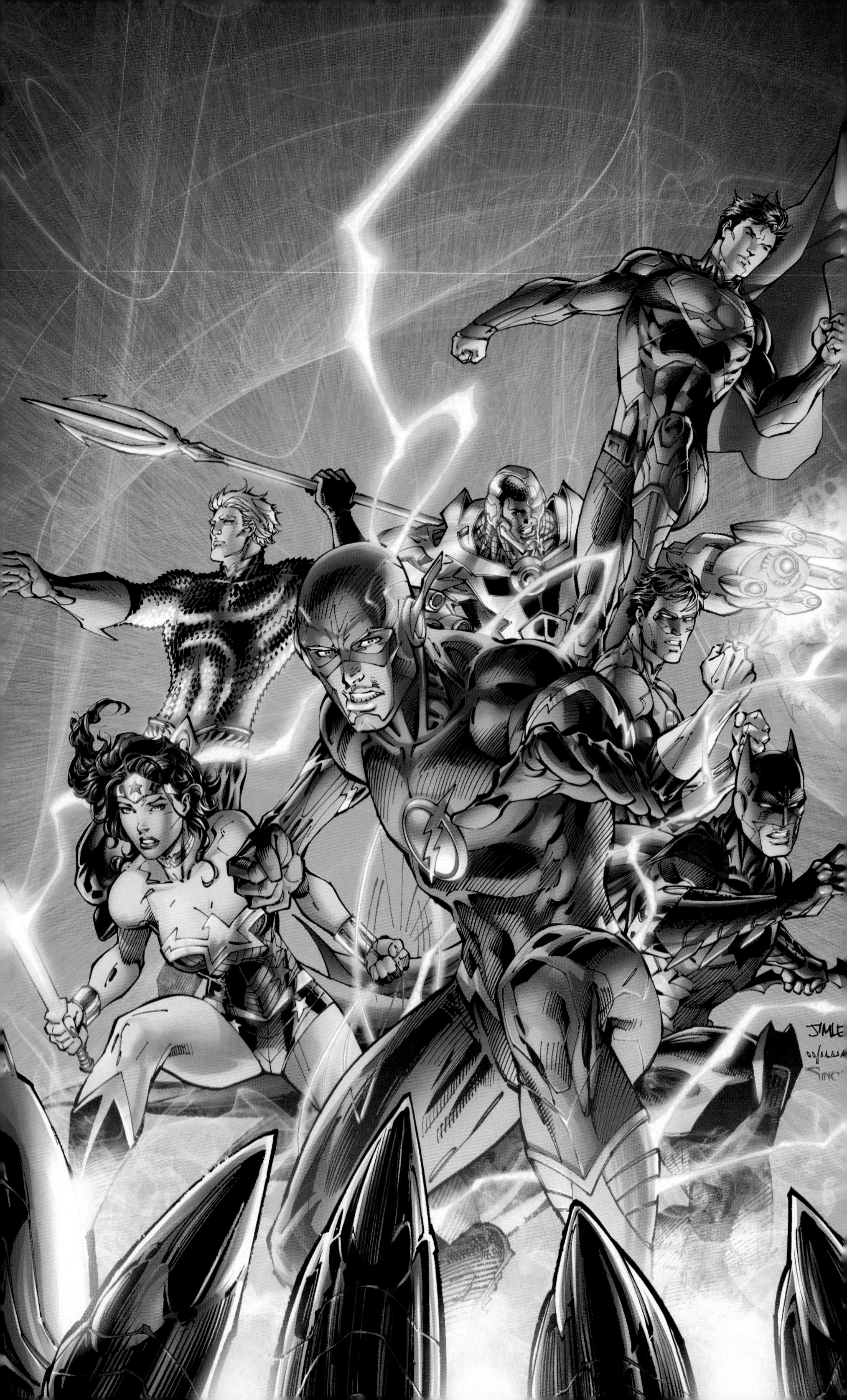

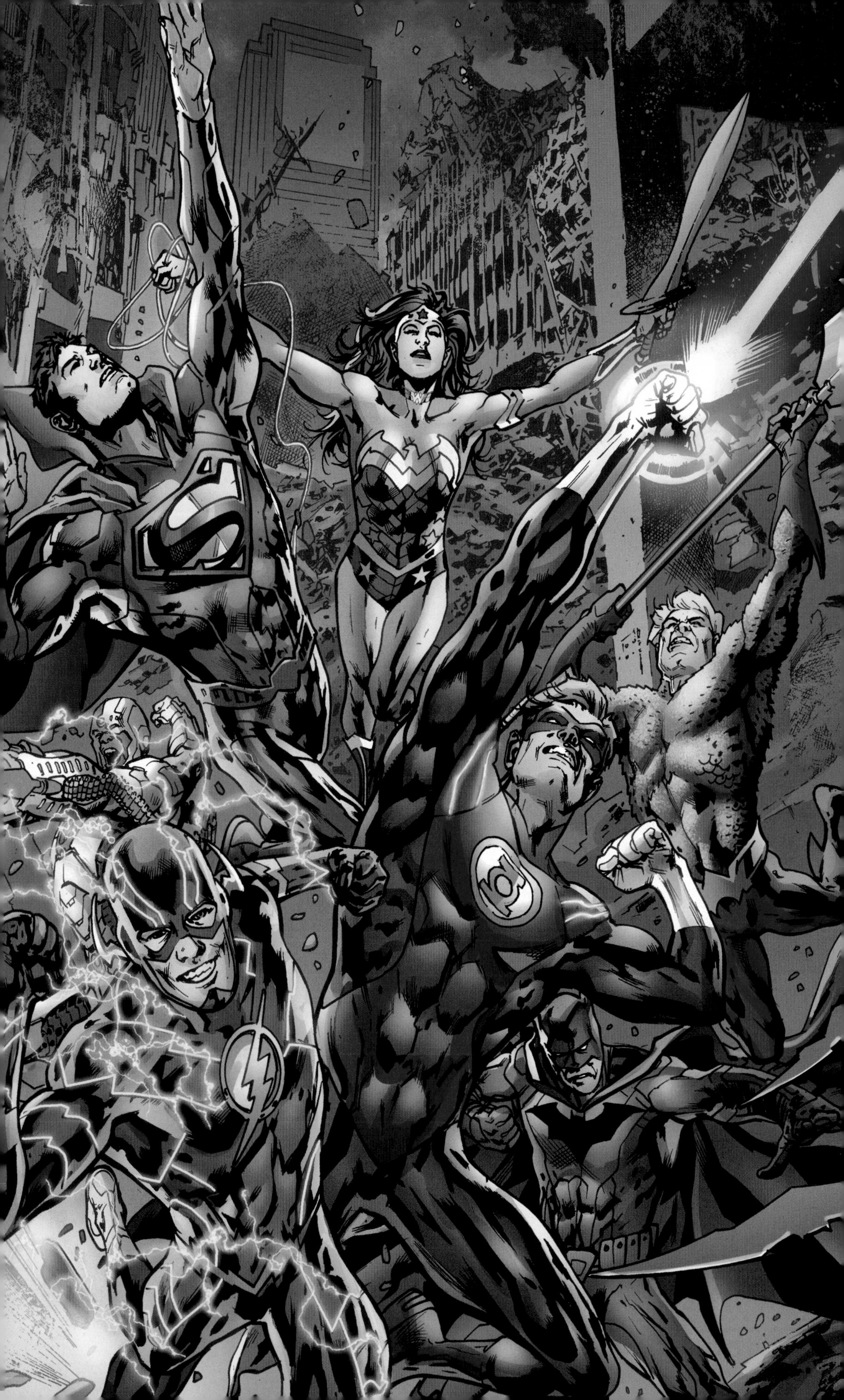

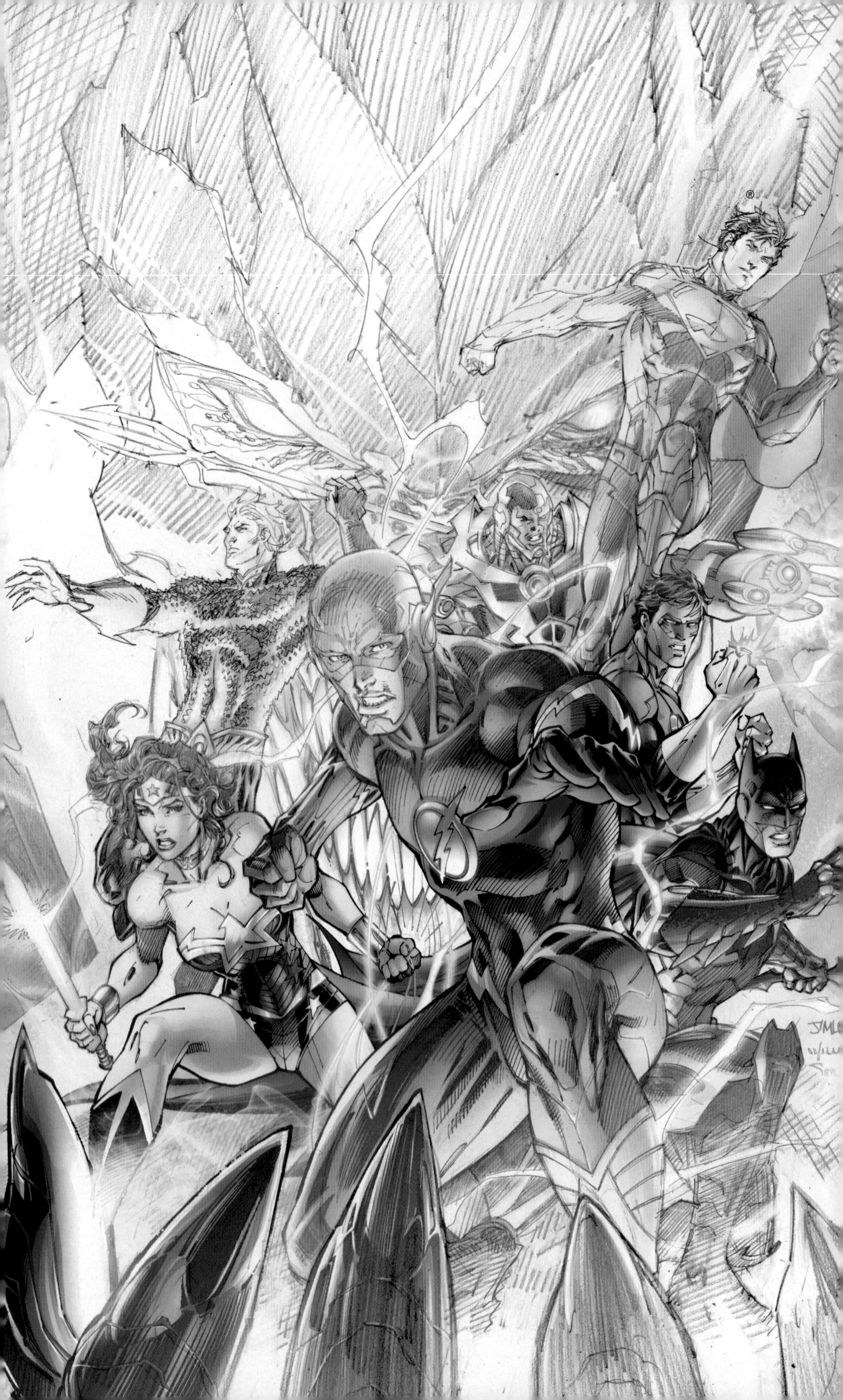

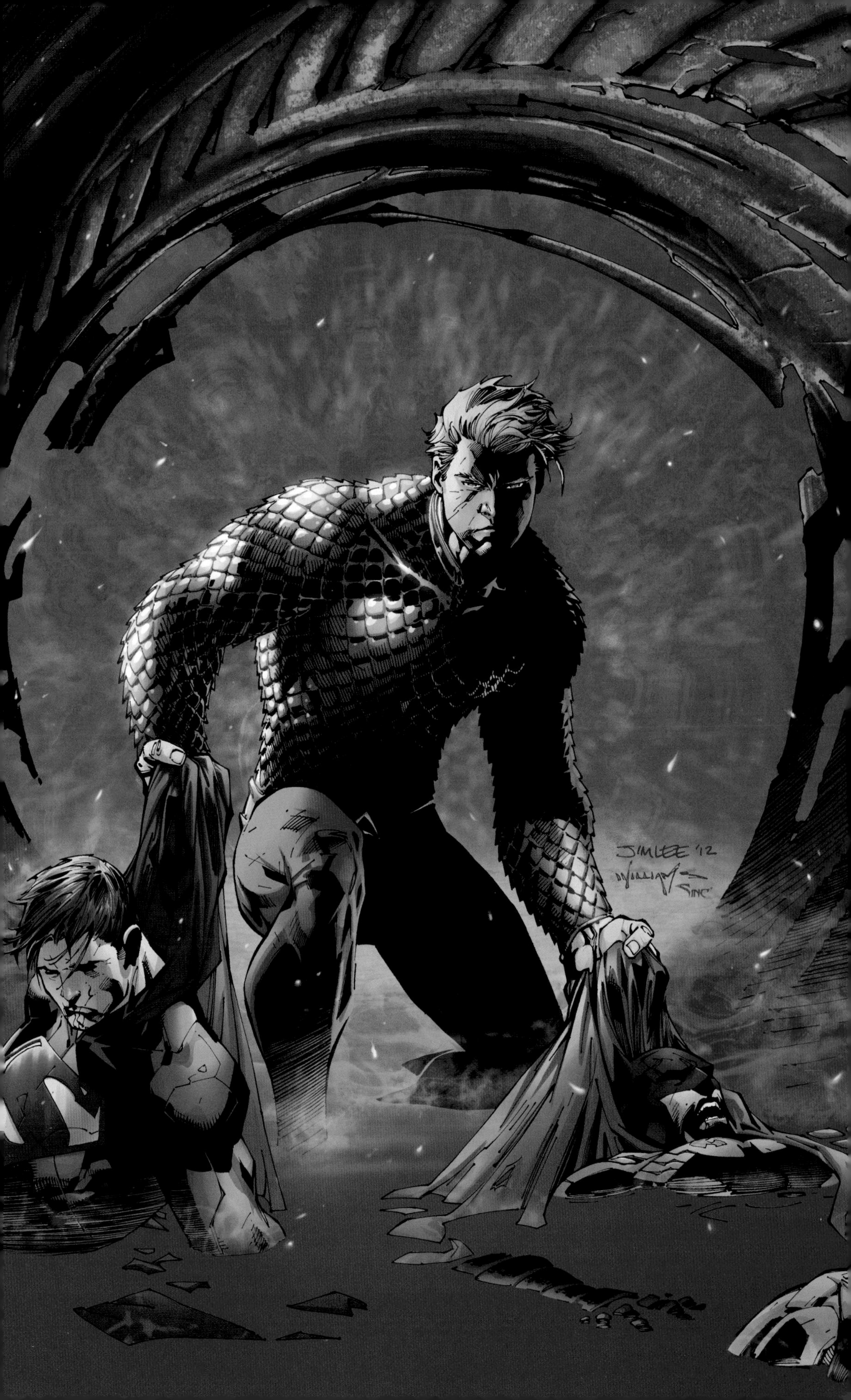
JIMLEE '12

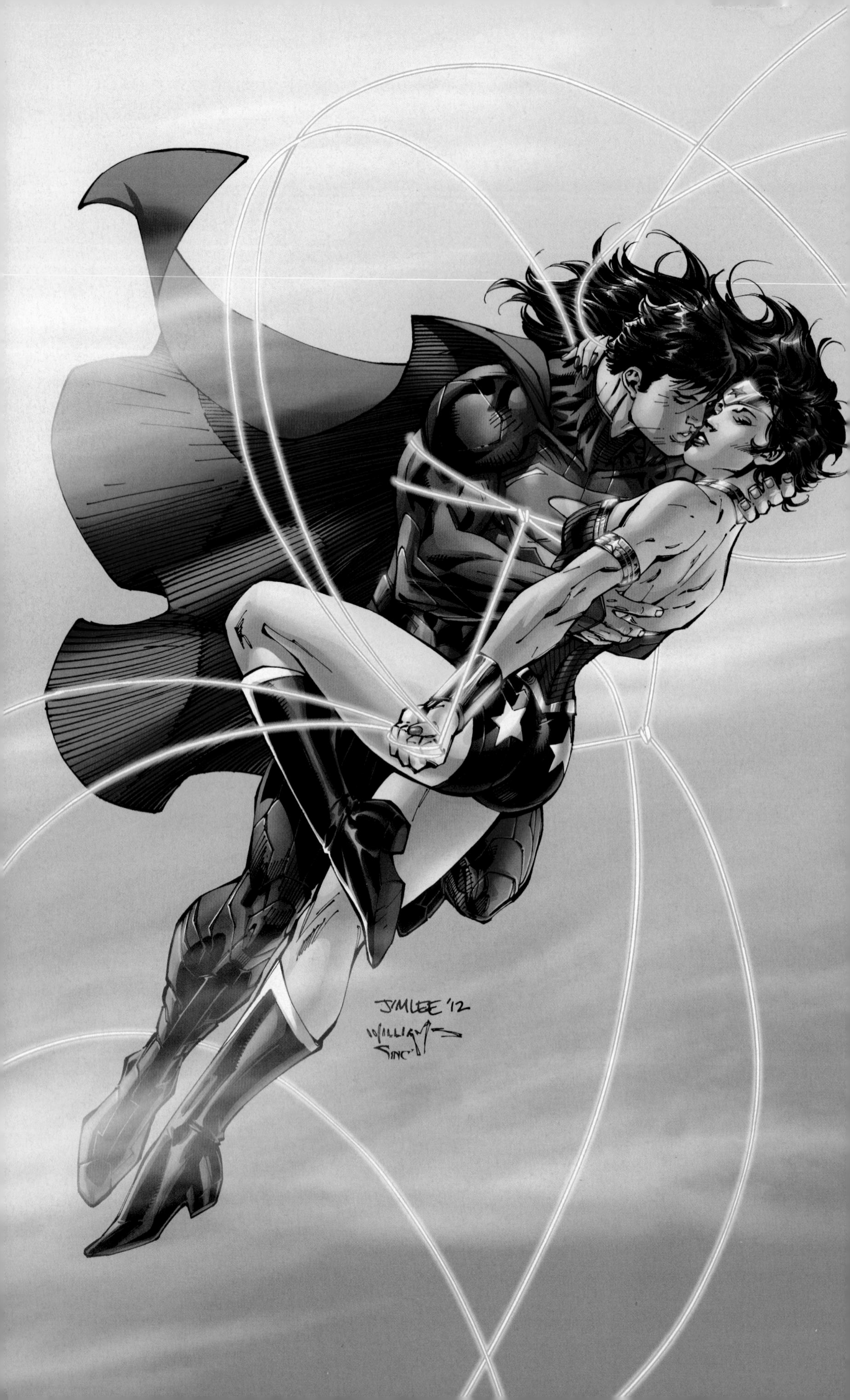
JIMLEE '12

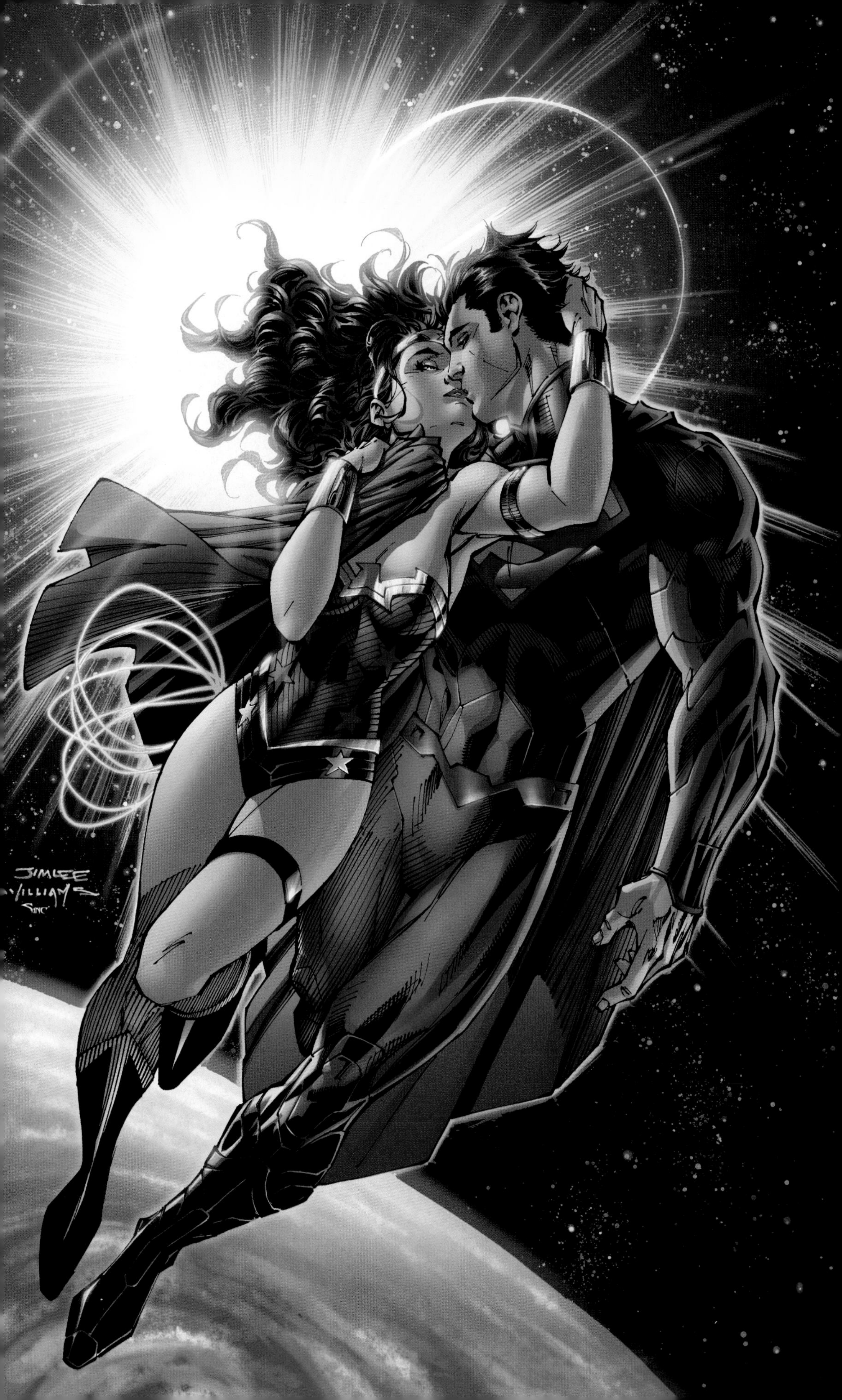
JIMLEE
SINC

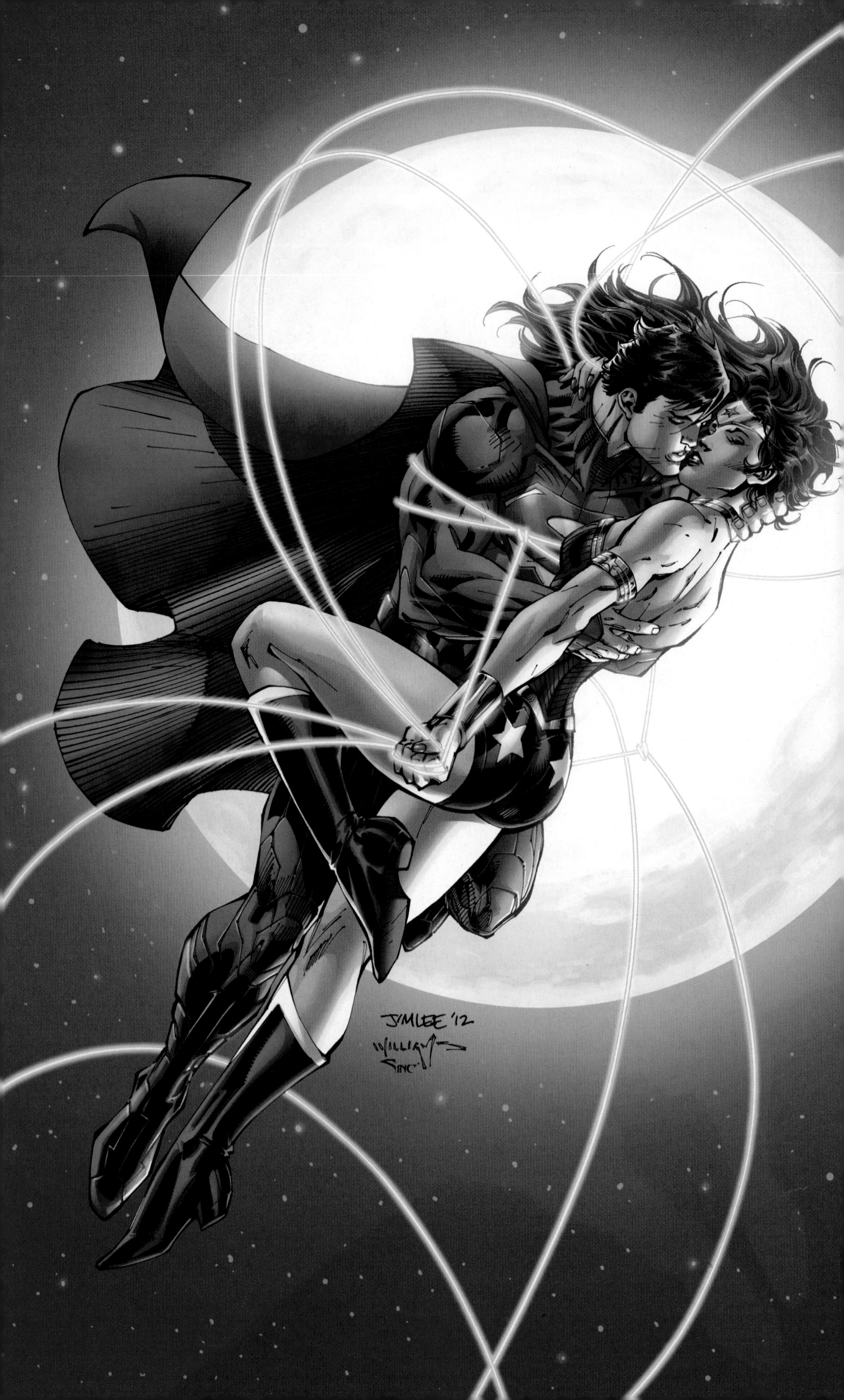

DC COMICS™

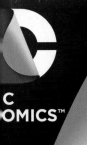

"Welcoming to new fans looking to get into superhero comics for the first time and old fans who gave up on the funny-books long ago."
—SCRIPPS HOWARD NEWS SERVICE

START AT THE BEGINNING!

JUSTICE LEAGUE VOLUME 1:ORIGIN

AQUAMAN VOLUME 1: THE TRENCH

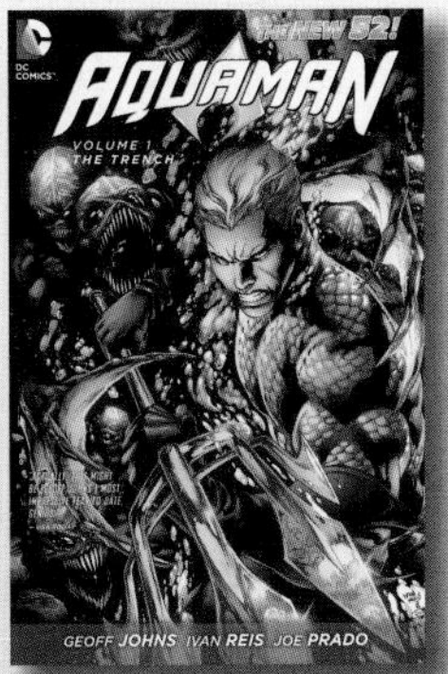

DC COMICS
THE NEW 52!
AQUAMAN
VOLUME 1 THE TRENCH
GEOFF JOHNS IVAN REIS JOE PRADO

THE SAVAGE HAWKMAN VOLUME 1: DARKNESS RISING

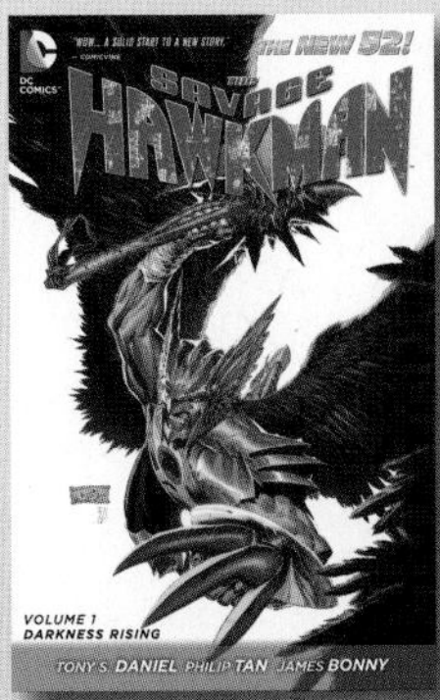

DC COMICS
THE NEW 52!
SAVAGE HAWKMAN
VOLUME 1 DARKNESS RISING
TONY S. DANIEL PHILIP TAN JAMES BONNY

GREEN ARROW VOLUME 1: THE MIDAS TOUCH

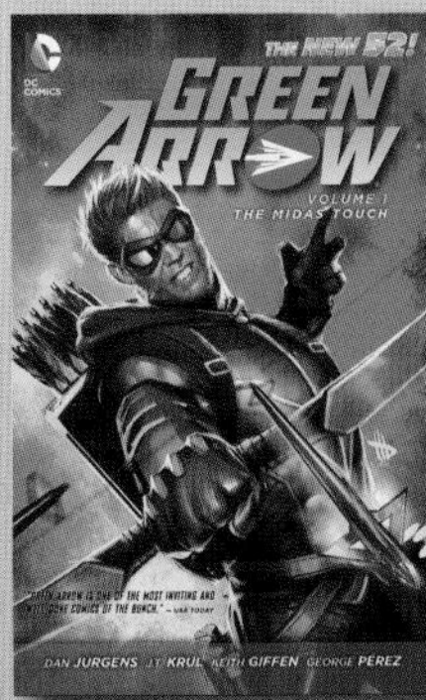

DC COMICS
THE NEW 52!
GREEN ARROW
VOLUME 1 THE MIDAS TOUCH
DAN JURGENS J.T. KRUL KEITH GIFFEN GEORGE PEREZ

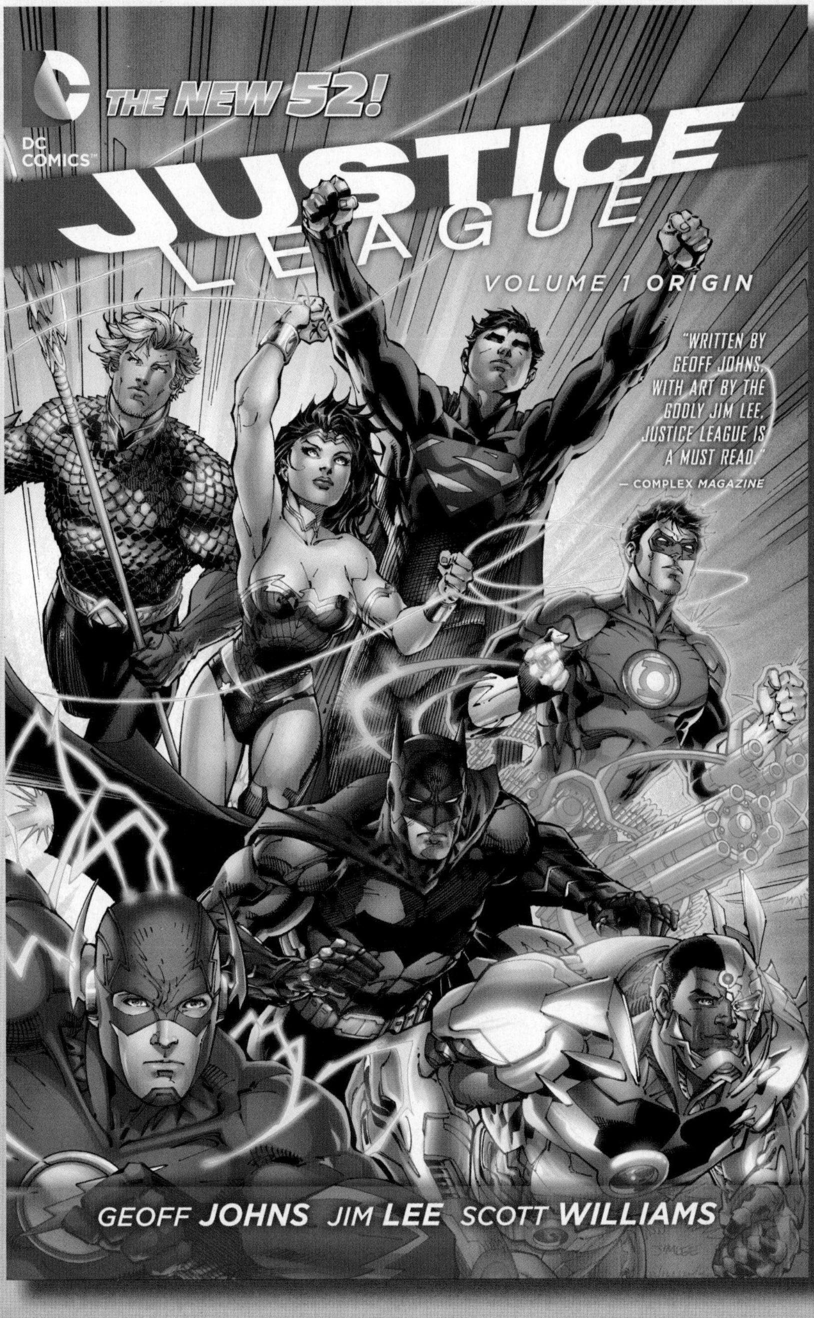

DC COMICS™
THE NEW 52!
JUSTICE LEAGUE
VOLUME 1 ORIGIN
"WRITTEN BY GEOFF JOHNS, WITH ART BY THE GODLY JIM LEE, JUSTICE LEAGUE IS A MUST READ."
— COMPLEX MAGAZINE
GEOFF JOHNS JIM LEE SCOTT WILLIAMS

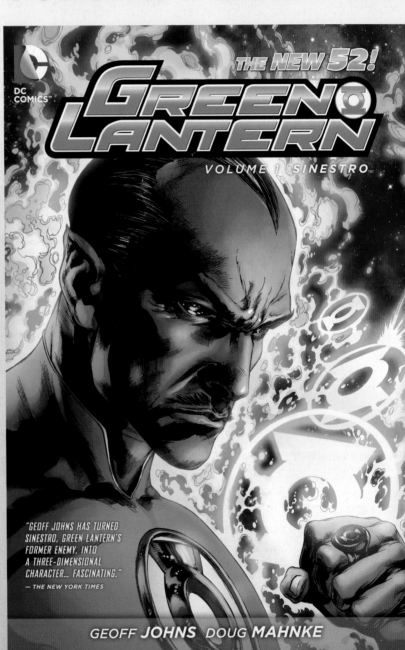

C COMICS™

FROM THE ARTIST OF *JUSTICE LEAGUE*
JIM LEE
with JEPH LOEB

SUPERMAN: FOR TOMORROW VOL. 1

with BRIAN AZZARELLO

SUPERMAN: FOR TOMORROW VOL. 2

with BRIAN AZZARELLO

ALL-STAR BATMAN AND ROBIN, THE BOY WONDER

with FRANK MILLER

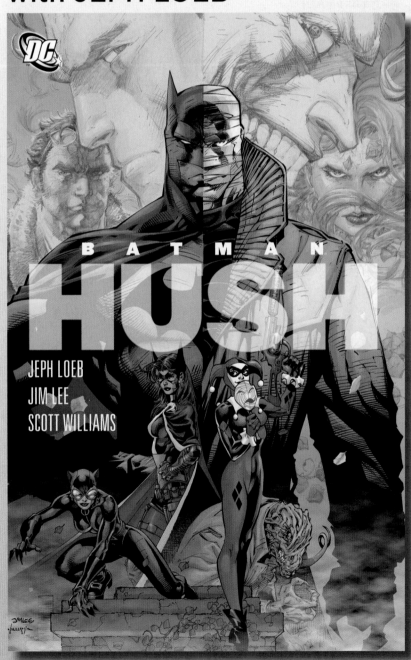

BATMAN HUSH

JEPH LOEB
JIM LEE
SCOTT WILLIAMS

DC COMICS™

FLASHPOINT
GEOFF JOHNS with ANDY KUBERT

FLASHPOINT: THE WORLD OF FLASHPOINT FEATURING BATMAN

FLASHPOINT: THE WORLD OF FLASHPOINT FEATURING GREEN LANTERN

Read the Entire Epic!

Flashpoint

Flashpoint: The World of Flashpoint Featuring Batman

Flashpoint: The World of Flashpoint Featuring The Flash

Flashpoint: The World of Flashpoint Featuring Green Lantern

Flashpoint: The World of Flashpoint Featuring Superman

Flashpoint: The World of Flashpoint Featuring Wonder Woman

"Heroic comic-book art at its finest" – ENTERTAINMENT WEEKLY / SHELF LIFE

GEOFF JOHNS · ANDY KUBERT · SANDRA HOPE

FLASHPOINT

"A soaring, if radical, tale that uses superheroes in ways that may surprise both first-time readers and long-time fans."
– THE ASSOCIATED PRESS